What Others Are Saying About *A Securities Regulation, Litigation, and Enforcement Handbook*

Paul Saunders has written the most readable handbook I have come across in my many years of law practice, judging, and law school teaching. He has taken a difficult and dense subject and made it understandable to all levels of readers—law students, practitioners, and interested non-lawyers. The sprinkling of questions throughout the book are thought provoking and tantalizing. I constantly thought "how would I answer that." His writing style is clear, crisp, and concise. Believe it or not, I couldn't put it down. As good a read as the best novels, biographies, or history books that I so enjoy. I highly recommend its use in classrooms, law libraries, and personal bookshelves. If you want to understand the securities markets—this is your best choice.—Hon. Shira A. Scheindlin, United States District Judge (Ret.), Fellow, College of Commercial Arbitrators, Of Counsel, Stroock & Stroock & Lavan, LLP

Paul Saunders' *A Securities Regulation, Litigation, and Enforcement Handbook* is a welcome addition to a very crowded field. It is written in a succinct, and non-technical style. In particular, key cases are presented with careful attention to procedural context that then shapes how holdings are framed and understood. By providing a close reading of regulations and cases, Mr. Saunders is able to state applicable principles clearly without sacrificing nuance or understating gray areas, which are consistently and precisely highlighted. This will be a wonderful resource for anyone striving to provide nuanced advice or formulate litigation strategy.—Owen C. Pell, Retired Partner Of Counsel, White & Case LLP

Paul Saunders would be on any list of all-time greats of securities litigators. In this magnum opus, he distills a half century of experience into a comprehensive treatment of that subject. It is remarkable how clear he can be, even as he captured the nuances that many would miss. Every serious student of securities law will want this book.—John Sexton, Benjamin Butler Professor, Dean Emeritus, and President Emeritus at NYU

In addition to being a mentor and friend, Paul is one of the finest securities litigators of his generation. He is one of the few litigators ever to take multiple securities cases to trial, and he has been deeply involved in the development of the law in this area for nearly fifty years. This book condenses his decades of practicing and teaching securities litigation at the very highest levels into a detailed, comprehensive compendium of knowledge. Written in Paul's trademark approachable style, this is both a practical and scholarly guide that will be invaluable to practitioners, clients and students alike.—Timothy Cameron, Partner, Cravath, Swaine & Moore LLP

This book hits the sweet spot for practitioners and students who want to understand the fundamentals of securities law with enough sophistication to appreciate why this is such a deep, challenging, and fascinating subject, and then put that knowledge to practical use.—Donald Langevoort, Thomas Aquinas Reynolds Professor of Law. Georgetown University Law Center

In addition to its thorough discussion of the law of securities regulation and securities enforcement, this handbook provides a useful roadmap through the ways and means of litigation, written by a practitioner who has spent many years trying cases as well as many years in the classroom. To that extent, it is different from the ordinary casebook or textbook and combines a scholarly discussion of securities laws with the practical perspective of a litigator. For that reason, it should become a valuable addition to the lawyer's library.—Robert Haig, Partner, Kelley Drye & Warren LLP

A Securities Regulation, Litigation, and Enforcement Handbook

A Securities Regulation, Litigation, and Enforcement Handbook

Paul C. Saunders

fastcase FULL COURT PRESS

A Full Court Press, Fastcase, Inc., Publication.

Printed and bound in the United States of America.

10 9 8 7 6 5 4 3 2 1

ISBN (print): 978-1-949884-73-9

To Pat,
our sons Paul Jr. and Mike,
and our grandchildren Tatum, Erin, Will, Henry, and Ruby

Contents

Preface

This Handbook had its creation when I began teaching Securities Litigation and Enforcement at Georgetown University Law Center many years ago and had a second birth more recently when I began teaching Securities Regulation at the Elisabeth Haub School of Law at Pace University. But the real genesis of this handbook was in my decades of practicing law. I began my legal career as an Army JAG lawyer in Korea and Washington DC, where I tried and appealed general courts-martial. I then joined the firm of Cravath, Swaine & Moore, LLP, where I spent the rest of my career as a trial lawyer. As it happened, many of my trials, including jury trials, involved the securities laws. I was fortunate to have tried many securities cases before very good federal judges who knew the law and made certain that I did as well.

As a result, this Handbook is a bit different from a traditional casebook or law textbook. It contains and represents the reflections of a trial lawyer who is, somewhat by happenstance, also a law professor. The question that is presented, time and time again in the classroom and the courtroom, is "what would you do under these circumstances?" As trial lawyers and law students well know, that is an easy question to ask, but a difficult one to answer. I hope that this Handbook will help the readers answer that question whenever it is posed.

The purchase and sale of securities is at the center of our economic system. But for far too long it was unregulated and exploited by unscrupulous robber barons who took advantage of the naïveté of investors to make millions. Prior to the stock market crash of 1929 and the Great Depression, there were no federal securities laws, only state "blue sky" laws that were largely ineffective. Investors were encouraged to buy stocks "on margin" without having any idea what they were buying. After a comprehensive investigation, Congress adopted the Securities Act of 1933 on the eve of President Franklin Roosevelt's inauguration in order to require corporations that were issuing securities to provide full and truthful disclosure about what they were selling. A year later, the Securities Exchange Act of 1934 was enacted to regulate the securities exchanges and to prohibit deceptive devices and contrivances in connection with the purchase and sale of securities.

In the decades that followed, the federal securities laws became the most important federal vehicle we have for prohibiting fraud in the purchase and sale of securities and for insuring that investors are told the whole truth about what they are buying and selling. This is a tall order, and the resulting statutes, rules, and regulations are often complex, opaque, and sometimes even unintelligible. One of the objectives of this Handbook is to simplify the federal securities laws and to remove some of their opaqueness. But its more important objective is to assist lawyers in advising their clients about the purposes and consequences of the federal securities laws, thereby assisting them in delivering the rule of law to those who they represent. It is my hope that, in doing so, they will reflect and enhance the essential values of our shared honorable profession.

January 2022

Acknowledgments

I would like to acknowledge three groups of colleagues and friends who helped me write this Handbook. First and foremost were my students, who asked the right questions and who helped me shape the right answers. Second, my colleagues at the Cravath firm kept my work on the straight and narrow and never failed to give me help when I asked for it. I single out LizAnn Eisen, Steve Burns, Dave Stuart, Tim Cameron, Dan Slifkin, and Kimberley Drexler for special thanks. Third, I would like to acknowledge and thank the many scholars whose works on the U.S. securities laws I have studied and used for many years. In particular, I thank my friends and colleagues at Georgetown Law, Professors Don Langevoort and Christopher Brummer, whose works I have respected and relied upon, and my colleague at the Haub School of Law at Pace University, Associate Dean Jill Gross. I would also include in this category six law professors I have never met, Professor Steven Choi at NYU Law, Professor Adam Pritchard at Michigan Law, Professor Donna Nagy at the Maurer School of Law at Indiana University, Professor Richard Painter at the University of Minnesota Law School, Professor Margaret Sachs at the University of Georgia Law School, and Professor Marc Steinberg at the Southern Methodist Law School, all of whose works I have studied and used extensively in my courses and in this Handbook.

My thanks to all.

January 2022

A Securities Regulation, Litigation, and Enforcement Handbook

Chapter 1

Overview of the Securities Markets and Securities Regulation[1]

The History of Federal Securities Regulation

The history of and the need for federal regulation of the securities market begins in the nineteenth century, long before the stock market crash of 1929 and the Great Depression. In the early nineteenth century, for example, *caveat emptor* was the watchword, and the equivalent of today's securities regulators were the journalists, who wrote about business fraud.[2] P.T. Barnum's "A sucker born every minute" was more than a tale. The out-of-control market characterized by the railroads and the oil barons gave birth to the Sherman Antitrust Act of 1890. But the securities markets, marked by periodic crashes as they were in the nineteenth century, were hotbeds of fraud. For example, in 1880, after his presidency, Ulysses S. Grant invested in a securities firm created by one of his sons, Buck, and a friend of his, Ferdinand Ward. The firm of Grant & Ward turned out to be a giant Ponzi scheme in which the same securities were used over and over again as collateral for loans. Before the firm crashed into bankruptcy, Grant told his wife: "Ward is making us all rich—them as well as ourselves."[3] The cartoonist in *Harper's Weekly* referred to the firm as "Smash, Bang & Co." There was, of course, no regulation to speak of.

Shortly after Herbert Hoover took office as President in 1929, the stock market crashed, followed by the Great Depression. This crash and Depression

---

[1] The primary focus of this Handbook is on the regulation and enforcement of the laws relating to the offer and sale of equity securities. There are many nuances in the offer and sale of debt securities that are not covered in this Handbook.

[2] This is still true today. The exposure of the activities of Theranos is one of many current examples of the importance of journalists to private companies.

[3] Ron Chernow, *Grant* (Penguin Press) (2017), 919; Edward J. Balleisen, *Fraud: An American History From Barnum to Madoff* (Princeton Univ. Press) (2017), 14.

were no doubt caused in large part by the financial problems caused by World War I. The unemployment that followed was soon corrected and by the end of the year more than a million people had been put back to work.[4] But the underlying problems of "rags to riches" and easy credit, plus the widespread use of margin to buy securities, led not only to a plethora of fraud and discontent, they soon led to the market crash of 1929. Although by 1932 the stock market, still below its pre-crash high, had crept its way into positive territory, the economy remained in tatters. It has been estimated that of the $50 billion in new securities that were marketed during the period immediately before the crash, more than half became worthless.

The 1932 Senate Banking Committee hearings revealed the shambles left by the rampant speculation and market manipulation practiced by greedy securities dealers. Presidential candidate Franklin Roosevelt campaigned against the fraud in the markets, claiming that Hoover was exploiting the American people on behalf of the "not more than five human individuals" who controlled America's wealth, and he promised reform.[5]

Congress considered introducing bills to impose federal regulation on the securities markets, but President Hoover and congressional Republicans resisted. FDR campaigned on securities regulation—"letting in of the light of day" (FDR speech at the 1932 Democratic Convention accepting the presidential nomination).[6]

Ferdinand Pecora (a former prosecutor), chief counsel to the Senate Banking Committee, led hearings in which the committee investigated a wide variety of efforts to manipulate the markets; how companies used public relations to manipulate news reports; insider trading (e.g., Harry Warner and Mrs. David Sarnoff); how companies put politicians and executives on "preferred lists" for stocks at low prices before public offerings; and high salaries (e.g., $1.2 million to the chairman of National City Bank) and interest free loans.

The committee's 400-page report formed the basis for the securities laws. As a result, within months after the election, FDR's advisors drafted legislation

---

[4] According to the National Bureau of Economic Research, the national unemployment rate in 1928 was 2 million, and it declined to 1.5 million in 1929. Unfortunately, it rose again in 1930 to 4.3 million. NBER, "The Measurement and Behavior of Unemployment" (1957) (out of print).

[5] Campaign Speech, Columbus, Ohio, https://presidency.ucsb.edu/node/288091.

[6] Jean E. Smith, *FDR* (Random House) (2007), 276-277; The American Presidency Project, *Address Accepting the Presidential Nomination at the Democratic National Convention in Chicago*: "I list an important place for that prize statement of principle in the platform here adopted calling for the letting in of the light of day on issues of securities, foreign and domestic, which are offered for sale to the investing public," https://www.presidency.ucsb.edu.

to regulate *both* new issues and stock exchanges On the eve of the introduction of the bill that became the Securities Act of 1933, President Roosevelt sent a message to Congress that was annexed to a bill that dealt only with new issues: "[P]ut the burden of telling the whole truth on the seller."[7] Congress agreed and passed the bill that separated new issues from a bill regulating stock exchanges, which later became the Securities Exchange Act of 1934.

The first draft of the new-issue legislation allowed the government to judge the merits of new issues. There was much opposition and Professor (later Justice) Felix Frankfurter, Jim Landis, Ben Cohen, and Tommy ("the Cork") Corcoran were brought in to fix the draft. They proposed a British model: full disclosure by the issuer, not a review by the government/regulators of the merits of a proposed offering. The Securities Act of 1933 passed in two months. The 1933 Act was not popular. Some said it was too weak, others said it was too strong and would hold back the economy.

Because of political considerations, Congress agreed on concurrent federal and state jurisdiction.[8] This will become important later in this Handbook. The second step in the federal regulatory scheme was the Securities Exchange Act of 1934, and it was far more politically ambitious than the 1933 Act.

Predecessors of the Federal Securities Laws: State "Blue Sky" Laws

State securities laws existed prior to the federal securities laws of the 1930s. "Blue sky laws" are state laws that were originally designed to prevent "speculative schemes that have no more basis than so many feet of 'blue sky' over Kansas." The first blue sky law was enacted in Kansas in 1911. It regulated the offering of securities, required the licensing of brokers and dealers, and prohibited misinformation. There are many different accounts as to where the term "blue sky" came from; one was that rainmakers promised farmers rain, but after taking their money, delivered only "blue skies." Blue sky laws have largely been replaced by the Uniform Securities Act of 1956 (amended in 1985 and 2002) that has been adopted in one form or another by forty-one jurisdictions, one of which is *not* New York.[9]

---

[7] March 29, 1933, FDR press conference, https://www.presidency.ucsb.edu/exerpts-from-the-press-conference-146.

[8] Pursuant to Section 22 of the 1933 Act, except for the Securities Litigation Uniform Standards Act with respect to securities class actions based on common law or state law, no securities case brought in a competent state court may be removed to a federal court. SLUSA will be discussed later in this Handbook.

[9] The times may be changing. On December 1, 2020, New York's Attorney General Letitia James announced the adoption of rules that would modernize at least

Nature of the Securities Markets

Most securities markets are places in which securities are bought and sold and provide issuers with access to capital and liquidity and investors with a ready market for selling their securities or buying additional securities.

1. *Primary Markets.* In these markets, issuers can raise capital by selling registered securities in public markets or through unregistered private placements. They provide fora in which buyers and sellers can easily find sellers and purchasers, and learn about other transactions that might inform their buying and selling decisions. From a company's early seeding, to investing by an "angel," to venture capital, investing is usually carried out directly between the issuer and the investor. However, once an issuer has equity securities trading on a public market, it is rare for issuers to sell equity securities directly to end purchasers. Rather, investment banks facilitate the process by working with the issuer to provide information and by purchasing equity securities for resale to their customers and others.
   a. *Initial Public Offerings* (IPOs). These are used by firms distributing equity capital via a registered offering for the first time. However, many IPOs involve sales of securities by selling shareholders so the issuer does not actually "raise capital." This is sometimes referred to as a "traditional" or underwritten IPO.[10] Once the SEC has declared the relevant registration statement effective, the equity securities are typically purchased by underwriters who take the risk of being able to resell them to customers. However, the risk is largely theoretical, given the way IPOs are priced and distributed.
   b. *Private Placements.* These are direct sales of unregistered equity securities to sophisticated purchasers. They do not take place on or through exchanges but instead are privately negotiated and may or may not include a financial intermediary.
2. *Secondary Markets.* (Trading Transactions) These transactions are not between the issuer and the investor but are between traders who buy or sell to other investors either in the public market or

some of New York's securities laws, making them more consistent with federal laws. In particular, the new rules would harmonize New York's procedures with federal Regulations D and A, a change that was first recommended by the New York State Bar Association in 2002!

[10] There are other possibilities, including "direct listings" and Special Purpose Acquisition Corporations (SPACs).

in private transactions. The transactions typically take place on exchanges, which are becoming increasingly reliant on technology to execute trades.[11] The exchange floor is where floor brokers negotiate certain trades, although exchange floors and brokers are becoming increasingly rare. For example, there are far more electronic stock exchanges in New Jersey than there are in New York City. The NASDAQ market, a combination of three markets, is a good example of an exchange that is entirely an electronic network in which most transactions are consummated using desktop computers.[12] Today, Alternate Trading Systems have replaced the market-making intermediary and use computers to link sellers and purchasers by matching bids and asks.

3. *Functions of Securities Markets.*
   a. *Capital Formation.* This occurs when issuers sell securities to raise capital.
   b. *Liquidity.* This exists when investors are able readily to sell securities in a public market.
   c. *Risk Management.* The essence of an investment decision by an investor is to compare the value of money today with its expected value sometime in the future in order to decide whether a particular investment (or sale) is worthwhile. One of the goals and benefits of the securities registration system is to make sure that investors have at least some of the information they need to make a wise investment decision. That is why our securities laws mandate certain disclosures and prohibit deception and fraud through omission or commission.
4. *Participants in the Securities Markets.*
   a. Individual investors;
   b. Institutional investors;
   c. Issuers (businesses, governments, agencies, not-for-profit organizations, mutual funds, others), including those who securitize pooled obligations that are packaged and sold; and
   d. Broker-dealers, investment companies, commercial banks, accounting firms that prepare and vouch for the accuracy of issuer financial statements, lawyers, and others.
5. *Operation of the Markets.*
   a. *Information.* All market investors depend on information about the securities being bought or sold, the financial

---

[11] *See, e.g.*, Michael Lewis, *Flash Boys* (W.W. Norton) (2014).

[12] *See* Alan Palmiter, *Securities Regulation* (7th ed.) (Wolters Kluwer) (2017), pp. 2-3.

performance of the issuer, the future prospects of the issuer, and many other types of information.

b. *Efficiency*. In theory, public markets are said to be informationally efficient markets in which the prices of securities reflect ("impound") all information available to the public. We will see that this is an important hypothesis that underlies securities class actions, among other things, but it remains a hypothesis and has often been questioned.[13]

There are three types of hypothetical market efficiency:

1. *Weak Form*. This implies that a security is efficient with respect only to past stock prices. This means that past stock prices or trends cannot be used to identify over- or under-valued stocks. For example, the fact that a security is trading at a three-year high or low would not contain any value-relevant information. This is called a "martingale" in statistics, and in securities literature is called the "random walk" in which future performance cannot be predicted by past performance.[14]
2. *Semi-Strong Form*. In this theory, all publicly available information is impounded into the market price. The release of private information will move the stock price, but once it is public, it can no longer be used to earn risk-adjusted returns; in other words, investors cannot beat the market by using publicly available information. This is consistent with the idea that insider trading on private information is potentially profitable. But can all publicly available information actually be impounded in a stock price? We know that this is not, in fact, the case; take, for example, the so-called internet bubble of the 1990s, called "irrational exuberance" by the Federal Reserve Board Chairman Alan Greenspan.[15] A more recent example is the dramatic increase in the price of GameStop, a retailer of video games, whose stock price was inflated by purchasers of stock and options who allegedly intended to create a "short squeeze" for hedge fund owners of

---

[13] *See, e.g.*, Justin Fox, *The Myth of the Rational Market: A History of Risk, Reward and Delusion on Wall Street* (Harper Collins) (2014).

[14] *See* Stephen J. Choi & A.C. Pritchard, *Securities Regulation, Cases and Analysis* (5th ed.) (Foundation Press) (2019), 32-33.

[15] This phrase was used in a speech to the American Enterprise Institute in 1996 to warn that the markets might be overvalued. It later became the title of Nobel Prize winner Robert Schiller's 2000 book, *Irrational Exuberance*, about the stock market boom of the late 1990s.

the stock, driving the price of the stock far higher than its intrinsic value. As expected, the "bubble" ultimately burst.[16]

3. *Strong Form.* This implies that a security is efficient with respect to private as well as public information. If the stock price is strong-form efficient, then the disclosure of even the most closely held secret would not move the price. Most economists agree that the equity market is not strong-form efficient and that such a form is, in fact, not possible.

In 1976, Eugene Fama, who was one of the principal developers of the efficient market hypothesis, wrote that "an efficient capital market is a market that is efficient in processing information. The prices of securities observed at any time are based on 'correct' evaluation of all information available at that time. Prices 'fully reflect' available information."[17] Fama won the Nobel Prize in Economics in 2013.

However, economists soon realized that stock prices could and did deviate from their fundamental value and that markets did, in fact, over- or under-react to information.[18] Robert Schiller also won the Nobel Prize in Economics in the same year as Fama, even though their theses were diametrically opposed.

There are two types of principal markets for public trading of securities: exchange markets, in which buy and sell orders are matched in a continuous auction, and over-the-counter markets, in which buying and selling takes place between firms that have access to information about prices being offered by other firms. NASDAQ is today an over-the-counter market in which members are linked by computers and can quote prices and make trades with each other. The use of advanced technology is changing the way securities markets operate.

Today, an increasing proportion of trading occurs off exchanges, on platforms run by high-frequency traders. Nearly every major brokerage firm in the United States now routes orders to these market makers and receives a portion of the money that they earn on the spread between bid and ask prices. This system, known as payment for order flow, helps brokers make enough money on the back end so they can more easily charge zero commissions for trades. However, because the deals between the brokers and the market makers are opaque, the SEC wants to open them to more sunlight and perhaps change the rules. New SEC Chair Gary Gensler has asked the SEC staff to "enhance and update" the rules around market structure. He noted that some countries,

---

[16] This can happen in many different ways. Consider, for example, a company that outperforms its guidance to analysts but upon announcing its supposedly "good" results, its stock price drops.

[17] Eugene Fama, "Efficient Capital Markets: A Review of Theory and Empirical Work," *The Journal of Finance*, Vol. 25, No. 2 (1969).

[18] *See* Robert Schiller, *Irrational Exuberance* (Broadway Books) (2001).

such as Canada and Australia, have banned payment for order flow and that Europe considers there to be "an inherent conflict between best execution and these payments."[19]

Federal Securities Laws

The Securities Act of 1933. The 1933 Act is the principal legal framework for the offer and sale of securities in United States. The fundamental premise of the U.S. securities laws is disclosure by the issuer, not a qualitative evaluation by a governmental entity, and its purpose is to ensure "full and fair disclosure of the character of securities sold in interstate and foreign commerce and through the mails." It applies mainly to primary markets—that is, offers and sales by issuers—and in general, requires that new issues of stock be registered with the SEC (originally with the Federal Trade Commission) by the filing of a registration statement whose principal content is a "prospectus" containing specified information about the issuer. The Securities Act also erected a scheme of liability for any misinformation in connection with the distribution of the new securities. The scheme is a combination of regulatory oversight and private litigation.

Section 5 is the heart of the 1933 Act and provides that securities cannot be sold or delivered, absent an exemption, unless a registration statement has been filed with the SEC, and declared effective. Offers of securities cannot be made unless a registration statement is on file and complies with Section 10, which governs prospectuses and their content. Failure to register the offer and sale of securities, absent an exemption, and otherwise to comply with the statute, carries criminal penalties, administrative sanctions, and the threat of private civil liability. There is an express private right of action for those who purchase securities in a public offering by means of a registration statement and who were defrauded by materially false statements or omissions in the registration statement. As we will see, however, such cases are relatively rare because of difficult pleading requirements. Although the Securities Act regulates public offerings that are registered with the SEC, the Exchange Act, by contrast, regulates secondary markets such as stock exchanges.

The Securities Exchange Act of 1934. The 1934 Act created the SEC with broad enforcement powers; it regulates the securities industry, in particular the stock exchanges and securities firms, prohibits the use of any "manipulative or deceptive devise or contrivance" in connection with the purchase or sale of a security registered on a national securities exchange (or "any security not so registered"), regulates margin for purchasers of securities, requires periodic

[19] Avi Salzman, "Gary Gensler Indicates That the SEC Has Meme-Stock Trading and Bitcoin in Its Sights," *Barron's*, June 10, 2021.

disclosure by public companies, regulates proxy voting and, at least in theory, regulates insider trading in the stock of public companies. It has been amended many times since 1934.

In general, the rights of aggrieved investors under the Exchange Act are limited in scope and utility. In the beginning, there was no private right of action under the 1934 Act (with a few exceptions), but lower courts began to hold that a private right of action was implied. The U.S. Supreme Court sided with those decisions in *J.I. Case v. Borak*, 377 U.S. 426 (1964), in which the shareholder plaintiff sought rescission or damages caused by a consummated merger that was authorized by a proxy statement that allegedly contained false and misleading statements in violation of Section 14(a) of the 1934 Act. The Supreme Court held that it was "the duty of the courts to be alert to provide such remedies as are necessary to make effective the congressional purpose.... It is for the federal courts to 'adjust their remedies so as to grant the necessary relief' where federally secured rights are invaded." Thus was sanctioned the implied private right of action under the 1934 Act.[20]

The chief purpose of the 1934 Securities Exchange Act is the protection of investors. But as noted, the 1934 Act did not create an express private right of action. Was that intentional or an oversight?

Both statutes are primarily concerned with the timeliness, adequacy, and accuracy of disclosures and with "fair and honest markets." Justice Louis Brandeis once said that "Sunlight is said to be the best disinfectant." Congress chose disclosure as the best way to prevent fraud.

There are several other federal laws relating to securities:

- *Sarbanes-Oxley Act of 2002.* Regulates accounting firms that act as auditors of public companies, created the Public Company Accounting Oversight Board, and imposed obligations and liability on certain corporate officers.
- *Glass-Steagall Act (repealed in 1999).* Separated commercial banking from investment banking; over time, the separation disappeared and was ultimately destroyed by the Gramm-Leach-Bliley Act of 1999, which although it required separate financial regulations, permitted the functional units to exist in the same corporate entity or under common ownership.

---

[20] Since the Supreme Court remanded the case for further proceedings, *Borak* left many open questions, including whether there was strict liability under the 1934 Act or whether negligence or intent was required, whether loss causation was required, and whether "eyeball" reliance on the false statement was an element of the cause of action. Later cases would answer all of those questions.

- *Dodd-Frank Wall Street Reform and Consumer Protection Act (Dodd-Frank) (2010)*. Adopted the so-called Volcker Rule[21] that limited the ability of banks to engage in proprietary trading, limited their investment to 3 percent of their core capital in hedge and private equity funds.
- *Jumpstart Our Business Startups Act (JOBS) (2012)*. Intended to encourage investment in small businesses by easing offering and reporting obligations.
- *Public Utility Holding Company Act of 1935 (repealed in 2005)*. Limited public utilities to single integrated systems such as gas or electric.
- *Investment Company Act of 1940*. Required certain funds and investment companies to register with the SEC and have independent boards.
- *Investment Advisers Act of 1940*. Required investment advisers to disclose their interests in transactions executed for their clients and prohibited fraud.

State Securities Laws: The New York Martin Act

New York State's Martin Act is believed to be one of the most extreme blue sky laws in the United States.[22] It was enacted in 1921 but was hardly used in the following decades. It is extreme because it creates civil and criminal liability for a misrepresentation or omission of material fact "by any person, partnership, corporation ... who shall have employed or employs ... any deception, misrepresentation, concealment, suppression, fraud, false pretense or false promise ... and which has operated or which would operate as a fraud upon the purchaser." [NB. This is a contracted version of a much longer sentence.]

The statute is very complicated and hard to follow. My hypothesis is that there are in fact few people alive today who have ever read the Martin Act from cover to cover. Although for many years it was hardly used, in recent years it has been invoked against Merrill Lynch, Salomon Smith Barney, and Credit Suisse Group AG. What makes the Martin Act especially severe is that it punishes securities fraud both civilly and criminally based only on evidence of a misrepresentation or omission of a material fact or other conduct that deceives or misleads the public, or even tends to do so, in the sale or promotion of a

---

[21] Paul Volcker was Chair of the Federal Reserve of the United States from 1979 to 1987.

[22] It is found in Article 23-A of New York's General Business Law, §§ 352c & 353 (McKinney 1996).

security within or from New York. *See People v. Federated Radio Corp.*, 244 N.Y. 33 (1926).

Of particular note is that neither proof of scienter (intent) (except in the case of felonies) nor proof of an actual purchase or sale in reliance on the fraud is required. In addition, the New York Attorney General's discovery powers are extremely broad. The AG may conduct private investigations into fraudulent practices, require sworn statements from witnesses, compel the attendance of witnesses and examine them under oath, *without the presence of counsel.* The AG may also compel the production of all relevant or material documents and may grant immunity to witnesses.

Probable cause is not required for the commencement of an investigation. A public investigation requires a court order, known as a Section 354 order, which may be granted *ex parte.* In civil matters, the AG may seek a preliminary injunction and permanent injunctive relief. The injunctive power is so broad that the AG may permanently enjoin a defendant from selling securities in New York merely because the defendant failed to respond to a question or produce a document when ordered to do so. Misdemeanor criminal prosecutions may be based on any fraud or false statement if the person making the false statement knew the truth, could have known the truth, or did not make any reasonable effort to ascertain the truth.

Felony prosecutions require proof of intent to violate the act to defraud ten or more persons and to obtain property from one or more of those persons. There is now a six-year statute of limitations, after N.Y.C.P.L.R. § 214(2) was amended in 2019, following a decision by the New York Court of Appeals holding that the statute of limitations was only three years.[23] There is no express or implied private right of action under the Martin Act. *CPC Int'l Inc. v. McKesson Corp.*, 519 N.Y.S. 2d 804 (1987). However, private actions founded in fraud may still be maintained so long as the claim is not based entirely on a violation of the Martin Act. *Assured. Guar. (UK) Ltd. v. J.P. Morgan Inv. Mgmt. Inc.*, 939 N.Y.S. 2d 274 (2011).

Required Federal Public Company Disclosures

The Securities Act of 1933 and the Securities Exchange Act of 1934 were intended to protect investors by, among other things, promoting transparency. In general, they do so by requiring and promoting disclosure about the company and its business in a timely manner. Congress "chose to place a heavy burden on parties with superior access to, and control over, information about securities: those who offer them." *FHFA v. Nomura Holding America, Inc.*,

[23] *People v. Credit Suisse Sec. (USC) LLC*, 31 N.Y. 3d 622 (2018). Full disclosure: my firm represented Credit Suisse in that case.

104 F. Supp. 3d 441 (S.D.N.Y. 2015) (Judge Denise Cote). It was hoped that such disclosures would enable informed decision making by investors. However, disclosure is only required of "material" information and only if there is a "duty" to disclose. A second purpose was to expose corporate wrongdoing.

Under Section 13 of the 1934 Act, every issuer of a security registered pursuant to Section 12 shall file with the SEC, "in accordance with such rules and regulations as the Commission may prescribe as necessary or appropriate for the proper protection of investors and to insure fair dealing in the security":

> (1) such information and documents (and such copies thereof) as the Commission may require issuers to keep reasonably current the information and documents required to be included in or filed with an application or registration statement ... and
>
> (2) such annual reports (and such copies thereof) ... and such quarterly reports (and such copies thereof), as the commission may prescribe.

In today's jargon, those required documents are the annual report on Form 10-K (Form 20-K for foreign private issuers) and the quarterly reports on Form 10-Q (no equivalent required for foreign private issuers). In addition, Form 8-K, sometimes referred to as a current report, requires the timely disclosure of current information, among other items, that would be material to changes in a company's financial condition or operations. There is not a direct equivalent reporting form for disclosures by foreign private issuers.

Information Required to Be Disclosed by Public Companies on Form 8-K

In general, the SEC requires U.S. domestic public companies to make disclosures about certain current relevant facts concerning the corporation's finances and operations. In their textbook *Securities Regulation*, Professors Stephen Choi and A.C. Pritchard have listed the following types of information that must be disclosed on a Form 8-K[24] within four business days after the events occur.[25] They include information about the following, to which I have added three additional types of information:

---

[24] This form, and many others, can be found on sec.gov. *See, e.g.*, https://www.investor.gov/introduction-investing/investing-basics/glossary/form-10-k.

[25] Stephen Choi & A.C. Pritchard, *Securities Regulation, Cases and Analysis* (5th ed.) (Foundation Press) (2019), 206-224. I have used this textbook-casebook in my classes, and I highly recommend it.

1. The registrant's business and operations, including bankruptcy, shutdowns, and contracts outside the ordinary course of business.
2. Financial information, including disposition of more than 10 percent of the assets, off-balance sheet arrangements, certain costs, and material impairments.
3. Securities and trading markets, including delisting, unregistered sales of equity securities, and modification of shareholders' rights.
4. Matters relating to accountants and financial statements, including changes in the auditor and the reasons for the change.
5. Corporate governance and management, including the existence of a code of ethics, changes in control, amendments of the charter or bylaws, suspension of trading, matters submitted to a vote of shareholders, and disclosures relating to shareholder-director nominations.
6. Asset-backed securities, including change of servicer or trustee, failure to make required distributions to holders, and disclosures relating to offerings registered on Form S-3.
7. Regulation FD (Fair Disclosure, discussed further below), including any disclosure the issuer elects to disclose through Form 8-K (following a private disclosure of material information).
8. Financial statements and exhibits, including such documents for businesses acquired by the issuer.
9. Certain M&A transactions.
10. Withdrawal of reliance on an audit opinion.
11. Waivers of the code of ethics for "named executive officers."
12. Other events, including anything that the issuer thinks would be important to shareholders.

Information Required to Be Disclosed in Form 10-K

Form 10-K prescribes an annual report filed by a corporation. It must include, among other things, information about the company's business, risk factors, legal proceedings, executive compensation, certain relationships and transactions, and accounting fees. Perhaps two of the most important parts of a Form 10-K are the Management Discussion and Analysis of Financial Condition and Results of Operations, known colloquially as the MD&A and audited financial statements. The MD&A must contain a narrative discussion of the company's operating results and financial condition and changes and, most important, a discussion of "known trends or uncertainties" that the company "reasonably expects" to affect the company's liquidity, capital resources, net sales, revenues, or income in the future. (Note that this is a requirement for a "forward-looking" statement that may be protected by a safe-harbor provision.)

The 10-Q

This is a quarterly report that contains much of the same information as the 10-K, with some limitations that make it easier to compile and file.

Regulations S-K and S-X

These are the regulations that set out in great detail the information that must be contained in Forms 10-K, 10-Q, and 8-K. Regulation S-K, for example, which describes primarily non-financial information, although it does govern the MD&A as well as the provision of the ratio of earnings to fixed charges and similar items, is 127 single-spaced pages long. Regulation S-X deals with financial information. NB: On November 19, 2020, the SEC substantially modernized, simplified, and improved the financial disclosure requirements of Regulation S-K, including Items 301, 302, and 303. The changes are effective commencing with the 10-K for the year ending December 31, 2021.

Regulation FD and the Problem of Selective Disclosure

In the 1990s, concerns were raised that companies were making selective disclosures to certain parties that enabled them to trade on the information or, if they were analysts, to inform their clients about the information in order to facilitate their trades in advance of the information becoming widely available to the public. As a result, the SEC promulgated Regulation FD (Fair Disclosure) that applies to U.S. domestic reporting companies and people who work for them. Unlike Regulation S-K, Regulation FD is only three-and-a-half pages. It is quite simple. If, absent a confidentiality agreement, an issuer or someone acting on its behalf discloses any material non-public information regarding the issuer or its securities to a broker or dealer, an investment adviser, an investment company, or a holder of the issuer's securities if it is reasonably foreseeable that that person will purchase or sell the issuer's securities on the basis of the information, then the issuer must disclose the same information publicly at the same time.

If the private disclosure was intentional, the public disclosure must be made simultaneously; if not, it must be disclosed "promptly." There is no private right of action for a violation of Regulation FD, and Regulation FD specifies that a failure to make a public disclosure is not to be deemed a violation of Rule 10b-5 under the 1934 Act.

Consequences

There are consequences for failing to tell the whole truth—which includes disclosing both the facts and the implication of those facts—in these required public disclosures. A good recent example is a $200 million fine that General Electric agreed to pay to the SEC for failing to explain in its financial disclosures that its reported profit growth in its power business "actually resulted from reductions in cost estimates for repairs and service for customers' power turbines." The company also failed to disclose that it had begun to use "deferred monetization" that allowed the company to report an additional $1.9 billion in increased cash flow without disclosing that it was "depleting future cash flows by moving them into the present."[26]

Enforcement of the Federal Securities Laws

The SEC is the principal enforcer of the federal securities laws but only the Department of Justice may bring criminal cases. Shareholders may also bring civil cases, both individual and class actions, seeking damages.

There is a tension between historical policies of preventing (and punishing) securities fraud and the potential for abuse in securities litigation. The Supreme Court has said that the securities laws have a "broad remedial purpose" (*Affiliated Ute Citizens v. United States*, 406 U.S. 128 (1972)) and should be interpreted not technically and restrictively but flexibly. *See SEC v. Capital Gains Res. Bureau*, 375 U.S. 180 (1963), and more generally *SEC v. Texas Gulf Sulphur*, 401 F.2d 833 (2d Cir. 1968). But in enacting the Private Securities Litigation Reform Act (PSLRA), Congress intended to make it harder to bring securities cases. In recent years, the Supreme Court has also made it more difficult to maintain securities cases, especially class actions. The tension between these two points of view still exists.

Role of the SEC

Basically, the SEC has civil jurisdiction to enforce the securities laws. It can bring administrative proceedings, issue cease-and-desist orders, seek "bar" orders prohibiting individuals or companies from participating in the securities industry, impose penalties, and seek disgorgement. It can bring civil actions in

---

[26] Al Barbarino, "SEC Fines GE $200M to Wrap Accounting Investigation," *Law 360*, Dec. 9, 2020. A private securities class action relating to some of the same claims was dismissed by Judge Cote of the U.S. District Court for the Southern District of New York for failing adequately to allege scienter, among other things. *In re General Electric Securities Litigation*, Opinion and Order, May 7, 2020.

federal court but criminal cases must be referred to and brought by the Justice Department, generally with the assistance of the SEC.

Role of the Department of Justice

The Department of Justice has responsibility for enforcing the securities laws that have criminal provisions. In particular, the Department enforces 18 U.S.C. §§ 1348 and 1349. These statutes prohibit executing a scheme or artifice to defraud any person in connection with any security registered under Section 12 of the 1934 Act or that is required to file reports under Section 15(d) of the 1934 Act, or to obtain, by means of false or fraudulent pretenses, representations, or promises, any money or property in connection with the purchase or sale of any security of an issuer that is required to file reports under Section 15(d) of the 1934 Act. Chapter 18 of 18 U.S.C. § 1349 prohibits attempts or conspiracies to commit an offense. Penalties include fines and imprisonment for not more than twenty-five years.

The Supreme Court's Role

In the creation of the implied private right of action and the encouragement of class actions, the Supreme Court could be said to have taken an activist role. Recently, some have described the Supreme Court's role with respect to the securities laws as that of a museum curator doing minor restoration, preserving artifacts, and some rearranging. According to Professor Eric Chaffee of the University of Toledo, "The days of an activist Court in the area of securities regulation have long passed."[27] That appears to be an overstatement. In this Handbook, we will discuss many recent examples of the Supreme Court's continued activism as well as some of its recent retreats.

Jurisdiction and Venue

Federal courts have explicit subject matter jurisdiction and also federal question jurisdiction in federal securities litigation. But the 1933 Securities Act also provides for concurrent federal and state jurisdiction for actions under Sections 11 and 12 of that statute. Why? As noted, politics in Congress was responsible. States that had active securities law practices did not want to lose them. As a result, cases brought in state court under the Securities Act are not removable except for "covered class actions" under the Securities Litigation Uniform Standards Act (SLUSA). But as we will see, in *Cyan v. Beaver*

---

[27] Eric C. Chaffee, "The Supreme Court as Museum Curator: Securities Regulation and the Roberts Court," 67 *Case Western Reserve L. Rev.* 847, 854 (2017).

County Employees Retirement Fund, 138 S. Ct. 1061 (2018), the Supreme Court recently ignored any ambiguity in SLUSA and restored securities class actions in state courts alleging violations of the federal 1933 Securities Act.[28] By contrast, the 1934 Exchange Act provides for exclusive federal jurisdiction. Personal jurisdiction is not dependent on state long-arm statutes. There is nationwide service of process for federal securities laws. *See* Securities Act Section 22 ("service in any district of which defendant is an inhabitant or wherever the defendant may be found"). Courts have the greatest possible reach consistent with the Due Process Clause. The defendant may even be served in a foreign country. *SEC v. Int'l Swiss Investments Corp.*, 895 F.2d 1272 (9th Cir. 1990). Minimum contacts with the United States are all that is required.

Implied Rights of Action Under the Federal Securities Laws

With certain exceptions noted above, the federal securities laws did not permit private rights of action by those who were injured by false or manipulative practices relating to the sale or the purchase of securities. Such actions were first recognized by lower courts in 1946 using tort principles. *Kardon v. National Gypsum*, 69 F. Supp. 512 (E.D. Pa 1946). *See J.I. Case v. Borak*, 377 U.S. 426, dealing with Section 14(a) of the Exchange Act and false or misleading statements in the solicitation of any proxy. In *Basic v. Levinson*, 485 U.S. 224 (1988), the Supreme Court said that private actions were a "necessary supplement" to government enforcement. But in *Central Bank v. First Interstate Bank*, 511 U.S. 164 (1994), the Supreme Court said that it would not recognize any more implied rights of action beyond those already recognized by the Supreme Court. Specifically, there would be no private rights of action against aiders and abettors, although the SEC may still bring such actions.

There were concerns that private securities litigation might be too abusive. For example, in *Blue Chip Stamps v. Manor Drug Stores*, 421 U.S. 723 (1975), the Supreme Court limited Section 10(b) to claims by actual purchasers and sellers, not those who were merely dissuaded from purchasing or selling. The Court was concerned with "vexatiousness" that might "frustrate or delay legitimate business activity." Later Supreme Court cases have echoed the same sentiment.

For example, the Supreme Court (and later Congress) also carved out certain "forward-looking statements" from liability and created the "bespeaks caution" defense for issuers and other sellers. The Supreme Court also made it

---

[28] In general, cases alleging violations of federal securities laws brought in state courts cannot be removed to a federal court. *But see California Public Employees Retirement Sys. v. WorldCom*, 368 F.3d 86 (2d Cir. 2004) (claims under section 11 brought in state court may be removed if they came within the purview of "the federal bankruptcy statute.").

clear that the securities laws were not meant to regulate corporate governance and that there was no federal remedy for inefficient, incompetent, or corrupt management. Note, however, that the Sarbanes-Oxley Act moved the law in the other direction (at least somewhat). In *Chiarella v. United States*, 445 U.S. 222 (1980), the Supreme Court said that "Section 10(b) is aptly described as a 'catch all' provision but what it catches must be fraud."

Recent Statistics

In the first half of 2021, securities class action filings fell to 112 from 150 in the first half of 2020. According to Cornerstone Research, this drop off was due to the reduction in merger-and-acquisition-related class actions.[29] Cases under the 1933 Securities Act in federal and state courts dropped 27 percent compared to the first half of 2020. The number of those cases filed in state courts more than doubled compared to the same period in 2020. One trend observed by Cornerstone Research was the increase in securities filings relating to Special Purpose Acquisition Companies.

The maximum dollar loss computed by Cornerstone Research, that is, the loss from the highest market capitalization during the class period to the first trading day after the end of the class period, fell from $991 billion in the second half of 2020 to $361 billion in the first half of 2021.

Perhaps as a result of recent Supreme Court cases discouraging such filings, the number of securities cases brought against non-U.S. issuers fell from seventy-four such cases filed in federal courts in the first half of 2020 to fifteen in the first half of 2021.

In the first half of 2021, most of the securities cases filed in federal courts were filed in the Second Circuit, followed by the Ninth Circuit. This was a reversal from the first half of 2020, when the filings in the Ninth Circuit were higher than those in the Second Circuit.

---

[29] Cornerstone Research, "Securities Class Action Filings, 2021 Midyear Assessment," https://www.cornerstone.com/Publications/Reports/Securities-Class-Action-Filings-2021-Midyear-Assessment.pdf.

Chapter 2

What Is a Security?

The definition of a "security" began as a matter of state, not federal, law. Today, however, most states look to the federal laws, not their own, for the definition. In fact, the Uniform Securities Act basically duplicates federal standards. Unfortunately, there is no widely accepted definition of a "security" under federal law.[1]

In *Marine Bank v. Weaver*, 455 U.S. 551 (1982), the Supreme Court wrote that the definition of "security" is "quite broad" and is meant to include "the many types of instruments that, in our commercial world, fall within the ordinary concept of a security." In other words, the definition of a "security" as the term is used in the federal securities laws includes, but is not limited to, the statutory definitions that Congress has provided. There are two lists of examples of securities in the federal securities laws; they are helpful but not sufficient. They are not definitional, only examples.

Statutes and Rules

Securities Act of 1933. Section 2(a)(1) contains a list of examples of what constitutes a "security." In general, it is a very broad term.

Securities Exchange Act of 1934. Section 3(a)(10) also contains a nearly identical list, with a few minor wrinkles.

But these lists are not exhaustive or even always applicable. For example, Section 2(a)(1) of the 1933 Act defines "security" as, among other things, "any note, stock ... transferable share [and] investment contract...." It goes on to include in the definition "any interest or instrument commonly known as a 'security' ..." but the statute explicitly exempts any definition of a security if "the context otherwise requires." So much for a bright-line test.

[1] *See generally*, Douglas M. Branson & Karl S. Okamoto, "The Supreme Court's Literalism and the Definition of 'Security' in the State Courts," 50 *Wash. & Lee L. Rev.* 1043 (1993).

One of the types of "security" listed in both the 1933 Act and the 1934 Act is an "investment contract." However, there is no other definition in the statutes. In the leading—and still valid—test first set forth in *SEC v. W.J. Howey Co.*, 328 U.S. 293 (1946) (the so-called *Howey in the Hills* case), the Supreme Court established a four-part test for determining what constituted an "investment contract" under the statutes: The transaction must be one in which (1) a person invests money, (2) in a common enterprise, and (3) is led to expect profits, (4) solely from the efforts of others. The ostensible purpose of the *Howey* test was to look at the economic realities of the transaction, but that is often hard to discern. In *Howey* itself, the Supreme Court, rejecting the decisions of the lower courts, held that an investment contract in which a purchaser bought a row of forty-eight citrus trees that were cultivated, harvested, and marketed by an affiliate of the seller, constituted a security. However, the court took a literal approach and declined the opportunity to consider the policy implications in determining what constituted a "security." Rather, it used the term "investment contract" to apply to novel schemes whenever they were encountered. For example, the sale of earthworms and the sale of "participations" in a pyramid scheme for distributing cosmetics both meet the definition of an "investment contract." The *Howey* court wrote that an investment contract "embodies a flexible rather than a static principle, one that is capable of adaptation to meet the countless and variable schemes devised by those who seek the use of the money of others on the promise of profits."

Why do we care about the definition of a "security"? There are several reasons:

- first and foremost, the federal securities laws only apply to transactions in "securities";
- the key provisions of the 1934 Securities Exchange Act, Section 10(b) and Rule 10b-5, only apply to transactions "in connection with the purchase or sale of a security";
- under most circumstances, most offerings of "securities" require registration with the SEC; and
- statutory disclosure rules apply to "securities."

In most cases, the issue turns on what is an "investment contract," a term used in both statutes and that formed the basis of the *Howey* decision. Note that although that term is used in both statutes as a part of the definition of a "security," there is no other definition of an "investment contract" in the securities laws. Post-*Howey* decisions have adopted a flexible, even expansive, interpretation of the four-part *Howey* test. The common law test looks at substance, not form, in order to define an "investment contract." It seems to be a legal term without any commercial significance.

In *Marine Bank v. Weaver*, 455 U.S. 551 (1982), the court considered the "if context otherwise requires" portion of the definition of security in the Exchange Act. At issue were certificates of deposit and the Supreme Court took note of the fact that such instruments were already extensively regulated by banking laws, especially those on depositor insurance. The court held that neither a certificate of deposit nor an agreement given as consideration for pledging the certificate to guarantee a bank loan was a security under the federal securities laws. "Congress, in enacting the securities laws, did not intend to provide a broad federal remedy for all fraud."

The Elements of the *Howey* Test Explained

A Person Invests His Money. In International Brotherhood of Teamsters v. Daniel, 439 U.S. 551 (1979), an employer-funded, fixed-benefit pension plan in which employees make no direct contribution and their participation is compulsory is not a security. There were two reasons: the plan's benefits were fixed and depended not so much on the investment returns as on the employee becoming eligible, and the ERISA statute already regulated such plans, making securities law protection less important.

In a Common Enterprise. In *SEC v. SG Ltd.*, 265 F.3d 42 (1st Cir. 2001), the court found a security when an offshore company created an online investment game that allowed players to buy a "virtual investment" and earn "virtual returns" that depended on the promoters and players luring other players into the game. The U.S. Court of Appeals for the First Circuit held that it was irrelevant that the enterprise was called a "game"; the question was whether it met the *Howey* test, and it did. There was horizontal commonality because the assets were pooled from many investors who all shared in the profits and risks, and there was vertical commonality because the investors' fortunes were tied to the success of the promoter, not the fellow investors. The court's decision was based on the horizontal commonality, largely because of the pooling.

Is Led to Expect Profits. In *United Housing Foundation, Inc. v. Forman*, 421 U.S. 837 (1975), a nonprofit co-op was created for low-income families who purchased shares of stock that allowed them to lease apartments. The tenants sued claiming false and material misrepresentations after the prices of the apartments rose. The Second Circuit held that the "stock" was a security or an investment contract, but the Supreme Court reversed. The purpose of the sale of the "stock" was to raise capital not to make a profit. Here, the purchase was motivated to use or consume the item purchased—to live in the apartment—not to make a profit. In addition, the co-op repeatedly called itself a nonprofit. So, calling something a "stock" does not necessarily make it a security.

Solely From the Efforts of Others. (Over time the word "solely" has morphed into "predominantly.") In *Williamson v. Tucker*, 645 F.2d 404 (5th Cir.

1981), the court articulated three tests for this criterion: (1) no legal control by the investor, (2) no capacity in the investor to control, and (3) no practical control to the point where the investor cannot replace the manager or exercise meaningful partnership powers. In *SEC v. Merchant Capital, LLC*, 483 F.3d 747 (11th Cir. 2007), the court applied all three *Williamson* criteria in finding that, even though a limited partnership had all the management attributes of a partnership under state law, it did not in practice give the limited partners the ability to remove the manager, and finding that they had no practical alternative to staying with the managing partner. Although in general, in a limited partnership the approach is to treat the interests of the limited partners as securities and the interests of the general partners as non-securities given their managerial role, this is not always the case if the limited partner can and does exercise some level of control. *See, e.g.*, *Steinhardt Group v. Citicorp*, 126 F.3d 144 (3d Cir. 1997).

A Stock Is Not Always a Stock

To some, the *Howey* test appeared to be a literalist test but that point of view ended with *United Housing Foundation, Inc. v. Forman*, 421 U.S. 837 (1975), in which, as noted, an investment that was literally called a "stock" was held not to be an "investment contract."[2] Justice Lewis Powell wrote that "we reject at the outset any suggestion that the present transaction, evidenced by the sale of shares called 'stock,' must be considered a security transaction simply because the statutory definition of a security includes the words 'any ... stock.'" The transaction at issue in that case was shares in a low- and middle-income housing cooperative that produced a favorable tax treatment. The sale of "stock" in order to be able to purchase an apartment in New York's Co-op City was not a security even though the instrument was called a "stock." "[T]he inducement to purchase was solely to acquire subsidized low-cost living space; it was not to invest in a profit." But, the Court said, "We do not suggest that the name is wholly irrelevant to the decision whether it is a security. There may be occasions when the use of a traditional name such as 'stocks' or 'bonds' will lead a purchaser justifiably to assume that the federal securities laws apply.... In the present case there can be no doubt that investors were attracted solely by the prospect of acquiring a place to live, and not by financial returns on their investments."

The *Forman* test abandoned the literal approach and instead adopted an "economic realities" approach that gave rise to the "sale of control of a business" line of cases. When a party transferred control of a business to another party who intended to participate actively in the ownership and management

---

[2] *Id.*

of the company, that was not the sale of a "security" because the purchaser was expected to have sufficient bargaining power to protect him- or herself. It did not matter whether the sale was structured as a sale of stock or a sale of assets.

However, the Supreme Court came back to the literal approach in *Landreth Timber Co. v. Landreth*, 471 U.S. 681 (1985). In that case, a purchaser of 100 percent of the unregistered stock of a privately held sawmill was able to sue the seller for making the sale without a registration statement and for making material misrepresentations under the federal securities laws. In this case, the purchaser decided not to run the business himself after the sale of the stock, and the seller continued to run the business. The seller's defense to the claim that stock should have been registered was to invoke the so-called "sale of business" doctrine under which, if an entire closely held corporation is sold, the "stock" of the corporation is not a security. Because the seller continued to run the sawmill after the sale, the court was skeptical whether the "sale of business doctrine" was applicable. The court held that "where an instrument bears the label 'stock' and possesses all of the characteristics typically associated with stock ... a court will not be required to look beyond the character of the instrument to the economic substance of the transaction to determine whether the stock is a 'security' within the meaning of the Acts." Back to the literalist test. A stock is a stock, it appears, except when it isn't.

In *Reves v. Ernst & Young*, 494 U.S. 56 (1990), the Supreme Court tried to resolve the split and to make sense of the issue when it articulated the so-called family resemblance test creating a rebuttable presumption that every "note" is a security unless it falls into a category of instruments that are not securities or bears a "family resemblance" to them. The Supreme Court did not create the "family resemblance" test but took it from a Second Circuit case, *Exchange Nat'l Bank v. Touche Ross & Co.*, 544 F.2d 1126 (1976), and expanded the test. It was never clear why the Supreme Court adopted the "family resemblance" test for things that are *not* securities, and not for things that were securities. However, the test works either way.

In *Reves*, a farmers co-op in the Midwest offered members uncollateralized demand promissory notes that had a variable rate of interest that was adjusted monthly. Because the notes were demand notes, they did not have terms less than nine months and therefore did not meet the statutory exemption for such notes. The co-op went bankrupt and the U.S. Court of Appeals for the Eighth Circuit rejected a securities fraud claim by the investors, holding that the "demand nature of the notes is very uncharacteristic of a security." The Supreme Court reversed, holding that the notes in question did not bear a "family resemblance" to items that were not securities. In doing so, the Supreme Court looked at four factors: the motivations of the investors, the plan of distribution of the instrument, the reasonable expectations of the investing public, and whether the existence of some other regulatory scheme reduces the risk of the instrument. Notes with a term less than nine months are more like commercial paper than securities. The "family resemblance" test between the note at issue and something that was clearly not a security was not met. In addition, the court ruled, "we have consistently identified the fundamental essence of a 'security' to be its character as an 'investment.' ... The advertisements for the notes here characterized them as 'investments' ... and there were no countervailing factors that would have led a reasonable person to question this characterization."

Most commentators have written that the *Reves* test is just another version of the *Howey* test, although the similarities are not very clear. Other commentators were critical, especially since the Supreme Court took a list of *examples* of securities appearing in the relevant statutes and married the list to the *definition* appearing in the *Howey* case, doing what one commentator described as "mixing oil and water."[3] Another commentator wrote that *Reves* appeared to have "come from another planet."[4] The take-away is that there is still no satisfactory definition of a "security." The *Reves* test remains unpredictable. In other words, a security is a security except when it is not. If you find that definition unhelpful, you are not alone.

Are All Notes Securities?

The 1934 Act provides that "a security means any note." But it also provides that "notes do not include currency, or any draft, bill of exchange or banker's acceptance which has a maturity at the time of issuance of not exceeding nine months, exclusive of days of grace, or any renewal thereof the maturity of which is likewise limited." Similar but not identical language is in the 1933 Act.

What does this language mean? Basically, the two statutes have different definitions of commercial paper. Why? There is a difference between a consumer and a commercial transaction, but notes issued in either case are not securities unless they pass the statutory test. A note that matures within nine months of a transaction is not a security. The exemption was intended to cover commercial paper—unsecured promissory notes issued by financially sound companies to finance current operations and sold to institutional investors. The lower courts had difficulty with the test, and that is why in the *Reves* case, 494 U.S. 56 (1990), the Supreme Court created the "family resemblance"

---

[3] Lawrence Page, "Even After *Reves*, Securities Do Not Have Families: Returning to Economic and Legal Realities Through a Connotative Definition of A Security," 1992 *U. Ill. L. Rev.* 249, 291-93 (1992).

[4] James D. Gordon III, "Interplanetary Intelligence About Promissory Notes as Securities," 69 *Tex. L. Rev.* 383, 404 (1990).

test. A note secured by a home mortgage, for example, is in the "family" of non-securities. As noted above, in *Reves*, the Supreme Court created four tests for a "family resemblance": (1) the motivation of the seller, (2) the plan of distribution (for example, a note given in a face-to-face negotiation to a limited group of investors is more likely not a security), (3) reasonable expectations of the investing public (if the notes are like investments, they are more likely securities), and (4) other factors reduce risk (e.g., a non-collateralized note is more likely a security).

Despite the criticism, the *Reves* test remains alive and well. In *Thompson v. People*, 471 P.3d 1045 (2020), the Colorado Supreme Court adopted the *Reves* test, overruling more than three decades of Colorado precedent. In that case, the appellant borrowed money to continue development on a real estate project without disclosing to the investors that the lots were in foreclosure and that his company had filed for bankruptcy. After defaulting on the promissory note, the appellant was charged with two counts of securities fraud and one count of theft. He was found guilty on all charges by a jury and sentenced to thirty years in prison. The appellant argued that the note at issue was merely a short-term loan to cover cash-flow problems and was not a "security." He argued that an earlier Colorado case, *People v. Milne*, 690 P.2d 829 (1984), had expanded the application of the *Howey* "investment contract" test to "investment notes" but that in *Reves*, the Supreme Court had rejected expanding the *Howey* test in that fashion. The Colorado court overruled its earlier *Milne* decision and explicitly adopted the *Reves* "family resemblance" test instead. Applying that four-factor test to the facts, the court held that the promissory note was a "security" under Colorado law (which was nearly identical to federal law on this point).

Can Digital Games Be Securities?

Yes. In *SEC v. SG Ltd.*, 265 F.3d 42 (1st Cir. 2001), a Dominican company created a computer game in which virtual shares of an enterprise existing only in cyberspace could be purchased for the entertainment of the users. One of the enterprises was labeled the "privileged company," and the website promised that shares of the privileged company would "unfailingly appreciate." Gamers could buy shares for cash, and they could sell their shares at posted prices. At least 800 people in the United States paid several thousands of dollars for shares in corporations, which funds were deposited in Latvian or Estonian banks. Predictably, participants found it difficult to redeem their shares and as new gamers were more and more reluctant to play, the site suspended all requests to withdraw funds and announced a reverse stock split, causing share prices to fall to 1/10,000 of their previous values. This was, obviously, a classic Ponzi scheme and the issue before the court was whether the shares in these virtual and otherwise fictitious companies were "securities." The district court granted the defendant's motion to dismiss the SEC complaint, pointing out that in *Howey*, the Supreme Court seemed to make a distinction between "commercial dealings" and "games." The First Circuit had little trouble concluding that the distinction between commercial dealings and games "does not translate into a dichotomy between business dealings, on the one hand, and games, on the other hand, as a failsafe way for determining whether a particular financial arrangement should (or should not) be characterized as an investment contract." The court applied the *Howey* test and concluded that the test had been met and that the motion to dismiss the SEC complaint should not have been granted.

Securitizations

A securitization is generally thought of as the pooling of non-liquid assets—typically loans such as residential mortgage loans—followed by the sale of an interest in the returns from the pool. Are such interests securities? Apply the *Howey* test to answer the question whether, in a particular case, securitizations result in the creation of securities.

The Dodd-Frank Act of 2010 seemed to treat them as securities and imposed requirements on the SEC to implement rules that prohibited underwriters of asset-backed securities (ABSs) from engaging in transactions that created conflicts of interest for a period of one year after the first closing date of the asset-backed security. In 2010, the SEC proposed rules that would give investors more information about ABSs—the same information they would receive if the ABSs were offerings that were publicly registered—and tools that would help investors analyze information about the specific loans within the pools. Some of the proposed rules were adopted in January 2011 and others were adopted in August 2014. Of significance, the SEC did not decide whether ABSs were or were not "securities" but perhaps the Dodd-Frank legislation obviated the inquiry. In any event, whether or not ABSs have "family resemblances" to non-securities, the SEC regulates them at least in part as if they were.[5]

Cryptocurrencies

Are cryptocurrencies securities? On July 25, 2017, the SEC issued its "Report of Investigation Pursuant to Section 21(a) of the Securities Exchange Act of 1934: The DAO," in order to advise "those who would use ... distributed ledger or blockchain-enabled means for capital raising to take appropriate steps to ensure compliance with the U.S. federal securities laws." The Report

[5] *See* http://www.sec.gov/spotlight/dodd-frank/assetbackedsecurities.shtml.

found that the offering of digital assets at issue in that report were investment contracts and, therefore, securities.

- The Digital Autonomous Organization was a virtual organization formed for the purpose of funding digital projects that would facilitate corporate governance and compliance with bylaws and governing laws. DAO Tokens were purchased by exchanging Ethers from Ethereum's blockchain. Applying the *Howey* test, in 2017 the SEC concluded that the Digital Autonomous Organization's tokens were "securities" but declined to take any enforcement action. To make the point clear, its DAO report provided that "offers and sales of digital assets by 'virtual' organizations [that meet the *Howey* test] are subject to the requirements of the federal securities laws."
- The holders were able to propose and vote on corporate governance projects, although there is no evidence that any were created. The holders would receive profits from successful projects. The holders did not have "meaningful control" of the process of selecting and managing the projects. This is discussed further in Chapter 21.

In a statement issued on December 11, 2017, Jay Clayton, then SEC chairman, wrote, "It has been asserted that cryptocurrencies are not securities and that the offer and sale of cryptocurrencies are beyond the SEC's jurisdiction. Whether that assertion proves correct with respect to any digital asset that is labeled as a cryptocurrency will depend on the characteristics and use of that particular asset." He continued: "[W]hile there are cryptocurrencies that do not appear to be securities, simply calling something a 'currency' or a currency-based product does not mean that it is not a security.... By and large, the structures of initial coin offerings that I have seen promoted involve the offer and sale of securities and directly implicate the securities registration requirements and other investor protection provisions of our federal securities laws."[6]

In its "Statement on Potentially Unlawful Online Platforms for Trading Digital Assets," March 2018, the SEC said, "If a platform offers trading of digital assets that are securities and operates as an 'exchange' as defined by the federal securities laws, then the platform must register with the SEC as a national securities exchange or be exempt from registration." The following day, Bitcoin fell 10 percent, falling below the key $10,000 level.

In a speech given on June 24, 2018, William Hinman, the SEC Director of Corporation Finance, said that whether digital assets should be considered

---

[6] Jay Clayton, "Statement on Cryptocurrencies and Initial Coin Offerings," SEC, December 11, 2017.

securities depended in part on the expectations of purchasers and whether "a third party—be it a person, entity or coordinated group of actors—drives the expectation of a return." In a 2018 case, *SEC v. Blockvest LLC*, Judge Gonzalo Curiel of the U.S. District Court for the Southern District of California, denied a motion by the SEC for a preliminary injunction that would have prevented an offering of a cryptocurrency, stating that more discovery was required before the SEC could demonstrate that the tokens at issue were "securities," Case No. 18 cv 2287-GPC (S.D. Cal. 2018) (sanctions lifted, April 17, 2020). Applying the classic Supreme Court four-part test for determining whether an investment contract is a "security" set forth in *SEC v. W.J. Howey Co.*, 328 U.S. 293 (1946) (an investment of money, in a common enterprise, with an expectation of profits solely produced by the efforts of others), the court held that there was insufficient proof that the investors had an "expectation of profits." (Later cases have tended to ignore the word "solely.")[7] The focus rather is on whether the investor provides essential managerial efforts.[8]

Recent Development on Cryptocurrencies

On December 22, 2020, the SEC sued Ripple Labs Inc. and two of its senior executives for selling 14.6 billion XRP tokens without filing a registration statement. The complaint, filed in the U.S. District Court for the Southern District of New York, alleges that the defendants were told by their law firm in 2012 that the XRP tokens might be considered "investment contracts" and thus securities, and the defendants were advised to consult with the SEC. Nevertheless, the defendants did not heed the legal advice, did not consult with the SEC, and continued to market the tokens. The complaint, which is long and detailed (seventy-one pages) follows the *Howey* path in alleging that the tokens met the elements of the *Howey* test and were investment contracts, not currencies. At issue is something called an "XRP," units (of something) that were marketed to purchasers who wished "to engage in speculative investment trading." They were related in some fashion to something called the "XRP Ledger" that "operates as a peer-to-peer database, spread across a network

---

[7] On February 14, 2019, the court reversed itself and granted a preliminary injunction because of evidence that the defendant had engaged in prior securities violations, including forged signatures and deliberate false declarations and because there was evidence that they would be repeated. 2020 WL 1910355 (S.D. Cal. Apr. 20, 2020). In November 2020, the SEC imposed "terminating sanctions" on Blockvest, resulting in a default judgment against it, depriving it of a trial. Among other things, Blockvest falsely claimed to have been registered and approved by the SEC and forged witness signatures on doctored affidavits.

[8] *See* Stephen Choi & A.C. Pritchard, *Securities Regulation: The Essentials* (Wolters Kluwer, 2008), 67.

of computers that records data respecting transactions." Each server on the network evaluates the proposed transactions from a subset of servers it trusts, known as the server's "unique node list." The company that sold the XRPs was a subsidiary of Ripple Labs, and it owned 80 percent of the outstanding XRPs. The founders owned the remaining 20 percent. Lacking financing, the owners of Ripple decided to sell XRPs to finance its operations. Purchasers were told that the XRPs were a "speculative investment." The Ripple owners acknowledged that the XRPs had some "securities-type characteristics." If you are confused by this, you are not alone. One of Ripple's lawyers, Andrew Ceresney, a former SEC Director of Enforcement, said that the SEC's complaint "stretches *Howey* beyond recognition." The subject is quite complicated and the trial is undoubtedly years away.

Simple Agreements for Future Tokens (SAFTs) are investment contracts offered by cryptocurrency developers to accredited investors. They are definitely considered securities and as a result must comply with all securities regulations. The purpose of these Tokens is to help developers raise money without violating securities regulations. When the investor buys a SAFT, the investor receives documentation indicating that if the developer creates a cryptocurrency or other product, the investor will be given access. The SEC has been vigilant in pursuing unregistered SAFTs. For example, in June 2019, the SEC sued Kik Interactive Inc. for making a $100 million Initial Coin Offering that was an unregistered securities offering involving the SAFT framework. Southern District of New York Judge Alvin Hellerstein granted summary judgment for the SEC. Applying the *Howey* test, Judge Hellerstein found that the Kik offerings were securities. Under the SAFT structure, Kik's investors purchased the right to receive future tokens, called "Kin," at a discount price in a subsequent offering pursuant to the SAFT. Kik had filed a Form D with the SEC in which it claimed that the offerings were exempt from registration. Judge Hellerstein disagreed.[9]

A Simple Agreement for Future Equity (SAFE) allows investors who put cash into a start-up to convert the stake into equity at a later date.[10]

---

[9] *SEC v. Kik Interactive Inc.*, Docket No. 1:19-cv-05244 (S.D.N.Y. Sept. 30, 2020) (opinion and order granting motion for summary judgment).

[10] *See* Investopedia, July 1, 2020.

Chapter 3

Materiality

Why Do We Care About "Materiality"?

As noted, securities markets are basically markets based on information but there can be a problem: too little or too much information can distort a market. To rectify that problem, the securities laws have developed the concept of "materiality." This concept is important in two different contexts. First, it used to define information that issuers or filers must publicly disclose and file with the SEC. Second, it acts as a definition of the types of misstatements or omissions that would constitute violations of the securities laws. Unfortunately, like the word "security" that we discussed in the preceding chapter, there is no definite or universal definition of the word "materiality."

What Is "Materiality"?

There is no definition of the word "materiality" in either the 1933 or the 1934 Act although, as we will see, the SEC has attempted various definitions in its rules. The prevailing definition comes from the Supreme Court case *TSC Industries, Inc. v. Northway Inc.*, 426 U.S. 438 (1976): "An omitted fact is material if there is a substantial likelihood that a reasonable shareholder would consider it important in deciding how to vote.... Put another way, there must be a substantial likelihood that the disclosure of the omitted fact would have been viewed by the reasonable investor as having significantly altered the 'total mix' of information made available." This test was similar but not exactly the same as the test articulated by the Seventh Circuit below. The Supreme Court substituted the word "would" for the word "might" in the Seventh Circuit test.

Some observers believe that the *Northway* test had two parts, the "substantial likelihood" part and the "total mix" part. However, recall that according to Justice Thurgood Marshall, the "real nature of the question being asked is this: is there a substantial likelihood that the omitted information would have assumed actual significance in the deliberations of the reasonable investor?"

Moreover, a close reading of the text makes it rather clear that the "total mix" part is merely one way of proving the "substantial likelihood" part. This is how the SEC reads the test, at least in some of its interpretations.

A few years after *Northway*, in *Basic v. Levinson*, 485 U.S. 224 (1988), the Supreme Court again endorsed the *Northway* test, making it clear that there was no "bright-line test" for materiality and that at least with respect to future events, "[materiality] will depend at any given time upon a balancing of both the indicated probability that the event will occur and the anticipated magnitude of the event in light of the totality of the company activity." This became known as the "probability and magnitude" test of materiality.[1]

And in *Matrixx Initiatives Inc. v. Siracusano*, 563 U.S. 27 (2011), the Supreme Court slightly modified the *Northway* test by changing the phrase "a substantial likelihood" to the phrase "it is substantially likely that ..."

The *Northway* test raises more questions than it answers. For example, who is a "reasonable investor"? Does it have to be a person who buys and sells securities? Does the investor have to understand how securities markets operate and have a more than basic understanding of financial documents? What is a "substantial likelihood" or "substantially likely"? Does there have to be a more than fifty-fifty chance that the event will occur or that the reasonable investor would consider it important? How could a "substantial likelihood" be proved? What does "significantly altered" mean?

Because *Northway* remains the current test for "materiality," let's take a closer look at the case. National Industries merged with TSC and did not disclose in the proxy statement that National had already taken control of TSC. Northway brought claims under 1934 Act Rule 14a-3 alleging that the corporate defendants failed to mention in their proxies that a change in control had already taken place when certain interests in TSC were transferred to National. It also alleged under Rule 14a-9 that the proxy statement failed to include material information concerning (1) the degree of National's influence over the management of TSC, including the favorability of the terms of National's acquisition proposal to the TSC shareholders, and (2) the fact that its investment banker had submitted an opinion letter to the effect that the merger would be less profitable to the TSC shareholders than earlier predicted. The *plaintiff* moved for summary judgment, and the defendant National cross-moved for summary judgment. The district court denied both motions. The U.S. Court of Appeals for the Seventh Circuit affirmed the district court except that it found that the failure to include the investment banker's adverse

---

[1] *See, e.g.*, J. Anthony Terrell, "Materiality in Review—Probability, Magnitude and the Reasonable Investor," Bracewell (2012), https://bracewell.com/sites/default/files/knowledge-center/Materiality%20in%20Review_1.pdf.

opinion letter violated Rule 14a-9 as a matter of law and that the motion for summary judgment should have been granted on that claim.

What gave rise to the Supreme Court's review of the case was the Seventh Circuit's articulation of the proper test for materiality, that it should include "all facts which a reasonable stockholder *might* consider important ... in the process of determining how to vote" (emphasis added). The question was whether "might" was the right test. It was not; the Supreme Court's new articulation did not include that word. The Supreme Court held that National's failure to include the banker's letter was not materially misleading as a matter of law, and therefore that Northway was not entitled to a decision of partial summary judgment on that claim.

Basic seemed to hold that materiality was a question of fact but some lower courts treat materiality determinations as questions of law. For example, *Longman v. Food Lion Inc.*, 197 F.3d 675 (4th Cir. 1999), held that a company's omissions with respect to its labor and sanitary problems were well known to the market and therefore not material as a matter of law. The better view, according to most courts, is that materiality is a *mixed* question of law and fact. In *Chadbourne & Parke LLP v. Troice*, 571 U.S. 321 (2104), the Supreme Court held—in substance but not words—that the question was a mixed question of law and fact; the issue was whether the representation that the covered securities would be backed by uncovered securities was *in fact* not true, and whether *in law* the securities were "covered securities" under the Securities Litigation Uniform Standards Act. The test adopted by the Supreme Court was only a slight variation from the *Northway* test, that materiality is "something that makes a significant difference in a decision to buy or sell a security." *Query*: Is "significant difference" essentially the same as "substantial likelihood"?

In some cases, the difference between "material" and "immaterial" can be quite subjective. For example, in *In re MCI WorldCom Securities Litigation*, 93 F. Supp. 2d 276 (E.D.N.Y. 2000), the court held that a statement denying the existence of actual pending merger negotiations was material because the truth "might have given a reasonable investor pause." But in *Philips v. LCI International, Inc.*, 190 F.3d 609 (4th Cir. 1999), the court held that the statement "We're not a company for sale" in the middle of merger negotiations was not material. Perhaps for this reason, few materiality determinations are made on a summary judgment motion.

A few additional points concerning materiality and class actions:

- In *Amgen Inc. v. Connecticut Retirement Plans and Trust Funds*, 133 S. Ct. 1184 (2013), the Supreme Court decided that to certify a class, the court need not decide whether the statement at issue was material, since that is a merits issue. But after *Halliburton v. Erica P. John Fund*, 573 U.S. 258 (2014) (*Halliburton II*), a defendant can defeat class certification by showing that the statement at issue did not have a price impact and therefore is not "material." This is discussed further in Chapter 10.

- Does a material misrepresentation always result in a price distortion or impact? Could the "price impact" be merely maintaining the stock price at a certain level? That question was posed to the Supreme Court in the *Goldman Sachs* case but the court declined to decide it. We will discuss that case at length in Chapter 10.
- In *Matrixx Initiatives Inc.*, 563 U.S. 27 (2011), the court held that the fact that adverse reaction reports to the use of a nasal spray were not rendered immaterial even though there were not enough of them to be statistically significant.

Who Is a "Reasonable Investor"?

The courts do not provide a clear, simple answer to this question. This is the result of a disagreement with respect to who is the object of the securities law's disclosure regime: is it a sophisticated analyst or an unsophisticated investor? Many of the SEC's required disclosure forms are clearly not intended for the unsophisticated investor but for a professional analyst (*see Wielgos v. Commonwealth Edison Co.*, 892 F.2d 509 (7th Cir. 1989)). Others must be written in "plain English," obviously for the benefit of the less than fully sophisticated investor (*see* Securities Act Rule 421 (the "plain English" rule); *Pinter v. Dahl*, 486 U.S. 622 (1988)). In *In re Merck & Co. Inc. Securities Litigation*, 432 F.3d 261 (3d Cir. 2005), the court held that "reasonable investors are the market." Does that make sense? Is the "reasonable investor" similar to the "reasonable person" of tort law? Could a jury be expected to decide who a "reasonable investor" is without substantial additional jury instructions? Who decides? Although, as noted, materiality is a mixed question of law and fact, it is most often decided by the court, not a jury.

Perhaps the best definition of "reasonable investor" came from the Seventh Circuit in *Flamm v. Eberstadt*, 814 F.2d 1169 (7th Cir. 1987), which considered whether preliminary merger negotiations should be disclosed. The court said that "to attribute to investors a child-like simplicity, an inability to grasp the probabilistic significance of negotiations, implies that they should not be told about new plants, new products, new managers, or any of the other changes in the life of a corporation. These new events—things with potential for boom or bust—are exactly the news on which sophisticated investors make most decisions.... Disclosures to the market as a whole cannot be limited to what is fit for rubes." The Supreme Court's *Basic* case quoted this case with approval.[2]

The Relationship Between Materiality and the Duty to Disclose

The duty to disclose that permeates the federal securities laws deals with *whether* and *when* information must be disclosed, whereas materiality deals with *what* must be disclosed. In either event, there is an overarching obligation of honesty. Having possession of material information does not, in and of itself, trigger a duty to disclose the information. But some material information must be disclosed. For example, events specified in Items 1-6 and 9 of Form 8-K must be disclosed. An example is Item 5.02, which requires the disclosure of the fact that a board director has resigned "because of a disagreement with the registrant" and "a brief description of the circumstances representing the disagreement." For this reason, as we will see below, the SEC has attempted to devise its own definitions of materiality for the purposes of disclosure requirements. To be sure, some filers are not enthusiastic about having to disclose information that may be embarrassing or detrimental to their businesses; that is where lawyers and accountants play an important persuasive role.

Whether or not there is a duty to disclose—and even if information is voluntarily disclosed—it must be true. The federal securities laws require honesty. There is a duty (1) not to make false statements about material facts, (2) not to omit a material fact so as to make a statement that is made materially false or misleading, (3) to correct materially false or misleading statements, and (4) to update certain statements that have become materially false or misleading. Note that some courts make a distinction between the duty to correct a false statement and the duty to update it when it later becomes false. (*See In re Burlington Coat Factory Sec. Lit.*, 114 F.3d 1410 (3d Cir. 1997), which contains a good and useful discussion of the differences between the two.)

Can there ever be too much disclosure? We know that the SEC has increased—and is continuing to increase—its required disclosures. This has

---

[2] For additional useful reading on the concept of the "reasonable investor," *see* Amanda Rose, "The 'Reasonable Investor' of Federal Securities Law: Insights From Tort Law's 'Reasonable Person' & Suggested Reforms," 43 *J. Corp. L.* 77 (2017); Tom Lin, "Reasonable Investor(s)," 95 *Bos. U. L. Rev.* 461 (2015); and Hon. Richard Posner, "Behavioral Finance Before Kahneman," 44 *Loy. U. Chi. L.J.* 1341 (2013) (Daniel Kahneman won the Nobel Memorial Prize in Economic Sciences in 2002 for his research that concluded that the average human being was rational but often made mistakes in routine decisions and for that reason, often needed help to make more accurate judgments and decisions." Kahneman, *Thinking, Fast and Slow*, Farrar, Straus and Giroux (2011).

given rise by some to the argument that such requirements have led to "information overload" and that "billions of consumers receive too much information as they move through daily life."[3] Under the so-called buried facts doctrine, some corporations have chosen to hide bad facts in their mandated disclosures by surrounding them with distracting and irrelevant information.[4]

A relevant case in point was the Enron scandal of the early 2000s. Enron was one of the most successful companies in the country but hard times and changes in business direction caused it to resort to "mark-to-market" accounting.[5] Because Enron had taken on enormous debt to carry it through before the contracts could actually produce revenue, it created "special purpose entities" (SPEs) to which its debt was transferred, taking it off the Enron balance sheet. These were enormously complex entities that few people understood, but Enron argued that its footnote descriptions of the SPEs were sufficient.[6] However, a close reading of the footnotes in Enron's financial statements discussed these SPEs in such detail that one accounting professor at Baruch College said that "most people would be hard pressed to understand the effects of these disclosures on the financial statements, casting doubt on both the quality of the company's earnings as well as the business purpose of the transaction."[7]

Malcolm Gladwell argues that Enron was not a puzzle but a mystery because it did not disclose too little information, but too much. Quoting Duke Law's professor Steven Schwarcz, Gladwell writes, "You can try to make

---

[3] Karen B. Schulz, "Information Flooding," 48 *Indiana L. Rev.* 755 (2015). To be fair, Professor Schulz does not agree with the premise she stated and in particular with the proposal by some politicians that mandatory disclosures be scaled back. Instead, she proposed using "information intermediaries."

[4] Troy Paredes, "Blinded by the Light: Information Overload and Its Consequences for Securities Regulation," 81 *Wash. U. L. Q.* 417, 419 (2003).

[5] "Mark-to-market" accounting permitted companies to book as current revenue on their balance sheets future contracts, even if there were no quoted prices upon which to base their estimates of future value. In 2000, for example, unrealized trades accounted for more than half of Enron's reported pretax profit.

[6] In a typical SPE transaction, Enron would transfer some its stock to an SPE in return for a note or cash. The SPE would then hedge a particular investment on Enron's balance sheet, using the Enron stock as the principal source of payment. One of the purposes was to move debt from Enron's balance sheet to the SPE's. Steven L. Schwarcz, "Enron and the Use and Abuse of Special Purpose Entities in Corporate Structures," 70 *U. Cinn. L. Rev.* 1309 (2002). According to the Senate Committee on Governmental Affairs Report on the "Role of the Board of Directors in Enron's Collapse," U.S. Gov't Printing Office July 8, 2020, Enron's 10-K filings for 1999 and 2000 listed almost 3,000 separate special purpose entities. It concluded that the Enron Board failed to provide sufficient oversight and restraint to stop management excess [and] contributed to Enron's collapse and bears a share of the responsibility for it."

[7] C. William Thomas, "The Rise and Fall of Enron," *Journal of Accountancy*, Apr. 1, 2002.

financial transactions understandable by simplifying them, in which case you run the risk of smoothing over some of the potential risks, or you can try to disclose every potential pitfall, in which case you'll make the disclosure so unwieldy that no one will be able to understand it." The idea, according to Schwarcz, "that the more a company tells us about its business, the better off we are—has become an anachronism."[8] Enron disclosed too much but did so in a confusing, largely unintelligible way. As a result, three of its senior executives, Kenneth Lay, its chairman; Jeffrey Skilling, its CEO; and Andrew Fastow, its CFO, were convicted. Lay died of a heart attack before he could be sentenced, Skilling was sentenced to twenty-four years in prison, and Fastow six.

For those struggling with the concept of materiality and mandated disclosures, the Enron lesson is instructive. Mandated material disclosures must be true, clear, and easy to understand. Beware of the "buried facts" doctrine that might tempt some to disguise the disclosure of bad facts with irrelevant and obtuse jargon that cannot be understood by the most accomplished readers. Auditors and especially lawyers must give candid and independent advice to their clients, especially when giving advice about required disclosures. Disclosures must be able to be understood by the "reasonable investor," however defined.[9]

Are There Quantitative Benchmarks for "Materiality"?

At one time, accountants and auditors took the position that information was not material unless it had a specified effect on a firm's financials, an effect such as 10 percent. However, in SEC Staff Accounting Bulletin No. 99 (1999), the SEC made it clear that "the use of a percentage as a numerical threshold, such as 5%, may provide the basis for a preliminary assumption that . . . a deviation of less than the specified percentage with respect to a particular item . . . is unlikely to be material. . . . But quantifying, in percentage terms, the magnitude of a misstatement . . . cannot appropriately be used as a substitute for a full analysis of all relevant considerations." In addition, SAB 99 made it clear that even small discrepancies can be *qualitatively* material. They could mask, for example, earnings trends or the failure of the firm to meet analysts'

---

[8] Malcolm Gladwell, "Open Secrets: Enron, Intelligence and the Perils of Too Much Information," *The New Yorker*, January 1, 2007.

[9] *See Kohn v. American Metal Climax, Inc.*, 322 F. Supp. 1331 (E.D. Pa. 1971), *modified* 458 F.2d 255 (3d Cir. 1972), *cert. denied*, 409 U.S. 874 (1972). ("The Securities Exchange Act requires more than disclosure, it requires adequate disclosure. The more material the facts, the more they should be brought to the attention of the public.")

expectations. Thus, courts must consider both quantitative and qualitative factors in assessing an item's materiality.[10]

In *Litwin v. Blackstone Group, L.P.*, 634 F.3d 706 (2d Cir. 2011), *cert. denied*, Oct. 3, 2011, the Second Circuit recognized the 5 percent starting point for a quantitative analysis of materiality but quickly added that "a quantitative analysis is not dispositive of materiality." The court then analyzed the six factors that courts and the SEC often consider when assessing materiality (unlawful conduct, omissions relating to a significant aspect of the defendant's business, market reaction to disclosure, hiding a failure to meet analysts' expectations, changing a loss into income, and affecting compliance with loan covenants) and concluded that the complaint should not have been dismissed by the district court. Of interest for subsequent discussion of Sections 11 and 12(a)(2) of the 1933 Act is the fact that the complaint in this case did not allege fraud but only that the offering document contained a material omission.[11] The complaint also alleged a violation of Item 303 of Regulation S-K, which requires that issuers such as Blackstone (which was issuing an IPO) "describe any known trends or uncertainties that have or that [it] reasonably expects will have a material favorable or unfavorable impact on new sales or revenues or income from continuing operations." Courts have held that an omission of a fact required to be stated under Item 303 will generally produce liability under Section 11. The case was later settled for $85 million.

The significance of *Litwin* is one of pleading. The case came to the Second Circuit after the district court had dismissed the complaint for failure adequately to plead a claim that is "plausible on its face" as required by the Supreme Court's leading pleading cases, *Bell Atlantic Corp. v. Twombly*, 550 U.S. 544 (2007), and *Ashcroft v. Iqbal*, 129 S. Ct. 1937 (2009). The Second Circuit was satisfied that the plaintiff had "plausibly alleged" material omissions in the registration statement, and that was sufficient. Thus, according to one observer, the court "minimiz[ed] the pleading obligations under Sections 11 and 12(a)(2) of the Securities Act of 1933, focusing its analysis on the importance of the allegedly misleading statements to a corporate segment rather than the public entity itself; and permitting a claim to be based on corporate and

---

[10] *See, e.g.*, *Ganino v. Citizens Utils. Co.*, 228 F.3d 154, 161-62 (2d Cir. 2000) citing *Basic*, 485 U.S. at 231.

[11] This case added to the body of case law that holds there is a private right of action under Item 303 of Regulation S-K. The Supreme Court attempted to resolve a Circuit split when it granted, then dismissed, a writ of certiorari in *Indiana Public Retirement System v. SAIC*, 818 F.3d 85 (2d Cir. 2016), cert. dismissed after settlement).

market developments that were publicly known but not specifically described in the registration statement at issue."[12]

With respect to its discussion of quantitative benchmarks for materiality, the court did not find that quantitative factors alone could support a materiality claim but it did reinforce the SEC's position that quantitative factors could be a useful starting point for a materiality analysis.

The Significance of a Relationship Between Materiality and Stock Price Changes

As we will see in much more detail when we discuss Section 10(b) and Rule 10b-5, courts have drawn a relationship between materiality and price impact. Many economists believe that if a public statement of information about a company does not cause a price impact (i.e., a statistically significant risk-adjusted difference between the return of the stock price and the return of the chosen portfolio of relevance), then it is not material.[13] But does the decision rest on the efficiency of the market? In *In re Merck & Co. Inc. Securities Litigation*, 432 F.3d 261 (3d Cir. 2005), Merck's stock price dropped after the *Wall Street Journal* revealed aggressive revenue recognition practices. As a result, an IPO of a subsidiary was canceled. Some details of the accounting practices had been disclosed by Merck two months before the *Wall Street Journal* article, and Merck's stock price rose. Although the court criticized Merck's lukewarm disclosure, it found that in an efficient market (is there really any such thing?), materiality is defined as "information that alters the price of the firm's stock." Here, the partial disclosure was followed by an increase in the stock price. The complaint was dismissed on the pleadings. Could the decision have gone the other way? If the company's disclosure constituted an incomplete representation, is it fair to let the company off the hook because of the market's response?

---

[12] Brad S. Karp, "Second Circuit Addresses Materiality Standard Under Federal Securities Law," Harvard Law School Forum on Corporate Governance, March 8, 2011, https://corpgov.law.harvard.edu/2011/03/08/second-circuit-addresses-materiality-standard-under-federal-securities-law/.

[13] As we discuss in Chapter 10, there is a body of case law, including the *Arkansas Teachers' Retirement Fund v. Goldman Sachs* group of cases, that raises the question whether public information about a company that does not have a measurable price impact can nevertheless "maintain" a price inflation introduced into the stock by an earlier misrepresentation.

The Difference Between a Material Statement and "Puffery"

The line between a statement of fact that may be relied upon by a reasonable investor and "puffery" is real but often hard to determine. Under the *Northway* "total mix" of information available test, it would seem that a statement of pure "puffery" would add nothing to the total mix of information available. A statement that Sunrise Pizza makes "the best pizza on the East Coast" is so obviously an exaggeration incapable of proof that no reasonable investor could realistically rely on it when determining the value of the Sunrise Pizza business. "Puffery" defenses are now recognized in virtually every Circuit.[14]

Can Statements of Opinion Be Material?

Recall that the federal statutes refer to "material statements of fact." Statements of opinion are typically not material because a reasonable investor would not make an investment decision based on an opinion. In *Virginia Bankshares, Inc. v. Sandberg*, 501 U.S. 1083 (1991), the Supreme Court held that if the person rendering the opinion actually believed it, then it was not actionable even if it was not reasonable or accurate. But that test has since been modified.

In 2015, the Supreme Court decided *Omnicare Inc. v. Laborers District Council Construction Industry Pension Fund*, 135 S. Ct. 1318 (2015), reversing the Sixth Circuit and remanding for further proceedings. The Supreme Court held that a statement of opinion does not constitute an untrue statement of material fact simply because the stated opinion ultimately proves incorrect. (Recall that Section 11 is a "strict liability" statute that does not require a showing of scienter.) In the first part of the court's opinion, it reaffirmed the general rule that a statement of opinion affirms the "fact" that the speaker actually holds the stated belief. If that is not the case, then the statement may be actionable. The statement can also be actionable if the speaker's supporting facts, if articulated in the opinion, are untrue.

But then the court went further and discussed an issue not discussed by the Sixth Circuit, namely, whether the statement of opinion also affirms the unstated fact that there is a reasonable basis for the opinion. The court held that that question had to be addressed from the perspective of a reasonable investor. For example, where, as in this case, the statement of opinion concerned a belief that the company was in compliance with applicable law, a reasonable investor might conclude that the speaker had consulted with legal counsel. Context is important, as are other qualifying statements that are

[14] Robert Kravitz, "Room for Optimism: The Puffery Defense Under the Federal Securities Laws," Securities Litigation Journal, ABA Section of Litigation, Vol. 19, No. 3 (Spring 2009).

made at the same time. The question to be answered is whether the omitted "fact" that the reasonable investor would assume is a part of the basis for the opinion (i.e., whether counsel were consulted before the statement of opinion was made) would have been material to a reasonable investor (i.e., whether there is a "substantial likelihood that a reasonable [investor] would consider it important.")

This appears to be a significant case as far as Section 11 liability is concerned. Is the same reasoning applicable to statements of opinion in claims made under Section 10(b)? Probably. Many district courts have already applied *Omnicare* to claims under Section 10(b). *See, e.g.*, *In re Genworth Financial Securities Litigation*, 2015 U.S. Dist. LEXIS 57600 (E.D. Va. May 1, 2015).

Can Forward-Looking Statements Be Material?

Although the SEC once took the position that companies should not disclose favorable forward-looking information, the SEC gradually agreed that forward-looking statements were not necessarily misleading and in some cases were helpful. In fact, SEC safe harbor rules (Rule 175, Securities Act; Rule 3b-6, Exchange Act) permitted forward-looking statements unless they were made without a reasonable basis or disclosed in anything other than good faith. Since 1989, the SEC has *required* the presentation of soft non-financial forward-looking information in the MD&As of certain filings, such as in annual reports and prospectuses. Under Rule 303 of Regulation S-K, companies must disclose trends and uncertainties that are "reasonably likely to result" in material changes to a company's financial position. The SEC's safe harbor rules, Rule 175 of the 1933 Act, and Rule 3b-6 of the 1934 Act seems to have been superseded in part—or at least complemented by—the safe harbor provisions of the Private Securities Litigation Reform Act (PSLRA).

Safe Harbors

As noted, for many years the SEC not only did not encourage corporations to make projections about future results, it affirmatively prohibited them.[15] Apparently the SEC was concerned that such statements might confuse investors. After a study and the creation of a commission to review the issue, the Wheat Commission, the SEC decided neither to encourage nor discourage forward-looking statements. Eventually, following the work of a subsequent advisory committee and the court-made doctrine of "bespeaks caution" that insulated forward-looking statements that contained appropriate cautionary

---

[15] Royce Barondes, "The Bespeaks Caution Doctrine: Revisiting the Application of Federal Securities Law to Opinions and Estimates," 19 J. Corp. L. 243 (1994).

language,[16] the SEC enacted Rule 175, a safe harbor rule in the Securities Act and Rule 3b-6, a similar rule in the Exchange Act, to protect forward-looking statements that were made in good faith.

The PSLRA, enacted in 1995 and incorporated into both the Securities and the Exchange Acts, similarly created a safe harbor for forward-looking statements, but the conditions of that safe harbor are very hard to meet. The U.S. Court of Appeals for the District of Columbia Circuit recently held that the meaningful language had to contain "substantive company-specific warnings based on a realistic description of the risks applicable to the particular circumstances.... The cautionary language need not necessarily mention the factor that ultimately belies the forward-looking statement ... or warn of 'all' important factors, so long as an investor has been warned of risks of a significance similar to those that were actually realized ... such that the investor is sufficiently on notice of the danger of the investment to make an intelligent decision about it according to her own preferences for risk and reward." *In re Harman International Industries, Inc. Securities Litigation*, 791 F.3d 90 (D.C. Cir. 2015) (quoting from *Harris v. Ivax Corp.*, 182 F.3d 799, 897 (11th Cir. 1999)).

How can you tell whether a statement is forward-looking? The Eighth Circuit has held that "the determinative factor is not the tense of the statement; instead, the key is whether its truth or falsity is discernible only after it is made." *Julianello v. K-V Pharm. Co.*, 791 F.3d 915 (8th Cir. 2015). Perhaps the most well-known case for such statements is *Harris v. Ivax Corp.*, 182 F.3d 799, in which the statement "the challenges unique to this period in our history are now behind us" was held to be forward-looking because its truth could only be verified after the statement was made. There are many other similar examples. Do you find that to be a useful test? Many believe—and I am one of them—that the test is somewhat subjective and difficult to apply consistently.

Can Forward-Looking Statements Be Actionable?

Until the *Omnicare* case discussed above, *Virginia Bankshares, Inc. v. Sandberg*, 501 U.S. 1083 (1991), stood for the proposition that an opinion was not actionable unless the maker did not believe the opinion or lacked a basis for holding the opinion. The same is generally true about failed predictions of future performance. After *Omnicare*, *Virginia Bankshares* may no

---

[16] *See generally*, Anand Das, "A License to Lie: The Private Securities Litigation Reform Act's Safe Harbor for Forward-Looking Statements Does Not Protect False or Misleading Statements When Made With Meaningful Cautionary Language," 60 *Cath. U. L. Rev.* 1083 (2011).

longer be good law. Even if forward-looking statements are actionable, however, the various safe harbors in the securities laws offer the maker considerable protection.

What if a Forward-Looking Statement Is Immaterial?

Few courts have addressed this issue but those that have done so suggest that a forward-looking statement can be material only "where it is sufficiently specific for an investor to reasonably rely on that statement as a guarantee of some concrete fact or outcome" and, of course, immaterial forward-looking statements would not be actionable. *City of Pontiac Policemen's & Firemen's Retirement System v. UBS AG*, 752 F.3d 173 (2d Cir. 2014). However, the court's articulation may be a bit of an overstatement since many public companies do give forward-looking information that is both material and actionable, absent qualifying for a safe harbor.

Various SEC Tests of Materiality

Following the *Northway* decision, the SEC began to incorporate various definitions of materiality into its rules.[17] For example, SEC Rule 405 under the 1933 Act defined "materiality" as follows: "The term material, when used to qualify a requirement for the furnishing of information as to any subject, limits the information required to those matters to which there is a substantial likelihood that a reasonable investor would attach importance in determining whether to purchase the security registered." A similar definition is contained in Rule 12b-2 under the 1934 Act.

As discussed in Chapter 1, the SEC requires various disclosures in its Regulations S-K and S-X, and it has characterized those required disclosures as those that are "material" to the reporting company. For example, Item 105 of Regulation S-K requires a disclosure of the "material" risk factors that make an investment in the offering speculative or risky.

The SEC has issued guidance in which it made it clear that most of the disclosures are required only if management concludes that they would have a "material" effect on financial conditions or operations. In addition, in several sections of its guidance, the SEC, paying lip service to the "probability" test, requires disclosures only of events that management determines are "reasonably likely" to occur. A similar limitation is found in the SEC's 2020 MD&A

---

[17] Many of these definitions are discussed in some detail by J. Anthony Terrell, "Materiality in Review—Probability, Magnitude and the Reasonable Investor," Bracewell (2012), https://bracewell.com/sites/default/files/knowledge-center/Materiality%20in%20Review_1.pdf.

guidance (Release No. 33-10890) in which, for example, the SEC clarified and simplified its guidance to require disclosure of material events and uncertainties known to management "that have a material impact on reported operations, as well as matters that are reasonably likely based on management's assessment to have a material impact on future operations." Anthony Terrell asks, and properly so, whether this recent articulation incorporates the *Northway* and *Basic* "substantial likelihood" language.[18] The SEC's guidance attempts to answer that question by stating that "known trends ... that are not remote or where management cannot make an assessment as to the likelihood that they will come to fruition, and that would be reasonably likely to have a material effect on the registrant's future results or financial condition were they to come to fruition, should be disclosed *if a reasonable investor would consider the omission of the information as significantly altering the mix of information made available in the registrant's disclosures.*" Does this sound familiar?

The SEC's requirements for disclosures of market risks, contained primarily in Item 305 of Regulation S-K, contain similar provisions that only "material" risks following "materiality assessments" need be disclosed.

With respect to the SEC's Regulation S-X, Terrell points out that somewhat surprisingly the SEC slightly changes its definition of "materiality" by providing that the term "material" limits the information required to those matters about which an *average prudent* investor *ought* reasonably to be informed" (emphasis added).

Various Accounting Tests for Materiality

In recent years, the accounting profession has attempted with varying degrees of success to create its own definitions of materiality. Anthony Terrell has studied those definitions and has concluded that "materiality remains a multifaceted enigma, perhaps reminiscent of the Hydra of Greek mythology. There is no bright-line test, no magic formula."[19]

For example, Terrell writes that although the Accounting Standards Codification teaches that its provisions do not apply to immaterial items in a financial statement, it contains no definition of materiality, although several releases from the Financial Accounting Standards Board, the entity selected by the SEC to set accounting standards, define loss contingencies and probabilities, concepts that could be used to define materiality. The FASB's Concepts Statement No. 2 defines "material" as follows: "The omission or misstatement of an item in a financial report is material if, in light of surrounding circumstances, the magnitude of the item is such that it is probable that the judgment

[18] *Id.* at 12.

[19] *Id.*

of a reasonable person relying upon the report would have been changed or influenced by the inclusion or correction of the item." However, its Concept Statement No. 8 substituted the word "could" for the word "would" after considerable criticism and debate over the use of the word "would."

The Public Company Accounting Oversight Board (PCOAB) adopted the *Northway* test and then applied three different materiality levels, based on the magnitude of the consequences of the material misrepresentation. Each magnitude level is a fixed amount but is merely a tool to assist the auditor in determining what misstatements in the financials would be material under the applicable laws.

Like FASB's Concept Statement No. 8, the American Institute of Certified Public Accountants (AICPA) has developed its own definition of materiality to be applied by auditors who are auditing financial statements, and it uses the phrase "could reasonably be expected to influence the economic decisions of users."

Terrell argues with some force that because both the Securities Laws and the accounting oversight boards use the word "material" for different purposes, it might have been preferable for the PCOAB and the AICPA to have used different terminology although he does not propose any.[20]

---

[20] *Id.* at 30.

Chapter 4

Registration of Securities Offerings

What Is a "Public Company"?

Most corporations in the United States are privately owned but because of their size, they face difficulty in expanding and in managing a larger enterprise. The concept of a "public company" first appeared in Section 12(a) of the 1934 Securities Exchange Act, which prohibited broker-dealers from effecting transactions on a national exchange unless the security was "registered" and the registration statement had become "effective." Ostensibly, the purpose of registration is to fulfill the promise of the 1933 Securities Act to "let in the light of day" and to require sufficient disclosure so that the purchaser would be sufficiently informed before making a purchase.

Before we discuss registration statements, we should briefly discuss the requirements that companies must meet to register classes of securities with the SEC. Section 12 of the 1934 Securities Exchange Act provides that it is "unlawful for any member, broker, or dealer to effect any transaction in any security (other than an exempted security) on a national securities exchange unless a registration is effective as to such security for such exchange ..." In other words, in addition to filing a registration statement with the SEC for a public offering, issuers must also file a registration statement with the exchange on which the security will be offered.

An Exchange Act registration under Section 12 has the effect of making the company responsible for the filing of the reports required by Section 13 of the 1934 Act. Section 12 registration is accomplished pursuant to Section 12(b) by the filing of an application that contains all the detailed information required by Section 12(b)(1)(A-L). A company, excluding banks, bank holding companies, or saving and loan holding companies, may voluntarily register under Section 12(g) and must register, unless exempted, if it has $10 million in assets and the number of its record securities holders is either 2,000 or more worldwide or 500 persons who are not accredited investors. Additional threshold requirements were added by the SEC in 2016 in order to implement the JOBS Act and the FAST Act.[1]

Form 10 was the basic form for registration under the 1934 Securities Exchange Act. In 1936, Congress added Section 15(d) requiring periodic disclosures from public companies for at least one fiscal year after the effective date of the registration statement. In 1964, Congress expanded the registration requirements further and required all issuers involved in interstate commerce whose assets and number of shareholders reach a certain level to register with the SEC.[2]

Under Section 12(g), companies that were not listed on a national exchange, including companies that traded on the NASDAQ, became public companies and NASDAQ became a national exchange.[3] The consequence was to increase the number of registration statements being filed. Nevertheless, the number of public companies in the United States has declined, perhaps because of the expense of being a public company. However, the process of "going dark" is very difficult, requiring delisting, ensuring that the company does not meet the "public company" requirements of Section 12(g) and complying with the requirements of Section 15(d) to suspend public company status.[1]

What Must a "Public Company" Disclose?

There are three principal disclosure documents that all U.S. domestic public companies must file with the SEC: Form 10-K, an annual report; and Form 10-Q, a quarterly report, and Form 8-K, which discloses certain specified events that are deemed to be important.[5] Under the SEC's EDGAR filing system, these documents are publicly available.

The SEC has also created a set of disclosure requirements for these documents, set forth in the applicable Form by reference to certain SEC regulations.

---

[1] https://www.sec.gov/info/smallbus/secg/jobs-act-section-12g-small-business-compliance-guide.htm.

[2] The 2012 Jumpstart Our Business Startups Act (JOBS) reset the thresholds as $10 million in assets and either 2,000 shareholders for a class of equity securities or 500 shareholders of a class of equity who are not accredited investors in issuers that are not banks. An "accredited investor" includes any natural person who has a high net worth.

[3] As a result, today over-the-counter trading is limited to the Over-the-Counter Bulletin Board and the "pink sheets."

[4] *See generally* Stephen Choi & A.C. Pritchard, "Cases and Analysis," *Securities Regulation, Cases and Analysis* (5th ed.) (Foundation Press) (2019), 201-202.

[5] *See* SEC, *How to Read a 10-K/10-Q*, https://www.sec.gov/fast-answers/amswersreada10khtm.html.

For example, Regulation S-K contains a list of non-financial information that must be disclosed, and Regulation S-X contains a list of financial information that must be disclosed. In fact, the SEC's form documents in most cases merely refer to the regulation numbers in those two regulations for required disclosures. For example, Item 11(k) of Form S-1 (the form used by U.S. domestic issuers engaging in a traditional underwritten IPO) requires issuers to disclose information relating to its executive officers and directors. Rather than specify the required information, Item 11(k) simply references Item 401 of Regulation S-K.[6] The documents and the required disclosures are all inter-related.

Form 8-K requires disclosure of "material definitive agreements" but pursuant to the Supreme Court's opinion in *Basic Inc. v. Levinson*, 485 U.S. 224 (1988), letters of intent for mergers and acquisitions that would generally be considered "material" need only be disclosed if they impose enforceable obligations, which a letter of intent typically does not do.[7] A requirement in Section 2 of Form 8-K for the disclosure of off-balance sheet arrangements was added after the Enron scandal of 2001, in which two Enron executives went to prison for off-balance sheet arrangements that resulted in convictions for securities fraud, wire fraud, and insider trading. Companies may also use Form 8-K to disclose anything that they consider relevant to their securities holders.

What Are Public Offerings?

Public offerings ("going public") are sales of securities to the public by corporations or other legal entities ("issuers"), usually through underwriters who agree to buy the securities and resell them for a price.[8] Note that there is no definitive definition of a public offering. Not all of a company's stock need be offered in an initial public offering, and it would, in fact, be fairly uncommon to do so. Some stock is usually retained by the existing shareholders of the company.

Public offerings are regulated by the 1933 Act and, in very limited circumstances, by state regulatory authorities. Excluding Special Purpose Acquisition Companies (SPACSs) that are discussed further below, the number of initial public offerings has fallen in recent years, just as the number of companies with

---

[6] Stephen Choi & A.C. Pritchard, *supra* note 4, 206.

[7] *Id.*, 209.

[8] Typically, underwriters commit to purchase securities pursuant to an underwriting agreement and are indemnified by the issuer against liabilities arising from misstatements or omissions in the registration statement, prospectus, and any free writing prospectuses and "road show" materials. The Financial Industry Regulatory Authority (FINRA) reviews the underwriting agreement to ensure that it is fair and reasonable and limits the underwriter's compensation.

publicly traded stock has fallen from about 8,000 twenty years ago to about 4,300 today. In 2000, there were 397 initial public offerings of securities in the United States; in 2019, there were only 235. In part this is a reflection of the fact that many companies decide to stay private longer in order to attain higher valuations prior to an IPO. That may be because the primary purpose of a public offering is to raise capital that is not readily available from other sources, or to provide liquidity to existing investors.

As we will see, since the passage of the 1933 Securities Act, public offerings have been highly regulated by the federal government, with very detailed and sometimes very obscure regulatory requirements and with strict civil liability consequences for certain errors. They are difficult and costly to prepare. Because there is no generally acceptable definition of what constitutes a public offering, the SEC, in 2005 issued a lengthy report, titled "Securities Offering Reform" (sometimes also referred to as the "Public Offering Report") that described in some detail new rules that "modify and advance significantly the registration, communications, and offering processes under the Securities Act of 1933."[9] The new rules involved three main areas: communications relating to registered securities offerings, registration, and other procedures in the offering and capital formation process, and delivery of information to investors. For example,

- Rule 135 is a safe harbor available for the pre-filing public announcement of an offering so long as the announcement made it clear that when an issuer, selling security holder, or a person acting on behalf of either of them "publishes through any medium a notice of proposed offering to be registered under the Act," the notice would not be deemed an offer if certain conditions were met. Those conditions included a statement to the effect that the notice did not constitute an offer and that the notice contained "no more than" certain allowable information contained in a long list set forth in the Rule such as "the name of the issuer," "the amount of the offering," "the anticipated timing of the offer," and a "brief statement of the manner and purpose of the offering, without naming the underwriters." Why does the Rule prohibit naming the underwriters? Why might an issuer need to issue such a press release prior to filing a registration statement related to the offer and sale of securities?[10]

---

[9] https://www.sec.gov/rules/final/33-8591.pdf.

[10] If an issuer can name the underwriters, then it is thought to be a road map to purchase. Thus, it is prohibited since the press release is not an offer. Why would an issuer need to issue such a press release? The information that an offering is coming may be material to existing shareholders. In an IPO, it is sometimes done to end

- Similarly, Rules 137, 138, and 139 provide a safe harbor for certain research reports written by investment banks (note that research reports are not issuer communications since they are solely the responsibility of the investment bank).
- Rule 163 provides that pre-filing offers by Well-Known Seasoned Issuers (WKSIs) constituting offers to sell or buy securities before a registration statement is filed are exempt from the prohibitions of Section 5(c) on offers to sell provided that certain conditions are met. However, communications on behalf of WKSIs, such as underwriter communications, are not exempt.
- Rule 163A provides that any communication by an issuer made more than thirty days before a registration statement is filed "that does not reference a securities offering that is or will be the subject of a registration statement shall not constitute an offer to sell ... or offer buy securities" under Section 5(c) provided that certain conditions are met and exemptions are followed, including a requirement "that the issuer takes reasonable steps within its control to prevent further distribution or publication of such communication during the 30 days immediately preceding the date of filing the registration statement." How the issuer is meant to calculate the beginning of the thirty-day period is not entirely clear. What would the communication be if it is not about an upcoming securities offering?
- Rule 168 (available only for reporting issuers) and Rule 169 (available for non-reporting issuers such as most IPOs) provide a safe harbor at all points of the offering process for the regular release or dissemination by or on behalf of an issuer of factual business information in the ordinary course of business so long as the timing, manner, and form in which the information is released or disseminated is consistent in material respects with the issuer's similar past releases of information. Note, a key difference between Rules 168 and 169 (aside from the categories of issuers to which they apply), is that Rule 168 permits reporting issuers to continue to release forward-looking information subject to the same general guidelines and Rule 169 does not. Note that neither rule provides a safe harbor for any communications that mention the offering or are disseminated as part of the offering activities.

---

inquiries or line up selling shareholders. Note that the underwriters do not like these announcements because they are not allowed to be named. Given the limited information that can be disclosed, the best practice is that a Rule 135 release be a standalone press release. If a company is releasing earnings and is planning to do a Rule 135 release, it should be done in two separate press releases.

- Rule 433(e) provides a safe harbor for historical information on an issuer's website so long as the information is separately identified as historical and is located in an area of the issuer's website that contains only historical information.
- Rule 134 provides a safe harbor for limited communications during the waiting period (remember that during the waiting period offers are permitted orally or pursuant to a statutory or free-writing prospectus but sales are prohibited). Note also that the information that may be included in a press release made in compliance with Rule 134 is strictly prescribed by that Rule and requires that legends be included in the press release. Significantly, underwriters may be named in a Rule 134 press release.

In other words, do not assume that a statement does or does not constitute a public offering or a prospectus. You must check the applicable rules!

Types of Public Offerings

There are today at least four common ways of conducting a traditional, underwritten initial public offering:

1. *A Firm Commitment.* This is an offering in which the issuer offers to sell its entire offering of securities to an underwriter who agrees to purchase the offering at a discount and to take the risk of selling the offering to investors. The discount taken by the underwriter (or a syndicate of underwriters) is called a "spread." The managing underwriter of the syndicate receives a higher discount or percentage of the spread for its efforts in putting together and managing the syndicate. A variation on the firm commitment offering is called a "bought deal" in which an underwriter agrees to buy the entire amount of securities at a discount to the market price—before the preliminary prospectus is filed—and then resells them over time at variable prices. These deals are only applicable once a company is public and could not be used in IPOs.
2. *A Standby or "Old Fashioned" Underwriting.* The issuer offers its securities directly to the public, and the underwriter or syndicate agrees to purchase any securities not purchased by the public, in return for a fee. Today, this method is typically used when securities are being sold to existing shareholders pursuant to a "rights" offering.

3. *A "Best Efforts" Underwriting.* The issuer offers an agreed amount of securities to the public, and the underwriter, acting as an agent, agrees to use its "best efforts" to find investors. This could be an "all or nothing" underwriting or a "minimum percentage" underwriting. These are typically used by smaller underwriters who are risk averse.
4. *An Auction.* Called a "Dutch Auction" by Professors Choi and Pritchard,[11] an auction sale is where investors bid for the number of shares they want and specify the amounts they are willing to pay.[12] When all the bids are received, the issuer sets the price at the lowest price that clears the entire offering. The winning bidders buy the shares for which they bid at the clearing price, and the bidders at the clearing price divide the remainder.

How and When Are Public Offerings Priced?

If there is an established market for the offered securities, the price is typically set slightly below the prevailing market price to make sure that the offering clears. If there is no existing market, the price range is usually set by agreement between the issuer and the underwriters (with input through the "testing the waters" communications with sophisticated investors) and finally determined after a road show, with the marking of the deal at the end of the waiting period. A road show is initiated by the lead underwriter on behalf of the issuer after the issuer has a substantially complete registration statement that has been through a complete SEC review. During the road show meetings with investors, the lead underwriter will collect feedback from the potential investors about their interest in the offering—both in terms of the size of the investment and price sensitivity. This is called "book building." This practice has given rise to a number of techniques used by underwriters, such as "laddering"[13] in which a customer who receives a security at the initial price will be required to purchase additional shares at a higher price after the

---

[11] Steven Choi & A.C. Pritchard, "Cases and Analysis," *Securities Regulation, Cases and Analysis* (5th ed.) (Foundation Press) (2019), 492.

[12] In a typical Dutch auction, used by flower sellers in Holland, the seller would set a price higher than it expected to receive, and then lower it to a price the seller is willing to accept, which then ends the auction. The U.S. Treasury Department uses a Dutch auction to fund the U.S. Government.

[13] An SEC Advisory Committee Report in May 2003 defined "laddering" as inducing investors to give orders to purchase shares in the aftermarket at pre-arranged, escalating prices in exchange for receiving IPO allocations, and stating that "[t]his conduct distorts the offering and the aftermarket and destroys investor confidence in the IPO process." *See* https://SEC.gov/rules/interp/33-8565.pdf.

IPO, and "flipping" in which purchasers take advantage of first day "pops" in price by selling shares immediately after they were purchased.[14] SEC 's Regulation M prohibits a distribution participant or an affiliated purchaser from bidding for or purchasing a covered security during a restricted period. It also prohibits inducing a purchaser to bid for a security that is the subject of a distribution otherwise than in the distribution. This is sometimes called an "anti-manipulation" rule and the purpose was to prevent aftermarket bids that could "undermine the integrity of the market."[15]

When Google went public in 2004, it used a modified Dutch auction to set the selling price in order to eliminate the first-day "pop." Google left money on the table, since its first-day price rose from $85 to $100 per share, although its shareholder base was widely distributed as Google wanted.

Categories of Issuers

The SEC has divided all issuers into four categories for the purposes of public securities offerings:

1. *Non-Reporting Issuers.* These are IPO issuers that are not yet required to file reports pursuant to Sections 13 or 15(d) of the 1934 Act.
2. *Unseasoned Issuers.* These are issuers that are required to file reports pursuant to those Sections but that do not satisfy the requirements of Forms S-3 or F-3 for primary offerings of securities.
3. *Seasoned Issuers.* Issuers that are eligible to use Forms S-3/F-3.

---

[14] The SEC has been somewhat ambiguous in its regulations of after-market bids or purchases after IPOs. *See, e.g.*, *Friedman v. Smith Barney, Inc.*, 313 F.3d 796 (2d Cir. 2002). This was an antitrust case in which the plaintiffs were investors who purchased stock in public offerings and who claimed that the prohibitions imposed by defendants, underwriters, and brokerage firms that disallowed resales during a specified period after the initial offering distribution violated the antitrust laws. The defendants claimed that there was antitrust immunity because the SEC had already undertaken to regulate aftermarket price stabilization. The court held that some price stabilization was permitted under the SEC rules and some was prohibited and that there was therefore no void for the antitrust laws to fill. The SEC's 2005 guidance reinforced Regulation M's prohibition of certain aftermarket activities, including "laddering" designed to stimulate a demand and to suggest that there is a scarcity of offered securities. *See* Shearman & Sterling, *SEC Issues Guidance on Regulation M and IPO Allocations*, https://www.shearman.com/~/media/Files/NewsInsights/Publications/2005/04/.

[15] http://www.sec.gov/interps/legal/slbmr10.htm.

4. *Well-Known Seasoned Issuers.* These are known as WKSIs and have outstanding equity with a worldwide market value of $700 million or more or have issued in the last three years at least $1 billion of non-convertible securities other than common equity, in registered primary offerings for cash.

The last three categories are known as "reporting issuers."

The JOBS Act of 2012 created a new category of issuer, known as "emerging growth companies" (EGCs), that have total annual revenues of less than $1 billion for the most recent fiscal year. These EGCs benefit from special registration procedures that are easier to comply with. For example, they may omit required financial statements from their confidential submissions, so long as the omitted information is believed not to be required at the time of the contemplated offering effective date.

A Typical Registration Statement Timetable

Prior to Filing the Registration Statement

1. The board of directors gives its approval to begin work on a public offering.
2. The company selects a managing underwriter (sometimes called a "representative") and gives the managing underwriter a mandate to begin work.
3. Securities cannot be offered; prospective purchasers cannot be contacted; a prospectus cannot be distributed; only a notice or press release meeting the requirements of Rule 135 is permitted (the names of the underwriters cannot be mentioned).
4. The managing underwriter ceases publication of research reports with respect to the issuer's securities, except pursuant to Rules 138 and 139. The managing underwriter cannot initiate research coverage; there are special rules for EGCs.
5. Publicity restrictions become applicable to the issuer—advertising, meetings with financial analysts, press releases, social media, and other press contacts should be evaluated within the framework of the offering rules.
6. The managing underwriter becomes a "prospective underwriter" for purposes of Regulation M.
7. An organizational meeting is held with the managing and other lead underwriters, underwriters' counsel, the issuer's counsel, and the issuer's auditors. If there is a significant shareholder, that shareholder will often attend. Timelines are discussed and

responsibilities are assigned, including with respect to the initial preparation of the registration statement and other relevant offering documents and agreements (e.g., underwriting agreement, lockups, comfort letter(s),[16] legal opinions, Rule 10b-5 statements, and other documents).

8. Due diligence begins and continues throughout the preparation of the registration statement. The goal of the due diligence process is to prepare an offering document that is free from material misstatements and omissions and to document the process such that if the statements ultimately turn out to be incorrect, the offering participants can establish defenses to liability to the extent an affirmative defense is available to them.
9. The managing underwriter and its counsel commence due diligence investigation.
10. Occasionally, the SEC is notified by telephone or a pre-filing conference is arranged if there are disclosure or other issues to discuss with the staff prior to filing/confidential submission.
11. Once the registration statement is ready for submission/filing, the document is sent to a financial printer to be put into the appropriate "EDGAR" format and filed.

Filing and Pre-Effective (or "Waiting") Period

1. Registration statement (which includes a preliminary prospectus) is now submitted to the SEC or publicly on file with the SEC, and the SEC makes a "review" or "no review" decision that is communicated to issuer's counsel.
2. Oral offers and written offers of the securities are permitted, but only using the statutory preliminary prospectus (including documents incorporated by reference in the prospectus). No other written material may be distributed. Oral statements are permitted. There are special rules for EGCs.

---

[16] A "comfort letter" is often requested by underwriters and is prepared by the issuer's auditors. The purpose is to help an underwriter prepare a due diligence defense under Sections 11(b)(3)(B) of the 1933 Act to a claim that there was a material misstatement or omission in the registration statement. This defense is discussed further in Chapter 8. A typical comfort letter affirms that the issuer's financials conform in all material respects with the applicable accounting requirements of the 1933 Act and related rules and regulations. It is not required by SEC rules or regulations. The Statement on Auditing Standards No. 72 provides guidance for the preparation of comfort letters. *See* https://media2.mofo.com/documents/faqsrelatingtocomfortletters.pdf.

3. Securities cannot be sold or delivered. Only nonbinding "circles" or indications of interest can be solicited.
4. Press release meeting Rule 134 requirements (which can now mention the names of the underwriters) can now be made.
5. Prospective syndicate members are invited to participate. An "invitation" message is sent pursuant to the provisions of the master agreement among underwriters.
6. FINRA filing is made by underwriters' counsel, and clearance of the underwriting agreement is obtained. FINRA reviews filings to make a determination of the fairness of the underwriters' compensation in connection with the offering.
7. Stock exchange preliminary listing application is filed and, if applicable, 1934 Act registration statement on Form 8-A is filed. As noted above, the registration statement is the core document through which the SEC carries out the congressional intent that the 1933 Securities Act "let in the light of day" for securities offerings is carried out. The 1934 Act registration statements are one-time registrations required for entire classes of securities and are triggered by listing on a national exchange or reaching a certain size. The 1933 Act and 1934 Act registration statements are often filed simultaneously.
8. Blue sky filings, if any, are made by underwriters' counsel. Most offerings are exempt following a change in the law in October 1996.[17]
9. If registration statement is being reviewed, SEC comments are received, discussed with the SEC, and one or more pre-effective amendments to the registration statement are filed/confidentially submitted. There are special timings for EGCs.
10. "Road show" is conducted.[18] The only written materials permitted are the preliminary prospectus, including incorporated documents. There are special rules for EGCs.

---

[17] Blue sky laws were largely irrelevant from 1997 until the expansion of exempt offerings by the SEC. Now, again, you have to pay attention to state securities laws. The National Securities Markets Improvements Act of 1996 amended Section 18 of the 1933 Act to create a class of "covered securities" that are no longer subject to state law registration requirements. However, they remain subject to state law antifraud laws.

[18] A useful discussion of road shows has been published by my partner, Craig Arcella, titled "Nuts and Bolts of Road Shows." *See* https://www.cravath.com/a/web/380/3285628_1.pdf.

11. Comfort letters should be finalized for delivery immediately following execution of the underwriting agreement.[19]
12. Underwriting agreement is finalized. If FINRA approval is required, FINRA will require seeing a relatively final version and receiving copies of the executed version after pricing.
13. Due diligence is ongoing, including, if applicable, discussions concerning disclosure updates, recent financial results, any other recent developments, and revised disclosures are considered.
14. Any further SEC comments discussed and cleared with the SEC. A further amendment may be filed. Necessity to "recirculate" the amended prospectus is reviewed. Preparations for "going effective" are made. Acceleration requests are filed.

Declaration of Effectiveness and Pricing

1. Registration statement is declared "effective" by the SEC pursuant to Rule 430A (registration statement must be complete except for "pricing related" information).
2. Syndicate members (other underwriters) return "acceptance" notices pursuant to the master underwriting agreement among underwriters.
3. The issuer and the managing underwriter have a "pricing call" during which the managing underwriter offers to purchase the securities from the issuer/selling shareholders based on the agreed terms. The agreed terms depend on the securities being issued, including quantum, price, interest rate, and other terms of the securities. The "pricing call" is done on a recorded line and forms a binding contract between the underwriters and the issuer/selling shareholders. The sale of securities is not subject to the statute of frauds. The pricing terms that the managing underwriter offers to the issuer are based on its book-building exercise, which is based on prior discussions with prospective purchasers and obtaining nonbinding indications of interest.[20]

---

[19] *See* footnote 16.

[20] Once this is done, underwriters like to call the accounts that have given non-binding indications of interest and confirm the orders. Each call represents a different "time of sale" for liability purposes, and that is why underwriters like to do it as soon as possible after pricing, and simultaneously. Generally comfort letters and Rule 10b statements speak of time of sale as the pricing call, although there is always a gap between the bring-down due diligence call and the actual time of sale to individual accounts.

4. The underwriting agreement is signed by the managing underwriter and the issuer. Note that the underwriters care about the underwriting agreement because it supports their due diligence (it typically includes extensive representations and warranties by the issuer) and includes the indemnification and contribution provisions for their benefit.
5. After the underwriting agreement is signed, the comfort letter is delivered.
6. A pricing press release conforming to Rule 134 may be issued.

Filing of Final Prospectus and Post-Effective Period

1. Sales of securities are now permitted, but sales cannot be confirmed or securities delivered unless preceded by or accompanied by a prospectus required by the relevant statute.
2. Supplementary, or "free-writing," material can be distributed to any person who has previously or simultaneously received a statutory prospectus, although NYSE and FINRA rules prohibit the publication of research by managing underwriters for forty days (following an initial public offering) or ten days (following a secondary offering). There are special rules for EGCs.
3. The managing underwriter engages in stabilization activities, if necessary (pre-effective stabilization can also occur, but is unusual and must be disclosed in the prospectus).
4. Sales of securities commence and confirmations are sent, accompanied by a final prospectus.
5. Final prospectus containing 430A pricing information is filed with the SEC not later than the close of business on the second business day after pricing.
6. Final blue sky action, if any, is undertaken by underwriters' counsel.
7. Final stock exchange listing application is filed.
8. Depository Trust Corporation (DTC) Letter of Representations is signed and delivered if the offering is a debt offering.
9. Closing is held at which securities are delivered and the purchase price paid, and opinions, certificates, and the second comfort letter are delivered.
10. "Tombstone advertising" meeting the requirements of Rule 134 appears in newspapers.

Communications During the Registration Process

Prospective issuers will want to communicate to prospective purchasers about their coming offers. During the "pre-filing period," those communications are limited, but, as noted, there are exceptions contained in Rules 135, 137, and 163, among others. Between the time an agreement or an understanding to issue and sell securities has been reached and the filing of the registration statement, the issuer is prohibited from offering to sell or buy, by means of a prospectus or otherwise, any security; the prohibition is partially lifted when a registration statement is filed.[21] Once the registration statement is filed, there is a "waiting period" during which it is unlawful to sell securities by any prospectus, but oral and certain written offers are not prohibited during this period.

The prospectus is required to meet the requirements of 1933 Act Section 10 (although not Section 10(a)). A "free-writing prospectus," defined in Rule 405, discussed further below, is permissible during this period, provided that it complies with the applicable rules. During the "post-effective" period, securities may be sold but they cannot be delivered unless they are accompanied by a prospectus that meets the requirements of Section 10(a), that is, a "final prospectus." Written communications may be used provided they are preceded by or accompanied by the final statutory prospectus meeting the requirements of Section 10(a). Note that SEC Rule 405 defines "written communications" and "graphic communications."

How Are Public Offerings Documented?

The short answer is that they generate lots of paper and work for securities lawyers. Some documentation, such as the registration statement, listing documents, and FINRA filings, are required by statute or regulation to effect a public offering. As discussed briefly above and in more detail below, the federal securities laws are premised on the delivery to investors of information that is free from material omissions and misstatements. As discussed in greater detail below, liability attaches to offering participants for "bad disclosure." The underwriters have a defense to that liability referred to as the "due diligence" defense. It is an affirmative defense and the underwriters have the burden of showing that they have undertaken a reasonable investigation into the issuer's affairs. Some offering documentation is provided to support the underwriters' due diligence defense. Typical documentation include the following:

---

[21] Rule 163 exempts WKSIs (but not their underwriters) during the pre-filing period, provided that the other Rule 5(c) conditions are met.

- *Registration Statement.* This is the most important document in the SEC registration process. It is filed with the SEC and includes the prospectus. In an initial public offering, this filing is typically prepared by a working group, including senior members of management of the issuer, investment bankers, and lawyers. The issuer's auditors will also review the entire document. If the issuer is already public, the registration statement will incorporate by reference the issuer's disclosure under the 1934 Act; accordingly, the registration statement is much shorter and does not demand as much time from the working group.
- *Road Show Presentation.* The road show presentation is a PowerPoint slide presentation that summarizes the key investment highlights of the offering. The first draft of the road show presentation is often prepared by the managing underwriter. The final presentation is used by management in one-on-one and group meetings during the marketing of the offering. In addition, management records a version of the presentation that is publicly available on one or more investor internet sites like "road show."
- *Comfort Letters, Legal Opinions, and Rule 10b-5 Statements.* Each of these documents forms part of the underwriter's reasonable investigation into the issuer. They are not mandated by statute or regulation, but the norm is for underwriters to receive these documents. Their absence in an offering is a "red flag" that cannot be ignored. A comfort letter is provided by the issuer's accountants and addressed to the underwriters and the outside directors of the board of the issuer. It covers the procedures performed by the accountants, including with respect to periods after the date of the last financial statements, and it ticks and ties most financial information to the issuer's internal records. Legal opinions from both the issuer's counsel and the underwriters' counsel are required and provide support for the underwriters' investigation into the basic legality of the offering and other key legal matters. The opinion typically will state that the securities and the offering are authorized, that the securities do not conflict with key agreements, that the issuer is not an investment company required to register under the Investment Company Act of 1940, and certain other items. The underwriter also receives a legal opinion from counsel to any selling shareholders. Why would an underwriter want such a legal opinion? Finally, the underwriters will receive a Rule 10b-5 statement from counsel to the issuer and counsel to the underwriters outlining the work that such counsel did in connection with the offering and that nothing has come to such counsel's attention as

part of that work that causes them to believe there are any material misstatements or omissions in the registration statement and final prospectus. These statements are the culmination of the due diligence process that starts with the organizational meeting and ends at the closing. The scope of any such examination is dependent on the facts and circumstances, including the nature of the issuer and the type of offering. It requires considerable judgment and market knowledge to know what a "reasonable" investigation is. Deviations from market practice can result in difficulty establishing a "due diligence" defense.

- *Underwriting Agreement.* This is an agreement between the issuer and the underwriters, usually signed by the managing underwriter, that specifies the price and amount of securities to be offered, and the allotment given to each underwriter. It may include a "green shoe" option, essentially a call option, allowing underwriters to buy more securities to satisfy demand.[22] A "green shoe" option is named after Green Shoe Manufacturing Co. (now known as Stride Rite Corp.), which was the first issuer to use this option. A "reverse green shoe" option, essentially a put option, permits underwriters to sell shares back to the issuer. The agreement typically indemnifies the underwriters if they become liable due to disclosure violations in the offering. It also contains other representations and warranties.
- *Agreement Among Underwriters.* This is an agreement among the underwriters, usually finalized just before the registration statement becomes effective, that authorizes the managing agent to act on behalf of the syndicate in negotiating with the issuer. It specifies the managing underwriter's compensation and imposes joint liability on the underwriters for selling the securities. There is usually a master agreement among underwriters so there is not typically any documentation beyond confirmation that an underwriter is participating.
- *Selling Group Agreements.* These are agreements entered into between underwriters and retail dealers that require all sales be at the offering price.

The Registration Statement

As noted above, the registration statement is required to register with the SEC pursuant to Section 6 of the 1933 Act any security that the issuer wishes

[22] FINRA imposes a cap of 15 percent of the original number of shares offered.

to offer publicly. It is the central document required by the 1933 Act. Section 5 of the Act prohibits the use of the mails or any means of interstate commerce to sell an unregistered security or a security whose registration is not in effect. Section 7 of the 1933 Act sets out in detail what must be contained in a registration statement, specifically, the information and documents described in Schedule A of the 1933 Act. Schedule A in turn lists thirty-two categories of information and documents that must be a part of a registration statement, including information that must be in the prospectus. Section 10 of the 1933 Act describes what must be in a prospectus, including anything required by SEC rules and regulations. SEC Rules 420 et seq., in turn describe in great detail what must be included in a prospectus, including the requirement that it be "legible" and in "plain English." There are different requirements for prospectuses that are used prior to an effective date (Rule 430), at the time of effectiveness (Rule 430A), and after the effective date (Rule 430B).

What Is a "Prospectus"?

A prospectus is a legal offering or a "selling" document. Under Section 2(a)(10), a prospectus is any prospectus, notice, circular, advertisement, letter or communication, written or by radio or television, that offers any security for sale or confirms the sale of any security *except* "free-writing material" sent after the effective date, if it is established that prior to the date of the communication, a written prospectus complying with Section 10(a) was sent or given to the person to whom the communication was made. It should be noted that this is the definition of a prospectus set forth in the definitions section (Section 2) of the 1933 Act. By contrast, Section 10, which does not purport to define a prospectus, sets forth what must be in a prospectus. In *Gustafson v. Alloyd Co. Inc.*, 513 U.S. 561 (1995), the Supreme Court (Justice Kennedy) muddied the water by essentially refusing to treat Section 10 as a definitional section, and the court held that "a prospectus under § 10 is confined to documents related to public offerings by an issuer or its controlling shareholders." For that reason, the court held that a contract of sale that was not held out to the public did not constitute a "prospectus."

Depending on the category of issuer, the prospectus must include or incorporate by reference information describing important facts about its business operations, financial condition, results of operations, risk factors, and management. It must also include or incorporate by reference audited financial statements. The seller of securities is not always the issuer and therefore not always the entity providing the information. Also, entities other than WKSIs are able to incorporate by reference. For example, companies using Form S1 can "backward" incorporate, not just forward incorporate. The prospectus must be delivered to everyone who buys the securities as well as anyone who has received an offer to purchase the securities.

In *SEC v. Manor Nursing Centers, Inc.*, 458 F.2d 1082 (2d Cir. 1972), the U.S. Court of Appeals for the Second Circuit held that underlying the statutory requirement that the prospectus contain certain information is the requirement that such information be true and correct. "A prospectus does not meet the requirements of § 10(a), therefore, if information required to be disclosed is materially false and misleading." This is a strict test, and some thought it was at odds with the due diligence and reasonable care defenses. As a result, some courts have limited the test to cases where the prospectus is "egregiously incomplete or permeated with misrepresentations."[23] Other courts have rejected the *Manor Nursing* rationale completely. *See SEC v. Blazon Corp.*, 609 F.2d 960 (9th Cir. 1979).

Free-Writing Prospectus

In 2005, the SEC modernized the public offering process by eliminating "outmoded restrictions," establishing exemptions, and changing permitted communications during the registration process. One of the most important modernizations was the creation of the free-writing prospectus. This document allows issuers and underwriters to communicate in writing about an offering with potential investors, outside of the traditional statutory prospectus. It should be remembered that such free-writing prospectuses are still subject to liability under 1933 Act Section 12(a)(1) for material misstatements or omissions.

Rule 433 sets forth the conditions for permissible post-filing free-writing prospectuses. There are no content restrictions for a free-writing prospectus other than a required legend, except that the information it contains cannot conflict with the information in the prospectus that is a part of the registration statement or periodic filings with the SEC. Issuers are required to file free-writing prospectuses with the SEC by the date of their first use, although certain free-writing prospectuses, such as electronic road shows[24] and preliminary term sheets, may not need to be filed if certain conditions are met. (Note that the word "filed" does not mean that the free-writing prospectus becomes part of the registration statement where it would be subject to liability under

---

[23] *See, e.g., Byrnes v. Faulkner, Dawkins & Sullivan*, 413 F. Supp. 453 (S.D.N.Y. 1976).

[24] Electronic road shows that do not originate live and in real time are considered free-writing prospectuses pursuant to SEC's Rule 405, since they are "graphic communications" as defined in that rule. Accordingly, road shows that are free-writing prospectuses must be filed with the SEC unless at least one bona fide version of the road show is readily available to an unrestricted audience electronically. *See* Rule 433(d)(8)(ii).

Section 11). Free-writing prospectuses that are not filed must be retained for three years.[25]

All issuers except WKSIs must already have a prospectus on file before they can use a free-writing prospectus. And, in the case of an IPO, the registration statement must include a price range before a free-writing prospectus can be used.

Articles in the news media that appear during offerings may be considered offers, but if so, they would be free-writing prospectuses. In that case, they must be filed with the SEC within four days. Not all media reporting or stories are free-writing prospectuses, however. Reporting that is based on information that is already part of a filing with the SEC the dissemination of which does not constitute an offer and where there is no participation by an offering participant, is neither illegal nor a free-writing prospectus.

The Advantages of Being a WKSI

There are certain advantages specific to being able to qualify as a WKSI, including registration statements that become automatically effective, an ability to register an unlimited amount of securities, and pay-as-you-go registration fee arrangements. WKSIs are issuers who have a worldwide public float of at least $700 million (based on voting and nonvoting common equity held by non-affiliates) or who have sold at least $1 billion in aggregate principal amount of non-convertible debt in registered primary offerings for cash in the preceding three years. Typically, the date of determination of WKSI status is any date within sixty days prior to the filing date of the issuer's most recent shelf registration statement or the time of the most recent amendment to the issuer's shelf registration statement or update pursuant to Section 10(a)(3) of the 1933 Act or its most recent Annual Report on Form 10-K or Form 20-F if the company has not filed a shelf registration statement or post-effective amendment in the previous sixteen months. A WKSI must have a class of securities registered under the securities laws or otherwise be required to file reports pursuant to Section 15(d) of the 1934 Act. The issuer must also have been subject to the 1934 Act reporting requirements for at least the twelve months immediately prior to the filing of Form S-3ASR/F-3ASR (the distinct EDGAR code used by WKSIs to trigger automatic effectiveness) and must not have any delinquent filings during that period. The issuer must also not be an "ineligible issuer"; that is, it must not have engaged in any "bad acts" within the prior three-year period.

[25] Not all documents submitted to the SEC are "filed." Some are merely "furnished." The difference is that certain liability provisions in the 1934 Act apply only to documents "filed" with the SEC.

As noted, unlike registration statements filed by ordinary issuers, those filed by WKSIs are automatically effective when filed, and are therefore not subject to an SEC review process prior to use in an offering. WKSIs also may incorporate information by reference in their filings, and they need not include a specific amount of the securities being registered. Securities omitted in the initial filing may be added by filing an automatically effective post-effective amendment. Generally, a registration statement of a WKSI consists of a cover page, a brief description of the business of the issuer, and a list of documents incorporated by reference.

WKSIs and other seasoned issuers also have more ability to communicate prior to the filing of a registration statement than do non-seasoned issuers. They may communicate ordinary course-of-business factual information and forward-looking information, such as earnings guidance and financial projections. They may also use a free-writing prospectus as soon as the preliminary prospectus is on file with the SEC. They may also use a free-writing prospectus prior to the date the registration statement is filed. And the free-writing prospectus must be filed at the same time the registration statement is filed, not when it is first used, as required of non-seasoned issuers. Electronic road show materials that are used as a free-writing prospectus need not be filed with the SEC.

Registration Statement Filing Forms

The various forms require to effectuate a registered offering in the SEC typically contain two parts: first, the prospectus (Part I of the required form); and second, technical information, undertakings, signatures, and exhibits (Part II of the required form). The actual form required to effectuate the offering will depend on the type of offering and the category of the issuer. Two of the key forms are Form S-1 and Form S-3. A list of all of the available forms follows:

- *Form S-1.* This is available to all issuers and requires the most comprehensive disclosures. It contains both company information and transaction information. Part I of Form S-1 is the prospectus; Part II contains additional information that an issuer does not have to deliver to investors but must file with the SEC, such as copies of material contracts, signatures of management, and other representations. If the issuer is current in its SEC filings for the past twelve months, it may incorporate information by reference in Form S-1 from its existing SEC filings but it may not "forward incorporate" information that it files in the future. This form must be filed by companies that do not qualify to use Form S-3 and are either non-reporting or non-seasoned reporting issuers.

- *Form S-3.* This form is used by large, seasoned companies that have been reporting companies for at least one year and, if they are issuing new equity securities, have a "public float"[26] of at least $75 million (with some exceptions). Under this form, filers may also incorporate certain existing and future documents such as annual, quarterly, and current reports by reference, and the prospectus will be streamlined to describe only the particular offering.
- *Form F-1/F-3.* Corresponding forms used by foreign private issuers.
- *Other Forms.* There are other forms for smaller reporting companies that do not contain all of the information required of larger issuers. In addition, using FAST,[27] issuers can "forward incorporate" certain filings that will be made after the effective date of an S-1 filing. There are also special forms for "emerging growth companies"[28] created by the JOBS Act of 2012.

What Happens After the Registration Statement Is Filed?

Under Section 5 of the 1933 Act, no securities may be sold in a public offering until the registration statement becomes effective. Once the issuer files a registration statement with the SEC, the staff examines it for compliance with pre-established disclosure requirements set forth in the form and in Regulation S-K, but it does not evaluate the merits of the securities offering or determine whether the securities offered are "good" investments or appropriate for a particular type of investor. The SEC staff generally provides any comments or questions it has on the registration statement within about thirty days after the first filing date of the registration statement. The issuer, together with its lawyers and accountants, provide answers, and makes the necessary amendments. The staff may raise additional comments, and the process continues until the SEC notifies the issuer that the issuer has "cleared" all of its comments and the registration statement is declared "effective." Once a registration statement is declared "effective," the issuer becomes subject to

[26] A "public float" is the aggregate value of the company's equity stock held by public investors who are not insiders or affiliates of the company.

[27] The FAST Act of 2015.

[28] Under Section 2a(19) of the 1933 Act, an "emerging growth company" must have total annual gross revenues of less than $1.07 billion during its most recently completed fiscal year and, as of December 8, 2011, not have sold common equity securities under a registration statement.

the reporting requirements of the 1934 Exchange Act (if not already subject to them), including the requirement to file Form 10-K reports, Form 10-Q reports, and current reports on Form 8-K. Although the SEC determines what the effective date is, there is a statutory scheme that provides some guidance, but the practice is that such issuers give the SEC as much time as it needs to complete its review:

- *Effectiveness.* The registration statement becomes effective automatically twenty days after its filing (or twenty days after an amendment) unless the SEC determines an *earlier* effective date or unless the filer is a WKSI whose registration statement becomes effective upon filing.[29]
- *SEC Review.* After filing, the SEC has ten days to review the statement for incomplete or misleading disclosures and give notice of its intention to issue a *refusal order* that keeps the registration statement from becoming effective. 1933 Act Section 8(b).
- *SEC Oversight.* Before or after effectiveness, the SEC can open an administrative investigation, and it may issue a *stop order* after effectiveness if it discovers a defect in the disclosure. If such an order is issued or if an investigation is underway, no offering activities are permitted. In practice, there are often negotiations between the SEC and the issuer's counsel in which they will informally agree to "make amendments" to the statement in order to give the SEC more time to review the filing. During that period, the SEC may issue a "comment" or "deficiency" letter making suggestions for improvement or asking questions. These letters are public records. The SEC has the power to delay effectiveness until its comments have been satisfactorily addressed. Practice note: It is a very good idea to be as cooperative with the SEC as possible!

What Is a "Shelf Registration"?

Section 6(a) of the 1933 Act states, "A registration statement shall be deemed effective only as to the securities specified therein as proposed to be offered." However, in 1983, the SEC created the practice of a "shelf registration" pursuant to which securities may be registered for a later sale, provided

---

[29] In practice, issuers other than WKSIs include a "delaying amendment" on the cover of the registration statement that delays the effectiveness until the date the SEC is finished with its review (or provides the issuer notice of "no review") at which time the amendment is removed and the process for declaring the registration statement effective is commenced.

that the registrant agreed to file a "post-effective" amendment disclosing any "fundamental" changes in the information set forth in the original registration statement.

A shelf registration can be used where there is no present intention to immediately sell all the securities being registered. It can be used for sales of new securities by the issuer (called "primary offerings") and resales of outstanding securities (called "secondary offerings") or a combination of both and for both fixed price and "at-the-market" offerings. The benefit of shelf registrations is that they enable an issuer to access the market quickly when needed or when market conditions are optimal.[30]

The rules for shelf registrations are set forth in SEC Rule 415 and in Item 512 of Regulation S-K. The rules were changed again in 2005 to streamline the process for making "continuous or delayed" offerings in the future.[31] Among other things, the 2005 changes eliminated the two-year limitation for shelf offerings. However, the two-year limitation remains for business combinations, and a three-year limitation—beginning on the initial effective date—remains for mortgage-backed debt offerings, continuous offerings lasting more than thirty days, and offerings made by Form S-3.

What about strict liability under Section 11 of the 1933 Act for misstatements in a registration statement when it "became effective"? Under Item 512 and Rule 430B and Rule 430C, post-effective amendments and prospectus supplements filed under Rule 424 are deemed to be a part of the registration statement for liability purposes.

What Is "Gun Jumping"?

Section 5 of the 1933 Act and the applicable Rules have strict prohibitions on what can be done prior to the effective date of a public offering. There are three relevant time periods:

1. *The Pre-Filing Period*. This is the period when a company is "in registration" but before a registration statement has been filed. There can be no sales or offers during this period, nor any "transport for the purpose of sale or delivery after sale." But what does "no offers" mean? Section 2(a)(3) of the 1933 Act defines "offers" in a very broad way: "every attempt or offer to dispose

[30] *See generally* Morrison/Foerster, "Frequently Asked Questions About Shelf Offerings" (2017).

[31] Rules 415(a)(5) and (6) were amended by the SEC effective December 1, 2005. The changes are described by the SEC at https://www.sec.gov/divisions/corpfin/guidance/415a5guidance6.htm.

of, or solicitation of an offer to buy etc." Why does such a restriction exist? What would be wrong with an early dissemination of information? Could misleading information poison the well? That seems to be what the SEC thinks. *See In re Carl M. Loeb, Rhodes & Co.*, 33 S.E.C. 843 (1959). Under the SEC's 2005 public offering rule reforms, certain pre-registration communications are permitted if made more than thirty days before the filing, and certain others are permitted with caveats. Regularly released information such as advertisements may still be released under certain conditions. Preliminary negotiations with underwriters are exempted from the prohibition. Certain research reports may still be made by non-participating brokers and dealers, with limitations, and issuers are permitted to announce an intention to make a public offering, although they cannot announce the identity of the underwriter or the expected offering price. Note that under Section 5(d), added by the JOBS Act, emerging growth companies may engage in oral or written communications with potential investors that are defined in Rule 144A and Rule 501(a) of Regulation D to determine whether such investors might have an interest in a contemplated offering either prior to or following the date of filing of a registration statement, subject to the requirements of subsection (b)(2) (prohibiting the transport of a security in interstate commerce for the purpose of sale unaccompanied or preceded by a prospectus). This is sometimes referred to as "testing the waters."

Similarly, under Rule 163, WKSIs are exempt from the prohibitions of Section 5(c) prohibiting offers before a registration statement has been filed, provided that any written communication that is an offer made pursuant to that rule will be a free-writing prospectus as defined in Rule 405 and a prospectus under Section 2(a)(10). The exemption is conditioned on the offeror's satisfying the conditions set forth in subsection (b) of Rule 163. That subsection requires a legend on written offers, filing with the SEC as soon as the registration statement is filed (subject to certain limitations with respect to the filing of free-writing prospectuses), and it prohibits certain "ineligible offerings."

Rule 163A provides that any communication made by the issuer more than thirty days before the date of filing of a registration statement *that does not reference a securities offering that is or will be the subject of a registration statement* shall not constitute an offer to sell, offer for sale, or offer to buy the securities being offered under the registration statement, provided that the issuer takes reasonable steps within its control to prevent further distribution or publication during the thirty-day period.

2. *The Waiting Period.* This is the period after the registration statement has been filed but before it becomes effective. There can be no sales or offers, except that oral offers by non-reporting issuers and WKSIs are permitted, as are preliminary negotiations and tombstone ads. There can be no transport for the purpose of sale or delivery after sale and there can be no transport of a prospectus unless it complies with Section 10. Any solicitation of interest must be phrased in a way that it cannot be "accepted," which would create a binding contract. With respect to the Section 10 prospectus, the definition is very broad; in effect, Section 10(a) would apply to any written selling effort. Under Section 10(b), the SEC can authorize the dissemination of a preliminary or "red herring" prospectus so long as it does not disclose the offering price or the underwriting.[32] Tombstone ads are permitted so long as they comply with certain limitations. In addition, free-writing prospectuses (e.g., brochures, news clippings, and other non-prospectus sales material) may be used during the waiting period.
3. *The Post-Effective Period.* Once the registration statement has been declared effective by the SEC, the deal can be closed, and the securities can be sold to the underwriters, provided that the issuer files a final prospectus with pricing information within fifteen days after the effective date. There can be no transport for the purpose of sale or delivery after sale unless it is accompanied by a prospectus that complies with Section 10(a). All other communications, including oral offers, are permitted, so long as the prospectus is available on the SEC website. Price-related information may now be disclosed in a filing if made within fifteen days after the effective date; if not, an amended prospectus is required.

When does the "in registration" period begin and end? The SEC takes the position that the "in registration" period begins when a managing underwriter is retained and that the registration period ends when there are no longer any prospectus delivery obligations.

[32] A "red herring" prospectus is a preliminary prospectus with a disclaimer in red ink on the cover page that it is not final and does not include price or the minimum number of shares being offered.

Effective Date

Under Section 8(a) of the 1933 Act, a registration statement's effective date shall be the twentieth date after the filing thereof or such earlier date as the SEC may determine. An amendment filed after the effective date of the registration statement, if the amendment on its face appears to the SEC not to be incomplete or inaccurate in any material respect, shall become effective on the date determined by the SEC.

It is possible for the registrant to request an acceleration of the effective date under Rule 461. It is the "general policy of the Commission, upon [such a request,] to permit acceleration of the effective date of the registration statement as soon as possible after the filing of appropriate amendments, if any." Some registrants choose to have the effective date delayed for a variety of reasons, and Rule 473 permits the filing of "delaying amendments" for that purpose.

Some filings, such as those made by WKSIs, which file their registration statements on Form S-8 or Form S-3 (or on Form F-3 for a dividend or reinvestment plan), "shall become effective upon filing with the Commission" under Rule 462. Also under that rule, a post-effective amendment filed solely to add exhibits to a registration statement, shall become effective upon filing. An automatic shelf registration statement, including post-effective amendments filed to register additional classes of securities, becomes effective upon filing with the SEC, pursuant to Rule 462(e). Under Section 12(g) of the 1934 Exchange Act, registration statements filed with the SEC pursuant to Rule 462(e) "shall become effective sixty days after filing with the Commission or within such shorter period as the Commission shall direct."

Special Purpose Acquisition Companies (SPACs)

Sometimes referred to as "blank check" companies or "public shells," SPACs have been around for decades as alternate investment vehicles, but they have recently been used by market participants as an alternative to the traditional IPO process or a direct listing. The number of SPACs increased dramatically in 2020 with such increase continuing into the early part of 2021. SPACs typically focus on technology, media, and health care investments.

SPACs have been described as "mergers in waiting." Generally speaking, a SPAC is a shell company with no operations. In the first stage, it registers an offer and sale of redeemable securities for cash through a conventional IPO underwriting, sells them to hedge funds and other institutions, and puts the proceeds in a trust until the "de-SPAC" transaction occurs. After the SPAC completes the IPO, it is referred to as "seeking" a target and has a specified period within which to find a target (twelve to twenty-four months). Once a target has been identified, as part of the transaction, the SPAC together with the target often raise additional equity capital through a PIPE (Private Investment in Public Equity) to backstop redemptions by holders of SPAC equity and to fund the acquisition and post-closing operations of a private operating company.

When a SPAC is formed, the sponsors of the SPAC pay a nominal amount for an equity stake (founders' stock or "promote") and an initial registration statement is filed with the SEC. The sponsors of the SPAC do incur cost associated with the IPO (typically 2 percent of the cash raised in the IPO plus $2-3 million on top of that). Capital is then typically raised through an IPO of units and is held in a third-party trust account after the IPO and until the "de-SPAC" transaction is consummated. After the IPO, units are typically separated into common stock and tradable warrants. There is a lock-up period after the IPO, which is typically longer than that for a traditional IPO. When an acquisition target is located, acquired and absorbed, the SPAC is then "de-SPACed." At that time, dissenting shareholders may redeem their common equity shares for the full price paid for the unit issued at the IPO and for this reason, an acquisition is often accompanied by a PIPE as a backstop. SPAC shareholders must vote—usually by proxy—to approve the acquisition. After the target is merged into the SPAC, the target becomes a publicly traded company and a "Super 8-K" must be filed within four days. Founders' shares and warrants are typically locked up for a year but can be released from the lockup if certain share price targets are achieved.[33]

SPACs can provide target companies a quicker path to public markets than conventional IPOs, including more flexibility regarding the discussion of financial projections with investors. Although a point of negotiation with targets, SPAC founders often receive a significant percentage (up to 20 percent of the target's public shares), giving them a strong incentive to complete an acquisition. It remains an open question whether the general investing public benefits from SPACs.

The SEC has recently become concerned about the risks posed to ordinary investors by SPACs, looking into such things as how underwriters are managing risks and the controls that have been put in place by banks to police deals internally. In early 2021, the SEC's then-Acting Chair Allison Herren Lee said that "[o]ne of the major issues is that the incentives of the SPAC sponsors are not aligned with the investors" and that "performance for most investors doesn't match the hype.... It feels a little bit like the Wild West out

---

[33] *See generally* "Private-Company CFO Considerations for SPAC Transactions," Deloitte, September 2020.

here. I think we need some more oversight."[34] Chair Gary Gensler added: "I agree with your assessment that we can do more to strengthen SPAC disclosures, especially around dilution. I've asked staff to look closely at each stage of the SPAC process to ensure that all investors are protected."[35]

In the first three months of 2021, 296 SPACs completed IPOs and raised more than $96 billion. This was more than the entire year 2020, which exceeded the entire previous decade. This increase in the popularity of SPACs led the SEC's then-Acting Director, Division of Corporate Finance, John Coates to continue Ms. Lee's concern over SPACs. In a public statement released on April 8, 2021, Coates reflected a concern about the role disclosure plays (or does not play) in the SPAC process: "In the initial offering by a SPAC, when the shell company is first raising funds to finance all (or more commonly a portion) of its hoped-for acquisition of the yet to be named target, disclosures clearly have a role to play under the federal securities laws. Investors need to know about sponsors and their financial arrangements, the procedural protections of the SPAC structure, and what kinds of returns the SPAC is likely to generate for investors absent a de-SPAC transaction or for those who choose to exit before the de-SPAC is completed.... If we do not treat the de-SPAC transaction as the 'real IPO,' our attention may be focused on the wrong place, and potentially problematic forward-looking information may be disseminated without appropriate safeguards."[36]

Can States Regulate Securities Offerings?

The short answer is that they can do so only in limited circumstances. Section 18 of the 1933 Act (the preemption rule) provides that "no law, rule, regulation or order ... of any State or any political subdivision thereof ... requiring or with respect to, registration ... shall apply to a security that is a covered security." A "covered security" is defined as, among other things, "any security that is listed on a national securities exchange." The state blue sky laws may still require registration of securities offerings for other than "covered securities" but under the Uniform Securities Act, these filings are simple to make, usually by a short-form filing if the registrant is a seasoned, healthy issuer. For other companies making non-preempted state filings, however, the process can be rigorous.

---

[34] Tom Zanki, "SEC Inquiry into Blank-Check Boom Could Be Just the Start," Law 360, Mar. 24, 2021.

[35] Tom Zanki, "SEC Panel Endorses Tougher Regs on SPACs ...," Law 360, Sept. 9, 2021.

[36] https://www.sec.gov/news/public-statement/spacs-ipos-liability-risk-under-securities-laws.

Chapter 5

Exemptions From Securities Act Registration

Because the benefits of a securities offering may sometimes outweigh the costs of registration with the SEC, the Securities Act exempts certain securities offerings from full-blown registration, and, indeed, from the applicability of the 1933 Act in its entirety. Lawyers and a full-blown due diligence process are expensive and so is putting together a group of underwriters. The protections afforded by this process may not be necessary in all cases, especially where the investors are sophisticated and/or the security is less risky because it is secured or of a short duration. Aside from the expense, some companies do not want to go public in order to keep their financial affairs private; sunlight may be the best disinfectant, but as the experience of certain executives who have recently experienced criminal charges demonstrates, some companies do not believe in disinfectants.

In 2012, Congress recognized that the cost of "going public" was often prohibitive, and it passed the Jump Start Our Business Startups Act (the JOBS Act) that provided that companies need not register with the SEC unless their equity securities are held by either 2,000 persons or "500 persons who are not accredited investors," not including equity securities held of record by persons who acquired such securities by means of an exempt "crowd-funding" offering or pursuant to an exempt transaction under an employee compensation plan.[1]

Section 3 of the 1933 Act begins "Except as herein expressly provided, the provisions of this title shall not apply to any of the following classes of securities ..." Similarly, Section 4, titled "Exempt Transactions" begins "The provisions of Section 5 shall not apply to ..." What are those securities and those transactions that have led the SEC to conclude that investors in such securities do not require the full-blown protections of a traditional public offering? This chapter will explore some of those offerings, including private placements,

[1] Marc Steinberg, *Understanding Securities Law* (7th ed.) (Carolina Academic Press) (2018), 53-54.

small offerings, "crowdfunding" offerings, and issuer exchanges. We will also briefly revisit state level blue sky registrations and exemptions (or the lack thereof) from those requirements. It should be recalled that even though certain offerings are exempt from registration requirements, in most cases, they remain bound by the antifraud provisions of Section 10b of the 1934 Act and other similar statutes and regulations.

What Securities Are Exempt From Registration?

There are two types of exemption, exempted securities and exempted transactions. The majority of securities offerings are made pursuant to a transactional exemption rather than through a registered offering.

Exempted securities are securities or categories of securities that are not required to be registered under Section 5 of the 1933 Act largely due to the intrinsic character or nature of the issuer itself. As the title suggests, transactional exemptions are based on the nature of the transaction and for each separate transaction (i.e., an offer and sale of securities), an exemption from registration must be "perfected."

The principal statutes relating to registration exemptions are Sections 3 and 4 of the 1933 Securities Act. Section 3 exempts certain securities and transactions, and Section 4 exempts certain transactions.

Section 3 Exemptions (Securities Exempt From Registration)

As noted, certain types of securities are exempted from the Section 5 registration requirements. In general, the rationale for such exemptions seems to be because such securities are either rare or have other safeguards, investors are otherwise protected.

- *Government securities.* Securities issued or guaranteed by federal governmental organizations are exempt from the Section 5 registration requirements (Section 3 (a)(2)). Firms that deal in municipal securities must provide investors with an "official statement" for offerings above $1 million (Exchange Act Rule 15c2-12). This now applies also to industrial development bonds. Why might the 1933 Act exempt all securities issued or guaranteed by the U.S. government? (*Hint*: they are considered safe.)
- *Commercial paper.* The 1933 Act exempts "any note, draft, bill of exchange, or banker's acceptance which arises out of a current transaction or the proceeds of which have been or are to be

used for current transactions, and which has a maturity at the time of issuance of not exceeding nine months, exclusive of days of grace, or any renewal thereof the maturity of which is likewise limited." In other words, "commercial paper." This exemption is not applicable to a commercial paper program that takes advantage of the Section 4(a)(2) exemption. Recall that notes are typically purchased by banks and other institutional investors, not the general public. It should be noted that because the 1934 Act completely excludes short-term commercial paper from its definition of "security," it is one of the few instruments that is completely free from any liability under Rule 10b-5 of the 1934 Act. *See generally Reves v. Ernst & Young*, 494 U.S. 56 (1990).

- *Railroad Trust Certificates* (Section 3(a)(6)).
- *Securities of an issuer exchanged with its own securities holders where no compensation or commission is paid.* For example, an exchange of common stock upon a conversion of outstanding convertible debt (but not upon an exercise of a warrant by payment of a cash exercise price) (Section 3(a)(9)). Section 3(a)(9) is a transactional exemption; accordingly the securities received by the holder retain the character of the underlying security (i.e., if the old security is restricted, so is the newly issued security. Also, note, the issuer of the old and new security must be the same entity. Generally, a parent company and its wholly owned subsidiary are considered two different issuers. Why might investment banks not like offerings done in reliance of Section 3(a)(9)? (*Hint*: no compensation for them?)
- *Securities issued in exchange for one or more securities, claims, or property interests (and partly for cash) where the exchanges have been approved by a court or agency* (Section 3(a)(10)).
- *Securities that are part of an issue offered and sold only to persons in the state where the issuer is resident, does its business and, in the case of a corporation, is incorporated* (Section3 (a)(11)). Because this exemption seems to apply very narrowly, the SEC has created a safe harbor in Rule 147 and its amendment, Rule 147A. Unfortunately, those rules are hard to interpret. For starters, Rule 147 begins with a sentence that contains a triple negative.[2] It goes downhill from there.
- *Securities of not-for-profit issuers* (Section 3(a)(4)). This exemption applies so long as none of the issuer's net earnings benefits

[2] "This section shall *not* raise any presumption that the exemption provided by section 3(a)(11) of the Act is *not* available for transactions by an issuer which do *not* satisfy all of the provisions of this section."

"any person, private stockholder or individual ... or any security of a fund that is exempted from the definition of an investment company."

There are also a number of other securities that are exempted from the application of the 1933 Act, largely because they are otherwise regulated, such as by laws under the Employee Retirement Income Securities Act, state insurance laws, and bankruptcy law (i.e., certificates issued by bankruptcy trustees). These are all listed in Section 3 of the 1933 Act.

The takeaway is that exempt securities are not very significant, but as we will see, the same cannot be said for exempted transactions.

Section 4 Exemptions (Transactions Exempt From Registration)[3]

The relevant parties for transactional exemptions for equity offerings are primary issuers of securities. For example, a corporation issuing authorized but unissued securities would be a primary issuer, but a shareholder seeking to transfer shares to another person would not be. In fact, individuals reselling their stock must register any offer or sale unless they perfect an exemption, usually pursuant to Section 4(a)(1) or Section 4(a)(7).

The party seeking an exemption has the burden of proving that it has perfected the exemption. A failure to carry that burden can lead to liability for failure to register the security. In many cases, the offering participants will seek a legal opinion from counsel to the issuer and counsel to the initial purchasers that "no registration" is required for the offering. These opinions are highly caveated and based on the specific facts and circumstances. And even if the exemption was perfected, there can still be liability under the antifraud statutes such as Section 17(a) of the 1933 Act and Section 10(b) of the 1934 Act. State blue sky laws may still be applicable as well.

Section 4 exempts seven types of transactions from the registration requirement, among which the most important are the following:

- All transactions by a person other than an "issuer," an "underwriter," or a "dealer" (Section 4(a)(1)).
- All transactions by an issuer not involving any public offering (Section 4(a)(2)). These are the so-called private placements that are subject to resale restrictions and that cannot be accompanied by a general solicitation (although a public company can make a public announcement subject to strict limits on the information included

[3] With thanks to Marc Steinberg, *Understanding Securities Law*, *supra*.

in the announcement), and securities that are subject to the Regulation D safe harbor for certain eligible private placements and that can be accompanied by a general solicitation. Simply put, these are offers as to which there is no dollar limit, and with respect to which the so-called *Ralston Purina* test applies: "Does the group of offerees need the special protection of the Securities Act ?" In that case, the Supreme Court held that the company had made private offerings to non-managerial employees who, the court observed, were not "financially sophisticated" and the company did not carry its burden of proving the perfection of an exemption. *SEC v. Ralston Purina Co.*, 346 U.S. 119 (1953). Although certain high-ranking employees could "fend for themselves" and had access to the same information that would be made available in a registration statement, most of the non-managerial employees did not. They were entitled to the protections of the registration requirement of the 1933 Act, and they could not "fend for themselves" because they were not sophisticated investors.

Several points can be made about the lower courts' reaction to Section 4(a)(2):

- A single non-conforming offer may invalidate an entire offering.
- There may be certain limits on how many offers can be made under a single Section 4(a)(2) exemption.
- The issuer cannot engage in general solicitation or advertising.
- The issuer should take precautions against resales, such as obtaining written commitments from the purchasers that they are acquiring the securities for investment purposes only and not with a view to distribution and placing a legend on the certificates (and, if there is a transfer agent, placing a "stop transfer" order in place).
- All offerees must be financially sophisticated or be advised by someone who is.
- Sophistication is not a substitute for the type of information that a registration statement would disclose.
- Ascertaining which offerees have access to registration-type information can be difficult.

There are several other types of exemptions from registration that should be understood:

- The so-called Section 4(1)(½) exemption is not written into law but instead relies on a combination of the exemptions provided in Section 4(a)(1) and Section 4(a)(2) to facilitate private resales of securities. This exemption was later codified, in a modified form, in Section 4(a)(7), as discussed below. For those transactions that cannot qualify for the exemption in Section 4(a)(7), sellers may still rely on the Section 4(1)(½) exemption. The market for offers and sales of securities pursuant to the Rule 144A is one such market that continues to rely on the Section 4(1)(½) exemption.

- All dealer transactions so long as the transaction does not involve certain elements, such as transactions taking place prior to the expiration of forty days after the first date on which the security was offered to the public by an issuer or through an underwriter and transactions constituting part of an unsold allotment to a dealer as a participant in the distribution of the securities by the issuer or through an underwriter (Section 4(a)(3)).
- Brokers' transactions executed upon customers' orders on any exchange or in an over-the-counter market but not the solicitation of such orders (Section 4(a)(4)).
- Transactions involving offers or sales by an insurer solely to one or more accredited investors, if the aggregate offering price of an issue of securities offered in reliance on this section does not exceed the amount allowed in Section 3(b) (an amount periodically set by the SEC), if there is no advertising or public solicitation and if the issuer files a notice with the SEC. This is sometimes called a "limited offering" exemption for small enterprises (Section 4(a)(5)).
- A "crowdfunding" exemption under Section 4(a)(6), which is discussed further below.
- Note that Section 4(a)(7), added by the 2015 amendments, exempts certain accredited investor transactions described in Section 4(d). The term "accredited investor" is defined in Rule 501 of Regulation D and include, for example, certain banks, employee benefit plans, and natural persons whose net worth at the time of the purchase exceeds $1 million. This exemption allows parties that have acquired restricted securities in a Section 4(a)(2) private placement to resell these securities in a further private placement by following the procedures under Section 4(a)(2). However, because Section 4(a)(2) applies only to issuers, the actual exemption for this kind of transaction is Section 4(a)(1) because the third party avoids being deemed either an underwriter or a dealer. Note that these securities retain their "restricted" status under Rule 144, and will be deemed not to have been issued in a public offering, and the transaction will not be deemed to involve a distribution for the purposes of Section 2(a)(11), which defines

the term "underwriter." The adoption of Section 4(a)(7) has provided a statutory basis for the private resale of restricted and control securities offering a greater deal of certainty that these offers and sales meet the requirements to be exempt from registration.

Section 3(b) Exemptions

The SEC has been focused on evaluating whether the existing offering regime finds the right balance between investor protection and facilitation of capital-raising activities for both businesses and investors. Generally, Section 3(b) empowers the SEC to exempt from registration small offerings, where the aggregate amount of the offering does not exceed $5 million during any twelve-month period. What has developed is a series of rules and regulations that provide a framework for small issuers to raise capital without going through the full-blown registration process. We have already discussed Section 4(a)(2), which is the general exemption for offerings by an issuer not involving a public offering. What does that mean? The SEC has created a framework that provides certainty for small issuers so that the cost to determine whether an issuer has complied with Section 4(a)(2) does not become cost prohibitive. The principal rules and regulations are Regulation A (Tier 1 and Tier 2), Regulation D (Rule 504 and Rule 506), and Regulation Crowdfunding (Section 4(a)(6)).

Regulation A is generally used by small businesses. It exempts certain private issuers (i.e., non-1934 Act reporting issuers) from the Section 5 filing requirements provided that the offerings share many of the characteristics of registered offerings. For that reason, Regulation A looks very much like Section 5, inasmuch as it substitutes an "offering statement" for a registration statement, requires delivery of an offering circular to each investor, and prohibits sales of securities until the offering statement has been "qualified." Within ninety days after qualification, each purchaser must receive a copy of the Final Offering Circular. Sales may only be made to "qualified purchasers."

Because Regulation A holders who wish to sell their securities might meet the definition of "underwriter" and therefore lose their Section 4(1) exemption, some observers have questioned how freely tradable the Regulation A securities really are, especially because many state "blue sky" laws do not recognize the Regulation A proxy registration structure, requiring state regulation instead.

The 2012 JOBS Act, creating what became known as Regulation A+, created two offering tiers, Tier 1 for offerings up to $20 million in a twelve-month period that required fewer disclosures and no ongoing reporting requirements, and Tier 2, for offerings up to $50 million in a twelve-month period, which requires the filing of certain annual and periodic reports with the SEC. Non-accredited investors are limited in the amount that they may invest in Tier 2 offerings. One of the problems that has been identified under Regulation A+ is that the lack of its protections of a rigorous filing regime permits "bad apples" to enter the market. As a result, Rule 262(d) requires issuers to include a description of any matters that would have triggered disqualification under the "bad actor" rule.

Regulation A offerings may be made publicly, using general solicitation and advertising, and can be sold to purchasers irrespective of their status as "accredited investors," subject to certain limitations on the amount that non-accredited investors may invest in Tier 2 offerings. Securities offered in a Regulation A offering are not considered "restricted offerings" for the purpose of resale but the SEC must issue a "notice of qualification" before any Regulation A sales can proceed. This is similar to a notice of "effectiveness" under Form A-1.

Regulation D has much more practical use and application and is discussed in detail below. It is a group of rules that sets forth three exemptions from the registration requirements of the 1933 Act. Rule 504 creates an exemption for capital-raising needs for small start-up companies with a $5 million offering limit within a twelve-month period. (The rule was amended in 2016; prior to that time, the limit was $1 million with a twelve-month period.) "Bad actor" disqualifiers apply but the offeror need not determine whether the purchaser is sophisticated, and there are no specific federal disclosures required. There are no express limits on the number of purchasers. In fact, under Rule 504, the issuer may conduct a "mini-public offering" where general solicitation is permitted and purchasers may acquire freely transferable securities. To do so, one of two conditions must be met: either the offering is registered under a state law requiring the public filing of a substantive disclosure document, or the securities are issued under a state law exemption so long as sales are made only to accredited investors. Rules 506(b) and (c) each provide separate exemptions.

Rule 505 was another exemption under Section 3(b) allowing sales to thirty-five non-accredited investors and an unlimited number of accredited investors and an upper limit of $5 million, but it was repealed by the SEC in 2016. Once the Rule 504 limit was raised to $5 million, there was no need for Rule 505.

The Importance of Private Placements and the SEC's Response: Regulation D[4]

With the decline in the number of public offerings, private placements that are exempt from registration have largely replaced public offerings as

[4] A reasonably comprehensive, although somewhat out of date, monograph on private and public offerings was prepared for the American Bar Association's Section of

sources of equity capital. According to the SEC, in 2019, issuers undertook private placements under Regulation D that raised raising a total of $1.56 trillion in new equity capital with average proceeds of $26.5 million. The majority of that capital was raised in offerings in reliance on Rule 506(b). Given the importance of Rule 506(b), a brief overview is provided below.

There are two sources of the exemption for private placements: a statutory exemption in Section 4(a)(2) of the 1933 Act for transactions not involving a public offering, and a safe harbor rule, Rule 506 of Regulation D for such transactions. Rule 506 was written in response to the criticisms of Rule 146, which was viewed as far more restrictive than was the case law interpreting the Section 4(a)(2) statutory exemption.

Regulation D and Rule 506(b)

Regulation D was adopted by the SEC in 1982. Its principal mandate was that in order to perfect an exemption under Rule 506, no advertising or general solicitation could be made.[5] This mandate stayed in place until the JOBS Act of 2012.[6]

Rule 506 was available to any issuer, except certain "bad actors." And unlike Section 4(a)(2), Rule 506 focuses on purchaser, rather than offeror, qualifications. There is no limit to the aggregate price of the securities offered or the number of offerees. There is, however, a limit of thirty-five non-accredited purchasers. Unlike its predecessor Rule 146, under Rule 506 there is no requirement that the issuer determine that the purchaser can bear the economic risk of the investment. However, "financial sophistication" determinations must be made for all non-accredited purchasers, and the issuer must "reasonably believe" that the non-accredited purchaser has the knowledge and experience in financial and business matters such that the purchaser is capable of evaluating the merits and risks of the prospective investment. The issuer is also required to provide a written disclosure to non-accredited purchasers regarding the limitations on resale.

Business Law 2010 Annual Meeting and is available online. Stanley Keller, *Integration of Private and Public Offerings Update*, Aug. 9, 2010, https://www.americanbar.org. This report was updated in March 2019. https://www.capitalmarkets.lockelord.com.

[5] Because the definition of "general solicitation" is somewhat elusive, the SEC has attempted to clarify it in several "no action" letters. In general, a solicitation to persons with whom the issuer had a substantive preexisting relationship is not considered a "general solicitation."

[6] Regulation D was criticized for not meeting its objectives. *See, e.g.*, Rutherford B. Campbell Jr., "The Wreck of Regulation D: The Unintended (and Bad) Outcomes for the SEC's Crown Jewel Exemptions," *The Business Lawyer*, Vol. 66, August 2011, 919.

Who is an accredited investor? Under Rule 501, accredited investors include certain entities and institutional investors as well as certain wealthy individual investors whose net worth exceeds $1 million and whose individual income exceeded $200,000 in each of the two most recent years, or exceeded $300,000 joint income with a spouse. Whether or not they do, in fact, accredited investors are deemed to have access to registration-type information and to possess investment sophistication.

Regulation D prohibited all general solicitation and general advertising until Congress directed the SEC in the 2012 JOBS Act to authorize the use by issuers of advertising and general solicitation, provided that all purchasers of the securities are accredited investors. The statute also provided that "offers and sales under [Rule 506] shall not be deemed public offerings under the Federal securities laws as a result of any general advertising or general solicitation." According to the SEC, the JOBS Act was intended, among other things, to reduce the barriers to capital formation, particularly for smaller companies. "It created new exemptions that permit issuers of securities to raise capital without SEC registration."[7]

In a rule change mandated by the JOBS Act, the SEC amended Regulation D in September 2013 to allow issuers to engage in general solicitation and advertising provided that the purchasers met certain criteria (accredited investors) and the issuer took reasonable steps to verify that they did. "General solicitation" includes advertisements published in newspapers and magazines, public websites, communications broadcasted over television and radio, and seminars where attendees have been invited by general solicitation or general advertising. The solicitation must be an "offer" of securities, but solicitations that condition the market for an offering of securities may be considered to be offers. The SEC adopted paragraph (c) of Rule 506 to make it clear that issuers can offer securities through means of general solicitation provided that:

- all purchasers in the offering are accredited investors,
- the issuer takes reasonable steps to verify their accredited investor status; and
- certain other conditions in Regulation D are satisfied.

The SEC's modified Rule 506 provides the factors that the issuer should consider in order to meet the "reasonable verification" requirement for ascertaining the sophistication of the purchaser. Basically, there should be an objective determination by the issuer (or those acting on its behalf) as to whether

---

[7] SEC Small Entity Compliance Guide, "Eliminating the Prohibition Against General Solicitation and General Advertising in Rule 506 and Rule 144A Offerings," modified Sept. 20, 2013, https://www.sec.gov/info/smallbus/secg/general-solicitation-small-entity-compliance-guide.htm.

the steps taken are "reasonable" in the context of the particular facts and circumstances of each purchaser and transaction. The SEC called this a "principles based" method of verification, a method described in some detail in Rule 506(c).

Notwithstanding the modifications to Rule 506, however, most issuers did not take advantage of the permissible general solicitation and advertising in Rule 506(c) and continued to use the traditional Rule 506(b) exemption. Apparently they believed that the use of solicitation and advertising would disclose information to competitors and would attract the attention of the SEC. And the verification requirement in Rule 506(b) was more lenient.[8]

Regulation D implemented several of the exemptions under Sections 3 and 4 of the 1933 Act for the requirements of registration under Section 5. Basically, Rule 506(b) allows companies to raise an unlimited amount of money in private offerings if certain requirements are met, including the prohibition of general solicitation and advertising to market the securities. Rule 504 of Regulation D, generally exempts offerings by issuers of securities not exceeding $10 million (less the aggregate offering price for all securities sold within the twelve months before the start of and during the offering of securities under Rule 504 or in violation of section 5(a) of the Securities Act). Regulation D also provides a safe harbor for exemptions under Section 4(a)(2) of the 1933 Act. In addition, Rule 506, which has no dollar limit, deems certain transactions, such as those that limit the nature or number of the purchasers, not to be "public offerings" under Section 4.

Rule 506 has two categories of offerings: those subject to limitations on the manner of offering and those not subject to those limitations. For the former, the offering must meet all of the terms and conditions of Rules 501 and 502, and it must be limited to no more than thirty-five purchasers. Purchasers who are not accredited investors must have "such knowledge and experience in financial and business matters such that he is capable of evaluating the merits and risks of the prospective investment, or at least the issuer reasonably believes that the purchaser comes within this description." For the latter, the conditions of Rules 501 and 502(a) and (d) must be met and all purchasers must be accredited investors. Rule 506(c) has a long list of the ways in which the issuer can verify the accredited investor status of the purchaser.[9]

---

[8] Manning G. Warren III, "The Regulatory Vortex for Private Placements," Legal Studies Research Paper Series, Paper No. 2017-9, University of Louisville Law, at 11-12.

[9] *See generally* SEC, "Small Business Exempt Offerings—Private Placements—Rule 506(b)," modified March 15, 2021, https://sec.gov/smallbusiness/exemptofferings/rule506b.

Of note is the fact that Rule 506(d) states that no exemption is available for sales of securities to "bad actors." (You can readily imagine what kind of persons are included in the eight definitions set forth in the rule.)

In general terms, accredited investor is defined in Rule 501(a) and, as noted above, include entities and institutions with a minimum of $5 million in assets, "natural persons" with a net worth of $1 million (or joint net worth with the person's spouse), and those with income of $200,000 in each of the preceding two years, with a reasonable expectation of reaching the same level in the current year. The Dodd-Frank Act has modified these limits a bit, and the SEC's 2012 rules have excluded the investor's primary residence in calculating equity and liabilities, with certain exceptions. One little-known aspect of Rule 506 is that securities issued in a 506-exempt offering are also deemed "covered securities" under the National Securities Markets Improvements Act of 1996 and are therefore exempt from certain state securities registration requirements.

Under Rule 502, the Rule 506 issuer must make a knowledgeable person available to answer questions from prospective purchasers and ensure that the purchasers receive "restricted securities" that contain a clear legend to the effect that they cannot be resold unless they are registered or qualify for a registration exemption. Alternatively, "other actions by the issuer may satisfy this provision," such as those described in Rule 502(b)(2)(vii) that set forth substantially all of the information that would be required in a registration statement, including audited financial statements.

Fair warning: Rule 506 is very long and complicated. Should you face this situation in your practice, you will need to study Rule 506 carefully if your client wants to take advantage of the safe harbor.

Regulation S

This regulation creates a non-statutory exemption from Section 5 for securities offered and sold outside the United States, and it creates three safe harbors:

1. *Category 1* offers and sales of securities of foreign private issuers for which there is "no substantial U.S. market interest" (SUSMI) (a defined term that is hard for foreign private issuers to meet) in the class offered, or in its debt securities, or in the underlying securities; an overseas offer that is "directed" to a single country; foreign government securities; and certain employee benefit plan offerings.
2. *Category 2* offers and sales of securities that do not qualify for Category 1 and that are either equity securities of a foreign private

issuer that is an Exchange Act reporting company that has filed all of its required reports for at least twelve months, debt securities of an Exchange Act reporting issuer that has made the required filings, or debt securities of any foreign private issuer that is *not* an Exchange Act reporting company.

3. *Category 3* includes all securities that do not qualify for Categories 1 or 2 such as equity securities of U.S. domestic companies, whether or not they are reporting companies, and debt of non-reporting U.S. domestic companies.

Rule 903 contains an issuer safe harbor that may be used by both U.S. and foreign issuers offering securities outside the United States for all three categories of securities.

Regulation S contains definitions and restrictions that further limit the availability of the Regulation S safe harbors for foreign private issuers, including, for example, that there must be an "offshore transaction" and that neither the issuer nor any distributor may engage in "directed selling efforts" to condition the U.S. market for the securities. Note that the Supreme Court case *Morrison v. National Australia Bank Ltd.*, 561 U.S. 247 (2010), that held that the federal securities laws do not have extraterritorial reach, is now under serious attack, at least as far as cases brought by the SEC are concerned. This will be covered in detail in Chapter 19. As a practical matter, Regulation S offerings are often combined with offerings in the United States that are made in reliance on another exemption (e.g., Rule 144A debt offerings).

Regulation Crowdfunding

In the JOBS Act, Congress created a "crowdfunding" exemption to registration. Generally, this occurs when small amounts of securities are sold to large numbers of investors. "Crowdfunding" is a creature of the internet. For example, suppose your teenage sister or daughter wants to create a business to sponsor a group of rock bands and she turns to various websites that allow her to solicit her friends to contribute money to her enterprise in return for CDs of the first few bands. (I know that sounds old fashioned.) So far, so good. But what if the solicitation offered a percentage of her profits in return? Is that an offer of a security? Does Section 5 of the 1933 Act apply to her efforts? Do the "gun jumping" rules apply?

In 2012, Congress adopted the Capital Raising Online While Deterring Fraud and Unethical Non-Disclosure (CROWDFUND) Act (seriously!). This Act exempted equity crowdfunding from Section 5, and the SEC adopted Regulation Crowdfunding to implement it. Among other things, that regulation limits crowdfunding sales to $1 million during a twelve-month period and provides that the issuers may receive the proceeds of the offer only after they meet or exceed a target. Investors are subject to caps based on their annual income and net worth. Crowdfunding transactions must be conducted through a broker or a funding portal (a specially created intermediary for crowdfunding transactions). Crowdfunding is not available for foreign issuers, issuers that are required to file reports under Sections 13 and 15(d) of the 1934 Act, investment companies as defined in Section 3 of the Investment Company Act or that are excluded from that definition under sections 3(b) or 3(c), and any other categories of issuers designated by the SEC. Offering statements must be provided to the SEC and to intermediaries, who pass them on to investors. Resales are restricted, and blue sky laws are preempted. Between May 2016 and December 2018, there were 1,351 crowdfunding filings with the SEC. Professor Marc Steinberg of Southern Methodist University Law School has asserted that the crowdfunding exemption may well be little used because it imposes substantial regulatory costs and requirements that go beyond existing exemptions and because it raises liability concerns.[10]

Section 3(a)(11) Exemption

This section provides an exemption from registration with respect to any security that is part of an issue offered and sold only to persons resident within a single state or territory, where the issuer of such security is a person resident and doing business, or if a corporation, incorporated by and doing business within such state or territory. The apparent notion of the statute is that this intrastate exemption will apply to an offering where the investors in a local enterprise will have adequate familiarity with the enterprise and that the issuers will be relatively small and less able to bear the burden of federal registration. As noted, this section is implemented by the SEC in Rule 147, a safe harbor rule, that was later amended in 2016 as Rule 147A, which permits issuers to be incorporated or organized in a state or territory different from that where the intrastate offering is made, provided that the issuer can show the in-state nature of its business. The two rules contain explicit requirements for an exempt intrastate offering, such as that the issuer must obtain a written representation from each purchaser as to his or her residence.

---

[10] Marc Steinberg, *Understanding Securities Law* (7th ed.) (Carolina Academic Press) (2018), 89 *et seq. See also* SEC, "Investment Lawyer's Reference Guide, Regulation Crowdfunding (Reg CF)," Feb. 14, 2020, https://sec.gov/info/smallbus/secg/rccomplianceguide-051316.htm.

U.S. SECURITIES AND EXCHANGE COMMISSION

Division of Corporation Finance, Office of Small Business Policy
Overview of Capital-Raising Exemptions*

Type of Offering	Offering Limit Within Twelve-Month Period	General Solicitation	Issuer Requirements	Investor Requirements	SEC Filing or Disclosure Requirements	Restrictions on Resale	Preemption of State Registration and Qualification
Section 4(a)(2)	None	No	None	Transactions by an issuer not involving any public offering. *See SEC v. Ralston Purina Co.*	None	Yes. Restricted securities	No
Rule 506(b) of Regulation D	None	No	"Bad actor" disqualifications apply	Unlimited accredited investors Up to thirty-five sophisticated but nonaccredited investors in a ninety-day period	Form D Financial statement requirements for non-accredited investors consistent with Regulation A	Yes. Restricted securities	Yes

Type of Offering	Offering Limit Within Twelve-Month Period	General Solicitation	Issuer Requirements	Investor Requirements	SEC Filing or Disclosure Requirements	Restrictions on Resale	Preemption of State Registration and Qualification
Rule 506(c) of Regulation D	None	Yes	"Bad actor" disqualifications apply	Unlimited accredited investors Issuer must take reasonable steps to verify that all purchasers are accredited investors	Form D	Yes. Restricted securities	Yes

Regulation A: Tier 1	$20 million	Permitted; before qualification, testing-the-waters permitted before and after the offering statement is filed	U.S. or Canadian issuers Excludes blank-check companies, registered investment companies, business development companies, issuers of certain securities, certain issuers subject to a Section 12(j) order, and Regulation A and reporting issuers that have not filed certain required reports "Bad actor" disqualifications apply No asset-backed securities	None	Form 1 A, including two years of financial statements Exit report	No	No
Regulation A: Tier 2	$75 million			Non-accredited investors are subject to investment limits based on the greater of annual income and net worth, unless securities will be listed on a national securities exchange	Form 1 A, including two years of audited financial statements Annual, semi-annual, current, and exit reports	No	Yes

Type of Offering	Offering Limit Within Twelve-Month Period	General Solicitation	Issuer Requirements	Investor Requirements	SEC Filing or Disclosure Requirements	Restrictions on Resale	Preemption of State Registration and Qualification
Rule 504 of Regulation D	$10 million	Permitted in limited circumstances	Excludes blank-check companies, Exchange Act reporting companies, and investment companies "Bad actor" disqualifications apply	None	Form D	Yes. Restricted securities except in limited circumstances	No

Regulation **Crowdfunding; Section 4(a)(6)**	$5 million	Testing the waters permitted before Form C is filed Permitted with limits on advertising after Form C is filed Offering must be conducted on an internet platform through a registered intermediary	Excludes non-U.S. issuers, blank-check companies, Exchange Act reporting companies, and investment companies "Bad actor" disqualifications apply	No investment limits for accredited investors Non-accredited investors are subject to investment limits based on the greater of annual income and net worth	Form C, including two years of financial statements that are certified, reviewed, or audited, as required Progress and annual reports	Twelve-month resale limitations	Yes
Intrastate: Section 3(a)(11)	No federal limit (generally, individual state limits between $1 and $5 million)	Offerees must be in-state residents	In-state residents "doing business" and incorporated in-state; excludes registered investment companies	Offerees and purchasers must be in-state residents	None	Securities must come to rest with in-state residents	No

Type of Offering	Offering Limit Within Twelve-Month Period	General Solicitation	Issuer Requirements	Investor Requirements	SEC Filing or Disclosure Requirements	Restrictions on Resale	Preemption of State Registration and Qualification
Intrastate: Rule 147	No federal limit (generally, individual state limits between $1 and $5 million)	Offerees must be in-state residents	In-state residents "doing business" and incorporated in-state; excludes registered investment companies	Offerees and purchasers must be in-state residents	None	Yes. Resales must be within state for six months	No
Intrastate: Rule 147A	No federal limit (generally, individual state limits between $1 and $5 million)	Yes	In-state residents and "doing business" in-state; excludes registered investment companies	Purchasers must be in-state residents	None	Yes. Resales must be within state for six months	No

* All offers and sales of securities in the United States must be registered with the SEC or conducted pursuant to a federal exemption from registration. This chart provides a summary of certain exemptions and related requirements contained in the Commission's rules and regulations; it is not a substitute for the rules and regulations. Additional information can be found at www.sec.gov/smallbusiness.

Other Exemptions

Rule 701 was adopted by the SEC in 1988 under Section 3(b) and modified in 1999. This rule provided an exemption from registration for offers and sales of securities for certain compensation benefit plans adopted for the participation of employees, officers, directors, consultants, and advisors of an eligible company. An "eligible" company is one that is not subject to the periodic reporting requirements of the 1934 Act and for that reason, it is a rarely used exemption.

Chapter 6

The Law of Resales: Secondary Market Transactions, Underwriters, Control Persons, and Rules 144 and 144A

As we have seen, the principal purpose of the Securities Act of 1933 was to establish a framework for the offer and sale of securities that was premised on disclosure. Unlike the purchase of a loaf of bread that can largely (although not entirely) be inspected by the buyer before a purchase, the purchase of a security without disclosure about the character of the security and what it represents would largely be a crapshoot. Congress decided that the solution to this problem was the public registration of securities with the SEC with a full disclosure of the relevant facts as a predicate to the offer and sale of securities to the public. But does that always occur?

May a purchaser who bought registered securities from an issuer resell them? Under common law, you might think—correctly—that the answer is clearly yes. But under the 1933 Act, the answer is not so clear.[1] Section 5 makes it unlawful for "any person" to offer or sell a security unless the security is the subject of a registration statement or qualifies for an exemption from the registration requirement. The holder—the person who bought the registered securities from the issuer—cannot take advantage of the issuer's original registration statement; it legitimizes only original sales by the issuer. If the holder wants to sell, the holder must either register the securities itself—an unlikely scenario since the holder would not have the necessary access to the required information for a registration—or qualify for an exemption.

[1] *See generally* Andrew J. Pitts et al., "In Brief: Private Placements of Securities in the USA," Lexology, March 25, 2021, https://www.lexology.com/library/detail.aspx?g=dc6d7446-875f-0702c1937c96.

The most likely available exemption is found in Section 4(a)(1) of the Securities Act, pursuant to which all offers and sales of securities are exempt from the registration requirement except those made by an "issuer, underwriter, or dealer." In other words, if the seller is not one of those three, the seller is free to sell the security in question without limitation. Section 4(a)(2) of the Securities Act exempts "transactions by an issuer not involving a public offering." Under this section an issuer may sell a security in a "private placement" without registration under the Act.

Section 2(a)(11) defines an "underwriter" as one who has purchased with a view to "distribution." For the purposes of that statute, a "distribution" is the same as a sale or a public offering. What does it mean for a purchaser to purchase from an issuer "with a view to distribution"? What if the purchaser sold the securities a month after purchasing them? Two months? Three months? There is probably a rebuttable presumption in those cases that the purchaser made the purchase with a "view to distribution." If the resale is deemed to be a "transaction" rather than a "distribution," there is no limitation on the resale.

Does there have to be a connection or relationship between the purchaser and the issuer for the presumption to apply? One of the definitions of "underwriter"—the second definition in Section 2(11)—requires such a relationship, but in *SEC v. Chinese Consolidated Benevolent Ass'n*, 120 F.2d 738 (2d Cir. 1941), *cert. denied*, 314 U.S. 618 (1941), the Second Circuit held that a holder could be considered an underwriter even if there were no direct connection between the two.

There is another way out for the holder, however. The holder can prove that at the time of the purchase, the holder had an "investment intent." How to prove that? There are at least two ways: first, prove that the subsequent sale took place after there was a change in the holder's circumstances in a dramatic way,[2] or second, prove that the securities were held for an appropriate period of time, say, three years.

In reality, the SEC has largely ignored such resales because the strict application of a no-resale rule would significantly impact the post-offering trading of the issuer's securities. The fact that there is a registration statement already on file probably influenced the decision.

But what if the securities being offered and sold were not registered? What if the securities qualified for one of the exemptions to registration (discussed in an earlier) and were sold to the purchaser without a registration statement on file? If the holder of the security wanted to resell it without the registration statement, wouldn't the sale run afoul of the very thing that Congress sought

---

[2] *See* Thomas Lee Hazen, *The Law of Securities Regulation*, § 4.24 (2d ed.) (West Academic Publishing) (1990).

and intended to prevent, a sale with no disclosure? Remember that such securities are called "restricted securities" for a reason.

What are the restrictions on resale of unregistered—restricted—securities? We know that if our holder of restricted securities acquired the securities in order to resell them, there is a problem. Similarly, there is a problem if the holder is selling the securities "for the issuer." However, there are solutions to this conundrum, and we discuss them below.

Under What Circumstances May a Purchaser of "Restricted Securities" or a "Control Person" Who Owns Securities of the Issuer Resell Them?

Let's assume for discussion purposes that the holder who wishes to sell the securities purchased them in a private placement and therefore that they are "restricted securities."[3] How can the holder resell those securities? There are actually five ways in which that can be done lawfully:

1. in a registered offering;
2. in a further private placement (this is the Section 4(1)(½)[4] exemption described in Chapter 5);
3. in a sale to the public in a transaction not involving a "distribution";
4. in a sale to a Qualified Institutional Buyer (QIB) who purchases for its own account (assuming that the securities that are not publicly traded); and
5. in an offshore transaction under Regulation S.

To take advantage of one of those possibilities, our holder would have to take care not to be deemed an underwriter by showing that the holder did not purchase with a view to distribution. Our holder would also need to establish that he or she is not a "control person."

---

[3] In fact, Rule 144(a)(3) has eight definitions for the term "restricted securities." Probably the most common one is the first one: "securities acquired directly or indirectly from the issuer . . . in a transaction or series of transactions not involving any public offering under Section 4(a)(2)."

[4] Because Section 4(a)(2) applies only to issuers, the actual exemption would be found in Section 4(a)(1) since the third party would avoid being deemed an underwriter or a dealer. That is why the exemption (now codified in modified form in Section 4(a)(7)) is more properly referred to as a Section 4(a)(1)(½) exemption.

Underwriters

Why does it make a difference if the holder is deemed to be an underwriter? If the holder is an "underwriter" (*see* Section 2(a)(11)), the "transaction" might not be exempt from 1933 Act registration requirements because it would be deemed to be a "distribution." Are there any available exemptions? Probably not. If the holder purchased the securities for the purpose of ("with a view to") resale, and if the purchase was part of the "initial distribution" of the security, it is part of the public offering and is subject to the rules applicable to public offerings. If the resale of the securities takes place after the initial distribution under the public offer is complete,[5] and the resale takes place through a broker, there should not be a problem.[6]

Control Persons

Under Section 15 of the 1933 Act, any person who "controls any person liable under Sections 11 of 12 (the civil liability sections) shall also be liable jointly and severally with and to the same extent as the controlled person to any person to whom the controlled person is liable" with certain exceptions. Thus, control persons who purchase stock with a view to reselling it in a distribution might be underwriters, unless they hold the securities for a sufficiently long period of time.

Section 4(a)(1)(½)

As we have seen, this is *not* an actual rule but it is based largely on case law. If the control person is selling the security to a person with the ability to "fend for him- or-herself," there is no "distribution" under Section 2(a)(11) and therefore there is no "underwriter" in the control person's transaction. Recall, however, that in *SEC v. Ralston Purina Co.*, 346 U.S. 119 (1953), the Supreme Court held that in order for a sale not to be a "distribution," all of the purchasers would have to have the same information that would be found in a registration statement.

---

[5] An "initial distribution" is complete when all of the securities in the offer have been purchased.

[6] In *Ackerberg v. Johnson*, 892 F.2d 1328 (8th Cir. 1989), the appeals court held that "the mere involvement of a broker qua broker in a secondary transaction by persons other than the issuer, underwriter or dealer is insufficient to vitiate the exemption."

Rule 144

This rule, promulgated in 1972, is the best known and most commonly used vehicle for solving the problem of the resale of restricted or control (affiliate-owned) securities. To recapitulate, restricted securities are securities acquired in unregistered, private sales from the issuing company or from an affiliate of the issuer. Investors typically receive restricted securities through private placement offerings.

Basically, Rule 144 permits a limited number of resales of restricted securities so long as the seller is not engaged in a "distribution" (i.e., is not an underwriter), and other conditions are met.

Rule 144 provides a safe harbor that addresses these difficult issues. Under Rule 144, a complying person or entity is not an "underwriter," and therefore the transaction is exempt from the restrictions of Section 5 by virtue of Section 4(a)(1) because no underwriter is present in the transaction. This matter is complicated, however, and there are number of requirements that must be met before Section 144 can be invoked.[7] For example, among those requirements are the following:

- There is a holding period of six months for restricted securities issued by Exchange Act reporting entities and one year for non-reporting issuers during which no resales are permitted. If the issuer of the securities is subject to the 1934 Act reporting requirements and the holder has held the securities for at least six months but less than one year, the holder may sell the securities as long as the holder satisfies the current public information condition.
- Adequate current information with respect to the issuer must be available. For a reporting issuer, it must have been subject to reporting requirements under the Exchange Act for at least ninety days and have filed all required annual and quarterly reports for the preceding twelve months. For a non-reporting issuer, specified information, including information regarding the nature of its business, the identity of its officers and directors, and its financial statements must be publicly available.
- Volume limitations must be observed. If the holder is an affiliate of the issuer, the number of equity securities the holder may sell during any three-month period cannot exceed the greater of 1 percent of the outstanding shares of the same class being sold, or if the class is listed on a stock exchange, the greater of 1 percent

[7] *See* Andrew J. Pitts et al., "In Brief: Private Placements of Securities in the USA," Lexology, March 25, 2021, https://www.lexology.com/library/detail.aspx?g=dc6d7446-875f-0702c1937c96.

or the average reported weekly trading volume during the four weeks preceding the filing of a notice of sale on Form 144.[8]

- Affiliates must file a notice of proposed sale with the SEC on Form 144 if the sale involves more than 5,000 shares or the aggregate dollar amount is greater than $50,000 in any three-month period.
- The securities must be sold either in a broker's transaction subject to normal commissions or in a riskless principal transaction in which, among other things, the transaction is permitted to be reported as "riskless" under the rules of a self-regulatory organization. Such transactions are those in which the broker or dealer, after having received an order to buy or sell, buys or sells the security as "principal to the market."

Even if all of the above required conditions are met, the holder cannot sell the restricted securities to the public until the restrictive legend is removed from the certificates. Only a transfer agent can remove the legend. The transfer agent will not remove the legend unless the holder has received the consent of the issuer—usually in the form of an opinion letter from the issuer's counsel—that the restrictive legend can be removed. Holders are advised by the SEC to contact the company that issued the securities to ask about the procedures for removing a legend.[9] It can be a complicated process. If a dispute arises as to whether the legend can be removed, the SEC will not intervene. Removal of a legend is a matter solely in the discretion of the issuer of the securities. State law, not federal law, covers disputes about the removal of legends.

Rule 144A Private Resales of Securities to Institutions[10]

Rule 144A offerings are the result of a series of no-action letters issued by the SEC in the late 1980s and early 1990s allowing subsequent registered exchange offers. Rule 144A is a non-exclusive safe harbor exemption from the registration requirements of the Securities Act for resales of certain securities to qualified institutional buyers (QIBs). QIBs include certain entities that, in the aggregate, own and invest on a discretionary basis at least $100 million in securities of unaffiliated issuers. A registered broker-dealer qualifies as a QIB if

---

8 https://www.sec.gov/reportspubs/investor-publications/investorpubsrule 144htm.html.

9 SEC Fast Answers, *"Restricted" Securities: Removing the Restrictive Legend*, https://www.sec.gov/fast-answersrestrictm.html.

10 An excellent summary of Rule 144A has been prepared by the law firm Morrison Foerster, "Frequently Asked Questions About Rule 144A Equity Offerings" (2017), https://media2.mofo.com.

it owns and invests on a discretionary basis at least $10 million in securities of unaffiliated issuers. Prior to the JOBS Act, Rule 144A sales could only be made to QIBs but after the JOBS Act, securities may be offered to persons other than QIBs, including by means of general solicitation, provided that securities are sold only to persons that the seller and any person acting on behalf of the seller reasonably believe are QIBs.

Rule 144A is largely unrelated to Rule 144, and it has completely transformed the debt market. Rule 144A applies to the private resale of securities to institutions. As noted, it is basically a safe harbor provision. Any person other than an issuer may rely on Rule 144A for the sales of unregistered securities to an institution that qualifies as a QIB or who the seller reasonably believes is a QIB.

So-called Rule 144A Offerings (which are most commonly done as Section 4(a)(2) private placements to investment banks, followed by resales to QIBs), became the norm beginning in 2008 for executing high-yield bond offerings and acquisition financings.[11] Today, as a result of Rule 144A, hundreds of billions of dollars of securities are sold to qualifying institutions without having been registered with the SEC. Rule 144A transactions include offerings of debt or preferred securities by public companies, offerings by foreign issuers that do not want to become subject to U.S. reporting requirements, and offerings of common securities by non-reporting issuers (the so-called "back-door IPOs"). There are several requirements for Rule 144A sales:

- Securities being offered under Rule 144A must not be "fungible" with or substantially identical to, a class of securities listed on a national securities exchange or quoted in an automated inter-dealer quotation system. For example, American Depositary Receipts (ADRs) are considered to be of the same class as the underlying equity security.
- The buyers must be QIBs who purchase for their own accounts or that of another QIB and who own or invest on a discretionary basis at least $100 million in the aggregate of securities of non-affiliates (other than bank deposits and loan participations, repurchase agreements, and securities subject thereto, and currency, interest rate and commodity swaps).
- The following entities may qualify as QIBs:
    - an insurance company as defined in Section 2(a)(13);

[11] DDJ Capital Management LLC, "A Large but Often Misunderstood Segment of the High Yield Bond Market," November 2018, https://www.ddjcap.com/ddj-thought-piece-144as-a-large-but-often-misunderstood-segment-of-the-high-yield-bond-market/.

- an investment company registered under the Investment Company Act or any business development company as defined in Section 2(a)(48);
- a small business investment company licensed by the U.S. Small Business Administration under the Small Business Investment Act of 1958;
- a plan established and maintained by a state, its political subdivisions, or any agency or instrumentality of a state or its political subdivisions for the benefit of its employees;
- an employee benefit plan within the meaning of Title 1 of ERISA;
- a trust fund whose trustee is a bank or trust company and whose participants are exclusively plans of a certain type, with certain exceptions;
- a business development company as defined in Section 202(a)(22) of the Investment Advisers Act of 1940;
- any IRS Section 501(c)(3) organization, corporation (other than a bank as defined in Section 3(a)(2) or a savings and loan association or other institution described in Section 3(a)(5)(A) or a foreign bank or savings and loan association or equivalent association), partnership or Massachusetts[12] or similar business trust or a foreign bank or savings and loan association; and
- an investment adviser registered under the Investment Advisers Act.

How, you might ask, would a seller determine that the intended purchaser is a QIB? Rule 144A(d), an amendment required by the JOBS Act, answers that question by providing that the sale is legitimate if "the securities are sold only to a qualified institutional buyer or to a purchaser that the seller and any person acting on behalf of the seller reasonably believe is a qualified institutional buyer" and that in making that determination, the seller and any person acting on its behalf are entitled to rely on one of four non-exclusive methods of making that determination, including such things as published financial statements.

Important Note: Under the JOBS Act of 2012, the SEC promulgated SEC Release No. 33-9415 (July 10, 2013) that permitted offers (but not sales)

---

[12] A Massachusetts Trust is a common-law unincorporated business association that is managed by trustees for the benefit of holders of certificates indicating their entitlement to a beneficial interest in the trust estate and in which the holders are entitled to the same limitations of personal liability as stockholders of private corporations.

of Rule 144A securities to non-QIBs so long as the other requirements of Rule 144A are met; sales can only be made to QIBs.

What if the purchaser cannot meet the requirements of Rule 144A? In that case, the seller might try to use the "Section 4(1)(½)" case law–derived exception. *See generally Gilligan, Will & Co. v. SEC*, 267 F.2d 461 (2d Cir. 1959) (a person purchasing restricted securities from an issuer is not an underwriter under Section 4(1) if the purchaser resells the restricted securities to persons who qualify as purchasers under Section 4(2) (that is, that they meet the *Ralston Purina* test) and who acquire the restricted securities in a private offering of the type contemplated by Section 4(2)).

Any person, other than the issuer or dealer, who offers or sells securities in compliance with the conditions set forth in subsection (b) of the rule (listing four conditions with subparts) may rely on Rule 144A for resales and shall be deemed *not* to be engaged in a distribution and not to be deemed an underwriter under Section 2(a)(11) and 4(a)(1) of the 1933 Act.

The Rule 144A Offering Process

The typical Rule 144A offering process is similar in many ways to a regular public offering process. Solicitation of offers is typically made using a "red herring" offering memorandum,[13] followed by a term sheet and pricing terms. Once the order is confirmed, there is a final offering memorandum similar to registered offering documentation that includes a purchase agreement, a comfort letter from the issuer's auditors, and a legal opinion from the issuer's counsel. In addition to that information, in the case of non-reporting issuers, the purchaser has the right to ask for a brief description of the seller's business, its most recent balance sheet, and the financial statement for the current and the two preceding years.

Every Rule 144A sale must be preceded by a "good" private placement under Section 4(a)(2). In fact, this is the way that the seller, which is typically an investment bank, receives the securities from the issuer before reselling them to another institutional investor.

Rule 144A purchases are deemed to be "restricted securities" under Rule 144(a)(3) and must be held for a designated period of time before resale, at which time they may be resold either pursuant to an effective registration statement or some other available exemption. But if the issuer is a reporting company and the holder of the restricted shares is not an affiliate of the company, the holding period is only six months, after which the securities may be

[13] As noted, a "red herring" memorandum receives its name from the red-ink warning language printed on its cover.

resold without limitation. If the issuer is not a reporting company, the holding period is one year.

Rule 144A offerings are often followed by SEC-registered exchange offers (known as AB exchange offers[14] or "Exxon Capital" exchange offers) in which the issuer offers to exchange the privately placed Rule 144A securities for similar securities that have been registered and that are freely resalable. This is the preferred means for providing holders of Rule 144A securities with freely tradable securities. However, this procedure is currently available only for non-convertible debt securities, certain non-convertible preferred stock, and initial public offerings of foreign issuers.

As noted, many Rule 144A offerings are for convertible debt and are accompanied by shelf registration statements to provide the seller the ability to deliver freely tradable securities to a subsequent purchaser. But there are limitations to this procedure. The SEC requires that the prospectus for a shelf registration contain a list of all beneficial owners of the restricted securities that will be resold pursuant to the shelf registration statement. This is virtually impossible in most cases. This is why the "Exxon Capital" exchange offer is preferred when available.

Safe Harbor

If all the conditions of Rule 144 and Rule 144A are met, there is a safe harbor providing that the person who sells the restricted securities on his or her own behalf or on behalf of an affiliate of the issuer will be deemed not to be engaged in a distribution, and the purchaser will receive securities that are not restricted securities. However, the Preliminary Note No. 1 of Rule 144A makes it clear that the antifraud provisions of the 1933 Act still apply. For that reason, the offering memorandum may look more like a prospectus for a registered offering.

There is an open question whether a Rule 144A offering is exempt from state regulation, pursuant to Section 18. It will be exempt if the issuer has a class of securities traded on the New York Stock Exchange, the American Stock Exchange, or the NASDAQ Market System, and the securities being resold in the Rule 144A transaction are equal to or senior to the issuer's securities listed on one of those exchanges. Section 18 also exempts the Rule 144A resale from state regulation if the resale is made to a "qualifying person," but that phrase has never been defined. However, most states will exempt resales made to QIBs.

---

[14] An A/B exchange is an exchange of newly registered and issued shares (A shares, usually convertible debt) are exchanged for restricted shares (B shares) obtained in a private placement. This is a way of making restricted shares freely tradable.

Chapter 7

Proxy Solicitation and Tender Offers

Proxy Solicitation

Prior to the enactment of the Exchange Act in 1934, state corporate laws authorized open-ended proxy solicitations of shareholders by corporate management in order to obtain nearly limitless authority to manage the corporations without the shareholders even knowing what they were voting for or against. In effect, this practice gave management a "rubber stamp" over any matters on which the shareholders might be asked to vote.

To rectify this problem, Section 14(a) of the Exchange Act prohibits solicitation of any proxy, consent, or authorization in respect of any security registered with the SEC in violation of any rules or regulations promulgated by the SEC. In addition, Section 14 prohibits any bank or other fiduciary from giving or refraining from giving, in violation of rules and regulations promulgated by the SEC, a proxy or consent in respect of any registered security and "carried for the account of a customer." That section also requires the promulgation of certain required information to holders of record of registered securities in connection with proxy solicitations.

The SEC's Proxy Regulation Regime

Under the authority granted under Section 14(a), the SEC has created an elaborate regime to regulate proxy solicitations by registered companies. The goal was to improve what is sometimes referred to as "corporate democracy," a struggle that still continues today. Rule 14a-3(a), perhaps the most important part of the SEC's regime, requires any person who solicits a proxy from public shareholders to file with the SEC and to distribute to shareholders specified information in a document known as a "proxy statement." Rule 14a-9 prohibits any false or misleading proxy statements. It is not clear whether this is a strict liability statute (most courts have said no), whether there is a scienter requirement for liability, or whether negligence is sufficient. There is also no express private right of action, although the *Borak*[1] case found that federal courts have the power to grant all necessary remedial relief, without deciding what should be done in that particular case.

Proxy Statements

Required proxy statements must contain information about the corporation, the background of all director nominees (if election of directors is an object of the proxy solicitation), management's compensation and conflicts of interest, and any other matter being voted on. If the vote is for directors, every shareholder must receive a copy of the corporation's most recent annual report containing information about the company's direction, operations, and current financial information. Interestingly, this may be the only federal or state law that explicitly requires such periodic communications with shareholders. Under Rule 14a-12, participants may make both written and oral communications to shareholders prior to the filing of a proxy statement, provided that all such written communications are filed with the SEC on the date of their first use, that no proxy card is furnished to the shareholders, that the shareholders are advised of the identity of the participants and their interests, and that they are advised to read the proxy statement when it is filed. However, no proxies may be sought before a proxy statement is filed.

Rule 14a-9 also provides that no solicitation may be made by means of a proxy statement that, at the time and under the circumstances under which it is made, is false or misleading with respect to any material fact or which omits to state any material fact necessary in order to make the statements contained therein not false or misleading or necessary to correct any statement in any earlier communication with respect to the solicitation of a proxy for the same meeting or subject matter that has become false or misleading.

Proxy Cards

Under Rule 14a-4, proxy cards sent to shareholders must specify who is making the solicitation, may relate to only one specific meeting, and must specify the matters and directors on which the shareholders are expected to vote. It must give the shareholders a chance to vote for or against (or abstain from) each matter, and it must give the shareholders the right to withhold

---

[1] *J.I. Case Co. v. Borak*, 377 U.S. 426 (1964). "Our finding that federal courts have the power to grant all necessary remedial relief is not to be construed as any indication of what we believe to be the necessary and appropriate relief in this case."

their vote for any and all directors. The proxy holder must follow the shareholder's instructions.

On April 16, 2021, the SEC reopened the comment period for its proposal to require universal proxy cards in all non-exempt solicitations in connection with contested elections of directors.[2] The proposed rules would establish new procedures for the solicitation of proxies, the preparation and use of proxy cards, and the dissemination of information about all director nominees in contested elections. The principal change would require the use of universal proxy cards that include the names of all duly nominated director candidates for whom proxies are solicited and it would require dissidents in a contested election to solicit the holders of shares representing at least a majority of the voting power of shares entitled to vote on the election of directors.

On November 17, 2021, a divided SEC agreed to require universal proxy cards in contested board elections, permitting shareholders to vote for any combination of nominees they wished, as they could if they were voting in person. SEC Chair Gary Gensler called this "an important aspect of shareholder democracy" that would put "investors voting in person and by proxy on equal footing." There will be a period of public comment for thirty days after the proposal is published in the Federal Register, followed by a Commission vote on a final version.

Soliciting Shareholders

Under Rule 14a-7, shareholders who themselves seek to solicit proxies from other shareholders may call upon management to mail their own shareholder solicitation materials, either separately or together with the company's own proxy materials, provided that the soliciting shareholder or shareholders pay the cost. This is sometimes known as the "common carrier" requirement. But management has an option: it can avoid the "common carrier" obligation by giving the soliciting shareholders the current list of names and addresses of shareholders or nominees who hold shares on behalf of the beneficial owners.

There is another limitation on the company's obligation to mail shareholder solicitations. Rule 14a-8 requires management to send, at corporate expense, "proper" shareholder proposals with the corporation's own proxy materials. The rule specifies which shareholders may make proposals, the procedures for their submission, management's obligations, and the procedures for

---

[2] Universal proxy cards name all of the company and activist nominees for election as directors and provide stockholders the ability to vote for any properly nominated director nominee. They mimic the choices that the stockholders would have if they attended in person. As of this writing, no Delaware corporation has adopted the use of universal proxies. https://corpgov.law.harvard.edu/2018/12/05/universal-proxies-what-companies-need-to-know/.

the SEC to review any management decision to exclude a shareholder solicitation. There are three permissible reasons for a management decision to exclude a shareholder's solicitation: to preserve management's decision-making prerogatives; to protect management's usual proxy solicitations from interference; and to filter out illegal, deceptive, or crackpot proposals.[3]

It should be noted that with respect to the nomination of directors, Rule 14a-11 (authorized by Dodd-Frank) required public companies to give shareholders access to the company-funded proxy materials for director nominations. If the nominating shareholder (or group of shareholders) held at least 3 percent of the company's voting shares, and held them for at least three years, the shareholder or group could nominate up to one-fourth of the company's board. The soliciting shareholder or group was required to give the company 150 days notice and to provide full information about its nominees.[4] Unfortunately, the rule never took effect.

Under Rule 14a-8(i)(7), management may refuse to allow a shareholder proposal to be submitted to other shareholders if it related to the "company's ordinary business operations." On November 3, 2021, the SEC Division of Corporate Finance issued a Staff Legal Bulletin that permits shareholder proposals that raise significant social or environmental issues that would have been excluded under previous staff bulletins. We can therefore confidently expect to see many more such shareholder proposals in the future.

Liability for Fraud

Under Section 10(b) and Rule 10b-5 of the 1934 Act, there is civil (and potential criminal) liability for any false or misleading statement or omission in any required proxy statement. The standard rules for Rule 10b-5 liability apply. First, the plaintiff may either be the SEC or any shareholder.[5] Second, the misrepresentation or omission must be material. Here, that would mean that there was a substantial likelihood that a "reasonable shareholder" would consider the false or misleading statement or omission to be important in deciding how to vote. Third, there must be a causal link, that is, that the proxy solicitation

---

[3] This description is taken from Alan R. Palmiter, *Securities Regulation* (7th ed.) (Wolters Kluwer) (2017) 373.

[4] This provision was challenged as a violation of the Administrative Procedure Act because the SEC failed to consider the economic consequences of the rule and to connect those consequences to efficiency, competition, and capital formation. In *Business Roundtable v. SEC*, 647 F.3d 1144 (D.C. Cir. 2011), the rule was vacated.

[5] *J.I. Case Co. v. Borak*, 377 U.S. 426 (1964), suggested but did not explicitly hold that there was an implied right for a private action under Section 10(b) and Rule 10b-5.

must be an essential link to the accomplishment of the transaction, but there is no requirement to prove reliance since it is presumed. (*See Mills v. Electric Auto-Lite Co.*, 396 U.S. 375 (1970)).

Proxy Solicitation Examples

During the past ten years, the SEC has significantly changed the form and content of how companies disclose executive compensation. The new rules are found primarily in Item 402 of Regulation S-K (which is nearly forty pages long) and require disclosure of all compensation and highlighting performance-based versus non-performance-based compensation. Dodd-Frank introduced additional corporate governance requirements and "say on pay" and "say on golden parachutes" votes. Rule 402 disclosures are also required by Item 11 of Forms 10-K and S-1, and Item 6 of Form 10 (for spin-offs).

Not all executive officers are included. Item 402 of Regulation S-K applies to only Named Executive Officers (NEOs) who are the chief executive officer, the chief financial officer, and the three other most highly compensated individuals who were serving as executive officers as of the end of the last fiscal year.

Item 402(b) of Regulation S-K requires a Compensation Discussion and Analysis (CD&A). This must include tables setting forth summary compensation, grants of plan-based awards, outstanding equity awards, option exercises and stock vested, pension benefits, and director compensation, among other things. The CD&A must discuss the objectives of the compensation programs, what they are designed to reward and not reward, each element of compensation, how the company chooses the amount for each element, competitive benchmarking, and many other related items. The company must also disclose the dollar value of earned base salaries and earned bonuses for the preceding three fiscal years. Each element of compensation, including perks and personal benefits, must also be discussed and disclosed unless they are directly related to the performance of the executive's duties (e.g., a larger office).

Item 407 of Regulation S-K(e) (Compensation committee) requires proxy disclosure of the issuer's processes and procedures for the consideration and determination of executive and director compensation, including the authority of the compensation committee and the extent to which that committee may delegate authority to other persons. It also requires discussion of the role of executive officers in determining compensation and the role of compensation consultants, including their fees and whether they provided "additional services" to the company.

Item 401 requires disclosure of the names, ages, positions, and terms of office of each director, director nominee, and executive officer.

Item 405 requires disclosure of each person subject to Section 16 of the 1934 Act who failed to file timely reports under Section 16(a) (short-swing transactions).

If shareholder approval is being sought for an employee benefit plan, the proxy statement must include a description of the material features of the plan, a new "benefits table," and whether the plan can be amended without a vote of shareholders. If the plan includes the ability to grant options, they must be described and the exercise conditions must be set forth. The statement must also list options granted or to be granted to each NEO, all current officers as a group, all current directors who are not executive officers, each director nominee and all employees, as a group (in addition to several other categories of recipients).

Item 5(a) of Schedule 14A requires a brief description of any substantial interest of each person who served as a director or executive officer since the beginning of the previous fiscal year in any matter to be acted upon other than elections to office. There are similar disclosure requirements in Item 3 of Schedule 14D-9 for tender offers and in Item 18(a)(5) of Form S-4 for stock-for-stock mergers.

Under SEC rules adopted in January 2011 to implement Section 951 of Dodd-Frank, shareholders of public companies subject to the proxy rules must be allowed to cast an "advisory vote" on executive compensation (say on pay), the desired frequency of an advisory vote on executive compensation (say on frequency), and compensation arrangements in connection with merger transactions (say on golden parachutes). A say-on-pay vote is required as a separate shareholder vote at the annual meeting of shareholders at which directors will be elected. Item 24 of Schedule 14A requires a statement that the company is providing a separate shareholder vote on executive compensation, as well as the general effect of the vote (e.g., vote is nonbinding).

Even though Section 953(b) of Dodd-Frank required the SEC to amend Item 402 of Regulation S-K to require disclosure of the median of annual total compensation of all employees (excluding the CEO), annual total compensation of the CEO, and the ratio of the two numbers, the SEC did not issue final rules until 2015, and the first pay ratio disclosure was included in 2018 proxy statements. It turns out that this is a complex calculation, and the SEC rules therefore require that the median employee compensation needs to be identified only every three years.

Dodd-Frank's requirement that the SEC develop clawback rules to recover incentive-based compensation erroneously paid to executive officers in the event of an accounting restatement has not yet been implemented by the SEC.

On December 16, 2020, shortly before the end of the Trump administration, the Department of Labor published a regulation titled "Financial

Factors in Selecting Plan Investments" and another titled "Fiduciary Duties Regarding Proxy Voting and Shareholder Rights" (the Proxy Voting Rule) that many thought were intended to have a chilling effect on fiduciaries who include so-called ESG (environmental, social, and governance) factors in their financial evaluation of plan investments. On March 10, 2021, the Department of Labor, under new leadership, announced that it would not enforce or otherwise pursue enforcement actions against a fiduciary for failing to comply with either regulation, stating that it intended "to conduct significantly more stakeholder outreach to determine how to craft rules that better recognize the important role that environmental, social and governance integration can play in the evaluation and management of plan investments, while continuing to uphold fundamental fiduciary obligations." In early June 2021, Gary Gensler, the new SEC chairman, similarly announced that the SEC would not enforce rules regarding proxy voting that were put in place during the Trump administration and that were seen as placing significant restrictions on shareholders' ability to engage companies on ESG issues through the proxy and shareholder proposal process.

Proxy Contests

In this section, we will briefly discuss how proxy solicitations have recently come back to life as alternatives to tender offers. The tender offer regulations will be discussed later.

Until recently, because of the difficulty of ousting incumbent management through proxy solicitations, tender offers had largely replaced them. However, it has become clear that tender offers, especially hostile tender offers, are difficult, expensive, and subject to onerous regulatory requirements. Thus, proxy contests have experienced a bit of a resurgence, depending, of course, on the goals to be achieved. If, for example, shareholder insurgents were concerned about a company's stock trading at a low price, they might attempt a proxy contest to force the company to sell assets and to distribute the proceeds to the shareholders. Proxy contests can also facilitate hostile takeovers. *Question for consideration*: How would a corporation seek to insulate itself from such a tactic? *Hint*: A staggered board.

The Proxy Advisors Issue

Proxy voting advice businesses, sometimes known as proxy advisory firms, are persons or entities that provide proxy voting advice, for a fee, that falls within the definition of a solicitation under Rule 14a-1(l)(1)(iii), as amended, and includes registrants who are conducting solicitations and are the subject of proxy voting advice.

On July 22, 2020, the SEC amended its rules governing proxy solicitations. The amendments aim to facilitate the ability of those who use proxy voting advice—investors and others who vote on investors' behalf—to make informed voting decisions without imposing undue costs or delays that could adversely affect the timely provision of proxy voting advice.[6]

The federal proxy rules contain exemptions from certain requirements, including the requirements to file a proxy statement. The new amendments include conditions that proxy advice businesses must meet to utilize two of these exemptions. They must (1) provide their clients with tailored and comprehensive conflicts of interest disclosure, (2) have policies and procedures designed to ensure that registrants that are the subject of proxy voting advice have such advice made available to them in a timely manner (in other words, "give the client what she needs when she needs it"), and (3) have policies and procedures designed to ensure that their clients are provided with an efficient and timely means of becoming aware of any written responses by registrants to proxy voting advice (in other words, "tell the clients what the company thinks of their advice"). The amendments also amend the definition of "solicitation" to specify that it includes proxy voting advice, with some exceptions. The amendments made changes to Rule 14a(1)(l), Rules 14a-2(b)(1) and 14a-2(b)(3), and Rule 14a-9.

Reaction was swift and critical. The Investment Adviser Association said that the amendments were a "bad policy" and that "it is hard for us to understand why the SEC felt compelled to issue additional guidance for advisers." Similarly, the Institutional Shareholder Services said that "while the rules adopted today may appear less draconian than originally envisioned, they nevertheless serve as a blow to institutional investors seeking to judiciously monitor portfolio companies." And SEC Commissioner Allison Herren Lee said that the rules were "unwarranted, unwanted and unworkable." The American Securities Association, however, praised the amendments as "a win for 'mom-and-pop' investors.... American companies of all sizes will now be able to weigh in on critical issues before investors vote and can be confident that voting is based upon accurate information."

---

[6] SEC Press Release, "SEC Adopts Rule Amendments to Provide Investors Using Proxy Voting Advice More Transparent, Accurate and Complete Information," July 22, 2020. "The majority of our Main Street investors participate in our public markets through the ownership of mutual funds and ETFs managed by professional market participants. Today's actions ensure that those who take on the responsibility of investing and voting on behalf of our Main Street investors have the accurate and decision-useful information necessary to make an informed voting decision for the benefit of those investors."

Tender Offers

During the 1960s, cash tender offers for the stock of publicly traded securities were increasingly common and somewhat troublesome.[7] More than 80 percent of the shares of U.S. corporations were held by individual shareholders, unlike today when they account for only about 30 percent. When cash tender offers were made, the individual shareholders had very little time to decide whether to tender their shares and learn about who the offeror was. While some of the offers were perfectly legitimate, others were being made by "corporate raiders," some of whom were true scoundrels who wound up in prison. "Green mail" was a well-known tactic to force corporations to capitulate to hostile takeovers or at least to live in fear of them. Unlike proxy solicitations and share-for-share exchanges, cash tender offers could be made without any filings or disclosure of relevant information. Something had to be done, and that "something" was the Williams Act, sponsored by Senator Harrison Williams of New Jersey.

The Williams Act of 1968 amended the 1934 Act by adding Sections 13(d) and (e) and Sections 14(d), (e), and (f), and in 1970 Congress gave the SEC broad rule-making authority. Essentially, those sections contained disclosure mandates that were intended to give shareholders information and sufficient time to make an informed decision as to whether or not to tender their shares. Of great significance, Section 14(e) makes it unlawful for any person to make an untrue statement of a material fact or to omit to state any material fact necessary in order to make the statements made not misleading, or to engage in any fraudulent, deceptive, or manipulative act or practice in connection with a tender offer or request or invitation for tenders or any solicitation of security holders in opposition to or in favor of any such offer, request, or invitation.

The disclosure obligations of Section 13(d), mandated by the Williams Act, required public notice within ten days of any person or group who becomes the beneficial owner of 5 percent or more of a company's outstanding stock. (When the Act was first passed, the percentage that compelled disclosure was 10 percent.) "Beneficial ownership" is the direct or indirect power to vote, sell, or determine the disposition of the relevant shares. The Schedule 13D notice must include the background and identity of those on whose behalf the stock was acquired, the source and amount of funds, the plans of the acquiror, the

---

[7] The term "tender offer" is not defined in the Williams Act, but the courts have used two tests for determining whether a series of purchases and offers is a "tender offer." The first is the so-called "eight-factor test" in which no single factor is determinative, and it is not required to have all eight factors. Among those is "the active and widespread solicitation of public shareholders." The second test is the "totality of circumstances" test that looks at whether there is a risk that the shareholders will not have the necessary information to make a carefully considered appraisal of the bidder's offer.

number of shares that are owned, and any contracts entered into with respect to the securities at issue. *Question*: Why would anyone want to do that and keep it secret? *Hint*: To establish a toehold.

Section 13(d) regulated purchases by the target of its own shares.

Section 14(d) regulated the substantive aspects of tender offers. For example, under Section 14(d)(1), cash tender offers must be accompanied by the information required by Section 13(d)(1), including the identity and background of the offeror, the source of funds, the purpose, special arrangements, and the like. The purpose of the disclosure is to protect shareholders from fraud, deception, and manipulation. In the early days, the disclosures were printed in their entirety in newspapers such as the *Wall Street Journal* and resulted in contentious litigation over their truthfulness.

Section 14(e) prohibits fraud and certain other practices in connection with a tender offer, including failure to comply with time periods and disclosure obligations.

The Williams Act has very strict and narrow timing requirements for the consummation of tender offers, and related litigation moved very quickly through the courts, where many judges were unfamiliar with the phenomenon of a hostile tender offer or the Williams Act.

When a tender offer is made, the target company typically provides what is known as a "stop, look, and listen" communication, in which it urges shareholders not to make a decision about tendering their shares until the target company takes a position as to whether or not it supports the offer. Rule 14e-2(a) requires the target to disclose its position not later than ten days after the commencement of the tender offer. The target has four options: to recommend acceptance of the offer, to recommend rejection of the offer, to express no opinion, or to state that it is unable to take a position. The target's position must be set forth on Schedule 14D-9, which must be filed with the SEC on the date of the communication.

Rule 14d-10(a)(2) provides that the bidder may not make a tender offer unless the consideration paid pursuant to the offer is the highest consideration paid to any *other* security holder during the tender offer. This is called the "best price" rule. The courts have had some difficulty defining "pursuant to the tender offer" and "during the tender offer." Courts have declined to hold that the expiration date constitutes the end of the tender offer for the purposes of the best price rule. To deal with this confusion, the SEC amended Rule 14d-10 to provide that there is no time restriction for the rule's application and exempting from Rule 14d-10 the negotiation, execution, or amendment of an employment compensation, severance payments, and other employee benefit arrangements to be made or benefits granted according to such arrangement, with respect to any security holder of the issuer, where the amount payable under the arrangement meets certain conditions, such as being paid or granted as compensation for past services performed. In short (and subject to many qualifications), this rule means that for the purpose of calculating the highest consideration paid to any other security holder for shares tendered into the tender offer, certain payments to shareholders need not be taken into consideration. The rule is complicated and has many exemptions, so be warned in the event that you find yourself trying to calculate what constitutes the "highest consideration paid" to any security holder for securities tendered into a tender offer.

Once a tender offer is made, Rule 14e-5 prohibits any purchases by the offeror outside the tender offer. In addition, offerors must leave tender offers open for twenty business days (offers for roll-ups must remain open for no less than sixty calendar days), they must pay the full consideration offered (or return the deposited securities) promptly after termination (or withdrawal), and they may not extend the length of a tender offer without notice by press release or other public announcement.

Takeovers that present potential antitrust issues were especially problematic, since they could be consummated before the antitrust agencies had time to react. In that situation, the only available remedy would be divestiture, an unwelcomed and difficult procedure.

The 1976 Hart-Scott-Rodino Antitrust Improvements Act changed the landscape and required that takeovers could not be consummated until twenty days after the Federal Trade Commission and the Justice Department's Antitrust Division were notified and supplied with detailed information concerning actual or potential antitrust issues, and the agency that had taken primary responsibility for analyzing the transaction (the clearing agency) agreed that all requested information had been produced. If the agency did not agree, the transaction could not be consummated until after the requested information had been produced. Once the information is produced, the agency must either seek an injunction to prohibit the consummation of the takeover or allow it to proceed.

The 1999 SEC Tender Offer Rules

The 1999 Rules are extensive and require disclosure of specified additional information in tender offers. For example, they require disclosure of any changes in disclosures, and the disclosure of any negotiations or transactions taken by target companies in response to tender offers. To reduce any imbalances between cash and stock tender offers, the SEC rules now permit stock exchange offers to commence upon the filing of a registration statement. The rules permit third-party exchange offers to commence on the filing of the registration statement coupled with the filing of a tender offer statement (Schedule TO), although the bidder cannot purchase any securities tendered in the exchange until the registration statement has become effective. Securities tendered in such a tender offer may not be purchased until after the expiration of twenty business days after the commencement of the offer (Rule 14e-1(a)). The bid may be extended by a public notice, and an optional offering period may be provided.

In July 2000, the SEC promulgated detailed comments on tender offers that result in the bidders holding 5 percent or less of the outstanding securities of the target (a mini-tender offer). The SEC published a series of disclosure guidelines that should be "considered" in such cases. It noted that although Section 14(d) was limited to tender offers that would result in the ownership of more than 5 percent of a class of securities, there was no similar limitation in Rule 14(e). The SEC noted that "we are concerned the substance of the disclosure in many of these offers is not adequate under Section 14(e) and Regulation 14E." As a result, "security holders faced with a mini-tender offer" are entitled to the protections of Section 14(e) and Regulation 14E. The new guidelines on mini-tender offers were intended to "reduce the risk that [offerors] will violate the antifraud provisions of the statutes and rules."

Although it is beyond the scope of this Handbook, readers should be aware that there are a number of defensive tactics that may be taken by target boards under state laws. For example, in *Unocal Corp. v. Mesa Petroleum Co.*, 493 A.2d 946 (Del. 1985), the business judgment rule may be invoked by a board in support of certain defensive measures such as staggered boards and "poison pills," provided that there are "reasonable grounds for believing that a danger to corporate policy and effectiveness existed" and that the actions taken were "reasonable in relation to the threat posed." As a result, the successful hostile takeover is fast becoming a thing of the past. In fact, because of the influence of institutional shareholders, it is nearly impossible for a minority shareholder individually to dictate the outcome of a proxy contest or otherwise take control of a company through accumulation of 10 percent (or even more) of the outstanding stock. Because this is a new and burgeoning area of the law, readers are on notice that study and care must be taken whenever these issues are encountered in practice.

Disclosure of Merger Negotiations

There is no obligation to disclose the existence of pre-merger negotiations. The SEC has taken the position that companies need not disclose otherwise secret merger negotiations if management thinks that disclosure would jeopardize the negotiations. Silence is not actionable unless there is a duty to speak. The Supreme Court held in *Basic v. Levinson*, 485 U.S. 224 (1988), that merger negotiations were material and footnote 17 of that decision is a long discussion of "no comment" responses as the equivalent of silence. Form 8-K mandates the disclosure of merger transactions only once consummated.

Recent Changes in M&A Litigation

Mootness Fees. Prior to 2013, shareholders who wished to challenge mergers and acquisitions would typically assert claims for breach of fiduciary duty based on flawed disclosure, inadequate price, and unfair process allegations. They would also typically bring such cases in Delaware state courts as well as in other state and federal courts. Many of the non-Delaware courts were not well versed in M&A issues, and the plaintiffs were able to leverage that uncertainty because the transaction parties would not want to risk a delay of closing by litigating. As a result, most non-Delaware cases would settle, and the defendants would exchange supplemental disclosures with no financial consideration to the class for a global release. The plaintiffs' lawyers would typically receive a fee award of about $500,000 because of the "benefit" that the additional disclosures would confer on the shareholders.

Beginning in 2013, however, the Delaware state courts began to crack down on such cases and settlements. They began to enforce forum-selection clauses in corporate bylaws, and they criticized certain settlement practices. One consequence was that many shareholder M&A cases were brought in federal court, not state court, alleging violations of Section 14 of the 1934 Act. In 2020, approximately 122 federal class actions challenging proposed mergers were brought in Delaware federal court, and approximately 450 non–class action federal challenges were brought in the same court, all by the same law firm. The non–class actions are favored by the plaintiffs' lawyers because they are able to sidestep the Private Securities Litigation Reform Act (PSLRA) restrictions and certification requirements by avoiding class actions. Existing law permits non-class plaintiffs to seek fee awards under the common benefit doctrine. These cases were then voluntarily dismissed after the defendants made immaterial and minor supplemental disclosures in return for what the lawyers called "mootness fees." No court approval is required for these settlements because they are dismissed before a class is certified.

In *In re Trulia Inc. Stockholder Litigation*, 129 A.3d 884 (Del. Ch. 2016), the Delaware Chancery Court, a state court, refused to approve a settlement that awarded attorney's fees without a meaningful benefit to the clients. At least one federal circuit, the Seventh, has endorsed the *Trulia* decision in rejecting a class action settlement that was a "disclosure only" settlement in return for an attorneys' fee of $370,000. In *In re Walgreen Co. Stockholder Litigation*, 832 F.3d 718 (7th Cir. 2016), Judge Richard Posner sharply criticized the practice: "It is inconceivable that the six disclosures added by the settlement agreement either reduced support for the merger by frightening the shareholders or increased that support by giving the shareholders a sense that they now knew everything.... The value of the disclosures in this case appears to have been nil." For good measure, Judge Posner added, "A class action that seeks only worthless benefits for the class should be dismissed out of hand."

Similarly, a federal district court in Illinois rejected a mootness fee settlement, finding that the proposed disclosure was "worthless to the shareholders" and exercising its "inherent authority" to reject the mootness fee settlement and ordering counsel to return the fee to the company.[8]

As a result of these cases, "mootness fees" have declined relative to pre-*Trulia* fees. The usual fee is now less than $100,000, and fees in excess of $200,000 are unusual. It remains to be seen whether Congress will take action to limit these cases.[9]

Post-Closing Damage Cases. Rule 14a-9 prohibits a solicitation by means of a proxy statement or any other written or oral communication that, at the time and in the light of the circumstances under which it is made, is false or misleading with respect to any material fact or that omits to state any material fact necessary to make the statements therein not misleading. There is no scienter requirement, except for cases "sounding in fraud." In these cases, challenges to affirmative statements of opinion must plead both objective and subjective falsity, and challenges to omissions must plead "particular and material facts going to the basis for the issuer's opinion, whose omission makes the opinion statement at issue misleading to a reasonable person reading the statement fairly and in context." This is a quotation from the Supreme Court's 2015 *Omnicare* decision, discussed in Chapter 3. The court reminded us that making that showing "is no small task for an investor."

In these post-closing cases, the typical claims are breaches of the duty of care and the duty of loyalty. In the duty of care cases, there is nearly always exculpation for directors under Section 102(b)(7), so long as exculpation is in the corporate charter, not the bylaws. Duty of loyalty claims usually allege either conflict of interest or bad faith. The default rule for the standard of review is the "business judgment rule" that will uphold the decision of a director so long as the director was acting in good faith, with the care of a reasonably prudent person, and in the best interests of the corporation. *See, e.g., In re Synthes, Inc. S'holder Litig.*, 50 A.3d 1022, 1033 (Del. Ch. 2012). In any transaction in which corporate control passes to a third party, the so-called *Revlon* standard applies.[10] *See Paramount Communications, Inc. v. Time Inc.*,

---

[8] *House v. Akorn, Inc.*, No. 19-2408, N.D. Ill. This case was argued in the Seventh Circuit on April 14, 2020, and is awaiting decision.

[9] *See* Gregory Markel et al., "Abusive M&A Litigation Highlights the Need for Securities Reform," Law 360, March 4, 2021.

[10] *Revlon Inc. v. MacAndrews & Forbes Holdings, Inc.*, 506 A.2d 173 (Del. 1986).

571 A.2d 1140 (Del. 1989). This standard "examines whether the board's overall course of action was reasonable under the circumstances as a good faith attempt to secure the highest value reasonably attainable." *RBC Capital Markets, LLC v. Jervis*, 129 A.3d 816, 849 (Del. 2015).

The Corporate Governance Debate

It was long thought that "corporate governance," a term recently created to describe how corporations are managed and for whom, meant that the sole role of corporate management was to maximize the profits of the shareholders.[11] However, the phrase soon came to represent greater shareholder involvement in corporate management, perhaps brought on by changes in the capital markets, increases in information available about corporate management—including the excesses and derelictions exhibited by Enron and WorldCom—and social awareness that corporations are entities with social responsibilities of their own. What some have called an "obsession" with corporate governance has led to an entirely new field of best practices, shareholder democracy, shareholder activism, and increased board independence.[12]

The shareholder democracy movement was given a boost by two federal securities laws, the Sarbanes-Oxley Act of 2002 and the Dodd-Frank Act of 2010. These laws, brought on largely because of corporate scandals of large proportions, have transformed corporate governance from a profit-making enterprise to a favored response to things like income inequality, gender inequity, and social welfare. In a sense, shareholder democracy or modern corporate governance has become a metaphor for public policy or even government writ large in response to the financial crises most recently seen in 2008. Today, for example, there are calls for the required disclosure of a corporation's efforts in the areas of the ESG and human capital management issues.[13] The future of corporate governance and shareholder democracy remains to be seen. To be sure, they have not ended either inequality or corporate misfeasance or fraud, but the final chapter is yet to be written.

---

[11] This is sometimes called the "Friedman Doctrine," after the economist Milton Friedman.

[12] *See, e.g.*, Mariana Pargendler, "The Corporate Governance Obsession," 42 J. Corp. L. 359 (2016-2017).

[13] Prior to August 2020, the SEC's Regulation S-K, Item 101(c) required only disclosure of the number of employees in the company. The 2020 amendment now requires additional detail, such as information on full-time versus part-time employees and unionized versus non-unionized employees. The words "human capital" are not defined since they may evolve in meaning over time and may vary depending on the industry.

In fact, on February 24, 2021, then-Acting SEC Commissioner Allison Herren Lee reported that she had asked the Division of Corporation Finance to review the "extent to which public companies are following the SEC's February 2, 2010, guidance with respect to climate-related risks." The 2010 guidance asked companies to assess their climate-related disclosures based on such things as climate-related international accords and treaties, a company's legal, technological, political, and scientific developments, and climate-related laws and regulations.

On March 4, 2021, the SEC created a task force to "proactively identify" misconduct involving ESG issues, mining registrant information for potential violations, and evaluating and pursuing whistleblower tips relating to ESG concerns.

On May 24, 2021, Lee dispelled the "myth" that the existing disclosure rules already require issuers to disclose ESG material risks. "This is simply not true, and reflects a fundamentalist misunderstanding of the securities laws. The securities laws currently include little in the way of explicit climate or other sustainability disclosure requirements." The "myth," she said, is that there is already a duty to disclose climate and ESG matters, and that we "can rest assured that such disclosures are being made." They are not, she said.[14]

University of Pennsylvania law professor Jill E. Fisch has written that "mandatory disclosure [of ESG] will increase the reliability and comparability of disclosures. Regulation will also serve a role in managing expectations and relieving issuers of the burden or responding to a multiplicity of disclosure requests by shareholders, third-party standard setters and stakeholder groups." Others, such as West Virginia Attorney General Patrick Morrisey, have argued that "the Commission should stick to its core mission of requiring statements on matters that are material to future financial performance—not statements on issues that drive a political agenda.... This is federal overreach and political activism at its worst."[15]

---

[14] Address to a conference hosted by the American Institute of Certified Public Accountants, the Chartered Institute of Management Accountants, the Sustainability Accounting Standards Board, and the Center for Audit Quality. Al Barbarino, *SEC's Lee Rebukes "Myths" Related to ESG Disclosures*, Law 360, May 24, 2021.

[15] Al Barbarino, "Uber, Academics Back SEC's Push for Climate Disclosures," Law 360, June 10, 2021.

Chapter 8

Civil Liability Under the 1933 Securities Act

There are two main liability provisions in the 1933 Act: Section 11 and Section 12(a).[1] We will consider both in this chapter.

Section 11

This is a very straightforward section that authorizes a private right of action by a purchaser who purchased securities that were offered pursuant to a registration statement that contained an untrue statement of material fact or omitted to state a material fact required to be stated therein or necessary to make statements therein not misleading at the time the registration statement became effective.

Yet however straightforward Section 11 may appear to be, there are ambiguities that courts have struggled to resolve. The statute states: "In case any part of a registration statement when such part became effective, contained an untrue statement of material fact or omitted to state a material fact required to be stated therein or necessary to make the statements therein not misleading, any person acquiring *such security* ... may, either at law or in equity sue...." (emphasis added). What does "such security" mean? Note that the phrase has no antecedent in the statute. The courts have held that "such security" means that the person must have purchased a security issued under a specific registration statement, rather than under some other registration statement. *See, e.g.*, *In re Century Aluminum Co. Sec. Litig.*, 729 F.3d 1104 (9th Cir. 2013). This

[1] Section 12(a) could be said to contain two different liability provisions: Section 12(a)(1) applies to any person who offers or sells a security in violation of Section 5, and Section 12(a)(2) applies to any person who "offers or sells a security ... which includes an untrue statement of material fact or omits to state a material fact necessary in order to make the statements, in light of the circumstances under which they were made, not misleading."

interpretation has given rise to the so-called "tracing" obligation in which to establish standing the plaintiff must be able to "trace" the purchased share back to the offending registration statement. In IPOs, that is not difficult to do, since there is only one registration statement and one issue of stock. But in other offerings, it is nearly impossible to do.

In the leading case, *Barnes v. Osofsky*, 373 F.2d 269 (2d Cir. 1967), Judge Henry Friendly resolved the ambiguity in the statute by adopting a narrow interpretation of Section 11. In this case, the issuer had conducted a secondary offering—the company's stock was already publicly traded under a previous registration statement—and the company filed a new registration statement so that it could sell more stock. The plaintiffs alleged that the new registration statement contained material misrepresentations. The Second Circuit held that the plaintiffs had no standing because they could not prove that the shares they purchased had been issued under the new registration statement. Under the Second Circuit's interpretation, which has been widely followed ever since, "such security" meant a security purchased under the registration statement that is being challenged.

Another ambiguity concerns the phrase "In case any part of the registration statement, when such part becomes effective ..." This seems to suggest that different parts of the registration statement can become "effective" at different times. In fact, courts have held that that is true. For example, the filing of a post-effective amendment both includes the amendment in the registration statement and establishes a new effective date for the information for purposes of Section 11 liability. The remainder of the registration statement is still judged as of the original effective date and is not reset absent some specific reason for resetting the date.[2] Issuers must amend registration statements when "fundamental changes" occur in a shelf registration unless the issuer qualifies for Form S-3. Professors Choi and Pritchard remind us that the calculation of the "effective date" is somewhat complicated by the SEC's Rule 430B, promulgated in 2005, with respect to shelf takedowns.[3]

---

[2] Stephen Choi & A.C. Pritchard, *Securities Regulation, Cases and Analysis* (5th ed.) (Foundation Press) (2019), 580.

[3] *Id.* at 581.

Who Is Liable Under Section 11?

There are five categories of possible defendants in a Section 11 case:

1. "Every person who signed the registration statement;
2. Every person who was a director of (or performing similar functions) or partner[4] in the issuer at the time of the filing of the part of the registration statement with respect to which liability is asserted;
3. Every person who, with his [or her] consent, is named in the registration statement as being or about to become a director, person performing similar functions, or partner;
4. Every accountant, engineer, or appraiser, or any person whose profession gives authority to a statement made by him [or her], or who has, with his [or her] consent been named as having prepared or certified any part of the registration statement, or as having prepared or certified any report or valuation which is used in connection with the registration statement, with respect to the statement in such registration statement, report, or valuation, which purports to have been prepared or certified by him [or her]; and
5. Every underwriter with respect to such security."

Note that there is no explicit liability for lawyers based either on their drafting of the registration statement or their investigation of its accuracy, although in cases brought by the SEC, "aiding and abetting" liability is *probably* available.[5]

There are two requirements for a prima facie case of liability: the existence of at least one material misstatement or omission in the registration statement, and that the purchased shares can be traced to the registration statement. Although the statute does not say explicitly that the plaintiff must have either purchased shares in the public offering or is able to trace the purchase directly to the public offering, the Supreme Court has held that the words "such security" refer to securities purchased pursuant to a registration statement.

As noted, tracing shares that have been purchased on the open market or elsewhere back to the registration statement is difficult unless the offering was an initial public offering. In *Krim v. pcOrder.Com, Inc.*, an enterprising plaintiffs' lawyer attempted to do so by proving that as a matter of mathematical

---

[4] This word is not further defined in the statute.

[5] In *Lorenzo v. SEC*, 139 U.S. 1094 (2019), the Supreme Court noted that Section 20(e) of the 1934 Act gave the SEC authority to pursue those who "substantially assist" others in committing fraud under its "aiding and abetting" jurisdiction.

probability, there was a 1-(1-0.9958) to the 3,000th power probability that the lead plaintiff in a class action owned at least one share that could be traced to the registration statement out of the 3,000 shares he purchased. The Fifth Circuit was unimpressed and ruled that "statistical tracing" was unavailable. The plaintiff must prove that the purchased security was in fact part of the public offering. "Statistical tracing is not up to the task." The court recognized that "[w]hen Congress enacted the Securities Act of 1933, it was not confronted with the widespread practice of holding stock in street names.... That present market realities, given the fungibility of stock held in street name, may render Section 11 ineffective as a practical matter in some aftermarket scenarios is an issue properly addressed by Congress."[6]

There is no requirement in Section 11 for proof of scienter or causation, nor is there a requirement that the plaintiff relied on the misstatement or omission.[7] The plaintiff need not prove that he or she actually read the prospectus. Thus, the statute can be said to be one creating "strict liability."

Section 11 creates liability for false statements of fact and for omissions of discrete factual representations. What are they? A fact is "a thing done or existing ... or an actual happening" whereas an opinion is "a belief, a view, or a sentiment which the mind forms of persons or things."[8] But what if the statement contained in the registration statement is one of opinion? It has long been held that statements of opinion are not actionable so long as the speaker truly holds the stated opinion. *See, e.g., Virginia Bankshares, Inc. v. Sandberg*, 501 U.S. 1083 (1991).

---

[6] This "tracing" requirement essentially confines the plaintiffs to those acquiring securities issued pursuant to an initial public offering because proof that a security purchased on the open market originated from a specific registration statement can be difficult if not impossible. *See Krim v. pcOrder.com, Inc.*, 402 F.3d 489, 498 (5th Cir. 2005).

[7] There is an exception to this provision. "If such person acquired the security after the issuer has made generally available to its security holders an earning statement covering a period of at least twelve months beginning after the effective date of the registration statement, then the right of recovery under this subsection shall be conditioned on proof that such person acquired the security relying upon such untrue statement in the registration statement and not knowing of such omission, but such reliance may be established without proof of the reading of the registration statement by such person." *See APA Excelsior IIILP v. Premiere Techs., Inc.*, 476 F.3d 1261 (11th Cir. 2007) (Section 11 creates a conclusive "presumption of reliance" for any person purchasing the security prior to the expiration of twelve months); *but see FHFA v. Bank of America Corp.*, 2014 WL 7232339 (S.D.N.Y. Dec. 18, 2014) (rejecting the 11th Circuit's analysis).

[8] Webster's New International Dictionary 782 (1927); 7 Oxford English Dictionary 141 (1933); both quoted by Justice Elena Kagan in the *Omnicare* opinion.

However, that rule was substantially modified by the Supreme Court in *Omnicare, Inc. v. Laborers Dist. Council Constr. Indus. Pension Fund*, 135 S. Ct. 1318 (2015). Omnicare's registration statement included the following two statements:

1. "*We believe* our contract arrangements with other health care providers ... are in compliance with applicable federal and state laws."
2. "*We believe* that our contracts ... are legally and economically valid." (Emphasis added.)

In a class action brought under Section 11, the plaintiffs alleged that those statements were incorrect because the company's receipt of payments from drug manufacturers violated anti-kickback laws and that the company therefore "omitted to state material facts necessary to make its representations not misleading." It was conceded that the opinions were honestly held. The Supreme Court took the case to "consider whether the omission of a fact can make a statement of opinion like Omnicare's, even if literally accurate, misleading to an ordinary investor." The Supreme Court held that it could. "[W]hether an omission makes an expression of opinion misleading always depends on context.... Investors do not, and are right not to, expect opinions contained in those statements to reflect baseless, off-the-cuff judgments, of the kind that an individual might communicate in daily life." The Supreme Court remanded the case for further review, while noting that in order to prevail, "the investor must identify particular (and material) facts going to the basis for the issuer's opinion—facts about the inquiry the issuer did or did not conduct or the knowledge it did or did not have—whose omission makes the opinion statement at issue misleading to a reasonable person reading the statement fairly and in context. That is no small task for an investor."

What Defenses Are Available in a Section 11 Case?

The defenses set forth in Section 11(b) are somewhat confusing. Recall that under Section 11(a), there is a limited list of potential defendants, all of whom have some connection to the registration statement. The available defenses set forth in the statute can be better understood as applying to two categories of defendants: experts and all others.

First, all defendants, including experts, may escape liability by proving that the plaintiff "at the time of the acquisition of such security knew of such untruth or omission." (Section 11(a).)

Second, a defendant, including experts, may escape liability by showing that "before the effective date of the part of the registration statement with respect to which his liability is asserted, he had resigned from or had taken such steps as are permitted by law to resign from, or ceased or refused to act in, every office, capacity or relationship in which he was described in the registration statement as acting or agreeing to act and so advised the SEC and the issuer in writing that he had taken such action and that he would not be responsible for such part of the registration statement, or that if the registration statement became effective without his knowledge, upon becoming aware of it he forthwith acted and advised the SEC and gave 'reasonable public notice' that the registration statement had become effective without his knowledge." (Section 11(b)(1) and (2).) Obviously, these defenses are almost never asserted.

All defendants other than experts (who have no liability with respect to these parts) may also assert a defense under Section 11(b)(3)(A). Under that section, as regards any part of a registration statement *not* purporting to be made on the authority of an expert (a "non-expertised" portion), the defendant may prove that "he had, after reasonable investigation, reasonable ground to believe and did believe, at the time such part of the registration statement became effective, that the statements therein were true and that there was no omission to state a material fact required to be stated therein or necessary to make the statement therein not misleading."

One way to look at this is the following: experts have responsibility for "expertised" portions, and non-experts have responsibility for non-expertised portions of the registration statement.

As noted, experts have no liability whatsoever for the non-expertised portions of a registration statement, and they have specific defenses to the expertised portions. Those defenses are sometimes referred to as "due diligence."

Due Diligence

It is worth noting at the outset that the term "due diligence" does not appear anywhere in the 1933 Act or the 1934 Act or, indeed, in any rule adopted by the SEC. However, the word "diligence" does appear in Section 13.

Section 11(b)(3)(B) provides that with respect to any part of the registration statement made upon the authority of an expert, the expert may assert a defense if he had, "after reasonable investigation, reasonable ground to believe and did believe at the time such part of the registration statement became effective, that the statements therein were true and that there was no omission to state a material fact required to be stated therein or necessary to make the statements therein not misleading, or that such part of the registration statement did not fairly represent his statement as an expert or was not a fair copy or extract from his report or valuation as an expert."[9]

---

[9] It is unfortunate that the 1933 Act used the masculine pronoun throughout.

Section 11(b)(3)(C) sets forth a similar defense for an expert defendant with respect to statements in the registration statement made on the authority of an expert *other than himself*, but that section does not require that a "reasonable," or indeed any, investigation be undertaken by the expert defendant.

Subsection (D) contains a similar defense for statements in the registration statement made by "official persons" but that too does not require an investigation.

What is a reasonable investigation? The standard set forth in Section 11(c) is "that required of a prudent man in the management of his own property." But what exactly is that? In *Escott v. Barchris Construction Corp.*, 283 F. Supp. 643 (S.D.N.Y. 1968), the court opined, "To effectuate the statute's purpose, the phrase 'reasonable investigation' must be construed to require more effort on the part of the underwriters than the mere accurate reporting in the prospectus of 'data presented' to them by the company.... Underwriters must make some reasonable attempt to verify the data submitted to them."

The "red flag" analysis is also appropriate. In *In re WorldCom Inc. Securities Litigation*, 93 F. Supp. 2d 276 (E.D.N.Y. 2000), the district court denied the defendant underwriters' motion for summary judgment on its due diligence defense. Judge Denise Cote held that "if red flags arise from a reasonable investigation, underwriters will have to make sufficient inquiry to satisfy themselves as to the accuracy of the financial statements, and if unsatisfied, they must demand disclosure, withdraw from the underwriting process, or bear the risk of liability." The WorldCom underwriters neither demanded more disclosures nor withdrew from the process.

One of the issues raised by this defense is whether an underwriter may rely on certified financial statements. In her *WorldCom* opinion, Judge Cote clearly held that the underwriters of two WorldCom public offerings at issue were not entitled to rely on unaudited financials, even in the absence of red flags. But in his dissent from the Supreme Court's denial of certiorari in *Sanders v. John Nuveen & Co.*, 619 F.2d 1222 (7th Cir. 1980), *cert. denied*, 450 U.S. 1005 (2005), Justice Lewis Powell wrote that Section 11 means "almost by definition it is reasonable to rely on financial statements certified by public accountants." Perhaps, but according to Judge Cote, if "red flags" appear, "mere reliance on an audit will not be sufficient to ward off liability." What constitutes a "red flag," however, depends on the facts and circumstances of a particular case. "The question of what a reasonably prudent [person] should have known is particularly suited to a jury determination."

Note that lawyers who assist in the preparation of registration statements are not among the listed defendants in Section 11. That is somewhat surprising since it is typical for lawyers to prepare "due diligence" memoranda describing what underwriters and others did to fulfill their due diligence obligations.

In *In re WorldCom Securities Litigation*, Judge Cote explained the "due diligence" defense in some detail, taking note of the fact that it had not been well defined either by the courts or the SEC. Judge Cote concluded that it required an "investigation" of some sort, connoting a "thorough" or "searching" inquiry. It means "to inquire and examine into with systematic attention to detail and relationship." But there is an issue with respect to how much public knowledge can be attributed to shareholders, thereby absolving the underwriters or others of responsibility for seeing to it that it is disclosed. Although the Second Circuit has held, in *Siebert v. Sperry Rand Corp.* 586 F.2d 949, 952 (2d Cir. 1978), that underwriters can be relieved of the duty to see to it that developments that become "matters of public knowledge" are disclosed. Judge Cote wrote that there are also "serious limitations" on a defendant's ability to "charge its shareholders with knowledge of information omitted from a prospectus on the basis that the information is public knowledge and otherwise available to them."

For lawyers whose practice includes advising underwriters in public offerings, Judge Cote's *WorldCom* decision is a "must read" for you and your clients. It is the best exposition available about the responsibilities and pitfalls that underwriters may face if they ignore "red flags."

Rule 176, adopted by the SEC in 1982 set forth the SEC's view as to what constitutes reasonable investigation and reasonable grounds for belief. The SEC's conclusion was that whether a defense had been established must ultimately be proven in a case-by-case basis.[10] Rule 176 is considered by some to be unsatisfactory, especially since it was adopted as a part of the "integrated disclosure system" that attempted to merge the disclosure and other requirements of the 1933 Act and the 1934 Act and that permits certain issuers to include filings such as 10-Ks by reference, making traditional due diligence investigations by underwriters more difficult. In part because of such criticism, the SEC later made it clear in Rule 176(h) that whether or not the underwriter had any responsibility with respect to documents that were incorporated by reference was a factor to be taken into consideration in assessing due diligence.

This rule makes explicit the circumstances that may bear on the determination of what constitutes a reasonable investigation and reasonable ground for belief as those terms are used in Section 11(b).

Rule 176 contains eight relevant circumstances to be considered in determining whether or not the conduct of a person constituted "reasonable investigation" or a "reasonable ground for belief":

1. the type of issuer;
2. the type of security;

---

[10] *See* Adoption of Integrated Disclosure System, Securities Act Release No. 33-6383, March 3, 1982.

3. the type of person;
4. the office held when the person is an officer;
5. the presence or absence of another relationship to the issuer when the person is a director or proposed director;
6. reasonable reliance on officers, employees, and others whose duties should have given them knowledge of the particular facts (in the light of the functions and responsibilities of the particular person with respect to the issuer and the filing;
7. when the person is an underwriter, the type of underwriting arrangement, the role of the particular person as an underwriter, and the availability of information with respect to the registrant; and
8. whether, with respect to a fact or document incorporated by reference, the particular person had any responsibility for the fact or document at the time of the filing from which it was incorporated.

These eight grounds are generally considered somewhat unsatisfactory. For example, Paul Vizcarrondo Jr., of the Wachtell, Lipton law firm, has written that "Rule 176 codifies, without elucidating, the vague guidelines established by the case law."[11]

Affirmative Defenses

Negative Causation. This occurs when factors other than the misrepresentation or omission explain or contradict the depreciation in the stock value. This is a defense concerning the measure of damages. (Section 11(e): "If the defendant proves that any portion or all of such damages represents other than the depreciation in value of such security resulting from such part of the registration statement with respect to which his liability is asserted, not being true or omitting [etc.] ... damages shall not be recovered.")

Loss Causation. The *Dura*[12] standards should apply to claims under Section 11 (i.e., inflation in the price of the stock in itself is not enough; there must be a price drop after disclosure). However, since the notion of "price drop" has come under some scrutiny, especially in cases concerning "price maintenance," this proposition is likely on shaky ground.

Statute of Limitations. The applicable statute provides that the case must be brought one year from discovery of the violation and in no event more than

---

[11] Paul Vizcarrondo Jr., "Liabilities Under the Federal Securities Laws," Wachtell, Lipton, Rosen & Katz, August 2013, https://www.wlrk.com/docs/OutlineofSecuritiesLawLiabilities2013.pdf.

[12] *Dura Pharmaceuticals Inc. v. Broudo*, 544 U.S. 336 (2005).

three years after the security was "bona fide" offered to the public or more than three years after the sale (Section 13). This provision applies to claims under Section 11 and Section 12(a)(2). But what about the Sarbanes-Oxley Act, which increased the statute of limitations to two years/five years for claims "sounding in fraud"? It seems that that provision may apply only to claims that require proof of scienter, whereas Sections 11 and 12(a)(2) do not. *See In re Alstom SA Sec. Litig.*, 406 F. Supp. 2d 402 (S.D.N.Y. 2005).

Knowledge. As noted, there is no liability if the defendant can prove that the plaintiff knew of the misstatement or omission at the time of the acquisition of the security. This is extremely difficult to prove and is rarely even attempted.

Note that under the Private Litigation Securities Reform Act, there can be relative or proportionate responsibility, which the jury, or if no jury, the judge, is required to determine as a part of its verdict. Defendants who "knowingly" commit the violation remain jointly and severally liable, whereas the liability of defendants such as outside directors who did not "knowingly commit" the violation remains proportionate.[13]

Damages Under Section 11

The amount recoverable is limited to the difference between the price paid (not greater than the public offering price) and the value at the time the lawsuit is brought, or the price at which the security was sold in the market before the suit was brought, or the price at which the security was sold after the lawsuit was filed but before judgment is rendered, if such damages are less than the damages representing the difference between the amount paid for the security and the value, provided that the defendants that are liable for damages may reduce the damages by showing that the market depression in the price was due to factors other than the misstatement or omission. I recognize that is a mouthful; basically, Section 11 is a statute of full restitution, with several exceptions.

There are three damage formulations under Section 11:

1. *Formula One. Securities held at the time of judgment*: purchase price minus value at the time of the suit (Section 11 (e)(1)).
2. *Formula Two. Securities sold before the commencement of the lawsuit*: purchase price minus the sale price (Section 11 (e)(2)).

---

[13] If damages cannot be collected from the knowing defendants, non-knowing defendants will be liable, with certain financial and other limitations. Again, this rarely happens because the knowing defendants are almost always able to pay the damages rendered by the court or jury in those few cases that actually go to trial and verdict.

3. *Formula Three. Securities sold after commencement of the lawsuit but before judgment*: purchase price minus sale price *but* not more than Formula One.

NB: Formula One has the possibility of a windfall because the price is usually at its lowest just before the commencement of a lawsuit.

Direct Listings and Standing Under Sections 11 and 12

When securities are sold pursuant to an IPO, underwriters typically buy some or all of the offering at a pre-determined price so that they can be sold to customers. Because the underwriter wants to be sure that the price remains stable, the underwriter usually insists on a "lock-up" period of several months during which existing shareholders may not sell unregistered shares. Thus, if someone purchases shares during the lock-up period, those shares were necessarily registered, since the sale of unregistered shares is not permitted during the lock-up period. Such a lock-up period is common but it is not required by law. Companies can also make subsequent offerings of registered shares tied to new or updated registration statements. *See In re Century Aluminum Co. Sec. Litig.*, 729 F.3d 1104 (9th Cir. 2013).

In 2018, the New York Stock Exchange introduced a rule, later approved by the SEC, that permitted companies to sell their shares on the NYSE through a Selling Shareholder Direct Floor Listing (sometimes called a "direct listing").[14] In a direct listing, the company does not issue any new shares but instead files a registration statement to allow existing shareholders to sell their shares on the exchange. Preexisting shares must have been registered unless they met one of the Rule 144 exemptions. Shares made available through a direct listing are sold directly to the public and not through a bank or underwriter. There is therefore no lock-up agreement limiting the sale of unregistered shares.

The availability of a direct listing has recently given rise to a very controversial plurality decision of a panel in the Ninth Circuit, *Pirani v. Slack Technologies, et al.*, 13 F.4th 940 (9th Cir. 2021). This case concerns the standing of the plaintiff under Section 11 and Section 12(a)(2). Slack had gone public through a direct listing, releasing 118 million registered shares and 165 million unregistered shares into the public for purchase. Pirani had purchased 30,000 shares on the first day of issue and an additional 220,000 shares in the

---

[14] NYSE Listed Company Manual—Section 102.01B Footnote E, Aug. 26, 2020, https://nyseguide.srorules.com/listed-company-manual; SEC Approval 2018, 83 Fed. Reg. at 5653-54.

subsequent months. He sued Slack for misleading statements contained in its registration statement concerning service credits to customers. Slack moved to dismiss the complaint because Pirani could not show which of the shares he purchased were registered and thus met the pleading requirements under Sections 11 and 12. The district court denied the motion with respect to Section 11, holding that even if the shares Pirani purchased were unregistered, they were of the "same nature" as the registered shares. The court interpreted "such security" to include both registered and unregistered securities in a direct listing. The motion was granted with respect to Section 12(a)(2) because Slack had not issued any new shares in the offering.

The Ninth Circuit affirmed in an opinion written by Judge Jane Restani, a judge from the U.S. Court of International Trade sitting by designation. She concluded that interpreting Section 11 to apply only to registered shares in a direct listing would "essentially eliminate Section 11 liability for misleading or false statements made in a registration statement in a direct listing for both registered and unregistered shares," and she declined to require the plaintiff to prove that he had purchased only registered shares, notwithstanding the words of the statute.

Predictably, her opinion led to a spirited dissent from Judge Eric Miller, who noted that the interpretation of the words in Section 11 had been settled law for decades and that "such security" means "a security sold upon a registration statement," quoting from the House Report issued at the time the 1933 Act was passed. H.R. Rep. No.73-85 (1933). He similarly argued that Pirani lacked standing under Section 12(a)(2) since that statute requires that the sale of the security be made pursuant to a prospectus, which has been defined by the Supreme Court to be limited to documents that describe a public offering of securities by an issuer. "[W]hatever the merits of the policy considerations, they are no basis for changing the settled interpretation of the statutory text." We have not heard the end of this issue. Stay tuned.

Section 12(a)(1)

This section creates liability and a private right of action for "any person who offers or sells a security in violation of Section 5 [the registration statement requirement] using any means or instruments of transportation or communication in interstate commerce or of the mails, by means of a prospectus or oral communication, which includes an untrue statement of material fact or omits to state a material fact necessary to make the statements, in light of the circumstances in which they were made, not misleading [the purchaser not knowing of such untruth or omission.]"

Section 12(a)(2)

This section adds liability for any person who offers or sells a security, "whether or not exempted by the provisions of Section 3, other than paragraphs (2) and (14) of subsection (a) thereof." After the Supreme Court's decision in *Gustafson v. Alloyd Corp.*, 513 U.S. 561 (1995), it seemed clear that Section 12 (a)(2) (formerly known only as Section 12(2)) applies only to registered public offerings and to all exempt offerings other than those exempted by paragraphs (2) and (14) of Section 3(a), but *not at all* to secondary market trading.

But the *Gustafson* majority opinion by Justice Anthony Kennedy was roundly criticized by academics. One called it "the most poorly reasoned, blatantly results-driven securities opinion in recent memory."[15] The question before the Supreme Court was whether controlling shareholders of Alloyd Chemical who purchased all of the outstanding shares pursuant to a private contract of sale agreement could seek rescission under Section 12(a)(2) because some of the representations and warranties in the contract proved to be untrue. The purchasers could have sought a price adjustment, but they chose to seek full rescission under Section 12(a)(2) instead. The question was whether the stock purchase agreement was a "prospectus" within the meaning of Section 12(a)(2).

Justice Kennedy, for the majority, focused on the definitions of "prospectus" found in Sections 2(10) and 10 of the 1933 Act. He argued backward from Section 10 and reasoned that since a prospectus under Section 10 must include a registration statement, then the prospectus referred to in Section 12(a)(2) can only relate to public offerings. Much of the criticism of that view came because another section of the 1933 Act, the definitions section, defined a prospectus more broadly, as "any prospectus, notice, circular, advertisement, letter or communication, written or by radio or television, which offers any security for sale or confirms the sale of any security." Kennedy essentially ignored that definition, applied the Latin doctrine *noscitur a sociis* (a word is known by the company it keeps), and ruled that Section 2's "prospectus" was inconsistent with its accompanying words and gave "unintended breadth" to the Act. He added that at the time the statute was passed, it was "well understood to refer to a document soliciting the public to acquire securities from the issuer." Justices Clarence Thomas and Ruth Bader Ginsberg dissented.

Some academics argued, with some force, that Justice Kennedy was concerned that extending Section 12(a)(2) liability to the secondary market would, in his words, "create vast additional liabilities that are quite independent of the

---

[15] Stephen M. Bainbridge, "Securities Act Section 12(2) After the Gustafson Debacle," 50 Bus. Law. 1231-32 (1995).

new substantive obligations the Act imposed.... It is not plausible to infer that Congress created this extensive liability for every casual conversation between buyer and seller in the secondary market."

Which "exempt offerings" are being referred to in Section 12(a)(2)? It could include offerings under Rule 147, Regulation A, and Rules 504 and 506 of Regulation D, but that is not clear.

In its 2005 securities offering reforms, the SEC attempted to blunt the force of Justice Kennedy's *Gustafson* opinion by creating "free-writing prospectuses" that could "provide more timely investment information to investors without mandating delays in the offering process."[16] It seems clear that such free-writing prospectuses, defined by Rule 405, could be a written communication for a public offering that is an offer to sell or buy a security but that falls outside the requirements of a statutory Section 10(a) prospectus. If that is the case, then they would fall under Section 12(a)(2)'s reach. Recall that under Rules 163 and 433, free-writing prospectuses need not contain any specific information other than a legend. Thus, the *Gustafson* decision might have been intentionally or unintentionally broadened by the SEC. A client memorandum prepared by the Kirkland & Ellis law firm in August 2005 wrote that "it is intended that appropriate liability associated with the expanded communications will be maintained as well. For example, under the new rules, free-writing prospectuses have the same liability as that which currently applies to oral offers and statutory prospectuses; written communications not constituting prospectuses ... will still be subject to the anti-fraud provisions of the securities laws." Whether that liability can be claimed under Section 12(a)(2) remains to be seen, however.

Who is the seller? *Pinter v. Dahl*, 486 U.S. 622 (1988), held that a seller is one who is a title-passer and also one who solicits the purchase and is motivated in part to serve his or her own financial interests or those of the security owner and is one who directly communicates with a purchaser. In other words, a "seller's seller" (e.g., an issuer who "sells" to an underwriter) was not liable under the statute because the underwriter, not the issuer, actually passed title to the buyer. For example, then, in a firm-commitment underwriting, the issuer is almost always absolved of liability either by contract or by the operation of law. However, in new SEC Rule 159A adopted in 2005, the SEC provided that the issuer in a primary offering of securities is considered to offer or sell the securities to the investors in the initial distribution of the securities regardless of the underwriting arrangement in instances where securities are sold pursuant to "any free-writing prospectus ... relating to the offering and prepared by or on behalf of the issuer or used or referred to by the issuer." In that case, the issuer becomes a "seller" for the purposes of Section 12(a)(1) and 12(a)(2), thus

[16] Securities Offering Reform, SEC Securities Act Release 8501 (Nov. 17, 2004).

potentially increasing the number of available defendants, although the SEC did not clarify exactly what "prepared on behalf of the issuer" meant. Rule 159 provides that liability attaches at the time of sale and that information conveyed to the investor only after the sale will not be taken into consideration. These questions remain largely open for further clarification by the courts.

The Elements of an Offense Under Section 12(a)(2)

There is liability for any person who offers or sells a security (whether or not exempted under Section 3, other than paragraphs 2 and 14 of subsection (a) of that section) (i.e., securities issued or guaranteed by the United States (etc.) or a religious, educational (etc.) not-for-profit entity):

- by means of interstate transportation or commerce or use of mails;
- by means of a prospectus or oral communication (thus excluding offerings made by a private placement memorandum or purchases in private transactions);
- which contains an untrue statement of material fact or an omission of a material fact necessary to make the statements, in light of the circumstances under which they were made, not misleading; and
- the purchaser did not know of such untruth or omission.

If those elements are met, the offeror is liable. There is no requirement to prove scienter or negligence. There is no "due diligence" defense available as such, but Section 12(a)(2) absolves the offeror or seller of liability if that person can prove that "he [or she] did not know, and in the exercise of reasonable care could not have known, of such untruth or omission." The defendant has the burden of proof of this defense. It is not entirely clear in the case law whether this is the same as the "due diligence" defense in Section 11. The Seventh Circuit has held that it is, but the SEC has taken the position that it is a less demanding standard.

Query: Is a claim brought under Section 12(a)(2) that "sounds in fraud" required to comply with the fraud pleading requirements in the Federal Rules of Civil Procedure? Probably, but that is not certain.

Damages Under Section 12(a)(2)

Unlike Section 11, Section 12's damages are not capped at the offering price but as a practical matter this does not mean very much. Section 12 permits rescission damages ("to recover the consideration paid for such security with interest thereon, less the amount of any income received thereon upon the tender of such security, or for damages if he (or she) no longer owns the security"). The defendant may reduce the damages if it can prove that the amount recoverable represents other than the depreciation in value resulting from the part of the prospectus or oral communication alleged not to be true or containing a material omission. Once again, this is rarely seen because it is very difficult to prove. The person purchasing the security may sue either at law or in equity in any court of competent jurisdiction (state or federal) to recover the consideration paid for such security with interest thereon, less the amount of any income received thereon, upon the tender of such security, or for damages if the plaintiff no longer owns the security. Note that the damages are not capped at the offering price, unlike in Section 11. Section 12(a)(2) damages are sometimes called "rescission" damages in which the security is given back to the issuer in return for the consideration paid, with interest less any income received.

Because damages under Section 12(a)(2) are rescissory, a defendant can reduce or eliminate damages altogether by showing that the amount claimed in rescissory damages did not result from the depreciation in the value of the security resulting from such part of the prospectus or oral communication with respect to which liability is asserted not being true or containing an omission. This is similar to the "negative causation" defense in Section 11.

What Defenses Are Available in a Section 12(a)(2) Case?

There is no liability if the defendant can prove that he or she did not know and in the exercise of "reasonable care" could not have known about the material misstatement or omission. Note that, unlike in Section 11, this defense may be raised by an issuer as well as any other defendant. As noted, there is some question whether this "due diligence" defense is the same "reasonable investigation" defense under Section 11. At least one court has held that it is: *Sanders v. John Nuveen & Co.*, 619 F.2d 1222 (7th Cir. 1980). The SEC, however, has taken the position that the standard of care under Section 12(a)(2) is less demanding than the standard of care prescribed in Section 11.

Statute of Limitations

Section 13 of the 1933 Act defines the statutes of limitations for claims under Section 11 and Section 12(a)(2). Since the words of the statute are quite convoluted, we will simply quote them here: "No action shall be maintained to enforce any liability created under Section 11 or Section 12(a)(2) unless brought within one year after the discovery of the untrue statement or the omission, or after such discovery should have been made by the exercise of reasonable diligence, or, if the action is to enforce a liability created under Section

12(a)(1), unless brought within one year after the violation upon which it is based. In no event shall any such action be brought to enforce a liability created under Section 11, or Section 12(a)(1) more than three years after the security was *bona fide* offered to the public, or under Section 12(a)(2) more than three years after the sale." If you are confused, you are not alone.

Does Sarbanes-Oxley suggest that a claim "sounding in fraud" is covered by the new two-year/five-year statute of limitations instead of the Section 13 limitation? Probably not, although this is unclear at the moment. In January 2021, Congress changed the statute of limitations for actions by the SEC seeking disgorgement in cases where intentional misconduct was alleged, but it made no changes to Section 13.

Crowdfunding and Liability Under Section 12(a)(2)

New Section 4A(c) of the 1933 Act creates an express private right of action by someone who purchased securities from an issuer who used the crowdfunding exemption from registration and who wishes to challenge a material misstatement or omission provided in the course of the offering. The same defenses are available as if the liability was created under Section 12(a)(2).

Does Section 12(a)(2) Apply to Private Placements Other Than "Crowdfunding"?

It could (arguably) apply to private placements. *Metromedia v. Fugazy*, 983 F.2d 350 (2d Cir. 1992) ("The section has ... consistently been applied to private as well as public offerings of securities.").

Controlling Person Liability and Section 15

Under Section 15(a), every person who controls any person liable under Sections 11 and 12(a)(2) of the 1933 Act shall be liable jointly and severally with and to the same extent as such controlled person to any person to whom such controlled person is liable, unless the controlling person had no knowledge of or reasonable ground to believe in the existence of the facts by reason of which the liability of the controlled person is alleged to exist. Section 15(b) provides aiding and abetting liability. Any person that knowingly or recklessly provides substantial assistance to another person in violation of a provision of this subchapter, or any rule or regulation issued under this subchapter, shall be deemed to be in violation of such provision to the same extent as the person to whom the assistance is provided.

A corollary provision in the 1934 Act, Section 20(a), creates liability for controlling persons, but provides a "good faith defense." Accordingly, Congress amended Section 15 of the 1933 Act to include a "no knowledge" or "reasonable ground" defense for the controlling person. According to Ralph Ferrara, former Special Counsel in the Office of General Counsel of the SEC, and Diane Sanger, Special Counsel, Office of the General Counsel of the SEC, the purpose of Section 15 was to impose liability on directors and other corporate officers who were using "dummy directors" to sign registration statements in order to evade personal liability.[17]

Controlling person liability is discussed further in Chapter 11.

Section 17(a)

This statute, which creates a right of action in the SEC or the Justice Department but does not create a private right of action, makes it "unlawful for any person in the offer or sale of any securities by . . . the use of any means or instruments or transportation or communication in interstate commerce or by the use of mails, directly or indirectly,

- to employ any device, scheme, or artifice to defraud, or
- to obtain money or property by means of any untrue statement of material omission, etc., or
- to engage in any transaction, practice, or course of business which operates or would operate as a fraud or deceit upon the purchaser."

As we will see later, this statute is a close parallel to Rule 10b-5 of the 1934 Act rules. This is not an accident since Rule 10b-5 was taken from Section 17(a). But there are a few notable differences and a few open questions. Section 17 applies to "the offer or sale" whereas Rule 10b-5 refers to "the purchase or sale." Moreover, only Section 17(a)(1) requires the proof of scienter; the other two sections do not. *See Aaron v. SEC*, 446 U.S. 680 (1980). But if the Justice Department is bringing a criminal case, it still must prove scienter under subsections (a)(2) and (a)(3) because Section 24 of the 1933 Act requires proof of willfulness for a criminal conviction.

Because there is no explicit statute of limitations for claims under Section 17(a) set forth in the 1933 Act the way there is for claims under Sections 11 and 12(a)(2), the general federal five-year statute of limitations applies. However, if the SEC or the DOJ are the plaintiffs, they may not take advantage of

---

[17] Ralph Ferrara & Diane Sanger, "Derivative Liability in Securities Law: Controlling Person Liability, Respondeat Superior, and Aiding and Abetting," 40 *Wash. & Lee L. Rev.* 1007 (1983).

the so-called *Merck* "discovery of the violation" date[18] for the beginning of the running of the statute, and the beginning date of the statute is the date on which the violation occurred, whether or not the SEC or DOJ discovered it on that date. *Gabelli v. SEC*, 568 U.S. 442 (2013).

However, on January 1, 2021, Congress explicitly authorized the SEC to seek disgorgement of any unjust enrichment as a result of a securities law violation and extended to ten years the statute of limitations if the disgorgement claim involves conduct that violates Section 17(a)(1) of the 1933 Act or Section 10(b) of the 1934 Act. The five-year statute for civil penalties remains in place.

Section 17 and "Partial Disclosure of the Truth"

The SEC recently brought charges under Section 17 for incomplete disclosures of the truth in a Form 6-K. Pearson, a multinational UK–based educational publishing and services company, offered school boards software for the purpose of tracking students' academic performance. The databases included the names, titles, and usernames and passwords of school personnel. In 2019, Pearson learned that a vast amount of its data had been hacked and stolen. More than 11 million rows of student data had been exfiltrated. In July 2019, four months after Pearson learned of the hack, it issued a report on Form 6-K (a form used by foreign private issuers for reporting material information with respect to such things as changes in business, management, financial condition and results of operations, and "any other information which the registrant deems of material importance to security holders"). The Form 6-K stated that "a risk of a data privacy incident ... could result in a major data privacy or confidentiality breach causing damage to the customer experience and our reputational damage, a breach of regulations and financial loss." Of course, the breach had already occurred, a fact not mentioned in the Form 6-K. The Form 6-K was obviously worded in an attempt to minimize the extent of the breach.

Shortly after the form was filed, Pearson issued a media statement that disclosed the incident in the blandest terms, such as there had been "unauthorized access and exposure of data." The media statement also mis-described the data that had been stolen.

The SEC investigated and concluded that Pearson's Form 6-K and media statement had violated Section 17(a)(2) and (3) of the 1933 Act (the

---

[18] *Merck & Co. v. Reynolds*, 559 U.S. 633 (2010) (the "two years/five years" statute of limitations begins to run once the plaintiff actually discovered or a reasonably diligent plaintiff would have discovered the facts constituting the violation. So-called "inquiry notice" or "storm warnings" are useful in the analysis, but they do not automatically begin the running of the statute.)

non-scienter portions) by making untrue statements of material fact. It imposed a fine of $1 million. Pearson also violated Section 13(a) of the 1934 Securities Exchange Act by filing the untrue Form 6-K.[19]

One takeaway from this case is that inadequate internal controls over the required internal control over financial reporting and disclosure controls and procedures required by Sarbanes-Oxley must be taken seriously and can result in liability. Although most public companies have good internal controls over financial matters, the Pearson experience teaches that the same internal control is required over cyber incidents and human resources. It is inadequate to report that a cyber event "might" occur if it has already occurred. A more serious takeaway is that when companies make public statements, they must tell the whole truth.

Section 17 and Open Questions

Does the Supreme Court's *Janus* decision[20] apply to Section 17(a)? In *Janus*, the court held that only the "maker" of an untrue statement of material fact could be liable under Rule 10b-5(b) and that the "maker" was the "person or entity with ultimate authority over the statement." In *Lorenzo v. SEC*, 139 S. Ct. 1094 (2019), the Supreme Court held that individuals who did not "make" false statements but who disseminated them to potential investors with intent to defraud can still be found to have violated subsections (a) and (c) of Rule 10b-5. "By sending emails he understood to contain material untruths, Lorenzo 'employ[ed] a device, scheme and artifice to defraud' within the meaning of subsection (a) of the Rule, § 10(b) and Section 17(a)(1). By the same conduct, he engage[d] in an act, practice or course of business that 'operate[d] as a fraud or deceit' ... under subsection (c) of the Rule.... [W]e take for granted that he sent the emails with 'intent to deceive, manipulate or defraud' the recipients." One of the significant results of that decision is that by implication, the *Janus* limitations do not apply to claims under Section 17(a)(1), and individuals who are not the "makers" of the false statements but who disseminate them with intent to defraud can be held liable under that section even if the conduct would constitute only secondary liability under Rule 10b-5(b). Recall that only the SEC and the DOJ can bring claims under Section 17.

Another open question is whether the defendant must have actually received the "money or property" under Section 17(a)(2). Some courts have said yes, others have said it is sufficient if the defendant's employer profits from

---

[19] *In the Matter of Pearson plc*, Securities Act of 1933 Release No. 10963, August 16, 2021. Order Instituting Cease and Desist Proceedings Pursuant to Section 8A of the Securities Act of 1933 and Section 21C of the Securities Exchange Act of 1934.

[20] *Janus Capital Group, Inc. v. First Derivative Traders*, 131 S. Ct. 2296 (2011).

the misrepresentation, and the employee's subsequent incentive compensation is derived from the employer's wrongful profit. Still others have said that it is sufficient if the defendant obtained money for his or her employer.

Still another open question is what constitutes negligent conduct under Section 17(a). Can evidence of industry practice and custom be received to determine whether the defendant's conduct rose to the level of negligence? The trend seems to be in the affirmative. *See, e.g.*, *SEC v. Shanahan*, 646 F.3d 536 (8th Cir. 2011).

One question that seems to have been answered is whether Section 17(a) creates a private right of action. The answer is almost certainly no. Although the Supreme Court has not yet weighed in, every circuit that has considered the issue has refused to recognize a private right of action. *Maldonado v. Dominguez*, 137 F.3d 1 (1st Cir. 1998) ("We have recently come to the same conclusion.").

Chapter 9

Civil Liability Under the 1934 Exchange Act Section 10(b) and Rule 10b-5, Part One

Section 10(b) of the 1934 Securities Exchange Act and Rule 10b-5 are the basis for most securities litigation. As interpreted, they are probably the broadest statute and rule in the securities laws. There is very little legislative history about them. (The only comment that was made during the meeting of the Commission that approved the rule was "We are against fraud, aren't we?".)

There is no express right of action for private plaintiffs. The private right of action was only implied by the courts. (But the PSLRA certainly now assumes the existence of a private right of action under Section 10(b).)

The Writing of Rule 10b-5

The rule was written in one day in 1942 by Milton Freeman, an SEC official in Philadelphia:

> It was one day in the year 1943 I believe. I was sitting in my office in the SEC building in Philadelphia and I received a call from Jim Treanor who was then the Director of Trading and Exchange Division. He said "I have just been on the telephone with Paul Rowan ... and he told me about the president of some company in Boston who is going around buying up the stock of his company from his own shareholders at $4 a share and he has been telling them that the company is doing very badly, whereas in fact the earnings are going to be quadrupled".... So he comes upstairs and I called in my secretary and I looked at Section 10(b) and I looked at Section 17, and I put them together, and the only discussion we had there was where

"in connection with the purchase or sale" should be, and we decided to put it at the end.

We called the Commission and we got on the calendar and I don't remember whether we got there that morning or after lunch. We passed a piece of paper around to all the commissioners. All the commissioners read the rule and they tossed it on the table indicating approval. Nobody said anything except Sumner Pike, who said "well, we are against fraud, aren't we?" That is how it happened.[1]

What Is Prohibited?

Rule 10b-5 expands on the sparse relevant wording of Section 10(b) (prohibiting any manipulative or deceptive device or contrivance) and lists in more detail the activities that are prohibited. They are listed below. Note that the last element, "in connection with the purchase or sale of any security," is not in itself a prohibition but applies to each of the preceding prohibitions.

- use of any means or instrumentality of interstate commerce or mails or any facility of any national securities exchange;
- to employ any device, scheme, or artifice to defraud;
- to make any untrue statement of a material fact or to omit to state a material fact necessary in order to make the statements made, in light of the circumstances under which they were made, not misleading; or
- to engage in any act, practice, or course of business which operates or would operate as a fraud or deceit upon any person;
- in connection with the purchase or sale of any security (not necessarily the plaintiff's).

"In connection with" has been interpreted broadly by the courts. In *SEC v. Texas Gulf Sulphur*, 401 F.2d 833 (2d Cir. 1966) (*en banc*), the Second Circuit said *any* misstatement violates Rule 10b-5 if it is reasonably calculated to influence investors. For example, it has been applied to "churning" customer accounts by brokers. *See Rizek v. SEC*, 215 F.3d 157 (1st Cir. 2000). Rizek invested in zero-coupon bonds and churned them for unsophisticated investors, ostensibly for their benefit. He argued that there was no proof of scienter, but the court found that he lied about what he was doing.

Does the "in connection with" need to be with respect to the shares purchased by the plaintiff? The cases suggest that the test is met so long as

[1] Milton Freeman, "Conference on Codification of the Federal Securities Laws," 22 Bus. Law. 793, 921-23 (1967).

the fraud "touches" the purchase or sale of any security by anyone. *See, e.g.*, *Superintendent of Insurance v. Bankers Life & Casualty Co.*, 404 U.S. 6 (1971) (court seems to reject by clear implication that the "in connection with" requirement had to relate to the value of the securities being purchased). But this is far from a settled issue, as we will see in a moment.

On the one hand, we know that when the SEC is a plaintiff or when the Department of Justice brings a criminal case under Section 10(b), there is no requirement that they prove reliance or causation. So the "in connection with" that they must prove clearly does not have to be with respect to purchases or sales that they made. Note that the "in connection with" requirement in the rule is the same no matter who is the plaintiff.

On the other hand, *Blue Chip Stamps v. Manor Drug Stores*, 421 U.S. 723 (1975), suggests that the private plaintiff must have actually purchased or sold securities. So does the fraud have to be "in connection with" that specific purchase or sale? Professor C. Edward Fletcher answers that question by writing that *Blue Chip Stamps* imposes a non-textually based standing requirement.[2] But what if the plaintiff is claiming reliance on the efficiency of the market, not on the actual fraud itself? Can it be said that the fraud was "in connection with" his or her actual purchase? Probably not, but she still has a cause of action if the fraud is "impounded" into the market price of the stock in question, even if she was unaware of it. But many cases confuse causation with the "in connection with" requirement. As Fletcher noted, "courts simply have been unable to articulate principles for the interpretation and application of this requirement."[3] Fletcher asserts—with good reason—that part of the problem is that actions under Section 10(b) and Rule 10b-5 come in too many different situations, and it is difficult if not impossible to define "in connection with" in a way that can easily be applied in those different situations.

A Brief History of "In Connection With"

Birnbaum v. Newport Steel Corp., 193 F.2d 461 (2d Cir. 1952), was the first appellate case to discuss the issue. In that case, the directors of Newport rejected an offer of a merger that would have been beneficial to the Newport shareholders and instead accepted a higher price from a rival steel user that wished to take control of Newport and use it as a "captive" supplier. The Newport shareholders sued under Rule 10b-5 claiming that a communication to them had been false and misleading. The district court held that under Rule 10b-5, the fraud could only be perpetrated on the purchaser or seller, and that

---

[2] *See* C. Edward Fletcher, "The 'In Connection With' Requirement of Rule 10b-5," 16 *Pepperdine L. Rev.* 913, n. 22 (1989).

[3] *Id.* at 928-29.

the rule had no relationship to breaches of fiduciary duty by corporate insiders resulting in fraud upon those who were not purchasers or sellers. The Second Circuit agreed. "While the rule may have been somewhat loosely drawn its meaning and scope are not difficult to ascertain when reference is had to the scheme of SEC Regulation and the purpose underlying the adoption of Rule 10b-5.... The Commission was attempting only to make the same prohibitions contained in Section 17(a) of the 1933 Act applicable to purchasers as well as to sellers.... The Commission simply copied Section 17(a), adding the words 'any person' in place of 'the purchaser' and a final clause 'in connection with the purchase or sale of any security'.... That section was directed solely at that type of misrepresentation or fraudulent practice usually associated with the sale or purchase of securities rather than at fraudulent mismanagement of corporate affairs." In other words, corporate mismanagement is not a violation of Section 10(b) or Rule 10b-5. Rather, the fraud must be "of the type usually associated" with the purchase or sale and the plaintiff must be an actual purchaser or seller.

In *Superintendent of Ins. v. Bankers Life & Cas. Co.*, 404 U.S. 6 (1971), there was an elaborate scheme by a manager to use Manhattan Casualty Co. assets to purchase its stock and sell it to a person named Begole (not further identified). The lower court said there was no violation because the transactions themselves were lawful. The Supreme Court held that it was "in connection with" a purchase or sale because Manhattan was injured as an investor through a deceptive device that deprived it of any compensation for its block of securities. It was irrelevant that fraud was committed by a manager because the fraud went beyond mismanagement. Because the fraud related to the recipients of the proceeds of the sale, it was irrelevant that the deception did not relate to the value of the security being sold. The deceptive practices *touched* the purchase or sale of a security. This was the key takeaway.

The leading "purchase or sale" case is *Blue Chip Stamps v. Manor Drugs*, 421 U.S. 723 (U.S. 1975), which adopted the *Birnbaum* test. In that case, the Supreme Court limited standing to persons who are purchasers or sellers and in that case, there were no purchasers or sellers. In *Merrill Lynch v. Dabit*, 547 U.S. 71 (2006), where the plaintiffs merely held their securities when, had they known the truth they would have sold them, there were no actual purchasers or sellers, but the Supreme Court said that *Blue Chip* was based on policy considerations, not a factual analysis, and in that case, the Court did not "define the words 'in connection with the purchase or sale.'"

Under the 1933 Act, "sale or sell" includes "every contract of sale or disposition of a security or interest in a security for value." *See* Section 2(3). *Dabit* distinguishes standing from violation and emphasizes that the Supreme Court has given a broad definition to "in connection with." Let us see just how broad the definition is.

In *SEC v. Zandford*, 535 U.S. 813 (2002), a broker persuaded an elderly man to open a joint investment account with his mentally retarded daughter. The broker had a general power of attorney. When the old man died, it turned out that all of the money was gone. The broker was indicted for wire fraud for selling the stocks in the elderly man's account. The SEC then sued him for violating Section 10(b) and Rule 10b-5. The Fourth Circuit reversed the criminal conviction, and the SEC's summary judgment, holding that the fraud was not "in connection with the purchase or sale of any security." The Supreme Court reversed the Fourth Circuit and held that the conduct was in fact "in connection with the purchase or sale of a security." Congress sought to "substitute a philosophy of full disclosure for the philosophy of *caveat emptor* and thus to achieve a high standard of business ethics in the securities industry." In addition, the Court held that in order to effect its remedial purposes, "the Act should be construed flexibly, not technically and restrictively." Note that Zandford defrauded his customers, sold their shares, and stole the proceeds. The victims did not buy or sell anything. The fraud merely "coincided" with the sale.

In 2014, the Supreme Court decided that "in connection with" does not reach fraud "in connection with" the sale of "securities" that didn't actually exist. *Chadbourne & Parke v. Troice*, 571 U.S. 377 (2014). Allen Stanford's Ponzi scheme sold certificates of deposit saying that they were "backed by marketable securities." The CDs themselves were not "covered securities" under the Securities Litigation Uniform Standards Act (SLUSA) because they were not traded on a national exchange. The Fifth Circuit held that "in connection with" means that there is a relationship in which the fraud and stock sale *coincide* or are "more than tangentially related." The Supreme Court said that the misrepresentation had to make a significant difference to someone's decision (other than the fraudster) to purchase or sell a covered security. The question was related to whether the case concerned a "covered security" under SLUSA (*see* Chapter 12) if there were in fact no securities purchased at all, even though Stanford said that he would purchase them.

The Supreme Court held that Section 10(b) does *not* apply to purchases and sales by the "fraudster" and does not apply to a fraud in connection with purchases that never took place. The case concerned whether a state court class action could be maintained even though SLUSA provided that "covered class actions" (based on purchases and sales of securities listed on national exchanges with more than fifty in the class) could only be pursued in federal court.

Stanford promised his investors that the CDs they purchased would have a fixed rate of return and told them that he would use the money to buy "highly lucrative" assets, including securities that might meet the SLUSA definition of "covered security." But he never bought any. Instead, the money was used to repay earlier investors; it was a classic Ponzi scheme. The plaintiffs filed a civil class action under state law. The issue was whether the fraud was "in connection with" the purchase or sale of a "covered security"? If it was, the state court case would be precluded by SLUSA.

The Supreme Court, Justice Stephen Breyer writing for a 5-4 majority, held that "a fraudulent misrepresentation or omission is not made in connection with the purchase or sale of a covered security unless it is material to a decision by one or more individuals (other than the fraudster) to buy or sell a covered security." *Note to readers: Don't get hung up on the phrase "covered security." It was an artifact of SLUSA that was not central to the core issue of the case.* The Supreme Court held that the "false statement must be material to another individual's decision to purchase or sell a statutorily defined security or covered security." In this case, nobody actually bought any securities. There was no "purchase or sale." But there was no purchase or sale in *Dabit* either.

Why does the Supreme Court exclude purchase decisions by the fraudster? That is not clear. In *Zandford* the broker was clearly the fraudster and he is the one who sold the shares. In *United States v. O'Hagan*, 521 U.S. 642 (1997), the insider, O'Hagan, committed insider trading by overhearing information about an upcoming hostile takeover and purchasing the securities in order to profit from an increase in price. His conviction was affirmed by the Supreme Court. He too was the "fraudster." Justice Breyer acknowledged that in earlier cases, such as *Dabit*, the Supreme Court held that the actionable fraudulent manipulation of stock prices could be material if it *coincided with* third-party securities transactions. And in *Zandford*, where the broker sold the client's securities and stole the proceeds, the Supreme Court held that the fraud and the purchase or sale of a security "must simply coincide" with a breach of duty in order to be actionable. The *Chadbourne* dissenters took issue with the majority's exclusion of sales by fraudsters.

The *Chadbourne* Court held that a broad definition of "in connection with" would interfere with state efforts to provide remedies for victims of ordinary state law frauds. In *Chadbourne*, the allegations were not tied to the purchase or sale of covered securities because there were none. "The sales constituted no relevant part of the fraud but were incidental to it." In a dissent, Justice Anthony Kennedy noted that *O'Hagan* held that the person or entity defrauded is not the other party to the trade and that the Court's decision in *Chadbourne* "is hard to square with *O'Hagan*." Allen Stanford, the fraudster, misrepresented that he would buy covered securities, and the fraud coincided with the misrepresentation. According to Justice Kennedy, the Court's holding that the purchase or sale must be made by someone other than the fraudster "engrafts a limitation that does not appear in the text." Other courts have held in earlier cases that contracts to sell are sufficient for liability even if no sale ever takes place. So is a contingent right to receive stock for value. *Yoder v. Orthomolecular Nutrition Institute*, 751 F.2d 555 (9th Cir. 1999). Does the fraud have an effect on a regulated market? What remains of this test after *Chadbourne*? *Hint*: not much.

Following *Chadbourne*, there is a split in the Circuits as to whether *Chadbourne* eliminates the "coinciding" test of *Dabit* (First, Third, and Ninth Circuits) or whether it is a one-off test that should be confined to the particular facts of that case (Seventh and Eighth Circuits). *See, e.g.*, *Jones v. Anderson*, 990 F.3d 692 (9th Cir. 2021), petition for writ of certiorari filed October 12, 2021.

"Puffing" and Statements of Opinion

"Puffing" is the making of a statement that no reasonable person would believe in or rely on in making a purchase or sale of stock. It is not actionable. Where is the line? For example, "We make the best pizza in New York." Is that actionable? Is it objectively verifiable?

Recent examples of "puffing" that have been held not actionable include "the company has continued to devote substantial resources to regulatory compliance and felt good about its progress,"[4] a proposed merger represented "a singular and unique opportunity to return value,"[5] and the company had "established procedures" toward achieving regulatory compliance.[6]

The conventional wisdom was that statements of opinion (subjective statements) are generally not actionable unless they are (1) objectively false and (2) disbelieved by the speaker when made. *Fait v. Regions Financial Corp.*, 655 F.3d 105 (2d Cir. 2011); *see also Rubke v. Capital Bancorp*, 551 F.3d 1156 (9th Cir. 2009); *Virginia Bankshares v. Sandberg*, 501 U.S. 1083 (1991).

However, as noted in Chapter 3, in 2015, the Supreme Court decided *Omnicare Inc. v. Laborers District Council Construction Industry Pension Fund*, holding that a statement of opinion does not constitute an untrue statement of material fact simply because the stated opinion ultimately proves incorrect. (Recall that Section 11 is a "strict liability" statute that does not require a showing of scienter.) In the first part of the opinion, the court reaffirmed the general rule that a statement of opinion affirms the "fact" that the speaker actually holds the stated belief. If that is not the case, then the statement is actionable. The statement can also be actionable if the speaker's supporting facts are untrue.

But then the *Omnicare* Court went further and discussed an issue not discussed by the Sixth Circuit, namely, whether the statement of opinion also affirms the unstated fact that there is a reasonable basis for the opinion. The

---

4 *Carvelli v. Ocwen Financial Corp.*, 934 F.3d 1307 (11th Cir. 2019).

5 *Gross v. GFI Group, Inc.*, 784 F. App'x 27 (2d Cir. 2019).

6 *Singh v. Cigna Corp.*, 918 F.3d 57 (2d Cir. 2019).

court held that that question had to be addressed from the perspective of a reasonable investor. For example, where, as in this case, the statement of opinion concerned a belief that the company was in compliance with applicable law, a reasonable investor might conclude that the speaker had consulted with legal counsel. Context is important, as are other qualifying statements that are made at the same time. The question to be answered is whether the omitted "fact" (i.e., whether counsel were consulted before the statement of opinion was made) would have been material to a reasonable investor (i.e., whether there is a "substantial likelihood that a reasonable [investor] would consider it important"). Does this mean that the issue cannot be decided on the pleadings but must be submitted to a jury?

Omnicare caused the Second Circuit to revisit *Fait*. In *Tongue v. Sanofi*, 816 F.3d 199 (2d Cir. 2016), the Second Circuit adopted the "expanded disjunctive" test of *Omnicare* rather than its earlier conjunctive test.

Omnicare appears to be a significant case as far as Section 11 liability is concerned. Is the same reasoning applicable to statements of opinion in claims made under Section 10(b)? Many commentators thought not, since Section 10(b) requires scienter and Section 11 does not. However, several district courts and at least two circuit courts have already applied *Omnicare* to claims under Section 10(b).[7] We can safely assume that an *Omnicare* argument will be made in most Section 10(b) cases involving statements of opinion, at least until the law evolves a bit further.

Omnicare also raises the question whether *Virginia Bankshares* is still good law. Recall that *Virginia Bankshares* was a Section 14 case, but the Supreme Court in *Omnicare* does not seem to think that distinction made a difference. Certainly any analysis of the actionability of an opinion must now take *Omnicare* into consideration, since it adds an additional element to the *Virginia Bankshares* test.

The core inquiry is whether the omitted facts would conflict with what a reasonable investor would take from the statement itself. But as the Court said in *Omnicare*, the "reasonable investor would not expect that *every* fact known to the issuer supports its opinion statement" (emphasis in original). In *Sanofi*, there were three groups of statements of opinion, generally opining that the Food and Drug Administration would approve a drug by a certain date and that the company was "very satisfied with where the progress is going" and "very pleased with the results of a clinical trial." There was ongoing conversation between the company and the FDA about the company's testing methodology, but that would be expected. The company's statement "fairly aligned

[7] *See, e.g.*, *In re Genworth Financial Securities Litigation*, 2015 U.S. Dist. LEXIS 57600 (E.D. Va. May 1, 2015); *City of Dearborn Heights Art. 345 Police & Fire Retirement System v. Align Technology Inc.*, 856 F.3d 605 (9th Cir. 2017); *Abramson v. NewLink Genetics Corp.*, 965 F.3d 165 (2d Cir. 2020).

with the information in the issuer's possession at the time." Issuers need not disclose a piece of information merely because it cuts against their projections, especially given the sophistication of investors. Could it be said that this is a "narrow view" of *Omnicare*? Is there another view?

In *In re Vivendi Securities Litigation*, 833 F.3d 223 (2d Cir. 2016), the Second Circuit tried to reconcile *Omnicare* with its earlier decisions that an opinion was actionable only if it was *both* objectively false and if the speaker disbelieved it (e.g., *Fait*). "*Fait* and *Omnicare* merely expanded upon an uncontroversial point already made clear by *Virginia Bankshares*: that although statements expressing opinions may not be grounds for liability when they are not false or misleading in context to a reasonable investor, such statements are 'not beyond the purview' of the federal securities statutes. . . . Indeed we made similar observations even before *Fait* or *Omnicare* (citing *In re Int'l Bus. Mach. Corp Sec. Litig.*, 163 F.3d 102, 107 (2d Cir. 1998) ('statements that are opinions . . . are not *per se* inactionable under the securities laws')."

However, in a summary order in *Cox v. BlackBerry Ltd.*, 2016 WL 4470928 (2d Cir. Aug. 24, 2016), the Second Circuit held that *Omnicare* "altered the standard previously applied by this Circuit." Which is it?

As noted, lower courts are continuing to apply *Omnicare* to Section 10(b) claims as well as to Section 18, Section 17(a), and Section 14(e) claims (e.g., statements such as "the merger is fair to stockholders").

Remember that some of those claims require scienter, that is actual knowledge of falsity or at least (for the pleading stage) knowledge of nonpublic facts that contradict public representations. This is an emerging area, however, because even *Omnicare* acknowledged that there may be facts that "cut against" the stated opinion. In *In re Advanced Auto Parts Inc. Sec. Lit.*, 220 WL 599543 (D. Del. Feb. 7, 2020), the court allowed an "opinion" claim to go forward where the plaintiffs alleged with particularity that the defendants made a series of statements projecting an increase in sales and operating margins at a time when it knew that such projections were not attainable based on information not disclosed to the shareholders, and made other specific allegations suggesting knowledge of falsity.

Subsequent cases have made it clear that under *Omnicare*, cautionary language accompanying an opinion acts as a pleading barrier to preclude liability when the opinion turns out to be incorrect. *See, e.g.*, *Jaroslawicz v. M&T Bank Corp.*, 962 F.3d 701 (3d Cir. 2020).

What Is "Bespeaks Caution"?

The "bespeaks caution" doctrine apparently had its genesis in a footnote in an Eighth Circuit opinion, *Polin v. Conductron Corp.*, 552 F.2d 797 (8th

Cir. 1977).[8] It is a court-made doctrine that gives certain forward-looking statements immunity from liability if they are accompanied by adequate disclaimers. For example, certain documents, especially "red herrings," contain explicit warning statements that their forward-looking statements might not be accurate predictions of future events. In other words, "Buyer beware!" *See In re AMDOCS Ltd Securities Litigation*, 390 F.3d 542 (8th Cir. 2004) (cautionary language that "bespeaks caution" makes statement immaterial as matter of law).

In *In re Prudential Sec. Inc. Ltd. Partner Lit.*, 930 F. Supp. 68 (S.D.N.Y.), Senior Judge Milton Pollack wrote one of the clearest opinions describing the parameters and the limitations of the "bespeaks caution" defense. In a case involving the leasing of used commercial aircraft, the plaintiffs alleged that the offering documents did not accurately describe the risk that the value of the aircraft would significantly decline in the future. Judge Pollack wrote that "the bespeaks caution doctrine allows courts to rule that a defendant's forward-looking representations contain enough cautionary language or risk disclosures to protect against claims of securities fraud." However, the cautionary language "must precisely address the substance of the specific statement or omission that is challenged." In addition, the language "does not protect material misrepresentations or omissions when defendants knew they were false when made." In an example that has been repeated in at least one case by the Second Circuit, Judge Pollack wrote: "The doctrine of bespeaks caution provides no protection to someone who warns his hiking companion to walk slowly because there might be a ditch ahead when he knows with near certainty that the Grand Canyon lies one foot away."[9]

Today, the "bespeaks caution" defense is rarely applied, in part because, as one court noted, "the line can be hard to draw"[10] and in part because it has been superseded by the safe harbor for forward-looking statements in SEC Rule 175 and later by the safe harbor in the PSLRA. In general, courts applying the "bespeaks caution" require proof that the speaker had no knowledge of any undisclosed facts that would undermine the accuracy of the statement. Going even further, the Second Circuit held in the *Iowa Public Employees Retirement* case that the doctrine did not apply to the omission from the forward-looking statement of "present facts" that might be inconsistent with the

---

[8] The footnote characterized an annual report as one that "bespoke caution in outlook and fell far short of the assurances required for a finding of falsity and fraud." *See* Andrew Fine, "A Cautionary Look at a Cautionary Doctrine," 10 *Brook. J. Corp. Fin. & Com. L.* 521 (2016).

[9] *See also Rombach v. Chang*, 355 F.3d 164, 173 (2d Cir. 2004).

[10] *Iowa Public Employees' Retirement System v. MF Global, Ltd.*, 620 F.3d 137 (2d Cir. 2010).

statement because the "present facts" were "ascertainable when the challenged statements were made" and therefore the doctrine was inapplicable.

What Is the Line Between a Misstatement and an Omission?

Like the "bespeaks caution" doctrine, the line between a misstatement and an omission is not always easy to draw. What are the consequences of characterizing something as a misstatement or an omission? One consequence is that for omissions, there is a presumption of reliance (but the defendant may still show that there was no duty to speak). Take *Johnson v. HBO Film Management Co.*, 265 F.3d 178 (3d Cir. 2001), as an example. (Transforming a misrepresentation into an omission (failed to say it wasn't true) swallows the *Affiliated Ute* presumption of reliance almost entirely.) Section 10(b) does not require a misstatement or omission. "Conduct itself can be deceptive." *Stoneridge v. Scientific Atlanta*, 552 U.S. 148 (2008); *see, e.g.*, Rule 10b-5(c). What if a corporation made a false statement in its annual report and then failed to say that it was false? Is that a false statement or an omission (or both)?

What About Forward-Looking Statements and Statements of Future Intent?

A material fact need not be a "fact" in the historical sense; it may include false statements of future intent. Projections are actionable if not made in good faith or if made with reckless indifference. When is there a duty to correct? There is a difference between a duty to correct and a duty to update. *See In re Burlington Coat Factory Securities Litigation*, 114 F.3d 1410 (3d Cir. 1997), for a good discussion of the difference. Generally speaking there is a "duty to correct" a statement that was false or misleading when it was made, and there is no duty to "update" a statement that was true when made but that became misleading due to subsequent events. But this area of the law is somewhat murky, and some have argued that there is (or should be) a duty to update statements that have become misleading.[11] Some courts recognize a "duty to update" if the statement "remains alive" in the minds of reasonable investors, but most courts are reluctant to do so.[12]

Under the PSLRA, there is a "safe harbor" for forward-looking statements. The PSLRA defines a "forward-looking statement" as falling into one of six categories:

---

[11] *See* Robert Rosenblum, "An Issuer's Duty Under Rule 10b-5 to Correct and Update Materially Misleading Statements," 40 *Catholic U. L. Rev.* 289 (1991).

[12] *See* Bruce Mendelsohn & Jesse Brush, "The Duties to Correct and Update: A Web of Conflicting Case Law and Principles," *Securities Reg. L. J.* (Spring 2015) 67.

1. Statements concerning a projection of revenues, income, etc.
2. Statements of plans or objectives of management for future operations, etc.
3. Statements of future economic performance.
4. Statements of the assumptions underlying the first three categories.
5. Reports by outside reviewer retained by the issuer to the extent that the report assesses a forward-looking statement made by the issuer.
6. Statements containing a projection or estimate on such other items as may be specified by rule.

To be protected by the PSLRA safe harbor, the forward-looking statement must be identified as such and must be accompanied by meaningful cautionary statements identifying important factors that could cause actual results to differ materially from those in the forward-looking statement, or the forward-looking statement must be immaterial or the plaintiff fails to prove that the forward-looking statement was made with actual knowledge that the statement was false, or if made by a business entity, made by or with the approval of an executive officer of that entity with actual knowledge that the statement was false or misleading. General statements about risk are not sufficient. There are special rules for oral forward-looking statements. See PSLRA Section 21(E) for details. There are exclusions for statements made by issuers who were convicted of a felony or misdemeanor within three years or who were the subject of a judicial or administrative decree.

Oklahoma Firefighters Pension and Retirement System v. Xerox Corp., 300 F. Supp. 3d. 551 (S.D.N.Y. 2018), is a thoughtful discussion of forward-looking statement liability and liability for other types of statements such as statements consisting of mere puffery. With respect to the former, this is one of the few decisions that actually finds that the safe harbor requirements of the PSLRA are met in order to insulate such a statement from liability. One of the forward-looking statements at issue was that "the really nice things about platforms" was that while "standing [them] up" involves some "pain"—future implementation "becomes a pretty replicable process" that leads to "scale and experience gains in that area." This was held to be a forward-looking statement that was protected by adequate cautionary language: "We have to modify for every engagement a little bit of the system but not as big a modification as before and that's one of the things that we are learning." Inactionable puffery included statements such as "[Xerox has] successful[ly] implement[ed]" a system and that it had "launched successfully" a contract. The court held that those statements "conveyed no meaningful, objective data that an investor would rely upon." The key distinction, the court held, between those statements and actionable statements is that these statements are non-verifiable.

"To describe the initial launch of an ... implementation in a given state as a 'success' does not give an investor an assessment that can be measured or verified."

Scienter

Under Section 10(b), a plaintiff must prove that the defendant acted with a "mental state embracing intent to defraud or deceive." *Tellabs, Inc. v. Makor Issues & Rights*, 551 U.S. 308 (2007). Is that the same as "intent"? *Tellabs* holds that, on a motion to dismiss, the court must consider "all plausible non-culpable" explanations for the conduct. There must be a "compelling inference of scienter." Look at the facts holistically; don't look at them in isolation. *Matrixx*, 563 U.S. 27 (2011): "Court must review 'all the allegations holistically' ... the absence of a motive allegation, though relevant, is not dispositive." Why did the defendant lie? To make a profit? To avoid reprimand? *In re Verifone Holding Securities Lit.*, 704 F.3d 694 (9th Cir. 2012), has a good description of the "holistic" test to be applied in determining scienter. *Tellabs* also says to look at the totality of circumstances. Note that the PSLRA never uses the word "scienter."

Scienter may be alleged (at least in the Second Circuit) by facts showing either (1) the defendants had the motive and opportunity to commit the fraud, or (2) strong circumstantial evidence of conscious misbehavior or recklessness. "Strong circumstantial evidence of scienter" could be shown by showing that defendants (1) benefitted in a concrete and personal way from the fraud, (2) engaged in deliberately illegal behavior, (3) knew facts or had access to information suggesting that their public statements were not accurate, *or* (4) failed to check information that they had a duty to monitor. *See ECA & Local 134 Ibew Pension Trust v. JPMorgan Chase*, 553 F.3d 187 (2d Cir. 2009); *Novak v. Kasaks*, 216 F.3d 300 (2d Cir. 2000). Is this test satisfactory? The tests seem to be far removed from scienter. *See Silicon Graphics Securities Litigation*, 183 F.3d 970 (9th Cir. 1999), which rejects it. *See also Bryant v. Avado*, 187 F.3d 127 (11th Cir. 1999) (rejecting it).

There is an issue about recklessness. It is generally held to be sufficient for proof of scienter, although the actual wording of the test sounds very much like intent. "Knew or must have known," most circuits have said is enough, but the Supreme Court has never decided the issue. In fact, the Supreme Court has expressly reserved the question. *Ernst & Ernst v. Hochfelder*, 425 U.S. 185 (1976). The Ninth Circuit has said that the "required state of mind" is that "the defendants made false or misleading statements either intentionally or with deliberate recklessness." *Zucco Partners v. Digimarc Corp.*, 552 F.3d 981 (9th Cir. 2009) ("extreme departure from standards of ordinary care such that danger of misleading buyers and/or sellers is either known to the defendant or is so obvious that the actor must have been aware of it.") Note that the phrase "must have been aware of it" suggests that actual knowledge is still required. "Must have been" is different from "should have been." Is this just a word game? *Sundstrand v. Sun Chemical*, 553 F.2d 1033 (9th Cir. 1977), adopted a reckless test: "blinded by conflict, wantonly ignored."

If the speaker honestly believes that the statement is true, the objective unreasonableness of that belief does not satisfy the recklessness standard. *Restatement of Torts*, Section 526. Circuits typically do not look to the common law of deceit but rather to the definitions of physical torts. As noted, in *Stoneridge v. Scientific Atlanta*, 552 U.S. 148 (2008), the Supreme Court said that Section 10(b) did not incorporate common law fraud. But the requirement for reliance seems to have been taken from common law fraud.

The most frequently cited case on "recklessness" is *Sundstrand*. "It is a highly unreasonable omission." "Extreme departure from standards of ordinary care which presents a danger of misleading buyers that is either known or is so obvious that the actor must have been aware of it." There is no scienter for "white heart, empty head." Is this definition inconsistent with *Hochfelder*, which said that "inexcusable neglect" is not sufficient for scienter? The PSLRA has codified a pleading requirement for scienter but has not defined it. The complaint must plead facts giving rise to a "strong inference" of the "required state of mind," but it does not say what that is. Elsewhere the PSLRA talks about joint and several liability for "knowing violations." In the oft-quoted case of *In re Silicon Graphics Securities Litigation*, 183 F.3d 970 (9th Cir. 1999), the Ninth Circuit spoke of a requirement for "deliberate recklessness." Is that a helpful concept? Should "deliberate recklessness" be enough as a matter of policy? The Supreme Court has never dealt directly with the question of recklessness as a substitute for intent or as an acceptable definition of scienter in Section 10(b) and Rule 10b-5 cases.

Collective Scienter

Before *Janus* there was a split in the Circuits as to whether "collective" or "corporate" scienter could be alleged by combining the mental state of one employee with the misrepresentation of another. Some Circuits said that at the pleading stage, the individuals who had scienter need not be identified. *See, e.g.*, *Teamsters Local 445 Freight Fund v. Dynex Capital Inc.*, 531 F.3d 190 (2d Cir. 2008). But *Janus* seems to say that only the mental state of those with "ultimate authority" over the misrepresentation can be imputed to the corporation. (This is sometimes referred to as the "traditional approach" to corporate scienter.) After *Janus*, the mental state of an employee who merely furnishes information for inclusion in a misstatement cannot be imputed to the corporation. What if no employee who made the statement with ultimate authority and scienter can be identified?[13] Note that, at least in the Second Circuit, a plaintiff may plead scienter as to a corporate defendant "by pleading facts sufficient to create a strong inference either (1) that someone whose intent could be imputed to the corporation acted with the requisite scienter or (2) that the statements would have been approved by corporate officials sufficiently knowledgeable about the company to know that those statements were misleading." *Loreley Fin. (Jersey) No. 3 Ltd. v. Wells Fargo Sec., LLC*, 797 F.3d 160, 177 (2d Cir. 2015). "Collective scienter" may no longer be possible after *Janus Capital Group, Inc. v. First Derivative Traders*, 564 U.S. 135 (2011). But what about scheme liability? *See Stoneridge v. Scientific Atlanta*, 552 U.S. 148 (2008). This area of the law is evolving.

Some Recent Developments

In *Christine Asia Co. Ltd. v. Ma*, 16-2519cv (2d Cir. Dec. 5, 2017) (summary order; no precedential effect), the Second Circuit held that there were "no bright-line rules" for scienter and that scienter can be established by showing "strong circumstantial evidence of conscious misbehavior or recklessness." A "reckless disregard of a known or obvious duty to disclose" can establish scienter, and so can conduct "that is highly unreasonable, representing an extreme departure from the standards of ordinary care." As noted, this was a summary order and is not precedential.

Is this a new test for scienter? What about the *Sundstrand* test ("knew or so obvious that the speaker must have been aware of it")? This issue has never been decided by the Supreme Court. Is there now a concept of "deliberate recklessness?" All circuits now recognize some form of recklessness for scienter, but the tests are slightly different.

Some courts allow the imputation of scienter to the corporation from the aggregate knowledge of all employees (the "collective scienter" theory). Other courts use a watered-down version of collective scienter by allowing imputation so long as at least one management-level employee had scienter.[14] *Janus* seems to say that only the mental state of the person with "ultimate authority" over the contents or the communication of the statement can be imputed to the corporation.

---

[13] *See, e.g.*, *In re Banco Bradesco S.A. Sec. Litig.*, No. 16-cv-4155, 2017 WL 4381407, at *45, 48 (S.D.N.Y. Sept. 29, 2017) (rejecting defendants' argument that a statement could not be "made" by a corporation where it was not attributed to a particular individual within the corporation, but nevertheless dismissing the claim because there was no basis to impute scienter to the corporation with respect to that statement).

[14] *See* Browning Jeffries, "The Implications of Janus on Issuer Liability in Jurisdictions Rejecting Collective Scienter," 43 *Seton Hall L. Rev.* 491 (2013).

What about the mental state of those who "contributed" to the statement? There is at least one post-*Janus* district court case that looks to the mental state of those who "order or approve" the statement or who furnish information or language for inclusion in it. *Kerr v. Exobox Techs.*, 2012 WL 201872 (S.D. Tex. Jan. 23, 2012).

In re Cornerstone Propane Partners L. P. Sec. Lit., 355 F. Supp. 2d 1069 (N.D. Cal. 2005) (collecting cases), held that violations of Generally Accepted Accounting Principles and SEC regulations do not in themselves establish scienter.

Zucco Partners LLC v. Digimarc Corp., 552 F.3d 981 (9th Cir. 2009), held that the timing of a resignation of a corporate officer is insufficient, in itself, to establish scienter, although *In re Adaptive Broadband Sec. Lit.*, 2002 U.S. Dict. LEXIS 117416 (N.D. Cal. Apr. 2, 2002), held that it "could add one more piece to the puzzle as circumstantial evidence."

"Core Operations" Scienter

In some courts, there is an emerging doctrine known as "core operations" scienter that imputes scienter to senior corporate officials who make false or misleading statements regarding matters within the "core operations" of the corporation. According to a litigation newsletter prepared by the law firm Quinn Emanuel, "In the Second Circuit, the doctrine originates from *Cosmas v. Hassett*, 886 F.2d 8 (2d Cir. 1989), in which a company announced that sales to China would constitute a significant revenue source for the company, despite Chinese regulations preventing exactly those sales. The Second Circuit imputed knowledge of the regulations to the defendant directors, given that 'the restrictions apparently eliminated a potentially significant source of income for the company.'"[15] The report notes that the Second Circuit has still not yet decided whether the doctrine survived the PSLRA.

In *Charles Paddock v. Dreamworks Animation SKG, Inc.*, CJ 14-06053 (SJO) (C.D. Cal. Apr. 1, 2015), the district court observed that in alleging scienter on the part of Dreamworks's CEO and CFO, "plaintiff appears to rely on the 'core operations' theory in its attempt to establish scienter." Citing the Ninth Circuit's *Reese v. Malone*, 747 F.3d 557 (9th Cir. 2014), the district court wrote that "in rare circumstances, such allegations may be sufficient without accompanying particularized allegations, where the relevant fact is of such prominence that it would be 'absurd' to suggest that management was without knowledge of the matter" but "[p]roof under this theory is not easy." In affirming the decision to dismiss the complaint, the Ninth Circuit did not

---

[15] https://www.quinnemanuel.com/the-firm/publications/article-january-2013-securities-litigation-update/.

mention the "core operations" theory. *Roofers Local No. 149 Pension Fund v. Dreamworks Animation SKG, Inc.*, February 17, 2017 (unpublished and not precedential Memorandum).

According to some academics, a "core operation" is a "fact material to the company's operations and its bottom line, and as such is something that is material to investors as well.... Generally a core operation is thought of as the firm's primary product or service."[16] However, this concept has not yet been warmly embraced by courts, largely (or at least in part) because: it appears to run afoul of the dual-pleading requirement of the PSLRA, the facts supporting the allegation of the "requisite state of mind" must be alleged with particularity, and that those facts lead to a "strong inference of scienter." At least five Supreme Court cases have suggested that a "core operations" inference might support an allegation of scienter (*Janus*, *Stoneridge*, *Merck*, *Matrixx*, and *Tellabs*) but that suggestion is not robust. Perhaps for that reason, lower courts have been reluctant to use the "core operations" theory alone as sufficient for allegations of scienter.[17]

For example, in *South Ferry LP v. Killinger*, 2008 WL 4138237 (9th Cir. Sept. 9, 2008), the Ninth Circuit held that inferring scienter from nothing more than the fact that the speaker had a senior management position in the company did not satisfy the pleading requirements of the PSLRA.

As late as April 2012, the Second Circuit stated that it had not yet decided whether the "core operations" doctrine survives the PSLRA as a viable theory of scienter.[18]

In *In re Biogen Inc. Securities Litigation*, 857 F.3d 34 (1st Cir. 2017), the First Circuit rejected the "core operations" theory as sufficient for pleading scienter as "inapt" because the plaintiffs did not plead the existence of "materially contradictory reasonably accessible data within the company" and, echoing *Tellabs*, the court emphasized the importance of evaluating the complaint as a whole, including plausible opposing inferences.

---

[16] Michael Kaufman & John Wunderlich, "Messy Mental Markers: Inferring Scienter From Core Operations in Securities Fraud Litigation," 73 *Ohio State L. J.* 507 (2012).

[17] *See generally* Gregory Markel & Martin Seidel, "Core Operations Doctrine May Undermine PSLRA," *N.Y. L.J.*, Apr. 29, 2010, p. 5.

[18] *See Frederick v. Mechel OAO*, 2012 WL 1193724 (2d Cir. Apr. 11, 2012); *but see New Orleans Employees Retirement Sys. v. Celestica Inc.*, 2011 WL 6823204 (2d Cir. Dec. 29, 2011) ("allegations of a company's core operations ... can provide supplemental support for allegations of scienter, even if they cannot establish scienter independently."); *see also In re Longtop Financial Technologies Ltd. Securities Litigation*, 2012 WL 2512280 (S.D.N.Y. June 29, 2012).

Chapter 10

Section 10(b) of the Exchange Act and Rule 10b-5, Part Two

Reliance or Transaction Causation

In order to understand the genesis of the requirement for "transaction causation" or "reliance" in cases alleging violation of Section 10(b), it is worth recalling three cases in which the Supreme Court, either directly or by implication, held that Section 10(b) came from the common law of deceit. In *Ernst & Ernst v. Hochfelder*, 425 US. 185 (1976), the Supreme Court held that because it used the words "manipulative or deceptive device or contrivance" the statute must be read to proscribe only intentional or knowing misconduct. That being the case, said Justice Lewis Powell for the majority, the statute must require proof of scienter for a violation. Similarly, in *Basic v. Levinson*, 485 U.S. 224 (1988), the Supreme Court held that the common law of deceit required "reliance" and since most cases under Section 10(b) did not include face-to-face transactions in which reliance could easily be proved, the court created a "presumption" of reliance in cases involving "fraud on the market." Finally, in *Dura Pharmaceuticals v. Broudo*, 544 U.S. 336 (2005), the Supreme Court, once again recalling the common law tort of deceit, required that "economic loss" and "loss causation" be proven as elements of a Section 10(b) violation.[1]

Accordingly, "transaction causation" or "reliance" is a required element of proof in private Section 10(b) cases unless the "misrepresentation" is a pure omission, which obviously cannot be "relied on" since it is not apparent. To prevail "[a] plaintiff must allege that *but for* the fraudulent statement or omission, the plaintiff would not have entered into the transaction." *Suez Equity*

---

[1] Under the common law tort of deceit, the elements were (1) false representation of past or existing material fact, (2) knowledge that representation is false or not knowing whether or not it was, (3) intent to induce another to rely on representation, (4) actual reliance, and (5) damages caused by reliance. *See* Michael Knauss, "Common Law Fraudulent Misrepresentation and Negligent Misrepresentation," https://www.gtlaw.com/en/insights/2015/1/common-law-fraudulent-and-negligent-misrepresentation.

Investors v. Toronto Dominion Bank, 250 F.3d 87 (2d Cir. 2001). The "but for" test was repeated in *Dura Pharmaceuticals Inc. v. Broudo*, 544 U.S. 336 (2005).[2]

As noted, the requirement of reliance is an entirely judicial-made requirement; it does not appear in any statute or rule. Even though the Supreme Court did not say explicitly that this requirement of proof came from the common law tort of deceit, there was an exchange of correspondence about reliance between Supreme Court Justice Harry Blackmun and Justice William Brennan referring to the common law fraud antecedent of securities fraud and the three cases cited above certainly reflect that lineage, even though later, in *Zandford*, 535 U.S. 813 (2002), and *Stoneridge v. Scientific Atlanta*, 552 U.S. 148 (2008), the Supreme Court stated that Section 10(b) did not "incorporate common law fraud into federal law." It is hard to reconcile these statements but there is no need to do so, since the requirement for proof of transaction causation is clear.

Stoneridge holds that transaction causation is related to the "in connection with" requirement. Is it? Is this part of the confusion between the two concepts, or is the Supreme Court correct? If so, how do we explain the fact that when the SEC is the plaintiff, there is no requirement to prove transaction causation?[3] I believe that a better reading of *Stoneridge* is that the Supreme Court overstated somewhat the relationship between the two concepts. They clearly are related if the result of the reliance is a purchase or sale, but in common law deceit, without the reliance there would be no fraud. In a fraud-on-the-market case where there is no face-to-face transaction, the causal link between the fraud and the decision to buy or sell is attenuated at best and non-existent at worst. Most people buy stock because they think that it is under-valued by the market, not because it is correctly priced.

Nevertheless, "transaction causation refers to the causal link between the defendant's misconduct and the plaintiff's decision to buy or sell securities. It is established simply by showing that, but for the claimed misrepresentations or omissions, the plaintiff would not have entered into the detrimental securities transactions." *Emergent Capital Investment Management v. Stonepath Group*, 343 F.3d 189 (2d Cir. 2003). This was not a class action. Does that make a difference?

The issue is whether or not the purchaser or seller relied on the defendant's fraud in making the purchase or sale. You will sometimes see transaction

---

[2] The "but for" test is not the principal holding of *Dura*. The principal holding has to do with pleading loss causation, not reliance.

[3] *See* Merritt B. Fox, "Demystifying Causation in Fraud-on-the-Market Cases," 60 *Bus. Law.* 507 (2005).

causation referred to as "causation in fact," although that characterization is not particularly helpful.

As noted, the requirement for transaction causation first appeared in *Basic v. Levinson*, 485 U.S. 224 (1988), although lower courts had discussed it for some time. The Supreme Court has said that the reliance element "ensures that there is a proper connection between a defendant's misrepresentation and a plaintiff's injury." *Amgen Inc. v. Connecticut Retirement Plans and Trust Funds*, 568 U.S. 455 (2013). However, that appears to sound more like loss causation rather than transaction causation.

Consider whether, as a matter of policy, reliance should be required at all. If, as we will see, reliance is presumed in an efficient market, what does it add? It is, of course, a rebuttable presumption but it is rarely rebutted. Some have suggested eliminating the requirement of reliance entirely.[4]

As noted, courts (especially the Second Circuit in *Emergent*[5] and *Suez*[6]) have said that transaction causation is a "but for" test. That is, "but for" the misrepresentation, the plaintiff would not have purchased the stock. Can this be understood to mean "would not have purchased the stock *at that price*" or does it mean not at all?

Does this make sense? The misrepresentation causes the price of the stock to be inflated, and yet the plaintiff still purchased it. In a perfectly efficient market, wouldn't the purchase decision be the same with the misrepresentation plus inflation as without it, at a correspondingly lower price?

Remember that the reliance requirement comes from common law tort of deceit. It works something like this: assume that I want to buy your car, and I ask you whether it was ever in an accident. You lie and say no. I buy the car. Without the fraud, I would not have bought your car. The fraud caused me to buy the car. So far, so good. But what if I did not ask you about accidents, but you volunteered during our price negotiations that the car had never been in an accident. Have you committed fraud or just lied? In this scenario, there is no evidence that I relied on the misrepresentation or even cared about it. Can it be said that "but for" the fraud, I would not have purchased the car? Probably not.

The fraud we are talking about in the securities context is fraud that impacts or "inflates" the price of stock and thereby induces the purchaser to buy the inflated stock. The amount of inflation in the price of the stock should exactly correlate with the fraud (or so the experts say, which is another topic

---

[4] *See* Daniel Fischel, "Use of Modern Finance Theory in Securities Fraud Cases Involving Actively Traded Securities," 38 Bus. Law. 1 (1982).

[5] *Emergent Capital Investment Management v. Stonepath Group*, 343 F.3d 189 (2d Cir. 2003).

[6] *Suez Equity Investors v. Toronto Dominion Bank*, 250 F.3d 87 (2d Cir. 2001).

entirely). This theory is not without its problems, however. If the purchaser was willing to pay a higher price for the stock than its true value would suggest, wouldn't the purchaser also be willing to pay a lower price if there was no price inflation caused by the fraud? How can it be said that "but for" the fraud, the purchaser would not have bought the stock when without the fraud, the price would have been lower. Don't purchasers like to "buy low and sell high"?

Assume that a mining company announces, falsely, that it has just discovered gold in Alaska. Let us further assume that on the day after the disclosure, the price of the company's stock went up $2, which was an increase of about 1 percent. Let's further assume that that price increase was statistically significantly higher than the increase in the market as a whole and similarly higher than the increase in the prices of comparably situated companies. In securities law terms, this increase would be called a "price inflation" due to the fraud. Does that daily increase, in and of itself, cause purchasers to buy the stock? Is it a "but for" cause? How would we know? How could that "but for" cause be proved in court? Do we really think that most purchasers bought their stock on the day in question because of the announcement of the discovery of gold in Alaska? Almost certainly not.

Dura says that the fraud caused the purchaser to buy the stock and pay $2 more than she should have. She was willing to do that because of the fraud, even though it caused the stock to be priced $2 more than it should have been. But without the fraud, the stock price would have been $2 lower. Why didn't she buy the stock when it was selling for $2 less? The true values, at least hypothetically, were exactly the same in either case.

Let's take this hypothetical a few steps further. Let's assume that on the day that the gold strike in Alaska was announced, the price of the company's stock did not change. More precisely, let's assume that there was no statistically significant change in the price of the stock when compared to the market as a whole or to comparable companies. Three years later, the company issued a press release stating that its disclosure of the gold mine three years ago was not true, that it had been manufactured by a rogue employee who has since been fired. The next day, the price of the stock declined $2, which was statistically significant when compared to the market and to comparable companies. Was that $2 drop caused by the disclosure of the fraud? Securities plaintiffs lawyers would say that it was. They even have a theory that the $2 drop in the price of the stock—the elimination of the $2 inflation—can be traced back to the day of the fraudulent announcement. That tracing back is called a "constant ribbon" and operates on the theory that the inflation has been in the price of the stock for three years.

There are at least two problems with this theory that should be addressed. First, *Dura* held that price inflation dissipates over time. Assuming that the original inflation was $2, shouldn't at least some of it have dissipated in three years? How would we determine whether that is true and how would we measure the dissipation? Second, in this hypothetical, there was no change in the price of the stock on the day after the announcement of the discovery of the potential gold mine. How do we know that the announcement caused a $2 inflation? How do we know that the announcement of the fraud three years later caused the price of the stock to drop by $2 because of the earlier fraud and not some other reason? Perhaps the market just concluded that the company was simply a lousy investment because it was populated by corrupt employees? If true, would that be evidence that the price was inflated three years earlier or would it be evidence of something else? Who knows?

One of the other problems with these hypotheticals is that there is little or no academic scholarship that proves them or concludes they have any relation to the real world. These theories are not scientifically based. In fact, Justin Fox's *The Myth of the Rational Market: A History of Risk, Reward and Delusion on Wall Street*[7] has debunked most of them. Nevertheless, the theories persist, and most Rule 10b-5 class actions are predicated on them. As we will see below when we discuss the recent *Goldman Sachs* case, even if there is no change in the price at the beginning of the class when the fraud theoretically occurred, securities plaintiffs lawyers and some courts have opined that however the inflation got into the price of the stock, we know that it was there because it disappeared when the fraud was revealed and therefore it must have been "maintained" by the company during the entire period by announcements of positive statements about the company's business.

You may not think that these theories hold water, but you must take them seriously because they are the basis for most if not all Rule 10b-5 class action litigation.

"Eyeball" Reliance

The most direct type of reliance is sometimes referred to as "eyeball" reliance. That occurs when the plaintiff actually reads the misleading statement and relies on it in making the purchase or sale decision. In *Amgen Inc. v. Connecticut Retirement Plans and Trust Funds*, 568 U.S. 455 (2013), the Supreme Court said that "the traditional (and most direct) way a plaintiff can demonstrate reliance is by showing that he [or she] was aware of a company's statement and engaged in a relevant transaction—e.g., purchasing common stock—based on that specific misrepresentation." Obviously, there cannot be a class action where the only reliance is "eyeball" reliance since it would be nearly impossible to put together a class of purchasers who actually knew about the alleged false statement and relied on it to make their purchases.

---

[7] Harper Business (2011).

Stanford Law Professor Joseph Grundfest, a former SEC Commissioner, has written that the only type of reliance that should be permitted in Rule 10b-5 cases is "eyeball" reliance. He reached that conclusion by analogy to Section 18 of the 1934 Act, which does require "eyeball reliance."[8] In *Halliburton II*, discussed below, the Supreme Court rejected that proposal.

Reliance is difficult to prove, and "eyeball reliance" rarely occurs. As a result, the courts have created certain presumptions to make the plaintiff's burden easier. These presumptions, to which we now turn, are the cornerstone of today's securities class actions. Without them, securities class actions would almost certainly not exist.

The "Efficient Market" Hypothesis and "Fraud on the Market"

The first presumption that we will consider is the "fraud on the market" presumption. This is a presumption that purchasers of securities on the open market assume that the market is efficient, that the securities are fairly priced, and that the prices are not tainted by fraud.

The leading case is *Basic v. Levinson*, 485 U.S. 224 (1988). In *Basic*, the Supreme Court recognized that requiring direct proof of reliance "would place an unnecessarily unrealistic evidentiary burden on the Rule 10b-5 plaintiff who has traded on an impersonal market." That is because, even assuming an investor could prove that she was aware of the misrepresentation, she would still have to "show a speculative state of facts, i.e., how [she] would have acted ... if the misrepresentation had not been made." *Basic* held that "our task, of course, is not to assess the general validity of the ['efficient market'] theory, but to consider whether it was proper for the courts below to apply a rebuttable presumption of reliance, supported in part by the fraud-on-the-market theory." The court went further: "The presumption is also supported by common sense and probability. Recent empirical studies have tended to confirm Congress' premise that the market prices of shares traded on well-developed markets reflects all publicly available information, and, hence, any material misrepresentations. It has been noted that 'it is hard to imagine that there ever is a buyer or seller who does not rely on market integrity. Who would knowingly roll the dice in a crooked crap game?'" *Halliburton v. Erica P. John Fund*, 573 U.S. 258 (2014) (*Halliburton II*), later held:

> [I]n an open and developed securities market, the price of a company's stock is determined by the available material information

---

[8] Joseph Grundfest, "Damages and Reliance Under Section 10(b) of the Exchange Act," 69 *Bus. Law.* 307 (Feb. 2014).

> regarding the company and its business. Misleading statements will therefore defraud the purchasers of stock even if the purchasers do not directly rely on the misstatements.... The causal connection between the defendants' fraud and the plaintiffs' purchase of stock in such a case is no less significant than in a case of direct reliance on misrepresentations.

This presumption of reliance on the market price is based on the "efficient market" hypothesis. This hypothesis, also Supreme Court–created but based on some economic theory, holds that when stocks are publicly traded, the stock price is determined by the market's evaluation of all available information about the company and that false information causes the market to value the stock erroneously. In other words, the first presumption created by the *Basic* Court is that "if a plaintiff shows that the defendant's misrepresentation was public and material and that the stock traded in a generally efficient market, he [or she] is entitled to a presumption that the misrepresentation affected the market price." *Halliburton II*, 573 U.S. at 279.

There is a second presumption created by *Basic*. "If the plaintiff also shows that he [or she] purchased the stock at the market price during the relevant period, he [or she] is entitled to a further presumption that he [or she] purchased the stock in reliance on the defendant's misrepresentation." These two presumptions are obviously based on the assumption that the market is "generally efficient." But *Basic* did not endorse any specific economic theory of market efficiency.

The *Basic* presumption is rebuttable. "Any showing that severs the link between the alleged misrepresentation and either the price received (or paid) by the plaintiff, or his [or her] decision to trade at a fair market price, will be sufficient to rebut the presumption of reliance.... [I]f despite petitioners' allegedly fraudulent attempt to manipulate market price, news of the merger discussions credibly entered the market and dissipated the effects of the misstatements, those who traded Basic shares after the corrective statements would have no direct or indirect connection with the fraud."

Basic has been criticized. *See, e.g.*, Donald Langevoort, "*Basic* at Twenty: Rethinking Fraud on the Market," 2009 *Wis. L. Rev.* 151 (2009) ("*Basic* is confused about the role of efficiency in the presumption of reliance; is reliance the only available 'common issue?'").

In 2003, MIT and later Yale economist Robert Shiller, author of *Irrational Exuberance*,[9] won the Nobel Prize in Economics for his work in which he showed that the variations in the prices of stocks and bonds over long periods occur in predictable patterns that reflect the irrational expectations of investors

---

[9] Princeton University Press (2000).

regarding the value of future returns (e.g., dividends). Shiller's work contradicted the once dominant assumption that markets are inherently rational, which was a theory developed by economist Eugene Fama, who coincidentally also won the Nobel Prize in Economics in the same year as Shiller. Shiller's scholarship was widely perceived as demonstrating that the *Basic* presumption of an efficient market in which all stocks are fairly priced based on all publicly available information was erroneous. In fact, at least two Supreme Court Justices have called for the elimination of the *Basic* presumption but the Court has nevertheless maintained it.

In fact, in June 2014, the Court, in *Halliburton II*, explicitly reaffirmed the *Basic* presumption of reliance. *Halliburton II* not only left *Basic* untouched but it upheld the continued use of the fraud-on-the-market doctrine as a basis for establishing reliance, including at class certification. The Supreme Court held that the "fraud-on-the-market" presumption was based on the "fairly modest premise" that "market professionals generally consider most publicly announced material statements about companies, thereby affecting stock market prices." The Court reaffirmed that the presumption was rebuttable and observed that "even those investors who believe that price integrity is supposedly marginal or irrelevant will, in any event, rely at least on the fact that market prices, however inaccurate, are not distorted by fraud." However, there have actually been few cases in which the presumption of reliance on the efficiency of the market has been rebutted. One such case was *GAMCO Investors, Inc. v. Vivendi S.A.*, 927 F. Supp. 2d 88 (S.D.N.Y. 2013), *aff'd* 838 F.3d 214 (2d Cir. 2016).[10]

Note, however, that the Court's opinion in *Basic* goes on to say that if the false information is not reflected in the price of the stock at the time of the misrepresentation (i.e., if there is no inflation in the stock price), there can be no claim because the statement would not be material and there would be no damage. That is because there would be no loss causation. To that extent, Justice Thomas's concurring opinion in *Halliburton II*, that the fraud must be incorporated into the stock price *at the time of purchase* for it to be actionable seems correct, but in general it has not been embraced by the courts. Would a price impact caused by a corrective disclosure be sufficient? This remains an open question and is discussed further below.

What if the alleged misrepresentations are general statements? If they are so general that no reasonable investor would have considered the information significant in deciding whether or not to buy or sell a security, then they are immaterial under the *Chadbourne & Parke* test for materiality.[11] Does that

---

[10] Full disclosure: I was lead counsel for Vivendi in that case.

[11] In *Okla. Law Enf't Ret. Sys. v. Papa John's Int'l, Inc.*, 2021 WL 371401, at *7 (S.D.N.Y. Feb. 3, 2021), the district court held that the alleged misstatement in

mean that they cannot have a price impact? We know that most securities cases are only brought if there is a price impact but how is a court to determine whether a general statement was so general that it could not have had a price impact? May the court rely on its own "commonsense judgment" in making that determination? Perhaps. In *Goldman Sachs*, discussed next, the Supreme Court agreed with the parties that "courts may consider expert testimony and use their common sense in assessing whether a generic misrepresentation had a price impact." Common sense? Isn't this a factual question? What does "common sense" have to do with it?

Goldman Sachs Group, Inc. v. Arkansas Teachers Retirement System[12]

This is the most recent Supreme Court case on the presumption of reliance on an efficient market and the price impact *vel non* of a misrepresentation. The litigation history of this case is long, somewhat confusing, and fortunately of little or no relevance to the Supreme Court's opinion. Basically, the plaintiffs in this securities class action alleged that Goldman maintained an artificially inflated stock price by making false and misleading generic statements about its ability to manage conflicts.[13] An example of one such generic statement was: "We have extensive procedures and controls that are designed to identify and address conflicts of interest." The plaintiffs relied on their *Basic v. Levinson* presumption of reliance on an efficient market in which all material misrepresentations would be impounded into the Goldman stock price.[14]

At the class certification stage, Goldman tried to rebut the presumption by showing, through expert testimony, that the statements in issue actually had no impact at all on the price of Goldman's stock. The plaintiffs responded that the statements had the effect of maintaining an inflation that was already in the price of the stock, the so-called "maintenance theory." Goldman further argued that the Second Circuit did not fully consider whether the generic nature of the statements in question affected their price impact. In the Supreme Court, the parties agreed that the generic nature of a statement was important evidence of price impact (or not) and should be considered at the class certification stage

---

the defendant's code of conduct was "vague, broad, and merely aspirational ... [and] no reasonable investor could have relied on the Code's vague assurances in making investment decisions."

[12] 141 S. Ct. 1951 (2021).

[13] It is not entirely clear how the inflation got into the stock price in the first place.

[14] Would such a statement meet the *TSC v. Northway*, test for materiality? (*TSC Industries, Inc. v. Northway Inc.*, 426 U.S. 438 (1976).)

and the Supreme Court held that the Second Circuit "may not have properly considered the generic nature of Goldman's alleged misrepresentations," and vacated and remanded the case to the Second Circuit to reassess the district court's price impact determination on that score.

The more difficult issue—the issue that divided the Supreme Court—was which side, plaintiffs or defendant, had the burden of proving lack of price impact at the class certification stage. After revisiting *Basic* and *Halliburton II*, the majority concluded that the defendant bore the burden of persuasion—by a preponderance of the evidence—that the misrepresentation *in fact* did not lead to a distortion of the price of the stock. The Court further held that notwithstanding *Amgen*, this showing could be made at the class certification stage even if the issue of the generic nature of the statement in question may also be relevant to materiality, which *Amgen* reserved for the merits.

Of some interest is the Supreme Court's negative view of the Second Circuit's decision in *In re Vivendi S.A. Securities Litigation*, which affirmed a holding that a disclosure that corrected an earlier misrepresentation resulted in a price drop that was "equal to the amount of inflation maintained by the earlier misrepresentation." The Supreme Court in *Goldman Sachs* noted that "that final inference—that the back-end price drop equals front-end inflation—starts to break down when there is a mismatch between the contents of the misrepresentation and the corrective disclosure." Of course, in the *Vivendi* case, there was no corrective disclosure that explicitly corrected a misrepresentation. The *Goldman Sachs* Court added that if the misrepresentation is generic, and the correction is specific, "it is less likely that the specific disclosure actually corrected the generic misrepresentation, which means that there is less reason to infer front-end price inflation—that is, price impact—from the back-end price drop."

Of even more interest is the Supreme Court's unwillingness to accept the theory of inflation maintenance on which the *Vivendi* opinion was based. The court observed in a footnote that "[a]lthough some courts of appeals have approved the inflation-maintenance theory, this Court has expressed no view on its validity or its contours. We need not and do not do so in this case." One could read that footnote as suggesting that the price-maintenance theory is not doing so well and in fact may be on its last legs.

In *IBEW Local 98 Pension Fund v. Best Buy Co. Inc.*, 818 F.3d 775 (8th Cir. 2016), a divided Eighth Circuit rejected the plaintiff's claim that an allegedly false statement in an analysts' conference call that admittedly had no price impact on the stock when it was made was nevertheless actionable because it "maintained" inflation that had been created by a non-actionable press release issued by the company two hours earlier. The court held that a price drop when a "corrective disclosure" was made three months later was not the type of price impact that *Halliburton II* had in mind and that the "overwhelming evidence of no 'front end' price impact rebutted the *Basic* presumption." The dissent argued that the majority erred by not recognizing the validity of the "price maintenance" theory.

As noted above, in his concurring opinion in *Halliburton II*, Justice Thomas disagreed with the majority's endorsement of *Basic*. "Logic, economic realities, and our subsequent jurisprudence have undermined the foundations of the *Basic* presumption, and *stare decisis* cannot prop up the façade that remains. *Basic* should be overruled." (Slip op. at 2.) He wrote:

> *Basic* took an implied cause of action and grafted on a policy-driven presumption of reliance based on nascent economic theory and personal intuitions about investment behavior. The result was an unrecognizably broad cause of action ready made for class certification. Time and experience have pointed up the error of that decision, making it all too clear that the Court's attempt to revise securities law to fit the alleged "new realities of financial markets" should have been left to Congress.

The fraudulent statement at issue must be a public statement (unless it is a pure omission). *Stoneridge v. Scientific Atlanta*, 552 U.S. 148 (2008). And there can be no reliance on a statement that is not public. ("Section 10(b) does not incorporate common law fraud into federal law.") *Stoneridge* also said that "Reliance is tied to causation, leading to the inquiry whether respondents' acts were immediate or remote to the injury" but the causation that *Stoneridge* is talking about is *loss* causation (i.e., the injury) whereas reliance is about *transaction* causation not loss causation. The confusion between transaction causation and loss causation continues even at the highest level.

Does the fraud-on-the-market concept take the place of transaction causation? Some have said so. In *Dura Pharmaceuticals Inc. v. Broudo*, 544 U.S. 336 (2005), the Supreme Court said that in a class action context, the presumption of reliance means that "the price of a publicly traded share reflects a material misrepresentation and that plaintiffs have relied upon that misrepresentation *as long as they would not have bought the shares in its absence*" (emphasis added). That is clearly a "but for" requirement. And that is transaction causation, not loss causation. But again, in an efficient market, a misrepresentation will cause the stock price to be inflated. Can it truly be said that without the misrepresentation, the purchaser would not have bought the stock (even at a lower price)? Is there any empirical evidence that that actually occurs? There does not appear to be any.

Most economists would say that "market efficiency" commonly means that the market price fairly represents the current, expected economic value of the future cash flows and future sale price of the security. Thus, an efficiently priced stock cannot be expected to trade at a price different from its economic value, or else the forces of the market would drive the market price toward that value. For example, in an efficient market, the price of an undervalued security would quickly rise, while the price of an overvalued security would quickly fall. The Second Circuit test is that the market price in an efficient market represents an accurate measure of the intrinsic value of the security. Does that mean that all publicly available information is impounded into the price of the stock? What does that have to do with intrinsic value?

A commonly accepted implication of market efficiency is that the price of a security should change rapidly and fairly to reflect (or "impound") any new value-relevant information about the company. If the price rises beyond the expected new value, it is said to "overreact"; if it does not fully incorporate the new information, it is said to "underreact."

Another economic implication of the efficient market hypothesis is that trades based on publicly available information cannot be expected to yield a positive risk-adjusted return, that is, a return in excess of what could be earned by another investment of similar risk. This is the theory behind investing in a passive index fund as opposed to an actively managed fund (or a so-called value fund[15]), that is trying to beat the market. If the market were truly efficient, it would not be possible to identify an undervalued or overvalued security. All stocks would be accurately priced.

There are not only theoretical challenges to market efficiency, there are empirical demonstrations as well. Take, for example, the studies of the strong return differential between growth and value stocks. Value stocks are those with low market-to-book ratios or low price-to-earnings ratios. Studies show that they have market risks comparable to growth stocks. That is inconsistent with the efficient market hypothesis. Mario Gabelli's trading methodology (looking for stocks whose "private market value" based on the value of its assets is higher than the market price and have a "catalyst" to unlock that value) is the opposite of reliance on the efficiency of the market accurately to price a stock. *Halliburton II* suggests that the market might be efficient if the price impact of the fraud occurs in a reasonable time but a value investor does not have a claim unless the price impact has already occurred at the time of purchase, and, even then, the presumption of reliance can be rebutted.

In a perfectly efficient market, the demand curve for stocks is perfectly flat. Perfect substitutes exist for every stock. Thus, in theory, adding shares to the market should not affect price. But some studies showed that, for example, adding a stock to the S&P 500 causes the price to jump, because index funds can now buy the stock. But the value of the underlying company or its stock

---

[15] *GAMCO Investors, Inc. v. Vivendi S.A.*, 927 F. Supp. 2d 88 (S.D.N.Y. 2013), *aff'd* 838 F.3d 214 (2d Cir. 2016).

did not change in value. The purchases were not based on better prospects for the company, but only because they could be made. Is that consistent with the efficient market theory?

How Do You Prove That a Stock Is Trading in an Efficient Market?

This question turns out to be rather difficult to answer. In recent cases, defendants have tried to rebut the presumption of reliance on an efficient market by showing that plaintiffs' experts had failed to find statistically significant stock price declines on the days of the corrective disclosures even though there should have been such declines in an efficient market. However, in *Villella v. Chemical and Mining Co. of Chile, Inc.*, 333 F.R.D. 39 (S.D.N.Y. 2019), the court held that only "some evidence" of market efficiency was required, and was sufficient in that case, even if "one cannot rule out random volatility."

Cammer v. Bloom, 711 F. Supp. 1264 (D.N.J. 1989), listed factors that courts should consider in deciding whether a stock is trading in an efficient market (these are referred to as the "*Cammer* factors"):

- Trading volume.
- Price movement in relation to news (i.e., is there a cause-and-effect relationship?).
- Availability of public information.
- Interest in the stock by professional analysts.
- Trading on a national exchange.
- Effectiveness of the arbitrage market.

Many appellate courts, including the First, Second, Third, Fourth, and Ninth, have adopted the *Cammer* factors as "useful analytic tools" "depending on the circumstances." But the Supreme Court has not adopted them. Recently, the Eleventh Circuit has held that it would not require district courts to apply the *Cammer* factors in every case but they should be "flexible" in their analyses. *Local 703, I.B. of T. Grocery and Food Employees Welfare Fund v. Regions Fin. Corp.*, 2014 WL 3844070 (11th Cir. Aug. 6, 2014).

The *Cammer* factors have been criticized because, even if they are present, they do not ensure market efficiency.[16] They were developed in 1989,

[16] *See, e.g.*, J.B. Heaston, "Kill *Cammer*: Securities Litigation Without Junk Science," 418 *William & Mary Business L. Rev.* 417 (2020) ("The birth and survival of the *Cammer* factors—so obviously unrelated to the financial economics of market efficiency—raise the question whether more such phenomena exist where a junk science that can prosper for decades because the parties to the litigation have distorted incentives to challenge the unreliable methodologies that are sometimes helpful for them.")

before a lot of the economic work showing the flaws in the efficient market hypothesis was done. The *Cammer* case is also confusing and quite tentative. But at the moment it is all we have.

The *Affiliated Ute* Presumption

This phrase refers to *Affiliated Ute Citizens of Utah v. United States*, 407 U.S. 916 (1971). These were three very complicated consolidated cases over restrictions placed by the United States on the ability of mixed-blood Utes to sell their stock (representing ownership interests in mineral rights) to non-Indians. The share certificates were placed in a bank. Two of the bank's assistant managers devised a scheme to acquire shares from the mixed-blood Utes for less than fair market value and then to sell them to non-Indians at a higher price. They received commissions on the sales. They never told the mixed bloods that they were able to resell the shares at a higher price or that they were getting commissions.

The court of appeals found that although there was a misstatement of a material fact, to wit, that the prevailing market price was the figure at which the purchases were made, there was no evidence of reliance on that misrepresentation. The assistant managers also omitted to tell the mixed bloods that they were getting commissions for selling the stock at a higher price, but the appeals court held that was not actionable because the plaintiffs did not rely on it.

The Supreme Court reversed. "It is no answer that these defendants may have made no positive representation or recommendation. The defendants may not stand mute while they facilitate the mixed-bloods sales to those seeking to profit in the non-Indian market.... *Under the circumstances of this case, involving primarily a failure to disclose, positive proof of reliance is not a prerequisite to recovery. All that is necessary is that the facts withheld be material in the sense that a reasonable investor might have considered them important in the making of this decision*" (emphasis added).

The case has been interpreted as standing for the proposition that a plaintiff need not prove reliance in a pure omission case. *See, e.g.*, *Stoneridge*, 552 U.S. 148 (2008), *but see Halliburton II*, 573 U.S. at 279.

Affiliated Ute is somewhat unsatisfactory. Is it a failure to disclose case? Does the presumption only apply if there is a duty to disclose? What was the duty to disclose? Is the result driven by the difficulty of proving reliance on an omission? Wouldn't it have been easy to prove that the mixed-blood Utes would not have sold if they knew the facts that were not disclosed? Was there an affirmative misrepresentation, as the court of appeals seems to have found?

Note that *Halliburton II* requires proof of a price impact in order for a fraud to be actionable but it never mentions omissions or *Affiliated Ute*. It remains to be seen whether the *Affiliated Ute* presumption remains the law after *Halliburton II*. Note that *Local 703*, 2014 WL 3844070, discusses the relationship between "confirmatory information" and *Affiliated Ute*.

The Second Circuit, in *Waggoner v. Barclays PLC*, 875 F.3d 79 (2d Cir. 2017), has reaffirmed that the presumption can only be applied in a case that is "primarily" an omission case. It cannot be used in a case in which the alleged omission relates back to a prior statement that later became inaccurate or in which the omission merely exacerbated the misleading nature of an affirmative statement. The court cited *Wilson v. Comtech Telecommunications Corp.*, 648 F.2d 88 (2d Cir 1981), for that proposition.

Binder v. Gillespie, 184 F.3d 1059 (9th Cir. 1999), held that the presumption should not be applied to cases that allege both misstatements and omissions unless the case can be characterized as one that primarily alleges omissions. Is the issue only one of pleading? Does the court have to make an independent assessment? Is the dissent persuasive? Judge Stephen Reinhardt says that "it is equally difficult to establish reliance on a misrepresentation and on an omission." Is that correct? What about the presumption of reliance on an efficient market? That is clearly easier to prove than reliance on an omission.

How would you rebut the presumption of reliance in an omissions case? (Assuming there is such a requirement.) Perhaps you could establish that the plaintiff was motivated by other factors in making the purchase and would not have relied on the omitted fact even if it had been revealed. As far as we know, this has never been tried.

"Fraud Created the Market" Presumption

This presumption only applies to primary securities offerings and is rarely seen. *Shores v. Sklar*, 647 F.2d 462 (5th Cir. 1981) (*Shores I*). The plaintiff purchased bonds in a primary offering. He never saw the offering circular, which was alleged to have been misleading. The Fifth Circuit held that a Section 10(b) claim was made out. The fraud was intended to and did bring the bonds onto the market fraudulently and the purchaser relied "on the integrity of the offerings on the securities market." He "reasonably relied on the bonds' availability on the market as an indication of their apparent genuineness." Would the bonds have been "unmarketable" absent the fraud? Does it help to call the fraud "manipulation"? Is the dissent persuasive? Upon remand, the district court refused to certify a class. When the case came back to the Fifth Circuit, it reversed, saying the "fraud on the underdeveloped market" presumption still applied. The Fifth Circuit has "tweaked" the "fraud created the market" presumption in *Regents of University of California v. Credit Suisse First Boston, Inc.*, 482 F.3d 372 (9th Cir. 2007).

Rebutting the Presumption of Reliance on an Efficient Market

Basic holds that a presumption of reliance can be rebutted by "any showing that severs the link between the alleged misrepresentation and either the price received (or paid) by the plaintiff, or his decision to trade at a fair market price, will be sufficient to rebut the presumption." The Supreme Court gave several "examples" of ways to rebut the presumption, including a showing that market makers were privy to the truth about the alleged misrepresentation and thus the market price would not have been affected by the misrepresentation. Is this really rebutting the presumption or is this another way of saying that the fraud would not have been material?

Plaintiffs often argue that because the Supreme Court asked "who would knowingly roll the dice in a crooked crap game," the rebuttal proof must be proof that the plaintiff would have made the purchase even if it had known about the fraud. That is certainly one way to rebut the presumption (*Stark Trading v. Falconbridge*, 552 F.3d 568 (7th Cir. 2009) (affirming dismissal because plaintiffs believed that defendants' public statements were misleading and purchased shares for the purpose of bringing a securities fraud suit)). But *Basic* would also permit rebutting the presumption by a showing that a plaintiff did not rely on the integrity of the market price. *Basic* presumed that "an investor who buys or sells stock at the price set by the market does so in reliance on the integrity of that price."[17] But what does "integrity of the market" mean? Does it mean that there is no fraud? Or does it mean that the plaintiffs did not care whether or not there was fraud?

That was the situation in *GAMCO Investors v. Vivendi SA*, 927 F. Supp. 2d 88 (S.D.N.Y. 2013), *aff'd* 838 F.3d 214 (2d Cir. 2016). The Second Circuit affirmed the district court's judgment in favor of defendant Vivendi on the complaint of plaintiff Gabelli Asset Management Corporation (GAMCO) that Vivendi had engaged in securities fraud. The district court had found that GAMCO did not necessarily regard the market price to be a true reflection of the objective value of the Vivendi stock, but made it clear that its decision was not based on that fact alone but rather on the evidence that even if plaintiffs had "known of the alleged misrepresentation, they would still have purchased the stock." Although the Second Circuit noted that it seemed unlikely that an investor, aware of fraud, would opt to purchase a given security, "the record at the trial simply does not establish that it was clearly erroneous for the district court to find that GAMCO, had it known of the liquidity problems at Vivendi,

---

[17] *See Harcourt Brace Jovanovich Sec. Litig.*, 838 F. Supp. 109 (S.D.N.Y. 1993) ("It is axiomatic under *Basic* that non-reliance on the integrity of the market is critical in rebutting the presumption of reliance in a fraud on the market case.").

would have made the choice to buy the same securities it purchased." This case is one of the few successfully to rebut the presumption of reliance.

It may also be possible to rebut the presumption by showing that it was unreasonable for a plaintiff to have relied on a defendant's misstatements, particularly if the investor is sophisticated. A sophisticated investor has a heightened standard of diligence and does not reasonably rely on a misrepresentation if the investor should have discovered the truth through "minimal diligence." *Cromer Fin Ltd v. Berger*, 137 F. Supp. 2d 452 (S.D.N.Y. 2001), quoting *Brown v. E.F. Hutton*, 991 F.2d 1020 (2d Cir. 1993).

Reliance must be "justifiable" or "reasonable." Even though this is an objective standard, many courts will consider the plaintiff's sophistication and access to information. *See, e.g.*, *Olkey v. Hyperion*, 98 F.3d 2 (2d Cir. 1996) (no reasonable reliance where oral statement is contradicted by a prospectus).

"Truth on the Market" Defense

If the market already has adequate information from other sources, then the alleged misrepresentation may be immaterial. Under *Basic*, the information must "credibly enter the market." In *In re Apple Securities Litigation*, 886 F.2d 1109 (9th Cir. 1989), the plaintiffs alleged misleading statements about Twiggy (a disk drive) and Lisa (a computer). The court said that the press portrayed Lisa as a gamble and at least twenty articles stressed the risk that Apple was taking. "The market could not have been made more aware of Lisa's risk." However, the court circumscribed its holding: "We stress the limits of our holding. Scrutiny by the press will not ordinarily excuse the type of unqualified exuberance expressed by Apple and its officers in this case. Even in a fraud on the market case, corporate insiders are not relieved of their duty to disclose material information where that information has received only brief mention in a few poorly-circulated or lightly-regarded publications.... In order to avoid Rule 10b-5 liability, any material information which insiders fail to disclose must be transmitted to the public with a degree of intensity and credibility sufficient to effectively counter-balance any misleading impression created by the insiders' one-sided representations."[18]

Can "truth on the market" be raised on a motion to dismiss or does the factual nature of the inquiry preclude a motion to dismiss? *Halliburton II* says that lack of price impact (i.e., no materiality) can be raised in opposition to class certification. Does that suggest that "truth on the market" can also be raised at that time? The Second Circuit has said that "normally" it is premature to raise it on a motion to dismiss. "The defense is intensely fact specific and

---

[18] Full disclosure: I successfully represented one of the defendants in an appeal from the jury verdict in this case.

is rarely an appropriate basis for dismissing a § 10(b) complaint." *Ganino v. Citizens Utilities Co.*, 228 F.3d 154 (2d Cir. 2000). Summary judgment may be appropriate if no reasonable jury could conclude that the misconduct was material in the light of information in the market from all sources. *Rand v. Cullinet Software*, 847 F. Supp. 200 (D. Mass. 1994).

The Maintenance Theory

If there is no price reaction when the false statement is made, it may be because the statement is immaterial. *In re Merck & Co. Inc. Securities Litigation*, 432 F.3d. 261 (3d Cir. 2005). But be careful. We are talking about inflation, not just price. In theory, there could be an increase or decrease in inflation even if there is no change in the price. Does this ever happen? It is theoretically possible but almost impossible to prove. It might occur when the market as a whole goes down and the price at issue remains the same.

The Supreme Court suggested in *Dura* that the effect of a misrepresentation may dissipate over time even if there is no corrective disclosure. In the oral argument of *Halliburton II*, several Justices suggested that if the misrepresentation did not have a price impact, then it was not material and the presumption would be rebutted. The *Halliburton II* majority opinion says so explicitly. In fact, that opinion says more than ten times that price impact is an essential requirement of a Section 10(b) action for misrepresentation. After *Goldman Sachs*, that may no longer be the law.

Can it be argued that although the misrepresentation had no price impact, it could still be actionable if it merely "maintained" the inflation? This is a very big issue in current securities litigation. Professors Hillary Sale and Robert Thompson of Georgetown Law have written that although the Supreme Court seemed to say in *Erica P. John Fund v. Halliburton*, 131 S. Ct. 2179 (2011) (*Halliburton I*), that if a misrepresentation did not affect the market price, an investor could not be said to have relied on the misrepresentation merely because he purchased at that price, that rendition "leaves room for price impact in the form of price support, or propping up a price, to be distinguished from moving the price up or down ... the lack of movement may be price impact in the form of price maintenance." They went on to say that *Halliburton II*'s discussion of price impact "is problematic unless it is reframed to include price stabilization."[19]

---

[19] Hilary Sale & Robert Thompson, "Market Intermediation, Publicness and Securities Class Actions," 93 *Wash. U. L. Rev.* 487 (2015). *See also* Jill Fisch, "The Trouble With *Basic* Price Distortion After *Halliburton*," U. Penn Law School Scholarship Repository, 2013 ("the failure of market prices to move in response to a misrepresentation does not establish the absence of a price distortion, particularly in cases

In *Glickenhaus & Co. v. Household Int'l*, 787 F.3d 408 (7th Cir. 2015), the Seventh Circuit suggested that a false statement that prevents a stock price from falling could nevertheless be actionable. The court said it was not directly measuring the inflation caused by the false statements but "the value of the truth" when discovered.[20] However, if *Halliburton II* is to be taken at face value, there must be evidence of price impact. Is such evidence at the time of a corrective disclosure sufficient? That question has not been settled, although the Eleventh Circuit has said yes.

In *In re Pfizer Inc. Securities Litigation*, 819 F.3d 642 (2d Cir. 2016), the Second Circuit reversed a district court's ruling that University of Chicago Law Professor Daniel Fischel could not offer expert testimony concerning his theory that repeated false messages to the market (concerning the risks of taking Celebrex) merely "served to maintain Pfizer's stock price at a constant inflated level" even if he did not offer any opinion as to who was responsible for the inflation at the start of the class period. The Second Circuit found that the exclusion was an abuse of discretion, but the court went on to say "To be clear, we do not decide in this appeal that Plaintiff's theory is either legally or factually sustainable. It might be that Plaintiffs' inflation-maintenance theory is deficient under Rule 10b-5." Apparently that issue was not raised in the district court, and that is why the court of appeals declined to decide it.

As noted above, in *Goldman Sachs Group, Inc. v. Arkansas Teacher Retirement System*, the Supreme Court declined to decide whether the inflation maintenance theory was valid. "We need not and do not do so in this case."

Loss Causation

The Private Securities Litigation Reform Act (PSLRA) requires the private plaintiff (but not the SEC) to prove that the fraud caused an economic loss. This is different from transaction causation. Loss causation is the "causal link between the alleged misconduct and the economic harm ultimately suffered by the plaintiff." *Emergent Capital v. Stonepath Group*, 343 F.3d 189 (2d Cir. 2013).

The requirement for loss causation is codified in the PSLRA: "The plaintiff shall have the burden of proving that that act or omission of the defendant alleged to violate this chapter caused the loss for which the plaintiff seeks

---

when the misstatement fraudulently conceals a change in status quo"). Note that this was written before *Halliburton II*. Should that change her conclusion?

[20] *See also Schleicher v. Wendt*, 618 F.3d 679 (7th Cir. 2010); *FindWhat Investor Group v. FindWhat.com*, 658 F.3d 1282, 1314 (11th Cir. 2011); *Castillo v. Envoy Corp.*, 206 F.R.D. 464 (M.D. Tenn. 2002); and *In re Bristol-Myers Squibb Sec. Litig.*, 2005 WL 2007 004 (D.N.J. Aug. 17, 2005).

to recover damages." Basically, loss causation is proven by showing that the price of a stock was "inflated" by the false statement, that is, that the price was higher than it would have been without the false statement, and that it declined once the truth had been revealed. But it is very difficult to know how much inflation is actually caused by a false statement and for that reason, courts look to see what happens to the stock price when the truth is finally revealed.[21] Those who purchase the stock during the period of inflation and either hold it or sell it after the fraud is revealed and the price drops, have incurred the loss caused by the price drop.

The *Glickenhaus* case posits that there are two types of inflation: "actual inflation"—the difference between the stock price and what the price would have been if the truth had been known, and "fraud-induced inflation"—the difference between the stock price and what the price would have been if the defendant had spoken truthfully. Does this make sense? Is there really a difference? There does not appear to be any.

The opinion also dealt with the subject discussed above, maintenance of the inflation: "Note too that a stock can be inflated even if the price remains the same or declines after a false statement because the price might have fallen even more.... So the movement of a stock price immediately after a false statement often tells us very little about how much inflation a false statement caused.... The best way to determine the impact of a false statement is to observe what happens when the truth is finally disclosed and use that to work backward, on the assumption that the lie's positive effect on the share price is equal to the additive inverse of the truth's negative effect." This is a complex way of describing the "constant ribbon" of inflation. Is this description consistent with *Halliburton II*?

The issue of price inflation caused by a false or misleading statement and maintenance of that inflation either by silence or by statements that are not in themselves false or misleading but that do not disclose the falsity of earlier statements continued to plague the courts after *Halliburton II*. *Glickenhaus* suggested that a false statement that merely maintained inflation by preventing a stock price from falling could nevertheless be actionable. *In re Vivendi Securities Litigation*, 833 F.3d 223 (2d Cir. 2016), went even further, and held that once inflation is in the stock price, even if the inflation got into the price not because of a fraudulent statement but "because the market arrived at a misconception on its own," the defendant would nevertheless be liable if its

---

[21] *See generally Glickenhaus & Co. v. Household Int'l*, 787 F.3d 408 (7th Cir. 2015) ("It's very difficult to know exactly how much stock-price inflation a false statement causes because it requires knowing a counterfactual: what the price would have been without the false statement.").

subsequent statements, although not false, served to prevent the inflation from dissipating by not speaking the whole truth. The court wrote that:

> [F]ramed as such, it becomes clear that, once a company chooses to speak, the proper question for purposes of our inquiry into price impact is not what might have happened had a company remained silent, but what would have happened if it had spoken *truthfully*. . . . [A] statement may cause inflation not simply by *adding* it to a stock, but by maintaining it.

In other words, allegedly false or misleading statements can have a price impact even if there were no change in the price of the stock. "Put differently, we agree with the Seventh and Eighth Circuits that securities-fraud defendants cannot avoid liability for an alleged misstatement merely because the misstatement is not associated with an uptick in inflation."[22] But where does the obligation to speak at all rather than remaining silent come from? The Second Circuit did not say.

Two leading cases from Second Circuit are *Waggoner*, 875 F.3d 79 (2d Cir. 2017), and *Goldman Sachs*, 594 U.S. ___ (2021). They both presented issues relating to price impact, in particular, the burden of proof of the defendant who challenges the lack of price impact caused by an alleged misrepresentation and the appropriate time to make that claim. In the *Goldman Sachs* case, the Supreme Court has now answered that question; the defendant has the burden of proving lack of price impact by a preponderance of the evidence at the class certification stage.

As noted above, there is a split in the circuits with respect to the viability of the so-called "inflation-maintenance" theory. The Seventh and Eleventh Circuits seem to have allowed that theory to be maintained but have not discussed how the presumption of reliance could be rebutted in such cases. *FindWhat Inv'r Grp. v. FindWhat.com*, 658 F.3d 1282, 1314 (11th Cir. 2011); *Schleicher v. Wendt*, 618 F.3d 679 (7th Cir. 2010). In *In re Pfizer Securities Litigation*, 819 F.3d 642 (2d Cir. 2016) (later settled), the court held that the district court abused its discretion when it precluded testimony from plaintiff's expert witness (Professor Fischel) but stressed that it was not ruling that the price-maintenance theory was legally or factually sustainable. "It might be that Plaintiffs' inflation-maintenance theory is deficient under Rule 10b-5."

---

[22] Full disclosure: I was one of the lead counsel for Vivendi in *In re Vivendi Securities Litigation*.

As discussed above, *Glickenhaus* (Seventh Circuit) and *Vivendi* (Second Circuit) have endorsed the price maintenance theory.[23] This issue is far from decided, however, especially since in the *Goldman Sachs* case the Supreme Court explicitly declined to approve or validate that theory.

The Fraud Must Be a "Substantial Contributing Cause of the Loss"

This is the holding of *Miller v. Asensio & Co.*, 364 F.3d 23 (4th Cir. 2004), and *Huddleston v. Herman & MacLean*, 640 F.2d 534 (5th Cir. 1981), *aff'd in part, Herman & MacLean v. Huddleston*, 103 S. Ct. 683 (1983); *but see Katyle v. Penn National Gaming, Inc.*, 637 F.3d 462 (4th Cir. 2011) (misrepresentation must be "one substantial cause" of the decline in value).

Loss causation cannot be established by proof that the fraud caused plaintiffs to buy the shares. That is "transaction causation." *See McGonigle v. Combs*, 968 F.2d 810 (9th Cir. 1992). And the loss must be "a foreseeable consequence of any misrepresentation or material omission." *Emergent Capital Inc. v. Stonepath Group*, 343 F.3d 189 (2d Cir. 2003). "The securities plaintiff must demonstrate a causal connection between the contents of the alleged misstatements or omissions and the harm actually suffered." That is typically done by proof that the purchase of stock was made after the fraud, when the price was inflated, and that the loss occurred after the corrective disclosure eliminated the inflation, resulting in a loss.

A classic example: There is a misrepresentation relating to the capacity of a vessel, but true statements about the non-availability of insurance. The vessel sinks; the stock is worthless because there is no insurance. There is a loss but it was not caused by the misrepresentation.

The leading case on loss causation is *Dura Pharmaceuticals v. Broudo*, 544 U.S. 336 (2005). That case held that the plaintiff must allege more than price inflation; there must be a subsequent decline in price when the facts became generally known and that decline must be proximately caused by the fraud. This is similar to common law fraud. But recall that the Supreme Court has said that "Section 10(b) does not incorporate common-law fraud into federal law," *Stoneridge*, 552 U.S. 148 (2008) (quoting *SEC v. Zandford*, 535 U.S. 813 (2002)).

What if the price rises after disclosure? Does the price increase negate loss causation? *Acticon v. China North East Petroleum Holdings Ltd.*, 692 F.3d 34 (2d Cir. 2012), held that a price rise after a fall resulting from corrective

---

[23] In the *Vivendi* case, the price maintenance theory was raised for the first time in the plaintiffs' closing argument. No expert economist mentioned the theory during the trial.

disclosure does not defeat a securities fraud claim at the pleading stage. But what about the proof stage? It depends on why the stock went up. Is there an actual out-of-pocket loss? Section 28 of the 1934 Act requires "actual damages." There is apparently no case in which this issue was actually considered in a trial on the merits.

How Do You Prove Loss Causation?

Loss causation is typically proved through an event study prepared by an economist. An event study is a statistical regression analysis that provides one way of examining the effect of an event, such as the disclosure of information, on the market price of a security. Its primary purpose is to determine whether a particular event is associated with a significant change in price. Specifically, it attempts to link the fraud and the corrective disclosure to price change.[24] In *Halliburton II*, the Supreme Court explicitly contemplated the use of event studies by defendants in class certification to rebut the presumption of reliance.

The steps in preparing an event study are as follows:

- Identify the event, usually the fraudulent public statement.
- Establish an event window for the purpose of measuring the effect of the event on the market price (some events may not affect the market price on the same day as the event but may do so on the following day).
- Establish a period of time with which to compare the event window to the stock in question's normal price fluctuations, or "volatility" so that they can be "controlled" during the regression analysis.
- Determine a method to calculate the "normal" or "expected" price change, called a "return," for the defendant company over the event window (the difference between the expected return and the actual return is called the "residual return").
- Estimate the return for the market as a whole.
- Estimate the returns for comparable companies.
- Run a regression model to isolate the firm-specific stock price return (the percentage daily price change) after controlling for effects of the market, the firm's industry and if appropriate, other non-firm-specific factors.
- Conduct a statistical test to determine whether the residual firm-specific return is significantly different from zero on the date

[24] *See* Jay Eisenhofer & James Banko, "Securities Fraud, Stock Price Valuation and Loss Causation," 59 *Bus. Law.* 1419 (2004).

of the event. If the information released on the event day is value-relevant to an investor, the residual return should be statistically significantly different from zero.

- Ensure that the observed return is not the result of normal fluctuations (the observed return should be sufficiently large that this occurs only a small percentage of the time).[25]

"[B]y comparing the predicted return with the actual return on the date of release of the supposedly correct information or immediately thereafter, the [event study] attempts to isolate the change in return earned by investors that is attributable solely to the allegedly withheld or false information." *In re Pfizer Securities Litigation*, 819 F.3d 642 (2d Cir. 2016). As noted, the difference between the two is called the "residual return." The sum of the residual returns associated with the corrective disclosures should, at least in theory, represent the amount of inflation caused by the fraud.[26]

One issue that those who conduct event studies have encountered is multiple company events on the same day as the suspected fraud. To separate the effects of different events on the same day on the firm's stock price, economists often use sophisticated econometric tools, but nevertheless this is a challenge that defendants can be expected to exploit.

Some have argued that requiring event studies is inconsistent with the Seventh Amendment because it "removes quintessential factual determination from the jury" and "allows the judge to usurp the jury's power to assess otherwise reliable expert analyses in reaching its factual determination."[27] Others have argued that while there are judicial statistical and logical limitations on the use of event studies, they remain "an indispensable tool for ensuring that investor losses are truly the result of fraud."[28]

What does the event study show?

- Fraud is typically revealed by a corrective disclosure that typically is accompanied by a price decline.
- But the so-called "leakage theory" posits that there are no explicit corrective disclosures but that the truth gradually "leaked" into

[25] Pavitra Kumar & Torben Voetmann, "Correct Application of Event Studies in Securities Litigation" (2021), https://www.eventstudytools.com/litigation.

[26] *See* Frederick C. Dunbar & Arun Sen, "Counterfactual Keys to Causation and Damages in Shareholder Class Action Litigation," 2009 *Wis. L. Rev.* 199 (2009).

[27] Michael J. Kaufman, "Regressing: The Troubling Dispositive Role of Event Studies in Securities Fraud Litigation," 15 *Stanford J. L. Bus. Fin.* 1 (2010).

[28] Martis Alex & Michael Stocker, "Role of the Event Study in Loss Causation Analysis," *New York Law Journal*, August 20, 2009.

the market. *Dura* suggests that the truth can leak out over time.[29] Not all courts accept this theory. Should they? It is very difficult for an event study to deal with the "leakage" theory.
- The event study will, at least in theory, distinguish between fraud and non-fraud events. But disaggregation is very difficult to do and there is no scientific way to do it. *Glickenhaus*: "It may be very difficult, if not impossible, for any statistical model to do this."
- Statistical significance must be shown, usually at the 0.05 level.

Because volatility of a stock price can affect the statistical likelihood that a stock price will reach a certain level purely by chance (because a highly volatile stock will be more likely to do so) an event study is typically based on an assumption that the volatility of the stock price during the class period under consideration was the same as during a preceding period during which there was no alleged fraud (sometimes called a "control period.") Columbia Law Professor Ronald Gilson, Michigan Law Professor Edward Fox, and Columbia Law Professor Merrit Fox have recently demonstrated that if there is a "crisis-induced increase in idiosyncratic volatility," the assumption with respect to volatility during the class period may not be correct ("it fails radically") and that as a result, "securities fraud actions succeed when they should not."[30]

"Materialization of Undisclosed Risk" Theory

The leading case for this theory of loss causation is the Second Circuit's opinion in *Lentell v. Merrill Lynch*, 396 F.3d 161 (2d Cir. 2005). The case was one of 140 class actions filed after the New York Attorney General revealed an investigation of Merrill Lynch for making only "buy" or "accumulate" recommendations for stocks with respect to which it was also acting as an investment banker. The district court dismissed the complaint for failure to allege loss causation. The Second Circuit affirmed, but articulated the "materialization" theory.

Citing Judge Winter's dissent in *AUSA Life Insurance v. Ernst & Young*, 206 F.3d 202 (2d Cir. 2000), the Second Circuit said that a misstatement or omission is the proximate cause of an investment loss "if the risk that caused the loss was within the zone of risk concealed by the misrepresentations or omissions alleged by a disappointed investor."

---

[29] *See also Glickenhaus & Co. v. Household Int'l*, 787 F.3d 408 (7th Cir. 2015), and *In re Flag Telecom Holding Ltd. Sec. Litig.*, 574 F.3d 29, 40-41 n.5 (2d Cir. 2009).

[30] Edward Fox, Merrit Fox & Ronald Gilson, *Economic Crisis and the Integration of Law and Finance: The Impact of Volatility Spikes*, 116 *Colum. L. Rev.* 325, 358 (2016).

The court also quoted *Castellano v. Young & Rubicam*, 257 F.3d 171, 188 (2d Cir. 2001), and said, "If the significance of the truth is such as to cause a reasonable investor to consider seriously a zone of risk that would be perceived as remote or highly unlikely by one believing the fraud, and the loss ultimately suffered is within that zone, then a misrepresentation or omission as to that information may be deemed a foreseeable or proximate cause of the loss." Do you find this language satisfactory or opaque? What is a "zone of risk"? Is this a jury question?

What must materialize? Is it the same risk that was hidden? Isn't it the case that for every bad thing that happens to a company, there is a risk that it would happen, however remote? If that is true, how do you prove that the "zone of risk would be perceived as remote or unlikely by one believing the fraud"? How could a jury be instructed to decide that question?

The court held that there were no allegations that the market reacted negatively to a corrective disclosure regarding the falsity of Merrill's "buy" recommendations or that Merrill misstated or omitted risks that did lead to a loss. It was not enough to allege that there was a disparity between the transaction price and the true "investment quality" of the stocks in question. The analysts' reports were full of risk assessments suggesting that the stocks were volatile and subject to substantial devaluation risk.

Take "liquidity risk" as an example. Isn't every company susceptible to a liquidity risk even if it is not revealed? If there is a "liquidity crisis" a year later, how do you know that it was the materialization of the risk that was hidden? Is that the right question? What if there are intervening events? What is a "liquidity crisis"? Is it a failure to pay bills when due? At least one expert, Economist Dr. Blaine Nye, has said so.[31] *In Vivendi S.A., Securities Litigation* (S.D.N.Y.) Trial Tr. Dec. 2009. Or is it merely the possibility that bills may not be paid?

The Second Circuit in *Vivendi* visited the loss causation issue and more particularly the question whether loss causation required that the allegedly false or misleading statements themselves, as opposed to the "underlying circumstance that is concealed or misstated," caused the loss. The Second Circuit chose the latter formulation. Quoting *Lentell* and its discussion of the "materialization of the risk" concealed by the defendant's conduct, the Second Circuit held that it was irrelevant to the theory that the undisclosed risk never actually materialized. "[I]t is enough that the loss caused by the alleged fraud results from the 'relevant truth ... leak[ing] out" (citing and quoting *Dura Pharmaceuticals v. Broudo*, 544 U.S. 336 (2005)). *Lentell* held that the materialization of the risk theory was based on the fact that a misstatement

[31] If that name sounds familiar, it should. While in graduate school, Dr. Nye was also an offensive lineman for the Dallas Cowboys football team.

or omission concealed *something* (the court's emphasis) from the market that when disclosed, negatively affected the value of the security.

The *Vivendi* court held that "corrective disclosure" and "materialization of risk" are not distinct theories and that liability may ensue even if the thing concealed "never ripens from a mere risk to an out-and-out disaster—unless a specific corrective disclosure issues." Is it the risk—or the failure to disclose the risk—that causes stockholders to lose money even if the risk never materializes? "[E]vidence presented at trial ... revealed the truth about Vivendi's liquidity risk, and that concealment of 'the *subject*' of Vivendi's alleged misstatements (emphasis in original)—its liquidity risk—was therefore the 'cause of the actual loss suffered' by Plaintiffs."

In other words, the undisclosed risk does not actually have to materialize in order for there to be liability or loss causation. It is sufficient if the undisclosed risk at some point becomes disclosed. Do you find this theory acceptable? It has not yet been endorsed by any other courts.

In fact, not all circuits recognize "materialization of an undisclosed risk" as a basis for proving liability or loss causation. For example, the Ninth Circuit does not. *See Metzler v. Corinthian Colleges*, 540 F.3d 1049 (9th Cir. 2008), and *In re Oracle Securities Litigation*, 2010 WL 4608794 (9th Cir. Nov. 16, 2010) (loss causation cannot be proved by the "impact" of the fraud but only by the market's reaction to the "fraudulent acts themselves"). However, in *Nuveen v. City of Alameda*, 2013 WL 5273097 (9th Cir. Sept. 19, 2013), the Ninth Circuit seemed to recognize the theory as "well established" and quoted from *Lentell.*

If there is no corrective disclosure, can there be loss causation? Yes, under this theory because the "materialization of the risk" takes the place of the corrective disclosure. See *In re Parmalat Securities Litigation,* 377 F. Supp. 2d 390 (S.D.N.Y. 2005), in which disclosure of a bond default was held to be the materialization of the alleged fraudulent scheme. See also *In re Scottish Re Group Securities Litigation*, 524 F. Supp. 2d 370 (S.D.N.Y. 2007), in which a stock price decline following disclosure of accounting problems was held to be the materialization of the risk from concealed internal control deficiencies.

The "materialization" theory was not sufficient to prove liability in *In re Omnicom Securities Litigation*, 597 F.3d 501 (2d Cir. 2010). In that case, a *Wall Street Journal* article in 2002 discussed accounting and disclosure practices at Omnicom (global marketing and advertising company). The article also discussed the resignation of Ronald J. Callender, an Omnicom outside director and chair of its audit committee. In 2001, after the internet bubble burst, Omnicom created Seneca Investments to hold its internet marketing and advertising companies. Media suggested that was done to get the companies off Omnicom's books but those reports did not cause a drop in stock price. But the day after the *Wall Street Journal* article, the stock dropped 20 percent. The complaint alleged that Omnicom failed to write down the value of its internet companies prior to the creation of Seneca, that the accounting for the transaction was fraudulent, and that Omnicom should have accounted for Seneca's losses.

The district court granted summary judgment. The Second Circuit affirmed. None of the 2002 disclosures even purported to reveal some then-undisclosed fact with regard to the specific misrepresentations in the complaint. "A negative journalistic characterization of previously disclosed facts does not constitute a corrective disclosure of anything but the journalists' opinions." Plaintiff's argument that Callender's resignation was the result of the Senaca fraud was rejected because the underlying facts had been known for a year. To survive a motion in a "materialization" case, the plaintiffs must establish more than "a tenuous connection between the alleged misstatements or omissions and the subsequent materialization of the undisclosed risk." To hold otherwise "would undermine the very investor confidence that the securities laws were intended to support."

Note that in *In re Flag Telecom Holdings Ltd. Securities Litigation*, 574 F.3d 29 (2d Cir. 2009), the Second Circuit said that the Supreme Court's *Dura* decision, which came three months after *Lentell*, "reaffirmed the analysis we laid out in *Lentell*" relating to materialization of the concealed risk. That conclusion may put too much weight on *Dura* since the Second Circuit's theory is not mentioned in that case.

The "True Financial Condition" Theory

Some plaintiffs and courts have developed a theory that when the company's "true financial condition" is disclosed, that is sufficient for loss causation even if it does not directly reveal any prior misrepresentation. *See In re Daou Securities Litigation*, 2005 WL 237645 (9th Cir. 2005). However, in *Erica P. John Fund v. Halliburton*, 131 S. Ct. 2179 (2011) (*Halliburton I*), the Supreme Court restated the *Basic* presumption and the *Dura* test, which signaled the end of the "true financial condition" test:

> The fact that a stock's price on the date of purchase was inflated because of a misrepresentation does not necessarily mean that the misstatement is the cause of the later decline in value. We observed that the drop could instead be the result of other intervening causes, such as changed economic circumstances, changed investor expectations, new industry-specific or firm-specific facts, conditions or other events. If one of those factors were responsible for the loss or part of it, a plaintiff would not be able to prove loss causation to that extent. This is true even if the investor purchased the stock at a distorted price, and thereby presumptively relied on the misrepresentation reflected in that price.

Chapter 11

Section 10(b) of the Exchange Act and Rule 10b-5, Part Three; Section 14 and Section 18

Primary Liability

In *Janus Capital Group v. First Derivative Traders*, 131 S. Ct. 2296 (2011), the Supreme Court continued its efforts to restrict private actions under Section 10(b). "We must give 'narrow dimensions' to a right of action Congress did not authorize."

At issue was a misstatement in a prospectus issued by Janus Investment Fund (JIF), a mutual fund created by Janus Capital Group. JCG is a publicly traded company that created a family of mutual funds, organized in a family trust known as JIF. JCG also created Janus Capital Management (JCM), an investment adviser, which was retained by JIF to govern the "management and administrative services" necessary for JIF's operation. JIF and JCM maintained separate legal identities. JIF issued prospectuses for several of its funds that suggested that the funds were not suitable for "market timing," a statement that could be read to suggest that JCM would implement practices to curb the practice. Apparently, however, there were secret agreements that permitted several of the funds to engage in market timing. When the fraud was discovered, investors began to withdraw their investments from JIF. As a result, JCM, which received its compensation as a percentage of the assets under management, lost revenue. JCG also derived a large part of its income from JCM's management fees; the loss in JCM's revenues caused a sharp decline in the price of JCG's stock (approximately 25 percent).

The complaint alleged a violation of Rule 10b-5b, one of three subsections of Rule 10b-5, and the only subsection that prohibited the "making" of untrue statements of material fact. The other two subsections prohibited any person "to employ any device, scheme, or artifice to defraud" and "to engage in any act, practice or course of business which operates or would operate as a fraud or deceit upon any person. "Making" is clearly different from "employing" and "engaging."

The question at issue was "who made the false statements?" The claim was that JCG failed to reveal a breach of fiduciary duty to JIF investors. Plaintiff First Derivative Traders represented a class of shareholders of JCG who suffered losses. They alleged that JCG and JCM had "caused" the false prospectuses to be issued by JIF for the benefit of its investors and were liable to the JCG shareholders for a violation of Rule 10b-5. The district court dismissed the complaint but the Fourth Circuit reversed, finding that the complaint adequately alleged that JCG and JCM, by participating in the writing and dissemination of the prospectuses, "made" the misleading statements. The Supreme Court reversed, holding that only the entity with "ultimate authority" over a statement can be its "maker." The maker must have ultimate authority over the statement's content and how to communicate it.

How does one "make" a statement? According to Justice Thomas' majority opinion in *Janus*, one makes a statement "by stating it." "To make any statement," the court said, is the approximate equivalent of "to state." It does not mean "to create."

Janus has far-reaching implications. Entities that are legally separate from issuers cannot be primarily liable under Section 10(b). "We will not expand liability beyond the person or entity that ultimately has authority over a false statement."

Let's look at the language of Section 10(b) and Rule 10b-5. It is unlawful for "any person, directly or indirectly, to make any untrue statement of material fact" in connection with the purchase or sale of securities. Recall that under Section 10(b), there is no secondary liability unless all of the requirements for primary liability have been met. And there is no private right of action for aiding and abetting. So what does it mean "to make"? The Supreme Court said that *Oxford English Dictionary* rules of construction say that where the term is followed by the noun form of a verb, the statement is approximately equivalent to stating the verb. Thus, the phrase "to make" would be the functional equivalent of "to state." Therefore, whichever entity can be said to "state" the prospectus is the entity that made the misrepresentation.

Justice Thomas concluded therefore that only the entity with "ultimate authority" over the statement, including its content and whether and how to communicate it, is the "maker." Does that necessarily follow? Is control the same as attribution? A footnote in the opinion suggests that either explicit or implicit attribution is necessary to establish that an entity "made" a statement and that more than mere "authority" over the statement is required. But the Supreme Court said that "attribution within a statement or implicit from surrounding circumstances is strong evidence that the statement was made by—and only by—the party to whom it is attributed."

Counsel for defendants analogized this to the relationship between the U.S. president and a speechwriter. You wouldn't say that the speechwriter "made" the speech. The plaintiffs analogized it to a playwright and an actor. You wouldn't say that the actor wrote the play. There is a reason why certain corporate subsidiaries have separate legal entities. Was this the right instance to pierce the corporate veil? Was there any evidence that the corporation adopted this form in order to justify a wrong or protect a fraud? The dissent in *Janus* analogized it to a statement made by a cabinet member, over whom the U.S. president had ultimate authority.

What about Section 20(b)? This section provides that "[i]t is unlawful for any person, directly or indirectly, to do any act or thing which it would be unlawful for such a person to do under the provisions of this title or any rule or regulation thereunder through or by means of any other person." That section is ambiguous. The implied private right of action under Section 10(b) was intended to be and has been applied narrowly. The Supreme Court: "The inexorable broadening of the class of plaintiffs who may sue in this area of the law will ultimately result in more harm than good."

Congress did provide for liability for secondary actors who "control" primary actors, so Congress did intend to limit primary liability for secondary actors. But it has repeatedly refused to extend primary liability to those who "participate" in a statement or who "help to create" the statement.

What about the liability of a major corporate shareholder? In the Southern District of New York, two judges came to opposite conclusions. In *City of Roseville Employees Retirement System v. Energy Solutions*, 814 F. Supp. 2d 395 (S.D.N.Y. 2011), Judge John Koeltl held that a jury could find that a controlling shareholder could exercise control over the content of a message issued by a subsidiary and had the ultimate decision whether to communicate it. Two weeks later, Judge Shira Scheindlin held, in *In re Optimal U.S. Litigation*, 813 F. Supp. 2d 351 (S.D.N.Y. 2011), that the controlling shareholder was not liable because the board could issue the statement in question (a prospectus) without consulting the controlling shareholder. Which one is correct?

Is the *Janus* rule only about legally independent third parties? Lower courts have differed on that question. In *Glickenhaus & Co. v. Household Int'l*, 787 F.3d 408 (7th Cir. 2015), the Seventh Circuit held explicitly that "nothing in *Janus* limits its holding to legally independent third parties."[1]

[1] *See also, e.g.*, *In re UBS AG Sec. Litig.*, No. 07-cv-1125, 2012 WL 4471265, at *10 (S.D.N.Y. Sept. 28, 2012); *In re Banco Bradesco S.A. Sec. Litig.*, 2017 WL 4381407, at *26; *but see City of Pontiac Gen. Employees Ret. Sys. v. Lockheed Martin Corp.*, 875 F. Supp. 2d at 374 (explaining that *Janus* "addressed only whether *third parties* can be held liable for statements made by their clients"); *In re Merck*, 2011 WL 344199 (D.N.J. 2011).

How, other than attribution, can a person be found to have "made" a statement? One district court explained that "in the post-*Janus* world, an executive may be held accountable where the executive had ultimate authority over the company's statement; signed the company's statement; ratified and approved the company's statement; or where the statement is attributed to the executive." *In re Fannie Mae 2008 Sec. Litig.*, 891 F. Supp. 2d 458, 473 (S.D.N.Y. 2012).

Does *Janus* affect the liability of corporate insiders such as officers and management? Some courts have found that it does not limit their liability. For example, in *In re Merck & Co. Inc. Securities Litigation*, 432 F.3d 261 (3d Cir. 2005), the district court held that *Janus* only applied where there were separate legal entities and did not alter the well-known principle that a corporation can only act through its employees and agents. *Merck* confirmed liability for a company's most senior executives (there, an executive vice president) assuming sufficient attribution. However, a month later, in *Hawaii Ironworkers Annuity Trust Fund v. Cole*, 2011 WL 3862206 (N.D. Ohio Sept. 1, 2011), the district court in Ohio said that the only relevant inquiry was whether the defendants had ultimate authority over the false statements in question. The court said that the Supreme Court decision did not turn on the separate legal entities. It disagreed with the *Merck* rationale. Note that in *Merck*, the speaker was the executive vice president who regularly made statements authorized and on behalf of the corporation, whereas in *Hawaii Ironworkers*, the defendants were simply delivering information under the direction of senior management. Does this make a difference? *See also City of Pontiac Gen. Employees Ret. Sys. v. Lockheed Martin Corp.*, 875 F. Supp. 2d at 374 (*Janus* interpreted narrowly and held CFO was responsible for false statements in press release).

What does "ultimate authority" mean in a modern corporation? Georgetown Law Professor Donald Langevoort suggests three possibilities: the speaker, some other corporate official, or the knowledge of multiple actors, even if no single one knew the truth. Even if an officer prepares a statement, does he or she have "ultimate authority" over it? Would *Janus* lead to eliminating liability for corporate officers altogether? What if there is no explicit grant of authority? What if no individuals are defendants, only the corporate entity? Who has scienter? In *In re Vivendi Securities*, 765 F. Supp. 2d 512 (S.D.N.Y. 2011), the court held that a jury finding exculpating the speakers did not mean that the corporation could not have scienter for the very same statements.

Does "ultimate authority" mean something different from "control" under Section 20(a)? *Janus* uses the words synonymously. Who has "ultimate authority" over informal messages such as analysts, conference calls, and press interviews? *Merck* says it includes the managers who initiate the publicity and the issuer.

In May 2014, the Fourth Circuit held that *Janus* does not apply to criminal cases. *Prousalis v. Moore*, 751 F.3d 272 (4th Cir. 2014). There is a split in the Southern District of New York as to whether *Janus* should be applied to SEC enforcement actions under Section 17(a) of the 1933 Act. In *SEC v. Kelly*, 817 F. Supp. 2d 340 (S.D.N.Y. 2011), Judge Colleen McMahon held that it should because the elements of Section 17(a) are "essentially the same" as Rule 10b-5. She said that the SEC cannot impose primary liability under Rule 10b-5(a) and (c) for a scheme based on a false statement where the defendant did not "make" the statement, even if he facilitated preparation of the misleading material, lest *Janus* be rendered meaningless. But in *SEC v. Pentagon Capital Management*, 844 F. Supp. 2d 377 (S.D.N.Y. 2012), Judge Robert Sweet held that it should not, because the word "make" does not appear in Section 17(a). He stressed the distinction between public and private actions. There is a circuit split but most courts say there is *no* private right of action under Section 17(a). See also *SEC v. Garber*, 2013 WL 1732571 (S.D.N.Y. 2013), in which Judge Scheindlin held that even if *Janus* applied, the "making" of statements in opinion letters could be attributed to those who solicited them and had "ultimate authority" over how to communicate them. Given that the Private Securities Litigation Reform Act (PSLRA) established a scheme of proportionate liability, does that presuppose that several persons can "make" a false statement?

Post-*Janus* Issues

After *Janus*, the SEC began adding claims of aiding and abetting and control person liability to its cases. Note that there is no "scheme liability" for just making misrepresentations that do not qualify under *Janus*. Consider Section 17(a)(1) of the Securities Act ("employing any device, scheme or artifice to defraud"). This requires proof of scienter. There is an open question whether *Janus* applies to such claims. *SEC v. Garber*, 2013 WL 1732571, seems to suggest that it does not apply to such claims. *But see SEC v. Kelly*, 817 F. Supp. 2d 340. And the structure of *Janus* seemed to be focused on private rights of action, not SEC cases.

In *Lorenzo v. SEC*, 139 S. Ct. 1094 (2019), the Supreme Court held that under certain circumstances, a person who does not "make" a misstatement may nonetheless be held primarily liable under the antifraud provisions of the 1933 Act, the 1934 Act, and the related SEC rules. In that case, Francis Lorenzo, an investment banker, sent emails under his own name to two clients that were "staggeringly false." He was charged with violating Rules 10b-5(a), (b), and (c). His defense, under *Janus*, was that he was not the maker of the statements because his supervisor directed him to send the emails. An SEC Administrative Law Judge held that Lorenzo had willfully or at least recklessly violated the 1933 and 1934 Acts and various SEC rules and imposed penalties. The SEC upheld the administrative law judge. On appeal, the U.S. Court of Appeals for the District of Columbia Circuit reversed the SEC's finding that Lorenzo violated Rule 10b-5(b), based on its conclusion that he was not the "maker" of the statement. But the court affirmed the SEC's other finding that Lorenzo violated Rules 10b-5(a) and (c) as well as Section 17(a)(1) since those rules do not speak in terms of "making" false statements. The dissent by now-Justice Brett Kavanaugh argued that those findings should also be set aside since the SEC had merely "repackaged" a fraudulent statement claim as a fraudulent scheme claim. The dissent argued that the majority's opinion constituted an "end run" around *Janus*, creating a split in the circuits, with only the D.C. and Eleventh Circuits holding that a misstatement *alone* can be the basis of a fraudulent scheme claim.

The grant of certiorari asked, somewhat argumentatively, whether "a misstatement claim that does not meet the elements set forth in *Janus* ... can be repackaged and pursued as a fraudulent scheme claim."

The Supreme Court, with Justice Kavanaugh recusing himself, answered that it could, and reversed the D.C. Circuit and held by 6-2 vote that the dissemination of materially misleading false statements with fraudulent intent constitutes a "device, scheme or artifice to defraud" even if it does not violate the "making false statements" provision. This is so, the Supreme Court said, since there is considerable overlap among subsections of the Rule, and since Rules 10b-5(a) and (c) speak of "devices," "schemes," and "artifices" to defraud, and since the 10(b) "making false statements" provision is not the only section that applies when the fraud occurs by means of a misstatement. Thus, a defendant *can* be held liable for false statements that they themselves did not "make" so long as the misstatement also constitutes a "device, scheme or artifice to defraud." Justice Thomas nevertheless opined that *Lorenzo* "eviscerates" *Janus* and renders it a "dead letter." Whether that is true, we can expect *Janus* cases to diminish and defendants to turn their attention to allegations of "scheme liability."

Aiding and Abetting

Aiding and abetting liability exists for those who render "substantial assistance" to a primary violator both in Section 15 of the 1933 Act and in Section 20(a) of the 1934 Act. Generally, courts have looked to the common law tort and criminal law concepts of aiding and abetting to understand how they would apply to the securities laws. Under those laws, there are three requirements: another party committed a violation of the law, the accused aider had a general awareness that the participation was part of an overall activity that was improper, and the accused aider assisted in the violation knowingly and substantially.[2]

The Supreme Court was never very enthusiastic about enforcing aiding and abetting liability. In *Ernst & Ernst v. Hochfelder*, 425 U.S. 185 (1976), the Court said that it need not consider whether civil liability for aiding and abetting is appropriate under Section 10(b) since a specific intent to defraud was required by that law.

Nevertheless, prior to *Central Bank of Denver v. First Interstate Bank of Denver*, 114 S. Ct. 1439 (1994), those who were not primary violators could still be held secondarily liable as aiders and abettors if they knew about the fraud and provided substantial assistance. And prior to the PSLRA, there was joint and several liability. However, in 1981, Professor Daniel Fischel suggested that there should be no aiding and abetting liability and, in *Central Bank*, citing Fischel, the Supreme Court held that there is no private right of action for aiding and abetting (although the SEC can still bring aiding and abetting cases, after the PSLRA).[3] Before the PSLRA, there was some reason to believe that the *Central Bank* prohibition applied to the SEC as well. But Section 20(e) of the 1934 Act (added by PSLRA and amended by Dodd-Frank) affirmed the SEC's right to sue aiders and abettors and added liability for any person who "knowingly *or recklessly*" gave substantial assistance to another person in violation of the Exchange Act. The SEC can also bring such cases under the 1933 Act. The Supreme Court clearly signaled that it would not create any more implied private rights of action than those that have already been recognized. That was reaffirmed in *Stoneridge v. Scientific Atlanta*, 552 U.S. 148 (2008): "The decision to extend the cause of action is for Congress, not us. Though it remains the law, the Section 10(b) private right of action should not be extended beyond its present boundaries."

Lower courts have continued to struggle with the imposition of aiding and abetting liability in a private action. For example, in *Klein v. Boyd*, 1998 U.S. App. LEXIS 2004 (3d Cir.), vacated, rehearing granted, 1998 U.S. App. LEXIS 4121 (3d Cir. 1998), the full U.S. Court of Appeals for the Third Circuit vacated a panel decision that imposed aiding and abetting liability on secondary actors (here, a law firm) that participated in the misrepresentation to such a degree that they could be considered "co-actors" facing primary liability under Section 10(b). But the case was settled before the full hearing could be held.

---

[2] Ralph Ferrara & Diane Sanger, "Derivative Liability in Securities Law: Controlling Person Liability, Respondeat Superior, and Aiding and Abetting," 40 *Wash. & Lee L. Rev.* 1007 (1983).

[3] Daniel Fischel, "Secondary Liability Under Section 10(b) of the Securities Act of 1934," 69 *Cal. L. Rev.* 96 (1981).

Secondary Liability

There is secondary liability under Section 15 of the Securities Act and Section 20(a) of the Exchange Act for those persons who "control" a person who is primarily liable. Section 20(a) provides, for example, that "[e]very person who directly or indirectly controls any person liable under any provision of this Act or any rule or regulation thereunder shall also be liable jointly and severally with and to the same extent as such controlled person to any person to whom the controlled person is liable, unless the controlling person acted in good faith and did not directly or indirectly induce the act or acts constituting the violation or cause of action." The plaintiff does not have to prove controlling person's scienter. There can be no secondary liability without primary liability. "Control" is not defined in the statute but the SEC has defined it as "possession, direct or indirect, of the power to direct or cause the direction of the management and policies of a corporation." *SEC Registration General Requirements*, 17 C.F.R. § 230.405.

Respondeat Superior Liability

This classic liability for corporate defendants is based on the common law of agency doctrine of *respondeat superior* in which a principal is responsible for the acts of an agent within the scope of his or her authority, and a master is responsible for the acts of a servant within the scope of his or her employment. There has been a general principle that courts may look to the common law doctrines, such as *respondeat superior*, when necessary to enforce federally created rights if necessary to carry out the policies contained in the federal statutes creating those rights. When applied to the securities laws, a corporation is liable for the acts of a corporate official who makes a false statement with scienter within the scope of his or her employment. One of the reasons why *respondeat superior* liability is rarely seen is because that definition is limited to liability for the "employer" whereas Sections 15 and 20(a) are broader. In addition, there is a question as to whether scienter is required in order to invoke *respondeat superior* in a securities case even though in common law, *respondeat superior* resulted in strict liability, without the defenses of good faith or due diligence being available. In 1981, the SEC argued in an amicus brief that the statutory defenses set forth in Sections 15 and 20(a) should be available in a case alleging *respondeat superior* liability, but courts remain split on the issue.[4] At least one

---

[4] Brief of the SEC, *amicus curiae, Sharp v. Coopers & Lybrand*, 649 F.2d 175 (3d Cir. 1981), *cert. denied*, 455 U.S. 938 (1982).

court has held that the secondary liability contained in Sections 15 and 20(a) are in addition to the remedies that are available under the common law.[5]

Even though common law *respondeat superior* liability was strict liability, courts that have applied it to securities cases have generally required proof of scienter. Scienter under *respondeat superior* is established by looking "to the state of mind of the individual corporate official or officials who make or issue the statement." *Southland Sec. Corp. v. INSpire Ins. Solutions Inc.*, 365 F.3d 353 (5th Cir. 2004). Courts have held that if agency principles were not meant to be a viable basis for liability under Section 10(b), then the text of that section would have to be modified to include the phrase "natural persons." *See In re Centennial Techs. Litig.*, 52 F. Supp. 2d 178 (D. Mass. 1999). Does *respondeat superior* survive *Central Bank*? The dissent in *Central Bank* says it is at risk. But some later cases have said it does survive. They have distinguished *Central Bank* because *respondeat superior* simply determines on whose shoulders to place responsibility for conduct that is indisputably proscribed. *See, e.g.*, *In re Global Crossing Ltd Securities Litigation*, 313 F. Supp. 2d 189 (S.D.N.Y. 2005). *See Suez Equity Investors LP v. Toronto Dominion Bank,* 250 F.3d 87 (2d Cir. 2001) (*Central Bank* did not shield business entities from being held liable for misstatements of their agents).

Scheme Liability

Stoneridge confirmed that there is no aiding and abetting liability for implied rights of action under Section 10(b), although there is such liability in SEC actions. The Supreme Court held that there is no liability unless there was reliance on the defendant's deceptive acts. In this case, there could not have been because the investors never knew about them. In other words, the implied right of action does not apply to non-speaking defendants.

In that case, the plaintiff purchased the stock of Charter Communication, which was alleged to have engaged in fraudulent practices to meet Wall Street expectations. The defendants Scientific Atlanta and Motorola were suppliers and customers who had no role in the preparation and dissemination of the statements. But the allegation was that they knew that the transaction had no economic substance. Were they liable for participating in a scheme to defraud? No. Even though the conduct could be proscribed by the statute, there was no demonstration of reliance. The court reiterated the two presumptions of

[5] *Marbury Management Inc. v. Kohn*, 629 F.2d 705 (2d Cir.) *cert. denied*, 449 U.S. 1011 (1980); *see generally* "Note: Vicarious Liability: Respondeat Superior Applicable in Cases Involving High Fiduciary Duties Despite Controlling Persons Provisions of Securities Exchange Act—*Sharp v. Coopers & Lybrand*," 12 *Seton Hall L. Rev.* 353 (1982).

reliance: fraud on the market and *Affiliated Ute*. But neither applied because neither defendant had a duty to disclose and the deceptive acts were never communicated to the public. The court was uncomfortable applying the private right of action beyond the securities market to the realm of ordinary business operations such as purchase and supply contracts because doing so might impinge on traditional state causes of action.

Section 14(a)

This statute and its accompanying Rule 14(a)(9), both discussed in Chapter 7, deal with the solicitation of proxies. Basically, they prohibit the solicitation of proxies, consents, or authorizations other than pursuant to the SEC's rules. "It shall be unlawful for any person . . . in contravention of such rules and regulations as the Commission may prescribe as necessary or appropriate in the public interest for the protection of investors, to solicit any proxy, or consent, or authorization in respect of any security (other than an exempted security) registered pursuant to section 12 of this title." Rule 14(a)(9) essentially prohibits proxies and proxy solicitations that contain materially false or misleading statements or omissions.

Neither the statute nor the rule mentions private enforcement. The Supreme Court's *Borak* decision has been cited in support of an implied private right of action, although that has been called into question because of the court's *refusal* to acknowledge a private right of action under Section 17(a) of the 1934 Act in *Touche Ross & Co. v. Redington*, 442 U.S. 560 (1979). The only plaintiffs who would have standing to sue are those who have the right to vote on the merger or other transaction. Although the Supreme Court has ducked the issue, lower courts have not imposed a scienter requirement for a violation, largely because there are no words in the statute or rule dealing with fraud or deception. Proof of negligence seems to be sufficient, although these are all still open questions.

Section 14(e)

This statute prohibits fraud in connection with a tender offer. It is also a part of the Williams Act that protects shareholders in tender offers. In *Schreiber v. Burlington Northern, Inc.*, 472 U.S. 1 (1985), the Supreme Court limited Section 14(e) by holding that conduct prohibited by that statute requires a misrepresentation or an omission, not merely a manipulation. At least according to the Ninth Circuit, scienter seems to be a required element of a violation. *Varjabedian v. Emulex*, 888 F.3d 399 (9th Cir. 2018). Whether there is an implied private right of action has not yet been definitively decided and is open to question.

Section 18

This section of the 1934 Securities Exchange Act allows a private action by anyone who buys or sells a security in reliance on a material misstatement in an SEC filing "at a price affected by the misstatement." Although proof of scienter is not required, proof of actual "eyeball" reliance is required. In addition, proof of a causal relationship between reliance and damages and between the misstatement and the price paid is required. There are no viable class actions under Section 18 of which I am aware, since it would be virtually impossible to establish a class every member of which actually relied in a false or misleading statement in an SEC filing. Although claims under Section 18 often show up in class action complaints, they never make it all the way to a trial and a verdict, because of the difficulties of proof. However, there is an increasing number of non-class action complaints under Section 18 being filed by institutional investors against banks. It appears that institutional investors are having little difficulty in establishing "eyeball" reliance in those cases.

Both the Second Circuit and a district court in New Jersey have held that because Section 18 "sounds in fraud," the two-year/five-year statute of limitations contained in Sarbanes-Oxley applies to those claims. *Dekalb County Pension Fund v. Transocean Ltd.*, 817 F.3d 393 (2d Cir. 2016); *Pentwater Equity Opportunities Master Fund Ltd. v. Valeant Pharmaceuticals Inc.*, Civ. No. 17-7552 (MAS), Memorandum Opinion, Sept. 14, 2018, D.N.J; *but see In re Able Labs Sec. Litig.*, 2008 WL 1967509 (D.N.J. Mar. 24, 2008).

Chapter 12

Securities Class Actions

Rule 23 of the Federal Rules of Civil Procedure

The modern class action rule was established in 1966. Prior to 1966, there were three types of class actions: "true," "hybrid" (involving rights to specific property), and "spurious" (which weren't really class actions at all because "class members" could opt out *after* an unfavorable judgment was entered). One of the purposes of the 1966 amendments to Rule 23 was to permit securities fraud litigation to proceed as a class action.[1]

Rule 23 requires that the four requirements of part (a) be established and that one of the part (b) requirements be established in order to maintain a class action. Usually it is (b)(3) that is established (a common question of law or fact predominates over questions affecting only individual members). For that reason, securities class actions are almost always (b)(3) class actions in which the common question of fact is reliance on the efficiency of the market.

Numerosity. ("So numerous that joinder of all members is impracticable.") This is usually not a problem in securities class actions. The general (largely unspoken) rule is that a group of forty or more claimants is sufficient to meet the numerosity requirement and is capable of joinder and is not "impracticable." *Orr v. Shicker*, 953 F. 490 (7th Cir. 2020). However, the Seventh Circuit has recently held that other factors such as geographical dispersion, small dollar value of each claim, and the ease of contacting the class members could also be taken into consideration by a court when ruling on numerosity. *Anderson v. Weinert Enterprises*, 986 F.3d 773 (7th Cir. 2021).

Typicality. ("Claims or defenses of the representative party are typical of the Claims or defenses of the class.") In *In re Flag Telecom Holdings Sec. Litigation*, 574 F.3d 29 (2d Cir. 2009), "in and out" traders could not be class representatives because there was no loss causation, and they will not "even conceivably" be able to prove that there was. Thus their claims were not "typical" of the class.

1 *See* Sherman Cohn, "The New Federal Rules of Civil Procedure," 54 *Geo. L. J.* 1204, 1214 (1966).

Common Questions of Law or Fact. The common question must predominate, making the class action superior to other available methods for fairly and efficiently adjudicating the controversy. Usually reliance on the efficiency of the market is the common question of fact. Commonality and typicality tend to merge into one another, as "both serve as guideposts for determining whether the named plaintiff's claim and the class claims are so inter-related that the interests of the class members will be fairly and adequately protected in their absence." *In re WorldCom*, 294 F. Supp. 2d 392 (S.D.N.Y. 2003), held that 1933 Act and 1934 Act plaintiffs may join a single class. *See Loftin et al. v. Bande*, 574 F.3d 29 (2d Cir. 2009). In *Wal-Mart Stores v. Dukes*, 564 U.S. 277 (2011), the Supreme Court (Justice Antonin Scalia) added to the commonality test a requirement for a showing that the "capacity of a class-wide proceeding [will] generate common answers apt to drive the resolution of the litigation." This is a new test and it remains to be seen how far it will go. *Wal-Mart* requires an analysis of the alleged common issue. "Any competently crafted class complaint literally raises common 'questions.'" But according to the Supreme Court, to support a class action, the common question must be one "whose truth or falsity will resolve an issue that is central to the validity of each one of the claims in one stroke." It bears repeating that this articulation is not in the Rule; it was created by the Supreme Court. *See, e.g., Grousman v. Motorola, Inc.*, 2011 WL 5554030 (N.D. Ill. 2011); *but see Public Employees Retirement Systems of Miss. v. Merrill Lynch*, 714 F. Supp. 2d 475 (S.D.N.Y. 2011) (class of mortgage-backed securities purchasers certified).

Class Representative. The class representative must be able to "fairly and adequately represent the interests of the class" and must not be subject to unique defenses that "threaten to become the focus of the litigation." This typically comes up when fraud-on-the-market is pleaded. The argument usually is that the representative plaintiff did not rely on the efficiency of the market but instead had "eyeball" reliance. Courts usually permit such cases to go forward anyway, at least at the class certification stage. As a practical matter, this issue usually disappears if the case actually goes to trial and the court has appointed a "most adequate plaintiff" under the PSLRA.

Professional Plaintiffs. Under the PSLRA (unless the court may otherwise permit), a person may be a lead plaintiff in no more than five securities class actions during any three-year period.

Lead Counsel. The "most adequate plaintiff" selects and retains lead counsel for the class, subject to the approval of the court. In *Pelletier v. Endo International PLC*, No. 17 cv 5114 (E.D. Pa. Feb. 14, 2021), the court removed and replaced a previously appointed lead counsel for the class after it was disclosed that the plaintiff acquired shares in the defendant company ninety-seven seconds *after* the publication of a *Bloomberg* article disclosing the alleged corrective disclosure in the stock price. The court not only replaced the "most adequate plaintiff" but also replaced class counsel, who had misled and "misdirected" the court about the timing of the purchase, which the court found "alarming." In *In re IPO Securities Litigation*, 471 F.3d 24 (2d Cir. 2006), the court held that in order to sustain a securities class action, the district court must determine that each of the Rule 23 requirements has been met (not just that there has been "some showing"). It must resolve all relevant factual issues (even if there is an overlap with a merits issue), and it should not assess any other merits issues and may circumscribe discovery relating to Rule 23 issues and the hearing to ensure that the motion to certify the class does not become a partial trial on the merits. Preponderance of the evidence is the test. *See Teamsters Local 445 Freight Div. Pension Fund v. Bombardier Inc.*, 546 F.3d 196 (2d Cir. 2008). *Query*: How do *Halliburton II* and *Goldman Sachs* affect this holding? Those cases permit a mini-trial on price impact at the class certification stage.

Time. The class must be certified at "an early practicable time." (Note that this Rule used to say "as soon as practicable" but that "did not reflect prevailing practice.")

Notice. Notice to all class members is required; be aware of the due process issues. *Phillips Petroleum v. Shutts*, 472 U.S. 797 (1985). Putative class members will be bound by the judgment in the class action unless they opt out of the class. That is why they must receive notice. The notice must be sufficient to satisfy due process. It must be "the best notice that is practicable under the circumstances, including individual notice to members who can be identified through reasonable effort." This usually includes mailing to purchasers identified by the company's transfer agent, and publication. A 2018 amendment to the rule provides that electronic notice may be made, provided the class has sufficient access to the internet. Notice must also give the absent plaintiff an opportunity to opt out, at least in cases seeking predominantly money damages. Notice must also describe the "binding effect of a class judgment on members." Rule 23(c)(2)(B)(vii). Would a U.S. class action judgment in favor of the defendant preclude foreign shareholders from bringing similar claims in foreign courts? That is, would a foreign court give preclusive effect to a U.S. judgment in favor of the defendant or would the foreign shareholder be able to sue again in a different country? Although some cases said that a positive answer to this question required a "near certainty," the *Vivendi* district court adopted a "more likely than not" standard. Is that satisfactory? In any event, there are no recorded instances of foreign shareholders suing a U. S. defendant in a foreign court after a U.S. court ruled in favor of the defendant.

Tolling. American Pipe v. Utah, 414 U.S. 538 (1974), held that the statute of limitations is tolled once a class complaint is filed. But what if the representative plaintiff had no standing to bring the case? Is the statute still tolled?

Be aware that a statute of limitations is different from a statute of repose, which is *not* tolled by the filing of a class action.

Subclasses. What purpose do they serve? (*Hint*: not much.)

Opt-outs. There are opt-outs in approximately 3 percent of securities class action cases that are settled. Why? To get a larger settlement? To bring an action in state court? Opt-outs usually occur in larger settlements. Fifty-three percent of class settlements greater than $500 million had opt-outs. Some lawyers make a practice of representing opt-outs. Why would the lawyers representing the class not want too many opt-outs? (*Hint*: higher fees.)

Settlement Issues. Notice and court approval are required. A defendant's support of class certification for settlement purposes does not preclude it from objecting to class certification if the court rejects the settlement. The 2018 amendments to the rule require the court to analyze four factors before approving a settlement: (1) the adequacy of representation by class representatives and class counsel, (2) whether settlement negotiations were done fairly at arm's length, (3) the adequacy of the relief provided under the settlement, and (4) the equity of treatment of class members relative to one another. In Chapter 17, we discuss the different requirements for court approval of SEC settlements. The 2018 amendments also require that parties seeking preliminary approval of a settlement give the court the information that they propose to share with the class members in the approval process and the materials that they intend to submit to the court at the final approval stage. The concept is that this new rule will reduce costs and delays and will decide issues at the beginning of the process rather than waiting until after class notice has been given.

The new 2018 rule specifies two "procedural" considerations that must be dealt with by counsel at the preliminary approval stage (if they are seeking preliminary approval): the adequacy of representation of the class and the arm's-length nature of the settlement negotiations. The new rule also specifies one substantive issue that counsel must address, whether the relief proposed for the class is adequate. In making that assessment, counsel must discuss the costs, risks, and delay of trial and appeal, the effectiveness of the proposed method of distributing relief to the class, the terms of a proposed attorneys fee award, including timing, and any agreement made in connection with the proposed settlement. The comments suggest that counsel should be prepared to discuss the proposed claims administrative process and the expected effectiveness of the notice plan.

The new rule also permits notification of a proposed settlement by "electronic or other appropriate means."

It also seeks to discourage objections to settlements by "bad objectors" who seek only personal gain and who seek to use "objections to obtain benefits for themselves rather than assisting in the settlement-review process" by requiring court approval of any consideration provided to an objector for withdrawing an objection before or after an appeal is taken.

Offers of Judgment. An issue has recently arisen regarding offers of judgment under Rule 68 of the Federal Rules of Civil Procedure that are made to a class representative and that would fully satisfy that person's claim. If the class representative refuses to accept the offer of judgment, is the claim moot? And if it is, what happens to the rest of the class she purports to represent? In *Szmczyk v. Genesis Health Care Corp.*, 569 U.S. 66 (2015), the Supreme Court held that where the plaintiff did not timely raise the issue of mootness in her opposition of a petition for a writ of certiorari, the court assumed, without deciding, that an unaccepted offer of full relief in an offer of judgment rendered the class-action allegations non-justiciable and that they too became moot when the claims of the class representative became moot. As expected, there was a vigorous dissent, led by Justice Elena Kagan. Because of the peculiar procedural posture of the case, the decision was unsatisfactory and was widely criticized.[2] Perhaps in response to the criticism, the Supreme Court later decided, in *Campbell-Ewald v. Gomez*, 136 S. Ct. 663 (2016), a case from the Ninth Circuit, that an unaccepted Rule 68 offer that would have fully satisfied a plaintiff's claim does *not* render the claim moot. ("An unaccepted offer has no force ... like other unaccepted contract offers, it creates no lasting right or obligation.") But is there still a "case or controversy"?

Interlocutory Appeals. Under Rule 23(f) of the Federal Rules of Civil Procedure, an interlocutory appeal is possible from an order granting or denying class certification, but the appeal is discretionary with the court of appeals. Those courts (primarily the Second Circuit) have circumscribed the Rule 23(f) procedure and have seriously limited it. It is the exception, not the rule. *Sumitomo Copper v. Credit Lyonnaise Rouse*, 262 F.3d 134 (2d Cir. 2004) (the appeal must involve a "fundamental issue"). Rule 23(f) petitions must be filed within fourteen days of the certification or decertification order.

Private Securities Litigation Reform Act (1995)

Prior to the PSLRA, most securities litigation was a race to the courthouse; the winner controlled the litigation, and the winning lawyers controlled the litigation and distribution of attorneys' fees among other lawyers who also filed cases but who lost the race to the courthouse.

---

[2] *See, e.g.*, "Report of the Committee on Federal Procedure, Commercial and Federal Litigation Section," NYSBA, NY Litigator, Fall 2015, Vol. 20, No. 1, p. 25. *See also* "Don't Try This at Home: The Troubling Distortion of Rule 68," 103 *Geo. L. J.* 723 (2015).

One of the purposes of the PSLRA was to put the clients back in charge. It was part of the Contract with America. It was passed in 1995 over President Clinton's veto. He did not like the pleading requirements, attorney sanctions, or the safe harbor. The defendants' bar favored the PSLRA, and the plaintiffs' bar was opposed to it, especially to the difficult pleading requirements.

The PSLRA proponents were exuberant: "We have made a giant stride for common sense, reasonable litigation in America. We will reform a broken system that has been a curse that stops companies from starting good, high paying jobs." (Senator Pete Domenici) Did that really happen? I think it was hyperbole.

The bill had widespread bipartisan support. One of its ostensible purposes was to prevent the filing of frivolous cases.

It is important to note that some parts of the PSLRA apply to all private securities cases and others apply only to class actions. No part of it applies to cases brought by the SEC.

Certification. The putative class representative must file a PSLRA certification together with the complaint. There are specific requirements in the PSLRA as to what must be in the certification, including a representation that the plaintiff did not purchase the relevant security at the direction of plaintiff's counsel or in order to participate in any private action arising from the 1934 Act. The certificate must also describe all of the plaintiff's transactions in the relevant security and identify any other action filed during the past three years in which the plaintiff sought to be the class representative. The certificate must also say that the plaintiff is willing to be deposed and testify, even though generally other members of the class do not need to agree to a deposition.

Lead Plaintiff. A "most adequate plaintiff" must be appointed as "lead plaintiff" by the court. That person has the right to appoint lead counsel. The lead plaintiff is not necessarily the first to file. Any member of the class may be appointed lead plaintiff, even if he or she did not file a complaint. The lead plaintiff must be appointed within ninety days of the filing of the complaint. Can multiple plaintiffs band together to become "lead plaintiffs"? Courts are split. What does the lead plaintiff actually do? In theory, control the litigation, but that does not always happen. Is there a difference between lead plaintiff and class representative in practice? Not really. Do the claims of the lead plaintiff have to be typical of those of the class? The statute is silent but presumably all of the other Rule 23 conditions also apply to the lead plaintiff. The PSLRA requires the appointment of a lead plaintiff that the court deems to be "most capable of adequately representing the interests of class members." There is a rebuttable presumption that the "most adequate plaintiff" is the person who has either filed a complaint or made a motion for appointment and who has the "largest financial interest in the relief sought by the class." Is this the person with largest loss or the most significant (to him or her) loss? Most courts choose the former.

Some courts apply the "Olsten-Lax" factors to determine which plaintiff has the largest financial interest. Under that test, courts examine "(1) the number of shares purchased during the class period; (2) the number of net shares purchased during the class period; (3) the total net funds expended during the class period; and (4) the approximate losses suffered." The last of these factors typically carries the most weight. *In re Diamond Foods, Inc., Sec. Litig.*, 281 F.R.D. 405, 408 (N.D. Cal. 2012). *See also In re Olsten Corp. Sec. Litig.*, 3 F. Supp. 2d 286 (E.D.N.Y. 1998); *Lax v. First Merchants Acceptance Corp.*, 1997 WL 461036 at *5 (N.D. Ill. Aug. 11, 1997).

The representative class plaintiff (not the lead plaintiff) must publish a notice of the filing of the lawsuit "in a widely circulated national business-oriented publication or wire service" within 20 days of the filing of the complaint. This is usually done on the plaintiff's counsel's website. Among other things, it must invite applications for "lead plaintiff." The lead plaintiff cannot receive any damage award that is larger than a pro rata share of the entire damage award.[3]

Lead Counsel. The lead plaintiff selects and retains lead counsel for the putative class, subject to the approval of the court. Lead counsel could be multiple firms. Courts sometimes require competitive bids. This is a significant role. Why? As noted, the lead counsel controls the assignments given to co-counsel and gets the largest share of any fee award at the end of the case.

Heightened Pleading Requirement. The statute requires the complaint to state with particularity facts giving rise to a *strong inference* that the defendant acted with the required state of mind, but that is not defined in the statute. Can this test be met with proof of recklessness (or "deliberate recklessness") (Ninth Circuit) or "motive and opportunity" (Second Circuit)? The Supreme Court has never decided that question but it appears that most courts are leaning in that direction. (Although *Matrixx* was a "deliberate recklessness" standard in the lower courts, the Supreme Court did not consider the issue because it wasn't raised in the certiorari petition.) Group pleading is not sufficient to prove scienter. Note that there are also special pleadings rules for pleading facts "on information and belief." "The complaint shall state with particularity all facts on which that belief is formed." That is one reason why you rarely see "information and belief" pleading in a securities class action. Note also that

[3] Note that in jury trials, there is almost never a lump-sum damage award but rather a jury finding with respect to the size of the daily inflation during the class period. A claims administrator later determines the amount to be awarded to each member of the class based on the length of time the member held the stock during the class period and when, if at all, it was sold. A court must later approve the awards to each class member.

some complaints name "unnamed" or "confidential" sources. This is permitted at the pleading stage but the confidential source must eventually be identified, at least once discovery begins. The issue is timing.

Stay of Discovery. There is a mandatory stay of discovery in the PSLRA pending a decision on a motion to dismiss, with two exceptions (necessary to preserve evidence or to prevent prejudice to a party); there is a corollary obligation on the defendant to preserve relevant evidence. The defendant is required to preserve all documents; data compilations, including electronically recorded or stored data; and tangible objects that are in the custody and control of the defendant and that are relevant to the allegations in the complaint. Should there be such a stay in non-securities cases pending decision on a motion to dismiss? This possibility has been discussed by a task force of the American College of Trial Lawyers, among others, but the plaintiffs' bar has been opposed to it.[4] Below we discuss the application of the "stay of discovery" rule to state securities class actions.

What if there is a parallel SEC case in which discovery is not stayed? Can class plaintiffs take advantage of that discovery? Usually not. Courts will generally prohibit that type of back-door discovery.

Rule 11 Determination. A mandatory Federal Rules of Civil Procedure Rule 11 determination that none of the lawyers violated Rule 11(b)'s prohibition against making misrepresentations to the court and making frivolous arguments must be made by the court upon "final adjudication of the action." (This may not apply to settlements in which there is no "final adjudication," but the law is unclear). The court must find that each party and each attorney complied with each requirement of Rule 11(b) of the Federal Rules of Civil Procedure as to any complaint, responsive pleading, or dispositive motion. If the court finds a violation, the court "shall impose sanctions" after giving the party or lawyer notice and an opportunity to respond.

Limitation on Damages and Proportionate Liability. As noted, there is a ninety-day look-back period. This means that damages cannot exceed the difference between the price paid or received and the mean trading price for ninety days after corrective disclosure, or if the class member sells the stock during the ninety-day period, the difference between the purchase price and the mean price during the ninety-day period beginning on the date of the corrective disclosure and ending on the date of sale. What if it is a "manifestation of an undisclosed risk" case with no corrective disclosure? There are as yet no cases that have discussed that possibility. The liable defendant is only liable to the extent of proportionate fault. The jury must answer special interrogatories in order to allocate the percentage of responsibility among the defendants.

---

[4] Full disclosure: I chaired that task force.

"Safe Harbor" for Forward-Looking Statements. This statutory safe harbor in the PSLRA is similar to the "bespeaks caution" defense created by the courts. In theory, it protects any oral or written forward-looking statement that is (1) identified as such and accompanied by meaningful cautionary language, or (2) is immaterial, or (3) if the plaintiff had actual knowledge of the fraudulent nature of the statement. Note that there are special rules for oral forward-looking statements in the PSLRA. This is rarely a successful defense because the "meaningful cautionary language" test is very subjective, and courts have held that it must relate directly to the alleged fraud. *See, e.g., Slayton v. American Express Co.*, 604 F.3d 758 (2d Cir. 2010).

Securities Litigation Uniform Standards Act (1998)

The Supreme Court has observed that the PSLRA was enacted "principally to stem 'perceived abuses of the class action vehicle in litigation involving nationally traded securities.'... But the [PSLRA] fell prey to the law of 'unintended consequences'.... Rather than face the obstacles set in their path by the [PSLRA] plaintiffs and their representatives began bringing class actions under state law. That phenomenon was a novel one—and an unwelcome one as well. To prevent plaintiffs from circumventing the [PSLRA] Congress again undertook to modify both securities laws. The result was SLUSA." *Cyan Inc. v. Beaver County Employees Retirement Fund*, 138 S. Ct. 1061 (2018).

In other words, because the PSLRA made it more difficult to bring securities cases in federal courts, many plaintiffs brought cases in state courts to avoid the PSLRA's strict pleading and other requirements. So Congress passed SLUSA to make sure that all securities fraud class actions based on state or common law are heard only in federal court.[5] To accomplish that, SLUSA amended the 1933 and 1934 Acts. Recall that under the 1933 Securities Act, there is concurrent jurisdiction between state and federal courts, and there is an explicit no-removal provision. Presumably the intent of SLUSA was to require that all securities fraud class actions be brought only in federal court. To accomplish that, Congress amended the 1933 Act but, as we will see, the amendment only prohibited securities cases in state courts alleging violation of common law or state law, not federal law. And because the 1934 Securities Exchange Act did not permit concurrent jurisdiction, cases involving Section 10(b), for example, may only be brought in federal courts. SLUSA did not affect that requirement.

---

[5] It remains unclear why Congress restricted SLUSA to state securities cases brought under state or common law, instead of under the 1933 Securities Act. It may have been an oversight.

There are five conditions for SLUSA's application:

1. The lawsuit must be a "covered class action" (a case brought on behalf of more than fifty people seeking damages and in which the questions of law or fact common to those persons, without reference to issues of individualized reliance on an alleged misstatement or omission, predominate over any questions affecting only individual persons or members);
2. The claim must be based on state statutory or common law;
3. The claim must concern a "covered security" (i.e., traded nationally and listed or authorized for listing on a regulated national exchange, even if the fraudster did not actually perform any trades);
4. The plaintiff must allege a misrepresentation or omission of a material fact; and
5. The misrepresentation must be "in connection with" a purchase or sale of a covered security (i.e., material to a decision by one or more individuals other than the fraudster to buy or sell).[6]

If those conditions are met, the state law claim may not be maintained in any court, whether state or federal. *Merrill Lynch v. Dabit*, 547 U.S. 71 (2006): "SLUSA does not actually pre-empt any state cause of actions. It simply denies plaintiffs the right to use the class action vehicle to vindicate certain claims." If a qualifying case is filed in state court, the case may be removed to federal court where it will be dismissed. Courts look at substance, not labels, in order to determine whether a case is a qualifying case. But remember, SLUSA did *not* affect the concurrent jurisdiction of state and federal courts to hear cases alleging violations of the 1933 Securities Act. As Justice Kagan wrote in *Cyan*, "State-court jurisdiction over 1933 Act claims continues undisturbed. SLUSA's text, read most straightforwardly, leaves in place state courts' jurisdiction over 1933 Act claims, including when brought as class actions." Note, however, that very few securities class actions are actually brought alleging 1933 Act violations, primarily because several relevant provisions of the 1933 Act require that the security in question have been acquired from or are directly traceable to the registration statement.

SLUSA also covers state law claims that were consolidated for any reason with "covered class actions" even if they were later deconsolidated. *But see Liberty Media Corp. v. Vivendi S.A.*, 842 F. Supp. 2d 587 (S.D.N.Y. 2012), in

---

[6] *See generally Marchak et al. v. JPMorgan Chase & Co.*, 84 F. Supp. 3d 197 (E.D.N.Y. 2015) (state law case removed to federal court and dismissed under SLUSA).

which the court deconsolidated state law claims *nunc pro tunc* more than a year after they were made when a motion to dismiss based on SLUSA was made.[7]

There is a "Delaware carve out" (Section 28(f)(3)(A) of the 1934 Act) that preserves covered class actions based on the statutory or common law of the state in which the issuer is incorporated (in either federal or state court) *but* that exception has been limited by caselaw to actions based on statements made by the corporation to its shareholders concerning "specific shareholder decisions" (such as a response to a tender offer). *See Madden v. Cowen*, 576 F.3d 957 (9th Cir. 2009).

In 2014, the Supreme Court decided in *Chadbourne & Parke LLP v. Troice*, 571 U.S. 321 (2104), that SLUSA did not preclude a state class action fraud case where the misrepresentations concerned a security that did not in fact exist and at most concerned the fraudster's own purchase of securities. Alan Stanford, later criminally convicted, told his clients that the CDs (not "covered securities") purchased by his offshore bank were backed by marketable securities (i.e., "covered securities"), but they weren't. The bank was bankrupt. The "in connection with" test in SLUSA was not met because the "fraudster" himself was going to purchase them. (He never did.) As we will see in the later discussion of insider trading, this creates a problem for insider trading cases. Why did the plaintiffs want to bring a state law cause of action against the law firm and accountants? (*Hint*: aiding and abetting liability is not available in private securities actions brought in federal court.)

One big question is whether the PSLRA's automatic discovery stay is applicable to state court actions under the 1933 Act. The PSLRA stays discovery during the pendency of a motion to dismiss in "any private action arising under" the Securities Act. The PSLRA does not limit the stay of discovery to Securities Act cases filed in federal court, and federal actions brought in state court clearly "arise under" the Act. How broad is the phrase "any private action"? Does it mean "in any court, state or federal, or is it limited only to cases brought in federal courts"?

The courts are split on the stay issue. In fact, three different judges in the same New York county considered the question and reached three different results. Compare *Greensky, Inc. Sec. Litig.*, 2019 WL 6310525 (N.Y. Sup. Ct. Nov. 25, 2019) (finding the stay inapplicable "by its terms but staying discovery to give effect to the PSLRA's policy of staying discovery until a plaintiff has demonstrated that its 1933 Act claims have merit") with *In re Everquote Inc. Sec. Litig.*, 65 Misc. 3d 226 (N.Y. Sup. Ct. N.Y. Cty. 2019) (applying the PSLRA stay) and *In re PPDAI Grp. Sec. Litig.*, 2019 WL 2751278 (N.Y. Sup. Ct. N.Y. Cty. July 1, 2019) (in which a different court held that the automatic stay provision of the PSLRA "would undermine *Cyan*'s holding that '33 Act

[7] Full disclosure: I was counsel for the defendant Vivendi in that case.

cases may be heard in state courts"). On July 2, 2021, the last day of its October 2020 Term, the U.S. Supreme Court granted a petition for certiorari in *Pivotal Software, Inc., et al. v. Zhung Tran*, No. 20-1541, in which the California Court of Appeal, First Appellate District, declined to enforce the PSLRA stay of discovery in a securities case pending in a state court. Unfortunately, on September 2, 2021, the Supreme Court suspended its review of this case and removed the case from its November 2021 calendar because the parties notified the court that they had reached an agreement in principle to settle the case. Stay tuned.

Shareholders who opt out of federal securities class actions are not precluded by SLUSA from bringing state law fraud claims in follow-on individual actions even if federal claims are time-barred. *North Sound Capital LLC v. Merck & Co.*, 938 F.3d 482 (3d Cir. 2019). This ruling offers plaintiffs yet one more way to avoid the heightened pleading standards and limitations periods of the PSLRA.

SLUSA and the Securities Act's Non-Removal Provision

With respect to jurisdiction, note that under 28 U.S.C. § 1441(a), an action within the jurisdiction of the federal courts (i.e., arising under any federal law or where there is complete diversity plus $75,000 in controversy) is removable unless "Congress has expressly provided otherwise." But Section 22(a) of the 1933 Securities Act says that there can be no removal to a federal court. So SLUSA amended that section to say "except as provided in § 16(c)." Section 16(c) provides that "covered class actions involving covered securities shall be removed." Section 16(b) provided that covered class actions brought under state law alleging untrue statements must be dismissed. Before the Supreme Court clarified the issue in *Cyan*, the lower courts were in a state of confusion.

New York Versus California

Federal courts struggled to understand SLUSA; it was at best ambiguous. Could federal securities class actions under the 1933 Act filed in state courts be removed or not? In two federal district court opinions issued less than a week apart, one in the Southern District of New York and the other in the Northern District of California, the courts came to opposite conclusions with respect to whether under SLUSA, a state case alleging only federal securities law claims under the 1933 Act can be removed to a federal court despite the concurrent jurisdiction that the 1933 Act creates and despite the provision in that act that precludes removal of such cases from a state court "of competent jurisdiction."

As noted, SLUSA amended the concurrent jurisdiction provision of the 1933 Act to provide that a "covered class action" (more than fifty class members alleging a violation of state or common law based on a false or misleading statement in connection with the purchase or sale of a security) may be removed from a state court to a federal court and dismissed. The issue in both cases was the same. May a case alleging only a violation of the 1933 Act, with no state law claims alleged, be removed to a federal court? In other words, is such a claim a "covered class action" even though it is not based on state or common law? The New York opinion followed other courts in New York and some elsewhere and held that because SLUSA provides that covered class actions may only be heard in federal court, the state courts are not courts "of competent jurisdiction." *Hung v. IDreamsky Technology Ltd.*, 2016 WL 299034 (S.D.N.Y. Jan. 25, 2016); *see also Knox v. Agria*, 613 F. Supp. 2d 419 (S.D.N.Y. 2009). By contrast, the California opinion reached the opposite conclusion, that only covered class actions with state or common law claims can be removed to federal court and then only for the purpose of dismissing the state law claims. The California court said that it was following what appears to be "emerging as the dominant view around the country." *Buelow v. Alibaba Group Holding Ltd.*, Case No. 15-cv 05179-BLF (N.D. Cal. Jan. 20, 2016).[8]

Cyan decided the issue, putting the lower courts out of their misery, and held that SLUSA did *not* prohibit the trial of federal securities cases under the 1933 Act in state courts because the language of SLUSA referred only to cases alleging violations of state or common law, even though Congress may have had something else in mind. The Supreme Court held that the correct reading of the statutory language in SLUSA—that Justice Samuel Alito characterized as "gibberish" during the oral argument—was that state court jurisdiction over purely federal causes of action under the 1933 Securities Act was alive and well. As is her wont (see *Omnicare*), Justice Kagan, for the majority, engaged in an extensive exegesis of the dictionary meanings of the words in the statute to support her conclusion that federal claims under the 1933 Securities Act could continue in state courts. One can confidently expect that as a result, more such cases will be brought in state courts alleging violations of the 1933 Act in order to avoid the procedural and pleading hurdles of the PSLRA, although because of the limited applicability of that statute, there may not be many such cases brought. According to Cornerstone Research, only twenty-eight such cases were filed in 2019.

---

[8] This case, which was ultimately settled, had a strange history. After it was referred to the Multidistrict Panel, the district court vacated its transfer order and remanded the case to the California state court.

Standing Issues

There is a distinction between individual standing and class standing. When can a putative class plaintiff represent a class of plaintiffs whose claims may not be identical to the claims of the putative class representative? What if the class representative is subject to a reliance challenge?

Consider *Gratz v. Bollinger*, 539 U.S. 244 (2003), in which the Supreme Court held that a white male who was only seeking admission to the University of Michigan as a transfer student after having been denied admission as an applicant could nevertheless represent a class of freshman applicants because his allegations about the use of race in transfer applications did not "implicate a significantly different set of concerns" from the use of race in freshman applications.

Supreme Court jurisprudence seems to stand for the proposition that a plaintiff has class standing if he or she plausibly alleges that he or she personally has suffered some actual injury as a result of the putatively illegal conduct of the defendant *and* that such conduct implicates the "same set of concerns" as the conduct alleged to have caused injury to other members of the class by the same defendants.

Thus, the injury does not have to be "the same." Now apply those principles to the mortgage-backed securities cases. In *NECA-IBEW Health and Welfare Fund v. Goldman Sachs*, 693 F.3d 145 (2012), the Second Circuit dealt with class certification issues in a case brought by a purchaser of certain mortgage-backed securities that were being marketed by a subsidiary of Goldman Sachs. The securities (certificates backed by pools of residential mortgage-backed securities) were sold in seventeen separate offerings. Each certificate represented a "tranche" of particular offerings. All of the offerings were covered by a shelf registration statement that was then supplemented by a Supplemental Prospectus that described the transaction details such as pricing information or information regarding the specific assets to be included in the vehicle from which the securities were issued.

The putative representative plaintiff bought only two certificates (i.e., certificates from only two of the seventeen offerings) that were based on mortgages originated by only two banks (Green Point and Wells Fargo), although the complaint talked about the origination practices of many other banks.

The complaint alleged violations of Section 11, 12(a)(2), and 15 of the Securities Act. Recall that Section 11 imposes strict liability on issuers and signatories of registration statements; negligence liability on underwriters; that no scienter, reliance, or loss causation is required; that Section 12(a)(2) imposes liability under similar circumstances against "statutory sellers" for misstatements in a prospectus; and that Section 15 imposes liability on controlling persons. The complaint alleged that certain statements in the shelf registration were false or misleading because they failed to disclose that the originating banks did not always follow their origination guidelines and gave mortgages to people who were not qualified. The district court held that the plaintiffs did not have class standing.

The appeals court reversed, holding that there *was* class standing for claims by purchasers of offerings that were backed by loans originated by originators who were the same as those who originated the loans in the same tranches that the class representative plaintiff purchased (i.e., certificates backed by mortgages originated by Green Point or Wells Fargo). There was also "tranche level" standing because the differences in payment priority among tranches did not raise "a fundamentally different set of concerns."

As to cognizable damages, the Second Circuit held that a diminution in the value of the certificates was sufficient to sustain the claim even though no payments were ever missed. Because the underlying loans were riskier than advertised, there was an increased risk that the mortgages might default, thus requiring a higher discount rate for the certificates and thereby diminishing their present value.

However, in *Plumbers Union Local No. 12 v. Nomura Asset Acceptance Corp.*, 632 F.3d 762 (1st Cir. 2011), the First Circuit held that named plaintiffs did not have standing to sue trusts whose certificates they did not buy, either in an individual capacity or representing a class containing members who did buy. The court reasoned that the named plaintiffs would not have a significant interest in litigating against banks that financed trusts from which they did not purchase. (The opinion has an amusing compilation of inconsistent statements from the Supreme Court on the standing issue. ("There is no recent holding by the Court that with perfect clarity resolves the issue before us.")) *American Pipe* tolling applied even to claims that original plaintiffs did not have standing to bring or otherwise could not properly allege a class action. *See Joseph v. Wiles*, 223 F.3d 1155 (10th Cir. 2000); *but see In re IndyMac Mortgage-Backed Securities Litigation*, 793 F. Supp. 2d 637 (S.D.N.Y. 2011), *aff'd*, 721 F.3d 95 (2d Cir. 2013), *cert. granted* Mar. 10, 2014; *cert. dismissed as improvidently granted*, Sept. 29, 2014 (collecting cases to the contrary).

Class Certification Requirements and Limitations

Must loss causation be proved at the class certification stage (in order to trigger the fraud-on-the-market presumption)? No. *Erica P. John Fund v. Halliburton*, 131 S. Ct. 2179 (2011) (*Halliburton I*), held that "Loss causation has no logical connection to the facts necessary to establish the efficient market predicate to the fraud-on-the-market theory." But *Halliburton v. Erica P. John Fund*, 573 U.S. 258 (2014) (*Halliburton II*), allows the defendant to prove a lack of price impact at class certification stage, but for what purpose? Arguably, it is for the purpose of showing that the market is not efficient, although in that case, the parties conceded that the market was efficient. The only other purpose that could be served at that stage by a showing of no price impact is a showing that the statement at issue is not material. Isn't that a merits issue?

Must materiality be proved by admissible evidence at the class certification stage? In *Amgen Inc v. Connecticut Retirement Plans and Trust Funds*, 133 S. Ct. 1184 (2013), the Supreme Court said no. Is this consistent with *Halliburton II*? How can this result be reconciled with the trend in the Supreme Court making it harder to maintain a securities class action? Georgetown Law Professor Donald Langevoort thinks that *Amgen* demonstrates that the Court sees the fraud-on-the-market class action as sui generis.[9] *Amgen* may no longer be good law since *Halliburton II* permitted the defendant to prove, at the class certification stage, that there was no price impact caused by the allegedly false statement and since *Goldman Sachs* seems to have confirmed that practice. Because the parties conceded market efficiency, that result seems to be inconsistent with *Amgen*. The philosophical question raised by Professor Langevoort was whether these cases in reality represent two different points of view, whether class actions should be permitted to continue even if they will ultimately not be successful because their in terrorem effect will ultimately promote settlement, or whether cases that are doomed to fail on the merits should be given an early burial.

What if the class plaintiff proves at the class certification stage that there is no "price impact"? Does that mean that the market is not efficient or only that the statement is not material?[10] Would a lack of price impact defeat an allegation of loss causation at the pleading stage?[11] Is this still good law after *Halliburton II* and *Goldman Sachs*? Can the lack of price impact defeat class certification? Yes, in the Second Circuit.[12] No, in the Seventh Circuit.[13] The Third Circuit

---

[9] Donald Langevoort, "Amgen and the Fraud-on-the-Market Class Action: Frozen in Time?" (draft) (Sept. 2013), http://wp-vip.law.columbia.edu.

[10] *See Nathenson v. Zonagen*, 267 F.3d 400 (5th Cir. 2001) (misrepresentation that does not affect the stock price rebuts the presumption of reliance on the efficiency of the market). *See also Halliburton II.*

[11] *See Acticon AG v. China N. East Petroleum Holdings*, 2012 WL 3104589 (2d Cir. Aug. 1, 2012) (Chinese reverse mortgage case) (price rebound after a corrective disclosure does not defeat an inference of economic loss at the motion to dismiss stage) (pre-*Amgen*).

[12] *See In re Salomon Analyst Metromedia Litigation*, 544 F.3d 474 (2d Cir. 2008) (defendants have the burden of showing no price impact of misrepresentation at the class certification stage).

[13] *See Schleicher v. Wendt*, 618 F.3d 679 (7th Cir. 2010) ("It is possible to certify a class under Rule 23(b)(3) even though all statements turn out to have only trivial effects on stock prices. Certification is appropriate but the class will lose on the merits").

agrees with the Second; the Fifth Circuit agrees with the Seventh. As we have seen, the Supreme Court in *Goldman Sachs* appears to have resolved the issue. Lack of price impact may be raised by the defendant at the class certification stage and the defendant has the burden of proof by a preponderance of the evidence. One suspects, however, that this debate is far from over.

Class Certification and Interlocutory Appeal

Remember, Rule 23(f) of the Federal Rules of Civil Procedure allows interlocutory appeals of orders granting or denying class certification. A recent Supreme Court case discussed that rule in a strange but interesting way. In *Microsoft v. Baker*, 137 S. Ct. 1702 (2017), the plaintiffs represented a putative class of purchasers of the Microsoft Xbox. The claim was that the Xbox disks became scratched and as a result the case was also known as the "scratched disk securities litigation." The motion to certify the class was denied by the district court because the individual issues predominated over the class issues. The case was then settled.

A few years later, the same plaintiffs' counsel brought a new case representing a different class making the same allegations. The court ruled the same way. A Rule 23(f) motion was denied by the Ninth Circuit. The plaintiffs then voluntarily dismissed the case and filed an appeal in which they tried to raise the issue of the denial of the motion to certify the class. The Supreme Court affirmed the refusal to consider the issue on the appeal, holding that Section 1291 did not contemplate such a procedure, since this was a naked and transparent effort to circumvent the "no interlocutory appeal" provision of Section 1291.

What was going on? Recall that 28 U.S.C. § 1292(b) requires a "final decision" for an appeal and that in *Coopers & Lybrand v. Livesay*, 437 U.S. 463 (1978), the Supreme Court held that the "death knell doctrine," which gave courts appellate jurisdiction over class certification denials that left the plaintiff without an economic incentive to go forward, did not apply to orders that were not final under § 1291, even though they effectively ended the litigation. Here, the plaintiff sought to have his class claims dismissed with prejudice but assumed that on appeal, he would be able to challenge the district court's order striking his class allegations (his Rule 23(f) motion had already been denied).

But the Supreme Court in *Microsoft v. Baker* had a different view. Because § 1291(b) was to be given a practical interpretation, it should not permit what Rule 23(f) and *Coopers & Lybrand* forbid. In other words, the district court's voluntary dismissal was not a "final decision" under § 1291(b).

Some have argued that what the Supreme Court was trying to avoid was a difficult issue concerning Article III of the Constitution: if Baker's claims were dismissed at his invitation, did he have Article III standing to challenge the district court's order? (In other words, was there still a case or controversy?)[14] The Supreme Court bypassed this issue by holding that the district court's order "misfired" in that it tried but failed to extinguish Baker's individual claims even though the order purported to end the litigation. The court's order striking the class allegations did not merge with the final judgment and was not reviewable on appeal.

This is a long way of saying that the decision whether or not to certify a class is often outcome determinative and that the courts have made it increasingly difficult to take an "interlocutory" appeal from such a decision.

Ascertainable and Suitable

Several recent cases have discussed the emerging requirement that a class must be "ascertainable" before it can be certified. In *Brecher v. Republic of Argentina*, 806 F.3d 22 (2d Cir. 2015), the Second Circuit held that for a class to be certified under Rule 23, there is an "implicit threshold requirement that the members of the class be readily identifiable" (quoting *Sandusky Wellness Ctr., LLC v. Medtox Sci., Inc.*, 821 F.3d 992 (8th Cir. 2016)). The doctrine, sometimes called the "ascertainability requirement," means that to be certified, the class must be "sufficiently definite so that it is administratively feasible for the court to determine whether a particular individual is a member." In the Second Circuit, that means only that a class be defined using "objective criteria that establish a membership with definite boundaries." *In re Petrobras Securities*, 860 F.3d 250 (2d Cir. 2017) (class decertified because it did not meet the predominance criterion). Note that the Second Circuit test did not address an administrative feasibility requirement "and we decline to adopt one now." Rather, the test should be whether there are objective criteria that establish a class membership with definite boundaries. "In other words, a class should not be maintained without a clear sense of who is suing about what. Ascertainability does not directly concern itself with the plaintiffs' ability to offer *proof of membership* under a given class definition, an issue that is already accounted for in Rule 23" (emphasis in original).

A good recent example of a case in which class certification was denied because the individual issues predominated over the common issues is *Royal Park Investments SA/NV v. Wells Fargo Bank N.A.*, 14 Civ. 9764 (S.D.N.Y. April 17, 2018). This was one of many putative class actions arising from alleged breaches by the trustee of a residential mortgage-backed security trust. In none of those cases was a class certified as an appropriate vehicle for prosecuting the case. Here, there were three issues set forth by the district court judge that would predominate over the common issues and that resulted in

---

[14] *See, e.g.*, *Microsoft v. Baker*, 131 *Harv. L. Rev.* 323 (2017).

an order denying a motion for class certification: (1) whether each putative member of the class had standing, (2) whether applicable statutes of limitations render the class member's claims untimely, and (3) whether damages would be calculated on a class-wide basis. The court concluded that there were two principal reasons why a class action would not be superior: first, given the individualized nature of the claims, management of the litigation would be difficult if not impossible; and second, and somewhat curiously, that the proposed class members were very sophisticated financial institutions with wealthy private investors who would have a strong interest in controlling the prosecution of their own actions. With respect the second reason, the court noted that in most class actions, the amounts in issue for the individual class members are typically small, rendering individual litigation uneconomical. But here, the individual amounts were large, and the individual members of the putative class were quite capable of litigating for themselves.

Parallel Proceedings

There are many examples of parallel proceedings in federal and state courts, sometimes leading to a "race to the courthouse." The courts are grappling whether in such cases, there should be a stay in favor of the other forum. Courts are looking to the "first to file" to decide which case should be stayed. Other courts are asking whether a stay will avoid duplication of effort or a more complete disposition of the issues. What if there are concurrent 1933 and 1934 Acts claims, the latter of which can only be brought in federal court? There are no appellate decisions yet on these issues.

Another way of putting the question is whether state courts hearing 1933 Act claims are required to impose the heightened pleading standards of the PSLRA? Some say yes (*Hoffman v. AT&T Inc.*, 2020 WL 2236189 (N.Y. Sup. Ct. N.Y. Cty. May 6, 2020) and some say no (*In re Netshoes Sec. Lit.*, 2020 WL 2893433 (N.Y. Sup. Ct. N.Y. Cty. June 2, 2020).

Some companies have included forum-selection provisions in their charters and bylaws, requiring that all 1933 Act cases brought against them must be brought in federal court. In *Salzberg v. Sciabacucci*, 227 A.3d 102 (Del. 2020), the Delaware Supreme Court upheld such a provision as facially valid and not in violation of Delaware public policy. As far as we know, no federal court has decided the issue. To put it bluntly, this area of the law is a mess. Stay alert and stay tuned!

Chapter 13

Securities Litigation Issues, Part One

Statutes of Limitations and Repose

The Sarbanes-Oxley Act increased the statute of limitations for Section 10(b). The action must be commenced within two years after discovery of the fraud and in no event more than five years after the fraud occurred. So far, this has not been extended to cases under Sections 11 and 12 because they do not "sound in fraud." Those sections have a "one year after discovery" limitation. In no event may the claims under those sections be brought more than three years after the security is "bona fide" offered to the public. Such a statute is sometimes called a "statute of repose." Unlike traditional statutes of limitation, statutes of repose may not be equitably tolled. Claims under Sections 9 and 18 of the Exchange Act have a one-year/three-year statute of limitation and repose.

In *American Pipe & Construction Co. v. Utah*, 414 U.S. 538 (1974), the Supreme Court held that "the commencement of a class action suspends the applicable statute of limitations as to all asserted members of the class who would have been parties had the suit been permitted to continue as a class action." But Section 13 of the Securities Act says that "in no event" shall an action under Section 11 of the Securities Act "be brought ... more than three years after the sale." In *Public Employees' Retirement System of Mississippi v. IndyMac*, 721 F.3d 95 (2d Cir. 2013) (*cert. dismissed as improvidently granted*, 2014), the Second Circuit held that *American Pipe* did not apply to the three-year period of Section 13 because either *American Pipe* is a species of equitable tolling, in which case it is inconsistent with *Lampf, Pleva, Lipkind, Prupis & Petigrow v. Gilbertson*, 501 U.S. 350 (1991) (equitable tolling does not apply to "statutes of repose"), *or* it is a form of "legal" tolling, in which case it would violate the Rules Enabling Act, which prohibits the creation of rules of procedure that change "substantive" rights. *But see Joseph v. Wiles*, 223 F.3d 1155 (10th Cir. 2000) (*American Pipe* does not apply to Section 13). Is there a difference between "legal" and "equitable" tolling? Is there a difference between a "statute of repose" and a "statute of limitations"? Yes. Do "statutes of repose" create substantive rights (e.g., a right to be free from having claims made against you) unlike "statutes of limitations"? Probably. Note that in *CTS Corp. v. Waldburger*, 134 S. Ct. 2175 (2014), the Supreme Court discussed the differences between statutes of limitation ("a time limit for suing") and statutes of repose ("another limit on the right to bring a civil action"), noting that even Congress sometimes confuses the two, and holding, without citation, that "statutes of limitation, *but not statutes of repose*, are subject to equitable tolling" (emphasis added). That case concerned the effect of a limitations-extending provision in the Comprehensive Environmental Response Compensation and Liability Act (CERCLA).

However, the Second Circuit later held that *CTS Corp. v. Waldburger* did not alter its controlling authority that the FDIC limitations-extending statute applied to all time limitations, including statutes of repose. The appeals court reasoned that the *CTS* holding was rooted in the text, structural and legislative history of CERCLA and that for that reason, it is not the case that a federal statute extending statutes of limitations must always be read to leave in place existing statutes of repose. *FDIC v. First Horizon Asset Securities Inc.*, 821 F.3d 327 (2d Cir. 2016).

The issue was finally resolved by the Supreme Court in *California Public Employees' Retirement System v. ANZ Securities*, 137 S. Ct. 2042 (2017), which held that Section 13's three-year time limit is a statute of repose and is not subject to equitable tolling.

When does the statute begin to run? Under *Merck & Co. v. Reynolds*, 130 S. Ct. 1784 (2010), a Rule 10b-5 claim begins to run when a hypothetical reasonably diligent plaintiff would have discovered facts constituting the violation. *Merck* rejected "inquiry notice" as a beginning of the limitations period for private Section 10(b) claims. "Inquiry notice" is merely a "useful tool" for determining when a reasonable plaintiff would have discovered the facts, the statute still requires "discovery."

There remains an issue whether "inquiry notice" remains the test for Securities Act claims as well. *Pension Trust Fund for Operating Engineers v. Mortgage Asset Securitization Transactions*, 2013 WL 5184064 (3d Cir. 2013), rejected "inquiry notice" for Securities Act claims. The issue was before the Second Circuit in *Freidus v. Barclays Bank PLC*, 2013 WL 4405291 (2d Cir. 2013), but the Second Circuit declined to deal with the "inquiry notice" issue, holding only that in that case there was "constructive notice."

But this discovery rule does not apply to the SEC as a plaintiff. *See Gabelli v. SEC*, 133 S. Ct. 1216 (2013). Mark Gabelli (Mario Gabelli's son) was charged with violating the Investment Advisers Act (illegal for advisers to defraud clients). He and another were charged with aiding and abetting a fraud from 1999 to 2002. Allegedly they allowed one investor in a fund to engage in market timing in exchange for its investment in a hedge fund even though they banned other investors from engaging in market timing.

The complaint by the SEC was not filed until 2008, six years after the alleged fraud occurred. It was governed by 28 U.S.C. § 2462 (the general federal five-year statute of limitations). The SEC argued for the application of the *Merck* discovery rule. The Supreme Court disagreed. It observed that no case has ever applied the discovery rule to the government. The Court said that most private plaintiffs do not spend their days looking for evidence of fraud. (Some lawyers often do.) By contrast, the SEC's central mission is to investigate potential violations of securities laws. Therefore, the discovery rule does not apply to SEC penalty actions.

The Complaint

Commences the Litigation. The complaint must allege a violation and a right to relief. Under Rule 8 of the Federal Rules of Civil Procedure, the complaint must contain "a short and plain statement of the claim showing the pleader is entitled to relief," but the Private Securities Litigation Reform Act (PSLRA) has added additional pleading requirements for securities cases. The adequacy of the complaint is almost always challenged in a securities case because such cases have so many special pleadings requirements. The complaint should be written in crisp, concise, and plain English. Each allegation must be "simple, concise, and direct." It can be used to establish the plaintiff's themes and theories, but that is not its principal function. The most important part of drafting a complaint is gathering of the relevant facts and meeting the relevant pleading standards.

You must draft a complaint that will survive a motion to dismiss because there will almost inevitably be one. You must plead every element of each cause of action. This requires careful review of the statutes on which the causes of action depend. You must also anticipate the defendant's arguments on a motion to dismiss.

Should "borderline" claims be included if there is a good faith basis for making the allegations? Perhaps, but there could be negative consequences by including such claims, including the loss of credibility.

Who are the potential audiences? The court, the client, defendant, insurance companies, the public, the shareholders, competitors, the jury (although in practice, most complaints do not make it into the jury room).

Often, plaintiffs will make allegations based on information supplied to them by confidential witnesses. This is done in an effort to meet their pleading burden, and it is permitted. Those confidential sources will eventually be identified through discovery, but where discovery is stayed pending a motion to dismiss, it is difficult if not impossible for courts to assess the sufficiency of allegations based on confidential sources. Aren't courts required to accept all factual allegations as true for purposes of a motion to dismiss? Yes. Is this true with respect to facts pleaded based on confidential sources? Perhaps. In any event, it has been my experience that more often than not, confidential sources are misquoted in a complaint.

It sometimes turns out that allegations based on confidential sources are not true. In *In re Millennial Media, Inc. Securities Litigation*, No. 14 Civ. 7923 (PAE), 2015 BL 169156 (S.D.N.Y. May 29, 2015), Judge Paul Engelmayer dealt with that issue by ordering the plaintiffs to provide affidavits from a "personally knowledgeable attorney" explaining the circumstances under which the confidential source allegation came to be included in the complaint and recounting the confidential source's version of the events. He also held that counsel's reliance on investigators created a significant potential for inaccuracy and that counsel must give the confidential source the opportunity to verify or refute that its quotes were accurate or presented in fair context.

In *Campos v. Sears Holdings Corp.*, 635 F. Supp. 2d 323 (S.D.N.Y. 2009), the court ordered limited discovery into the confidential source's allegations of scienter. Otherwise, the district court could not fulfill its obligation to weigh competing inferences under *Tellabs.*[1]

Notice Versus Fact Pleading

Bell Atlantic v. Twombly, 550 U.S. 544 (2007), and *Ashcroft v. Iqbal*, 129 S. Ct. 1937 (2009), required that the complaint be "plausible" and overruled the "no set of facts" language from *Conley v. Gibson*, 355 U.S. 41 (1957). The new rule provides that a claim will be dismissed only if "no plausible entitlement to relief can be shown on the face of the complaint." So-called "conclusory" allegations are ignored by the court when considering whether the complaint is "plausible." Courts have said that *Twombly* and *Iqbal* apply to securities cases even though the PSLRA has its own pleading requirements.

Obvious Alternative Explanation

In *Iqbal*, the Supreme Court held that a case must be dismissed if any explanation that the defendant gives to the court is more likely than the plaintiff's theory. The Supreme Court looked at the two proffered explanations

[1] *Tellabs, Inc. v. Makor Issues & Rights*, 551 U.S. 308 (2007). *See generally* Charles Davidow et al., "Best Practices for Dealing With Confidential Witness Allegations in Securities Fraud Complaints," 47 *Sec. Reg. & L. Rep. (BL)* 1483, July 27, 2015.

and determined that one was more likely than the other. The Court did not look at all possible explanations and did not require that the plaintiff's explanation be "substantially" more likely than the defendant's. As one lower court explained, "although the *Iqbal* opinion used phrases such as 'more likely' and 'as between,' it should not be read to say that a plaintiff should lose on the pleadings because a defendant had a more plausible alternative explanation. Rather, in light of the alternative explanation, plaintiff needed to allege more by way of factual content to 'nudge' his claim . . . across the line from conceivable to plausible." *McCauley v. City of Chicago*, 671 F.3d 611 (7th Cir. 2011).

By contrast, in *Twombly*, the Supreme Court not only compared two explanations and chose the one that was more likely, but it used the alternative explanation to determine that the plaintiff's explanation was "implausible."

The circuits have interpreted these cases in at least three different ways. The Third, Fourth, Fifth, and Ninth Circuits have given *Iqbal* a literal reading, and have dismissed cases where the alternative explanation is merely more likely than the pleaded explanation. The Sixth and Eighth Circuits have interpreted *Iqbal* as requiring more than mere notice pleading but less than an exclusion of all likely alternative explanations. The Second Circuit, in dictum, has rejected *Iqbal*'s plain meaning. *N.J. Carpenters Health Fund v. Royal Bank of Scotland Grp., PLC*, 709 F.3d 109, 121 n5 (2d Cir. 2013) ("The Supreme Court has not defined the phrase 'obvious alternative explanation'. . . . Whatever [it] means, the standard under Rule 8(a) undoubtedly remains less stringent than the 'heightened' pleading standard imposed by the PSLRA.")[2]

Glenn Greenberg argues that *Iqbal* could have more impact on pleading securities actions than is commonly assumed. With respect to loss causation, for example, he argues that "there almost always are intervening actions that can explain the loss." He continues: "If [courts] do follow the plain meaning of *Iqbal*, plaintiffs' securities lawyers will have a very difficult time winning cases, because they will need to have won the case before discovery." Is he correct? For example, wouldn't an event study, often performed before discovery has begun, eliminate the effect of possible alternative explanations for a loss caused by a corrective disclosure?

Do *Iqbal* and *Twombly* add anything meaningful to the pleading requirements of the PSLRA? The PSLRA already requires the pleading of sufficient facts to support "a strong inference that the defendant acted with the required state of mind." Doesn't *Tellabs* resolve the "obvious alternative explanation" issue by requiring that the allegations of scienter be "cogent" and "at least as compelling as any opposing inference one could draw from the facts alleged"? As noted, the Second Circuit seems to think so.

---

[2] *See* Glenn Greenberg, "The Impact of *Ashcroft v. Iqbal* on Securities Litigation," *NY State Bar Association Journal*, Feb. 2016, 21.

In *In re Century Aluminum Co. Securities Litigation*, 729 F.3d 1104 (9th Cir. 2013), the court affirmed the dismissal of a complaint in which the plaintiff alleged that he bought stock based on a misleading prospectus but could not plead sufficient facts to show that the stock he purchased was not already in the market." Citing *Iqbal* and *Twombly*, the court held that "when faced with two possible explanations, only one of which can be true and only one of which results in liability, plaintiffs cannot offer allegations that are 'merely consistent with' their favored explanation but are also consistent with the alternative explanation. Something more is needed," *Twombly* and *Iqbal* did not otherwise eliminate the special pleading requirements of Rule 9 or an allegation of fraud.

Remember that Rule 9(b) of the Federal Rules of Civil Procedure has a heightened pleading requirement for pleading fraud. Plaintiff "must state with particularity the circumstances constituting fraud or mistake." That rule still applies to securities cases covered by the PSLRA. After *Iqbal*, motions to dismiss have been granted in 15 percent more cases where the plaintiff was represented by counsel (or in 52 percent of cases in which a motion was made).[3]

The "group pleading" doctrine (*Wool v. Tandem Computers*, 818 F.2d 1433 (9th Cir. 1987)) said that Rule 9(b) was met by pleading the misrepresentation and, *where possible*, the role of the individual defendants in the misrepresentation. *Tellabs* left the issue open but *Janus*[4] probably closed the door. *Janus* requires proof that the "maker" of a misrepresentation had scienter. Thus, the "maker" of the statement has to be identified.[5]

PSLRA Certification Requirement

Each plaintiff seeking to be a class representative must file a sworn certification that he or she has reviewed the complaint and authorized its filing; that he or she did not purchase the security at issue at the direction of plaintiffs' counsel or in order to participate in the lawsuit; that he or she is willing to serve as a representative and will provide testimony at deposition and trial; set forth all of his or her transactions in the security at issue during the pendency of the class period; identify any other action filed during the preceding three years in which he or she served as a class representative; and state that he or she will not accept any payment beyond his or her pro rata share of any recovery, except as ordered by the court.

---

[3] *See* Alex Reinert, "Measuring the Impact of Plausibility Pleading," 101 *Va. L. Rev.* 2117 (2015).

[4] *Janus Capital Group, Inc. v. First Derivative Traders*, 131 S. Ct. 2296 (2011).

[5] *See, e.g.*, *In re Banco Bradesco S.A. Sec. Litig.*, 2017 WL 4381407, at *24-27 (concluding that group pleading doctrine does not survive *Janus*).

Other PSLRA Requirements

The PSLRA requires that the complaint must "specify" each misleading statement and set forth facts on which a belief that the statement is misleading was "formed."[6]

The PSLRA also provides "that in any private action in which the plaintiff can recover money damages only on proof that the defendant acted with the required state of mind, the complaint shall, with respect to each act or omission alleged to violate this title, state with particularity facts giving rise to a strong inference that the defendant acted with the required state of mind." Note that the statute does not use the word "scienter," but it is well understood that this is a reference to scienter.

Consider *Tellabs.*[7] In that case, Richard Notebaert, the CEO, allegedly falsely reassured investors that Tellabs was continuing to enjoy a strong demand for its products when he knew the opposite was true. The issue was whether or not in order to determine whether the pleading gave rise to a "strong inference of scienter," a court should consider "plausible opposing inferences." The Supreme Court said that in making that determination, the lower court *should* take into account "plausible opposing inferences." It then articulated what should be done if there are such opposing inferences. "Strong" means "powerful or cogent." "A complaint will survive, we hold, only if a reasonable person would deem the inference of scienter cogent and at least as compelling as any opposing inference one could draw from the facts alleged." What does "cogent" mean? "Convincing," "compelling," "forceful," "powerful," "appealing forcibly to the mind or reason."

Is this holding consistent with the Seventh Amendment? Is the Supreme Court weighing alternate inferences? Isn't that the sole province of the jury?[8] No court has gone this far, however.

Can there be a showing of "strong inferences" of corporate scienter without making such a showing with respect to an individual? Judges William Pauley and Richard Sullivan of the U.S. District Court for the Southern District of New York say yes. *Penn. Public School Employees Retirement System v. Bank of America*, 874 F. Supp. 2d 341 (2012) (S.D.N.Y. 2012); *In re UBS AG Securities Litigation*, 2011 WL 4059356 (S.D.N.Y. 2012); *see also Teamsters Local 455 Freight Fund v. Dynex Capital*, 531 F.3d 190 (2d Cir. 2008) (so-called collective scienter can be alleged without linking it to a specific individual).

---

[6] *See Dura Pharmaceuticals Inc. v. Broudo*, 544 U.S. 336 (2005).

[7] *Tellabs, Inc. v. Makor Issues & Rights*, 551 U.S. 308 (2007).

[8] *See* Professor Suja Thomas's work, including "Why Summary Judgment Is Unconstitutional," 93 *Va. L. Rev.* 139 (2007).

Do these decisions survive *Janus*? That issue remains unresolved. Some courts have said no.[9] It is worth noting, however, that in the Vivendi class action, the jury ruled in favor of the two individual defendants who were alleged to have acted with scienter but ruled against the corporation. The court upheld the jury verdict, finding that it was not necessary for the individuals to be held liable in order for the corporation to be held liable.

Is statistical significance required for scienter? In *Matrixx Initiatives v. Siracusano*, 563 U.S. 27 (2011), the plaintiff alleged that the defendant purposely decided to conceal the results of an independent report showing a negative health-related impact of a pharmaceutical product because the defendant knew it would have an adverse effect on the market. To support scienter, the plaintiff alleged that the defendant was sufficiently concerned about the report that it retained a consultant to review the alleged effects of the product. It alleged that the defendant asked a doctor to conduct animal studies, that the defendant convened a panel of physicians and scientists in response to the report, that the defendant prevented the study from using the name of its product in the public report, and that the defendant issued a press release suggesting that studies had confirmed that the product did not cause the reported health issues. In fact, it had not conducted any such studies, and the scientific evidence was insufficient to determine whether or not the product actually caused the reported health issues. The defendant argued that the scientific evidence was not statistically significant.

The Supreme Court held that in considering whether a plaintiff has met the "strong inference" test, "plausible opposing inferences" must also be considered. "A complaint adequately pleads scienter under the PSLRA only if a reasonable person would deem the inference of scienter cogent and at least as compelling as any opposing inference one could draw from the facts alleged." In making this determination, the court must review all the allegations holistically. The absence of a motive allegation, though relevant, is not dispositive. The court held that the allegations in that case gave rise to a cogent and compelling inference of scienter. Statistical significance is not required.

The PSLRA contains an exception for complaints against credit rating agencies. The complaint must only plead with particularity "facts giving rise to a strong inference that the credit rating agency knowingly or recklessly failed to conduct a reasonable investigation of the rated security with respect to the factual elements relied upon by its own methodology for evaluating credit risk, or to obtain reasonable verification of such factual elements ... from other sources considered to be competent and that were independent of the issuer or underwriter."

---

[9] *See* Browning Jeffries, "The Implications of Janus on Issuer Liability in Jurisdictions Rejecting Collective Scienter," 43 *Seton Hall L. Rev.* 491 (2013).

The PSLRA also has a requirement that loss causation must be proved by the plaintiffs but it does not say how. After *Dura*, the facts leading to loss causation must also be alleged. Some later cases have held that loss causation may be pleaded on the theory that the truth gradually emerged through a series of partial disclosures and that the entire series of partial disclosures prompted the stock price deflation. This is the so-called "leakage theory."[10] It is not universally accepted, however.

The PSLRA requires that misleading statements must be specified in the complaint with the reasons why each statement is misleading. How does this compare with the Rule 9 of the Federal Rules of Civil Procedure requirement for pleading fraud with particularity? It is probably more stringent.

Exhibits may be attached to a complaint, but there is a danger. What is it? (*Hint*: It may limit your options in the future.)

What are the reasons for suing individual officers as well as the corporation? The biggest one is usually insurance. Many D&O (directors & officers) insurance policies cover individuals but not corporations. Why do plaintiffs want to make sure there is insurance? (*Hint*: Settlement.) Another reason can be that it may also be useful to have a face for the jury to identify. But there are risks. In the Vivendi class action, the individuals were exonerated by the jury and the company was found liable whereas in *In re Apple Securities Litigation*, 886 F.2d 1109 (9th Cir. 1989), the individuals were found liable but the company was exonerated. (Not surprisingly, in that case the court promptly granted a JNOV, now called JMOL,[11] motion and ordered a new trial.)[12]

Demanding a Jury Trial

A jury demand may be done in the complaint or in a separate demand within fourteen days. Juries are demanded as a matter of routine. If the plaintiff does not, the defendant should. Why? (*Hint*: The defendant may want a jury and would be unable to have one if plaintiff did not ask for one.)

---

[10] *See Glickenhaus & Co. v. Household International, Inc.*, 787 F.3d 408 (7th Cir. 2015) (a leakage model "calculates every difference, both positive and negative, between the stock's predicted returns . . . and the stock's actual return during the disclosure period. The total sum . . . is assumed to be the effect of the disclosures.").

[11] Judgment Non Obstante Veridicto; Judgment as a Matter of Law. They are essentially the same; only the names have been changed!

[12] Full disclosure: I represented one of the individual defendants on that motion.

The Motion to Dismiss

Because of the special pleading requirements in securities cases, a motion to dismiss is made in almost every case. A motion to dismiss is addressed to the legal sufficiency of the complaint, assuming that all of the pleaded facts are true. By contrast, a motion for summary judgment can be made only when there are no material facts in dispute (whether or not pleaded in the complaint) and therefore the only issues to be decided are questions of law.

Under the PSLRA, motions to dismiss are expressly permitted and the complaint shall be dismissed for reasons that go beyond those in the Federal Rules of Civil Procedure. For example if the misleading statements are not specified and the reasons why the statements are misleading are not specified, or if the required state of mind is not established with particularity, the complaint must be dismissed.

Once a motion is made, all discovery is stayed unless the court finds that particularized discovery is necessary to preserve evidence or prevent undue prejudice. There is a corollary requirement that during any stay, all relevant documents shall be treated as if they were the subject of a continuing request for production of documents from an opposing party under the Federal Rules.

A federal court may also stay discovery proceedings in any private action in a state court as necessary in aid of its jurisdiction or to protect or effectuate its judgments in an action subject to a stay of discovery. This is meant to prevent plaintiffs from circumventing of the stay of discovery by bringing an action in state court and seeking discovery there. There is an open question, as yet unresolved by the Supreme Court, whether the automatic stay provision of the PSLRA applies to federal securities cases brought in state courts under the 1933 Securities Act. There is a split in the Circuits on this issue. *Jones v. Anderson*, 990 F.3d 692 (9th Cir. 2021), petition for writ of certiorari granted and then vacated because of settlement.

What is the purpose/benefit of the discovery stay? Because many securities class actions do not survive a motion to dismiss, it prevents unnecessary waste of money and effort. Some have argued that there should be a similar stay in all federal civil cases.

What Are the Usual Grounds for a Motion to Dismiss?

- Failure to comply with Federal Rules of Civil Procedure 9(b) and 12(b)(6).
- Failure to allege scienter with "plausibility."
- Failure to allege fraud with particularity.
- Failure to allege basis for allegation that statement is misleading.

- Failure to allege facts creating a "strong inference" of the "required state of mind."
- Failure to allege that others "actively participated in making or planning the false statements or other fraudulent acts" (see *Stoneridge v. Scientific Atlanta*, 552 U.S. 148 (2008)).
- The statements at issue are forward-looking statements accompanied by appropriate cautionary language as required by the PSLRA safe harbor.
- Statements at issue "bespeak caution" (in most circuits); ("Where an offering statement, such as a prospectus, accompanies statements of its future forecasts, projections and expectations with adequate cautionary language, those statements are not actionable." *Employers Teamsters Local No 175 v. Clorox*, 353 F.3d 1125 (9th Cir. 2004).) *See* Judge Robert Katzmann's opinion in *Wilson v. Merrill Lynch*, 671 F.3d 120 (2d Cir. 2011) ("be careful walking on this trail; you might fall into a ditch" is not a good enough warning if you know that the Grand Canyon is one foot away).
- Failure to allege loss causation facts (*Dura*).
- No duty to disclose.
- No duty to update.
- Opinions and puffery (mere expressions of general optimism are not material). If opinion is actionable, is it alleged to be objectively and subjectively false? (*See Fait v. Regions Financial Corp.*, 655 F.3d 105 (2d Cir. 2011).
- No responsibility for statements made by others (*Janus* issues).
- Oral statements inconsistent with the contents of a document furnished to the plaintiff.
- Information publicly disclosed elsewhere ("truth on the market").
- Absence of deception. (*See Santa Fe Industries v. Green*, 430 U.S. 462 (1977), deception is an essential ingredient of a Rule 10b-5 claim; forcing shareholders to sell at an unfair price by using available state law procedures was not actionable.)
- Statute of limitations. Usually this is raised as an affirmative defense because it may require reliance on material outside the complaint. But it could be raised in a motion to dismiss, especially if compliance with the statute is an element of plaintiffs' claim, such as in cases under Sections 11 and 12 of the Securities Act.

Answer and Affirmative Defenses

The first question that needs to be answered in a securities case is whether to answer the complaint or to move to dismiss it. Normally, the latter will be the preferred choice because the PSLRA has incorporated relatively rigorously pleading requirements that can be tested on a motion to dismiss the complaint. Under the Federal Rules of Civil Procedure, the defendant has twenty-one days from the service of the complaint to move against it or to answer it. A motion stays the answer date until after the motion is denied. If the motion is denied, the complaint must be answered within fourteen days after the court's decision.

The answer must contain "in short and plain terms [the party's] defenses to each claim asserted against it," and it must admit or deny the allegations asserted against it or state that the party lacks knowledge or information sufficient to form a belief about the truth of an allegation. (Rule 8.) The answer also must affirmatively state any affirmative defenses.

Due diligence defense must be pleaded. This applies usually to allegations in the complaint about statements made by those persons who are not authorized by the PSLRA to speak for the issuer and to take advantage of the safe harbor. Such a claim is usually defeated by a showing of good faith and due diligence. These are express defenses under Section 11 of the 1933 Act. To establish the defense, Section 11(b)(3)(A) requires the defendant to show that "he had after reasonable investigation, reasonable ground to believe and did believe" that the statements in the registration statement were true and that there was no omission that made the statements misleading. As noted in Chapter 8, there are different defenses for experts and non-experts. Equitable defenses such as in pari delicto, laches, and estoppel may also be pleaded.

In general, answers contain three possible responses to each factual allegation in the complaint: an admission, a denial, or a statement that the defendant is without knowledge or information sufficient to form a belief as to the truth of the allegation. This is generally known as a "DKI" answer and it has the same effect as a denial.

There are general and specific denials. A general denial is permitted where the defendant, in good faith, denies all allegations in the complaint, including jurisdictional grounds. Otherwise, the party must "either specifically deny designated allegations or generally deny all except those specifically admitted." If an allegation is not denied, it is deemed admitted. A "speaking answer" is also permitted, in which the defendant adds reasons why the factual allegation is being denied. It is not encouraged and should be used sparingly because it adds additional factual allegations that may or may not be sustained by subsequent proof, and it is unnecessary. If documents are referred to in the complaint, the relevant allegation may be denied "except the defendant refers to the [document in question] for its contents."

Answers must also contain certain defenses, otherwise they are waived. Those defenses are:

- lack of personal jurisdiction,
- improper venue,
- insufficiency of process, and
- insufficiency of service of process.

In addition, affirmative defenses are waived unless contained in the answer. In the Second Circuit, the *Twombly* standard applies not only to the allegations in the complaint but also to those in affirmative defenses pleaded in the answer, "but with the recognition that, as the Supreme Court explained in *Iqbal*, applying the plausibility standard to any pleading is 'context specific.'" *GEOMC Co. v. Calmare Therapeutics Inc.*, 918 F.3d. 92 (2d Cir. 2019).

Discovery

In class actions especially, discovery in securities cases is extensive and because the stakes are so high, the usual rules of proportionality are rarely applied. Note, however, that the 2015 amendments to the Federal Rules of Civil Procedure provide that material that is not "proportional" is not discoverable but the burden is on the objecting party to establish lack of proportionality. "Proportionality" is a difficult concept to apply to a securities class action, however, because discovery in those cases is almost always "one way" with most of it coming only from the defendant, except for discovery from plaintiffs' expert witnesses and other third-party witnesses. In addition, discovery of absent class members is not permitted. *See, e.g.*, *Cox v. American Cast Iron Pipe Co.*, 784 F.2d 1546 (11th Cir. 1986). A few additional points:

- Interrogatories are usually of limited utility.
- Requests for admissions are of even less utility.
- Document production, including electronic discovery, is usually extensive. Rule 26 contains a requirement for "initial disclosures" of documents and other information without awaiting a discovery request, although that requirement is sometimes honored in the breach, and also permits discovery "regarding any nonprivileged matter that is relevant to any party's claim or defense" so long as the rule of proportionality is observed. As a result, in practice, there are usually very few limitations on discovery in complex securities litigation.

E-Discovery

Electronic discovery is the search for relevant electronic evidence. It is ubiquitous and if done incorrectly, can result in sanctions. The key legal issues with e-discovery are proportionality (Rule 26(b)(1) Federal Rules of Civil Procedure), reasonable diligence (Rule 26(g)), selection of methods (*Hyles v. New York City*, 2016 WL 4077114 (S.D.N.Y. Aug. 1, 2019) (the producing party is in the best position to evaluate the necessary procedures and methodologies for preserving and producing electronically stored information)), and cooperation (Rule 26(f)). Potentially relevant documents must be preserved as soon as litigation or investigation becomes "reasonably foreseeable."

- E-documents are typically processed onto a review platform and non-discoverable documents are culled out.
- E-documents are then reviewed for responsiveness and confidentiality, often through the use of "Technology Assisted Review" (TAR), which typically uses machine learning and other artificial intelligence to review the documents. TAR is increasingly accepted by courts and has been shown to be more accurate than human review.
- Create a privilege log.
- Be aware of data privacy and protection restrictions.
- Good-faith cooperation is essential.
- The expanding "dataverse" of non-email messaging, social media, new collaboration tools such as Slack and Teams, cloud storage, mobile devices, multimedia, and geolocation data creates new issues, challenges, and risks.

Videotaped Depositions

Videotaped depositions are very common. Because they will be shown to the jury, the witnesses must be very carefully prepared. They should dress appropriately, for example.[13] Almost all cases require expert economic proof for such things as an event study. *Daubert* issues are almost always raised by motion. (*Daubert v. Merrell Dow*, 509 U.S. 579 (1993).) Note that *Daubert* motions often succeed, among other reasons, because there is very little scholarly literature on event studies and loss causation outside the realm of litigation itself, which *Daubert* found to be inadequate. As a result, Rule 702 was amended in 2011. An opinion will be permitted if an expert's scientific, technical, or other specialized knowledge will help the trier of fact to understand the evidence or to determine a fact in issue. This new test is so amorphous that it could be argued that it swallows the rule.

---

[13] *See* ABA Law Practice Management Section, "Video Depositions: Essentials, Resources" (2016).

Use of Experts

The proponent of the expert testimony has the burden of establishing the admissibility requirement with the district court acting as a "gatekeeper" to ensure that the "expert's testimony both rests on a reliable foundation and is relevant to the task at hand." *United States v. Williams*, 506 F.3d 151, 160 (2d Cir. 2007). There may also be expert testimony on damages, especially if rescission or rescissionary damages are sought. Should you depose experts as a matter of strategy? Most lawyers do, but there can be good reasons for not doing so. What could they be? (*Hint*: Previewing your cross-examination at trial and giving the expert an opportunity to revise her opinion.)

Discovery of Expert Work Product. Often, there are pretrial agreements limiting discovery of an expert's work product. In addition, Rule 26 of the Federal Rules, enacted in 2010, now protects drafts of expert reports and communications between experts and the retaining party's attorney, with three specific exceptions, relating to the expert's compensation, facts or data given to and considered by the expert, and assumptions provided to and relied on by the expert.

Chapter 14

Securities Litigation Issues, Part Two

Motions for Summary Judgment

Summary judgment motions are governed by Rule 56 of the Federal Rules of Civil Procedure. They may be filed at any time until thirty days after the close of all discovery (unless otherwise ordered). The rule provides that the motions "shall be granted if the movant shows that there is no genuine dispute as to any material fact and that the movant is entitled to judgment as a matter of law." Under Rule 56(d), the non-movant may show that it cannot present facts essential to justify its opposition. In that case, the court may defer consideration, allow time to get affidavits, or permit the non-movant to take discovery. This is one reason why summary judgment motions come after the close of discovery. Rule 56.1 statements of undisputed facts (required in some local civil rules) are increasingly disfavored. They take a long time to prepare and are rarely helpful. Courts are reluctant to grant summary judgment on scienter unless there is "no rational basis" for concluding that statements were made with scienter. *See In re Software Toolworkers Inc. Sec. Lit.*, 38 F.3d 1078 (9th Cir. 1994).

Unlike motions to dismiss, motions for summary judgment are not routinely made in securities cases because they are so fact intensive. Some say that such motions, even if unsuccessful, are useful to "educate the judge." However, they rarely serve that purpose. Motions for partial summary judgment may be helpful in clearing away extraneous issues. Courts disagree as to whether they can grant summary judgment on one element of a claim. Note that Rule 56(g) permits a court that does not grant all of the relief sought by the motion to enter an order identifying any material fact that is not genuinely in dispute and treating that fact as established.

After *Dura*, summary judgment on loss causation has become more likely. *See, e.g.*, *In re Mercury Interactive Corp.*, 2007 BL 210140 (N.D. Cal. July 30, 2007) ("failure to establish that the disclosure of the relevant wrongdoing played a significant role in the loss merits entry of summary judgment for failure to show loss causation.")

Orders granting summary judgment are not ordinarily appealable until the claims against all of the parties have been disposed of, but there are some exceptions. See Rule 54(b). An order denying summary judgment is not appealable except under 28 U.S.C. § 1292(b), which requires the consent of both the district court and the court of appeals. That rarely happens.

Trial Preparation in General

You should begin to prepare for trial at the earliest possible moment, even before any discovery has been taken. Confer with your clients, of course, but conduct your own investigation of the facts as well. What should you do with the results of discovery when it begins to come in? Prepare an outline of proof/order of proof, use it to prepare witnesses, use it to understand the issues, and use it to plan your affirmative or defensive cases. The outline will tell you how to prove or defend against each of the necessary facts and where additional work needs to be done. The outline of proof is a living document and should be updated constantly. At a trial, few exhibits are used, although many are discovered. Some use this fact to argue that there is too much irrelevant discovery in securities cases. The new amended Federal Rules of Civil Procedure Rule 26 requires proportionality, but it remains to be seen how that will be enforced.

Bear in mind that juries don't like deposition reading ("boring") but videotapes are slightly better.[1]

Motions in limine, which are motions asking the court to receive or exclude certain evidence for a variety of reasons, including relevance and prejudice, are standard. Start thinking about them early in your trial preparation. *In limine* is a Latin word meaning "on the threshold," which suggests that it should be made before the trial begins, so that the parties will know before trial what the evidence will or will not be.[2]

Use of jury consultants and mock trials is very common and is quite useful although expensive.

Begin preparing for trial from the first day the complaint is filed. While it is true that most securities cases do not go to trial, if you are not prepared to go to trial, you will be at a serious disadvantage when discussing settlement.

---

[1] *See* National Criminal Justice Reference Service, "Videotape on Trial—A View From the Jury Box" (1979), https://www.ojp.gov/ncjrs/virtual-library/abstracts/videotape-trial-view-jury-box.

[2] Philip Halpern, "Burden of Proof: Preparing a Case From Intake Through Verdict and on Appeal," American Bar Association, 2020, p. 256.

Read the model jury instructions early in the case so you know what you will be facing.[3] If the model jury instructions don't help your case, look for actual instructions from other trials. Remember that courts are not limited to using only the model jury instructions.

- Be creative.
- Begin preparing witnesses early.
- *Daubert* challenges to expert witnesses are commonplace.
- Write out your opening very early and constantly revise it. (But don't read it at trial!)
- In preparing for jury selection, use of a jury questionnaire is increasingly common. Samples are available from the Federal Judicial Center.

Expert witnesses calculate per-share inflation (i.e., "damages"). They rarely calculate an aggregate amount of damages. Why? (*Hint*: It may scare the jury and nobody can know how many successful claims will be filed by class members after the trial. In settlements, typically fewer than 25 percent of eligible claimants actually submit claims.)[4]

Opening Statements

Most trial lawyers believe (and I am one of them) that opening statements are the most important part of the trial. Why would that be true? (*Hint*: The jury's attention is at its highest during openings.[5]) Most cases are won or lost at the opening. (Some say 80 percent of jurors make up their minds during or immediately after the opening statements.[6]) Opening statements are not even mentioned in the Federal Rules of Civil Procedure. All of the law concerning opening statements is court-made law.

---

[3] *See, e.g.*, ABA, "Model Jury Instructions Securities Litigation," W3, Nexis.com.

[4] *See* Elizabeth Cabraser & Andrew Pincus, "Claims-Made Class-Action Settlements," 99 *Judicature* No. 3, Winter 2015, p. 81; Brian Fitzpatrick & Robert Gilbert, "An Empirical Look at Compensation in Consumer Class Actions," *Vanderbilt Law School Working Paper*, 2015. https://static.reuters.com/resources/media/editorial/.pdf.

[5] *See The Trial Process: Opening Statements*, Maurer School of Law ("Many trial practitioners asset that the opening statement is the most under-rated and overlooked part of the case."), https://pdf4pro.com/view/chapter-4-opening-statement-maurer-school-1ebce4.html.

[6] Donald Vinson, "Jury Psychology and Antitrust Trial Strategy," 55 *Antitrust L. J.* at 591 (1986) (based on a survey of 14,000 actual or surrogate jurors).

Most courts will not permit "argument" during opening statements. The line between "the facts" and "argument" is very thin. That is why lawyers use the phrase "the evidence will show . . ." even if they are really making an argument. Themes and credibility are important.

Key points for an effective opening statement include the following:

- Rehearse, rehearse.
- Don't read it.
- Don't promise more than you can deliver.
- Objections during opening. Don't! (Save them for a sidebar.)
- Keep it simple. Themes are important. Try for no more than three themes.
- Use of demonstratives is very common. It is almost unheard of to do a jury trial opening without them.
- Defendant should anticipate plaintiff's opening. The opening trial scene in the movie *A Few Good Men* is a good example of this. (Lt. Caffey anticipated his opponent's opening statement, which ended with these words: "These are the facts of the case and they are undisputed," and he began his opening statement by saying, "There was no poison on the rag and there was no intent to kill and any attempt to prove otherwise is futile because it just ain't true." In other words, the facts were very much disputed.)

Direct and Redirect Examination

The purpose of direct examination is persuasion. The key points for a direct examination include making a prima facie case and creating a record for appeal. How does a lawyer accomplish those objectives?

- Prepare a chronology.
- Create an order of proof for all elements and link them to witnesses.
- Create a direct outline.
- Some prepare Q&As; others use a list of facts to be established.

How to Prepare a Witness for a Direct Examination[7]

- Interview the witness thoroughly.
- Put witness at ease.
- Familiarize the witness with the case and your themes.

---

[7] This list is taken largely from Robert Haig, ed., *Business and Commercial Litigation in Federal Courts* (4th ed.) (Thomson Reuters) (2017). Full disclosure: I

- Emphasize the importance of truth telling.
- Review the witness's background.
- Elicit the witness's story:
  - Should it be told chronologically or thematically?
  - Is there a compelling narrative?
- Review the deposition with the witness.
- Discuss the use of documents and other exhibits.
- Review the testimony of other witnesses.
- Structure the direct:
  - Witness should know what to expect.
  - Clear presentation.
- Anticipate cross.
- Rehearse and videotape.
- Note that on cross, the witness may be asked about preparation; there will be a difference if the witness is your client; the attorney-client privilege may apply; for others, work product may apply, but it may not! For that reason, emphasize the obligation to tell the truth.

Techniques for Presentation of Direct

- Think about how to make it interesting:
  - Tell a story [but there may be a tension between telling a story and making a record for appeal].
  - Solve a puzzle.
- Let the witness do the talking.
- Accredit the witness for the trier of fact.
- Lawyer should be invisible.
- Short questions:
  - "Please explain."
  - "Tell us."
  - "What happened next?"
- Listen to the witness. Even the best prepared witness will be nervous and will say things you don't expect.
- Learn how to refresh recollection [you can use anything to do that, even if not admissible].
- Anticipate evidentiary issues.
- Learn how to ask non-leading questions; who, where, what, how, etc.

---

favorably reviewed this comprehensive multi-volume treatise for the *New York Law Journal* on several occasions.

- Eliminate jargon and "lawyerese."
- Use demonstratives.
- Prepare the witness's demeanor; it should be the same for direct and cross.
- Prepare the witness to deal with objections (largely to ignore them).
- Prepare the witness for cross.
- Tell the witness what to wear (neutral colors, no jewelry, nothing fancy).

Other Issues

- Experts
  - They will have prepared a report. Will it come into evidence?
  - Rules or agreement may limit whether experts can be asked about preparation.
  - They will not need much or any leading.
- Judge only versus jury
  - Judges will know the case, and therefore the direct can be structured to get to the issues more quickly; juries will need to be brought along more slowly.
  - Written direct in judge-only cases? This sometimes occurs when the court asks for it.
- Remember Rule 611 of the Federal Rules of Evidence: no leading questions on direct examination "except as necessary to develop the witness's testimony." What does that mean? Usually, a hostile witness or a child.
- The hostile witness
  - Can be led on direct.
  - Usually the adverse party or a witness identified with an adverse party will be declared hostile.

Redirect

- Purpose is rehabilitation.
- Keep it short. Don't just recapitulate the direct.
- When preparing for redirect, keep notes of the direct and annotate them as you go with possible points for the redirect.
- When your witness is on cross, there are only two things you have to do:
  - Listen to the testimony for possible objections.
  - Think about the redirect.

Cross-Examination

- The principal purpose of cross-examination is persuasion.
- That can be accomplished by casting doubt on the witness's testimony, either by discrediting it or showing incompetence.
- It can also be accomplished by eliciting helpful testimony.

Methods of Cross-Examination

- Use leading questions or leading assertions (e.g., "Isn't it a fact that . . .").
- Use positive statements (e.g., "The traffic light was red when you approached it, wasn't it?").
- Insist that the witness answer the question that you posed, not something else. The court will assist you in this effort. Do not allow the witness to "pontificate" or make a speech. Your questions must be clear, direct, and capable of being answered directly.

Preparing to Cross-Examine a Witness

- Have a theory of your case. Keep in mind the themes that you established during your opening statement.
- Have a theory of the witness (e.g., a liar, conflicted, confused, ignorant, helpful?).
- Use a modular or topical approach for your notes, not an outline, so that you can "go with the flow" of the testimony you are eliciting.
- Make a list of the points you wish to establish.
- Consider how best to establish them.
- Know when not to cross and when to stop.
- Anticipate objections.
- Witness control is absolutely essential.

The Rest of the Trial

Jury instructions in securities cases are relatively simple; be aware of the waiver issues if you do not object. You will be asked to propose jury instructions for the court's consideration. These would be in addition to the Model Jury Instructions for your jurisdiction. Remember that jury instructions that are not proposed are generally waived. Jury instructions must be disclosed to the parties by the court before the closing arguments, so that counsel can refer to them in the closing. In addition, remember that as a general matter, if there is no objection to a particular jury instruction, the objection is almost certainly waived for any appeal. Also remember that as a general rule, written copies of the jury instructions are given to the jury when it retires to deliberate.

Closing Argument

As a general rule, the party with the burden of proof—that is, the plaintiff—usually goes last. In that case, the defendant must anticipate the plaintiff's closing in its own closing argument. Repeat the themes set forth in your opening and use visual aids to remind the jury what those themes were and how you proved them. You may refer to the court's jury instructions in your closing. Practice tip: In preparing your closing argument, assume that you are going to lose. Ask yourself the five questions that the jury would like to have had answered during the trial in order to rule in your favor, but that were not in fact answered during the trial. What is your explanation for not answering them? If possible, answer them in the closing argument. Use this experience to prepare for your next trial.

If your opponent makes a statement in the closing that you find objectionable, you must call it to the court's attention either during the closing argument (usually not a good idea) or immediately after the closing at the sidebar. If you do not, your objection is most likely waived for any appeal.

Pre- and Post-Judgment Interest Issues

In some securities litigation, pre- and post-judgment litigation can become an issue but until the final amounts of payments actually made to class members, it is nearly impossible to calculate them. In addition,

- Pre-judgment interest is discretionary; the court can decide whether and if so at what rate.
- Federal law governs (there can be a complication if there are federal and state claims).
- Factors to be considered include whether pre-judgment interest is necessary to compensate the plaintiff fully, the degree of personal wrongdoing, the availability of alternative investment opportunities, and whether the plaintiff delayed in bringing or prosecuting the action and other fundamental considerations of fairness.
- Post-judgment interest is mandatory, but the rate is discretionary.

There must be a claims process if there is a verdict against the defendant. Why can't a final judgment be entered until after the claims process is finished? (*Hint*: Actual damages are an element of the offense.) Usually a claims administrator is retained by the winning plaintiff, with the approval of the court, and members of the class are notified of the verdict in the case, and given the opportunity to submit a claim to the administrator or to opt out of the class so that they can bring individual actions. Note that in reality, only about 20 percent of the class members typically submit claims. The claims administrator will adjudicate each separate claim, and that adjudication—either for or against the claim depending on such things like the date of purchase—will then be reviewed by the parties and the court. Once the court signs off on all the claims, judgment is entered, and the claims and counsel fees are paid by the defendant.

Settlements

"Claims made" settlements in securities cases are rare; "lump sum" settlements are now the norm. A "claims made" settlement is one in which the parties agree on the amount of settlement per share that will be paid, and the remainder of the agreed settlement is returned to the defendant if not enough valid claims are submitted to use up the settlement amount. A "lump sum" settlement is one in which the total amount of the settlement is distributed pro rata, no matter how many claims are made. Perhaps because of the increasing vigilance of the Delaware Chancery Court in overseeing settlements that skimp on benefiting the class in favor of benefiting the lawyers, federal courts are also becoming skeptical.

In *Pearson v. NBTY, Inc.*, 772 F.3d 778 (7th Cir. 2014), for example, Judge Richard Posner was outspoken in his criticism of lawyers who included a reversion clause, sometimes called a "kicker," in a settlement agreement. In that case, there were 12 million class members who alleged that certain pharmaceutical companies violated state consumer protection laws by making overly optimistic claims about their products.[8] The settlement amounts, after modification by the district court, included $1.93 million in fees to class counsel, and only $865,284 to the 30,000 class members who submitted claims (i.e., $5,000 for each member). The "kicker" clause provided that if the court reduced the amount of fees being awarded to class counsel—which occurred in this case—the difference would revert back to the defendants. Judge Posner called this a "gimmick for defeating objectors" since if the class cannot benefit from the reduction in attorneys' fees, then any objector would have no standing to object. Judge Posner wrote that the "simple and obvious way" for the court to correct an excessive attorneys' fee award was to increase the share of the settlement received by the class. Neither counsel nor the court could

---

[8] A federal court had jurisdiction because of the Class Action Fairness Act of 2005.

explain how negotiating first for class benefits could actually benefit a class, and the appellate court concluded that it could not "think of a justification for a 'kicker' clause; at the very least there should be a strong presumption of its invalidity."

Court approval of any class settlement is required. Rule 23(e)(2) of the Federal Rules of Civil Procedure requires that a settlement be approved only after notice to the class with an opportunity to opt out of the settlement, a hearing, and a finding that the settlement is "fair, reasonable and adequate." (Note that in approving an SEC consent decree, by contrast, the court does not make a finding of "adequacy." *See SEC v. Citigroup*, 752 F.3d 285 (2d Cir. 2014)). This case is discussed further in Chapter 17.

As noted, notice and opportunity to opt out and bring a separate action or to object must be given to the class. Note that the filing of the complaint tolled the statute of limitations. Claims administrators will distribute the settlement amounts following court approval. *Girsh v. Jepson*, 521 F.2d 153 (3d Cir. 1975), has nine factors that should be considered in approving a class action settlement, including complexity, duration of litigation, reaction of the class, stage of the proceeding, risks, ability of defendant to pay more, and reasonableness of settlement in light of best possible recovery and in light of litigation risks. *See also McReynolds v. Richards-Cantave*, 588 F.3d 790 (2d Cir. 2009).

Chapter 15

Insider Trading

What Is Insider Trading?

Many observers have said that insider trading is a clear wrong in search of a viable legal theory that would preclude or prevent it. There is no statute that explicitly prohibits it (except for Section 14(e) and Rule 14(e), which prohibit trading in connection with tender offers, and Section 16(b), which requires certain officers, directors, and 10 percent owners to return profits made or losses avoided on trades in the company's securities within any six-month period). Academics have argued that prohibiting insider trading preserves investor confidence in the integrity of the market, but others, such as Henry Manne, have argued that this is an illusion, since despite insider trading, there is a widespread and growing willingness in the American public to invest. Professor Donald Langevoort has called this "investor confidence" rationale a "useful myth."

Insider trading is a type of securities fraud, and civil and criminal insider trading cases are brought under Section 10(b) and Rule 10b-5. Insider trading has been considered common law fraud but only in those jurisdictions where officers and directors owe fiduciary duties to shareholders. Before the federal securities laws were enacted, some states, such as Massachusetts, required a face-to-face transaction for such a breach.

For there to be insider trading under the federal law, must the stock be sold on a national exchange? Probably not. Any sale that uses any means of interstate commerce or of the mails or of any facility of any national securities exchange would violate Section 10(b) so long as the other elements are met. The hard question is whether the other elements are met.

Under Section 10(b), insider trading occurs when a person or entity trades in any security on the basis of material non-public information about the security or issuer in breach of a duty of trust or confidence that is owed directly, indirectly, or derivatively to the issuer of that security or the shareholders of that issuer or to any other person who is the source of the material non-public information.

Cady, Roberts & Co.[1]

When William Cary became Chair of the SEC, he made it his mission to overturn a Massachusetts state court opinion, *Goodwin v. Aggasiz*, 186 N.E. 659 (Mass. 1933), that required a face-to-face transaction for insider trading liability. As Professor Langevoort has reminded us, Cary believed that state corporate law was moribund and perhaps even corrupt. His opportunity came in *Cady, Roberts & Co.*, which established a new federal corporation law. This seminal 1961 administrative decision was the first to establish the "abstain or disclose" rule. It also eliminated the previous state "face-to-face" rule.

Robert Gintel bought stock of Curtiss-Wright after being informed by his Cady, Roberts partner, who was on the board of Curtiss-Wright, that the company was going to reduce its dividend. His partner thought the information was public. The SEC brought an administrative action against Gintel. The SEC found that "the common law in some jurisdictions imposes 'on corporate insiders' particularly officers, directors, or controlling stockholders" an "affirmative duty of disclosure." The commission regarded the insider relationship primarily in terms of unequal access to non-public information, not merely one in which there was a common law fiduciary duty. "Abstain or disclose" was the result of the perception of the inherent unfairness of allowing one with access to non-public information to profit from it personally. But there was very little corporate law support for such a duty. As we will see, this theory has not been accepted by the Supreme Court.

"Abstain or disclose" means that the corporate insider must either abstain from personal trading (or tipping others) or ensure that the information he or she has is fully disclosed and disseminated to the market before trading. The SEC decision went beyond corporate employees and covers auditors, outside accountants, brokers, investment bankers, and counsel. They all owe a fiduciary duty to use information that has been entrusted to them only for the benefit of the corporation.

How Did the Prohibition Against Insider Trading Originate?

As noted, it originated as common law fraud first in state courts, then through the antifraud provisions of the state securities laws. Even before the federal securities acts were passed, the Supreme Court held that a corporate director who bought stock knowing that it was going to go up in price committed fraud. *Strong v. Repide*, 213 U.S. 419 (1909). The first state cases were based on a theory of "fraudulent nondisclosures" (or pure silence). But

---

[1] *In the Matter of Cady, Roberts & Co.*, 40 SEC 907 (1961); Donald Langevoort, "Rereading Cady, Roberts: The Ideology and Practice of Insider Trading Regulation," 99 *Colum. L. Rev.* 1319 (1999).

many states required a face-to-face transaction for liability. *See, e.g.*, *Goodwin v. Aggasiz*, 186 N.E. 659 (Mass. 1933). Some of the questions raised were whether corporate insiders owed a fiduciary duty to shareholders. As discussed further below, John Siffert, one of the prosecutors in the *Chiarella* case tells us that duty is the duty of loyalty. Also, some states permitted derivative actions against insiders who used inside information.

"Insider" is not defined by the securities laws but it is construed by courts to be a person or entity that by virtue of a fiduciary relationship with an issuer has knowledge of, or access to, material non-public information. Typically, this would include corporate officers. It also includes "temporary insiders." *See Dirks v. SEC*, 103 S. Ct. 3261 n.14. But the law goes far beyond corporate officers and covers, for example, any corporate employee.

The "Classic" Theory

This theory is based on a breach of a duty to the shareholder-seller. The theory is that true corporate insiders, such as officers, owe a duty to their shareholders and that when they use non-public, material information belonging to the company for personal gain, they are breaching that duty in a deceptive manner. The duty is similar to the duty of loyalty that is described in Delaware corporate law.[2] Thus, in *SEC v. Texas Gulf Sulphur*, 401 F.2d 833 (2d Cir. 1969), the officers breached that duty when they purchased stock just before the announcement of a valuable ore discovery. However, the *Texas Gulf Sulphur* court did not refer explicitly to a duty of loyalty nor, indeed, did it refer to a breach of any duty. Rather, the court said that under Rule 10b-5, "all investors should have equal access to the rewards of participation in securities transactions" and that "the insiders here were not trading on an equal footing with the outside investors." This led some to believe that Rule 10b-5 was violated whenever there was an imbalance of information between the purchaser and seller. That is not the law.

United States v. Chiarella[3]

Vincent Chiarella worked for Pandick Press, a financial printer, and learned about upcoming corporate takeovers by reading some of the documents that had been submitted to his company for printing in connection with tender offers. Chiarella deduced the names of the targets from the documents.

---

[2] *See* Delaware Supreme Court Justice Randy Holland's "Delaware Directors' Duties: The Focus on Loyalty," "Scholarship.Law.UPenn.edu," 11 *J. Bus. L.* 675 (2009).

[3] 455 U.S. 222 (1980).

Without disclosing his knowledge, Chiarella purchased stock in the targets and sold it as soon as the takeovers were announced. He made a profit of more than $30,000 over a fourteen-month period. His was the first criminal prosecution and the first Supreme Court insider trading case under Section 10(b). He was convicted, and his conviction was affirmed by the Second Circuit. However, the Supreme Court reversed his conviction. The Court noted the "abstain or disclose" rule articulated by the SEC, but disagreed with the SEC that mere possession of material non-public information alone triggered the abstain or disclose obligation. The Court held that the possessor is liable only if the trade breached an existing fiduciary duty. Chiarella, the Court ruled, had no duty to disclose his knowledge to a purchaser. He had no special confidential relationship with the parties to the transaction.

Although the *Cady, Roberts* obligation was not limited to corporate insiders but was flexible and extended to others who have a "special relationship" with a corporation or its insiders, Chiarella didn't have such a relationship with any of the companies whose stock he bought.

Chiarella was the first case to speak of a breach of a duty as a requirement for a successful insider trading prosecution. But what duty? It couldn't be a duty to disclose non-public information to the seller because Chiarella had no such duty. "[O]ne who fails to disclose material information prior to the consummation of a transaction commits fraud only where he is under a duty to do so." Similarly, "no duty could arise from ... [a] relationship with the sellers ... for petitioner had no prior dealing with them." Chiarella's conviction was reversed by the Supreme Court because he had no duty to the sellers. "A purchaser of stock who has no duty to a prospective seller because he is neither an insider not a fiduciary has been held to have no obligation to reveal material facts." The author of the majority opinion was Justice Lewis Powell, a corporate lawyer in private practice before his Supreme Court appointment. In a footnote, Justice Powell opined that tippees could inherit a tipper's fiduciary duty by becoming a participant "after the fact" or a "co-venturer." We will see that proposition re-surface in *Dirks*, which opinion Powell also authored.

The Supreme Court did not consider an alternate argument that Chiarella breached a duty to the acquiring corporation when he acted upon information that he obtained by virtue of his position as an employee of the printer employed by the corporation because that theory had not been submitted to the jury. If it had been submitted to the jury, do you think that the Supreme Court would have upheld a conviction?

If Chiarella had been an insider like the officers in *Texas Gulf Sulphur*, what would his duty have been? What is the nature of the "duty" or "fiduciary duty" that is violated when an insider or a temporary insider trades on inside information? John Siffert, the New York lawyer who prosecuted Mr. Chiarella, has written persuasively that the duty is one of loyalty. Trading or tipping for an insider's personal benefit, he points out, is a breach of the insider's duty of loyalty.[4] In *United States v. O'Hagan*, discussed below, the Court referred to the duty as "a duty of loyalty and confidentiality."

Dirks v. SEC[5]

This case further expanded this theory and developed the law of tipper-tippee liability. Raymond Dirks was an officer in a broker-dealer firm who specialized in investment analysis of insurance company stocks. He received information from a corporate insider of an insurance company that the company had vastly overstated its assets. Dirks shared that information with some of his clients, some of whom sold their stock in the company. The SEC charged Dirks with aiding and abetting a violation of Section 17(a) of the 1933 Act and Section 10(b) of the 1934 Act. Dirks was held liable and the finding was upheld by the U.S. Court of Appeals for the District of Columbia Circuit. Dirks petitioned the Supreme Court, which reversed in a divided opinion.

Dirks was not liable, the Supreme Court ruled, because there was no breach of duty by his tipper. The Court held that the tipper must have an improper purpose and must personally benefit. The disclosure must be for the purpose of receiving the benefit, and the tippee must know that. *Dirks* also said, perhaps in *dicta*, in the famous footnote 14, that "outsiders" may in certain circumstances, become fiduciaries of shareholders and thus be subject to the same duty to abstain or disclose. 103 S. Ct. at 3261 n.14. "The bases for recognizing this fiduciary duty ... [is that] they have entered into a special confidential relationship in the conduct of the business of the enterprise and are given access to information solely for corporate purposes.... For such a duty to be imposed, however, the corporation must expect the outsider to keep the disclosed nonpublic information confidential, and the relationships must at least imply such a duty."

Even if the person has no connection with the company, the law may still apply. First, if the person receives material non-public information from a corporate insider who breached a duty and received a benefit and trades on the basis of that information, the person can be liable as a tippee (assuming scienter and knowledge that the tipper received a personal benefit). Second, the person can be liable under the "misappropriation theory" for using information that was obtained in breach of a duty of trust or confidence. Justice Powell's theory, first articulated in *Chiarella*, was that the tippee could be a "joint venturer" with the tipper, who would share in the tipper's breach of duty by

---

[4] *See* John Siffert & Michael Herman, "Understanding Insider Trading after Newman as a Breach of the Duty of Loyalty," *N.Y. L.J.* Jan. 20, 2016.

[5] 463 U.S. 646 (1983).

receiving a "gift" of the inside information. According to an early Powell draft, this "gift" would also prove that the insider breach a fiduciary duty, which the tippee would share.

Even if one does not actually trade in securities, he or she could be liable if she learned the information from a corporate insider or someone else who breached a duty of trust or confidence and then shared it with someone who actually does trade in the securities, *and* he or she received a personal benefit. This is "tippee" liability. You must know or have reason to know about the breach of a duty of trust or confidence to be liable. If you are a tippee, must you also know that the tipper received a personal benefit? After *Newman*, discussed below, the answer was clearly yes. But after *Salman*, also discussed below, the answer may be less clear.

United States v. O'Hagan[6]: The "Misappropriation" Theory

James O'Hagan was a lawyer at the firm of Dorsey & Whitey in Minneapolis who heard about an upcoming takeover of Pillsbury Co. by Grand Metropolitan (Grand Met) in which his firm was involved. O'Hagan was not working on the matter and had no reason to know anything about it. O'Hagan was in debt and heard about the takeover through casual conversation in the hallways. He bought calls on Pillsbury stock. When the takeover was announced, O'Hagan exercised his calls and then sold the stock for a $4 million profit. O'Hagan was charged with criminal insider trading.

The Supreme Court (Justice Ginsburg) first noted that under the "classical" theory, trading on non-public information by an insider is a "deceptive device" under Section 10(b) because of a relationship of trust and confidence between the shareholder of a corporation and those who have received the non-public information because of their position with the corporation. [The Supreme Court said that this was the holding in *Chiarella*, but it was not. In fact, that theory had not been submitted to the jury in *Chiarella*, but four justices found that it had merit anyway.] The Court then noted that under the "misappropriation" theory, a person violates Section 10(b) when he or she misappropriates confidential information for insider trading purposes in breach of a duty to the source of the information. The Court referred to the duty as one of "confidence to the bidder or target company or their representatives." "The two theories are complementary, each addressing efforts to capitalize on non-public information through the purchase or sale of securities."

The indictment charged that O'Hagan breached a duty of trust and confidence that he owed to his law firm and to its clients. But what was the duty?

---

[6] 521 U.S. 642 (1997).

The stock he bought and then sold was not the client's stock, it was the target company's.

The Court made it clear that only "recognized duties" would suffice for liability. Assuming, as seems obvious, that O'Hagan was a temporary insider in the *Dirks* footnote 14 sense, his duty was not to use non-public information for personal profit, that is, loyalty. Understanding the duty this way makes all of these cases consistent and easier to understand. Thus, the mere disclosure or use of confidential information, negligent or otherwise, may breach a duty of care, but not a duty of loyalty unless it is accompanied by personal profit or benefit. And we know from *Chiarella* that mere imbalance in information absent a breach of duty does not result in liability.

Some commentators argue that O'Hagan's breach of duty was not "in connection with the purchase or sale of a security" because the seller of the stock on the open market was not the person deceived.[7]

Recall that *Santa Fe Industries v. Green*, 430 U.S. 462 (1977), held that conduct prohibited by Rule 10b-5(c) must include manipulation or deception and not merely a breach of duty. Who was deceived? Justice Ginsburg wrote that "the deception ... involves feigning fidelity to the source of the information." But who was the "source"? Was it Grand Met or Dorsey & Whitney? O'Hagan never met anyone from Grand Met. How could he "feign fidelity" to that corporation? And when did "feigning fidelity" become a crime?

The *O'Hagan* opinion has been roundly criticized. Critics note that Justice Ginsburg seems to have confused "deceit" as the word is used in Rule 10b-5(c) with "theft," which is entirely different. Nor does the Court deal with the question whether O'Hagan was actually an "insider." Perhaps most troublesome was the fact that the Court's conclusion that O'Hagan's purchases of calls and his exercise of them after the merger was announced was "in connection with the purchase of" a security. Recall that *Chiarella* held that there has to be a relationship with the two parties to the transaction in order for the fraud to be "in connection with" a purchase or sale. Justice Ginsburg claimed that the *O'Hagan* decision was consistent with *Chiarella* but it ignored that requirement. Instead, Justice Ginsburg wrote that the fraud was perpetrated on the source of the information, not on the purchaser or seller, citing a law review article that claimed that the real injury caused by insider trading was traders whose purchases or sales were crowded out, forcing them to widen their bid-ask spreads. No other Supreme Court opinion reached that

---

[7] Richard Painter et al., "Don't Ask, Just Tell: Insider Trading After United States v. O'Hagan," 84 *U. Va. L. Rev.* 153 (1998).

conclusion.[8] *O'Hagan* was the only misappropriation theory case ever taken up by the Supreme Court.

The SEC took the position that "insider" should not be limited to officers, directors, or controlling shareholders but should include any person who has a special relationship with the corporation. *See SEC v. Lund*, 570 F. Supp. 1397 (C.D. Cal. 1983). Would that definition have fit O'Hagan? What "special relationship" did he have with Grand Met?

Rule 10b5-2

In response to *United States v. Chestman*, 947 F.2d 551 (2d Cir. 1991) (*en banc*) (tipper and tippee were married; conviction reversed because there was no fiduciary relationship proven), the SEC attempted to codify this duty of trust or confidence in Rule 10b5-2(b). That rule provides that a duty of trust or confidence exists when a person agrees to keep information confidential; there is a history, pattern, or practice of sharing confidences where there is a mutual expectation of confidentiality; or information is obtained from a spouse, parent, child, or sibling, but the recipient may demonstrate that there is no expectation of confidentiality. The rule applies to any purchase or sale of a security on the basis of material non-public information misappropriated in breach of duty of trust or confidence.

In that rule, the SEC deliberately set out to adopt a "broader approach" than *O'Hagan*. *See* Proposed Rule: Selective Disclosure and Insider Trading, 64 FR 72590-01 (Dec. 28, 1999). ("We believe there is a good reason for the broader approach we propose today....") But courts have been reluctant to enforce this rule, and commentators have said it is inconsistent with case law and the statute.[9] Remember that *Santa Fe Industries v. Green*, 430 U.S. 462 (1977), held that a violation of Section 10(b) requires deception, not just a breach of duty.

Among the other problems with the rule, it attempts to impose liability whenever the purchaser obtained non-public information confidentially even

---

[8] *See* David Bayne, "Insider Trading: Ginsburg's *O'Hagan*: Insider Trading Ignored," 53 *U. Miami L. Rev.* 423 (1999) ("The serious errors perpetuated by Ginsburg's *O'Hagan* warrant the ready prediction that the Supreme Court will soon revisit the law of Insider Trading toward cleaning up the mess.")

[9] *See, e.g.*, Ryan Davis, "Trimming the 'Judicial Oak': Rule 10(b)5-2(b)(1), Confidentiality Agreements, and the Proper Scope of Insider Trading Liability," 63 *Vanderbilt Law Rev.* 1469 (2010).

if she is not an insider or "temporary insider" or a true tippee. No court has gone that far.[10]

In *United States v. McGee*, 763 F.3d 304 (3d Cir. 2014), the Third Circuit rejected a claim that Rule 10b5-2(b) exceeded the SEC's rulemaking authority, giving it *Chevron* deference.[11] ("Although we are not without reservations concerning the breadth of misappropriation under Rule 10b5-2, it is for Congress to limit its delegation of authority to the SEC or to limit misappropriation by statute.") *See also SEC v. Corbin*, 729 F. Supp. 2d 607 (S.D.N.Y. 2010).

In *SEC v. Cuban*, 634 F. Supp. 2d 713 (N.D. Tex. 2009), *rev'd on other grounds*, 620 F.3d 551 (5th Cir. 2010), the district court invalidated Rule 10b5-2(b)(1) because a promise to keep information confidential does not create a duty of disclosure under the misappropriation theory unless the promise also contained an undertaking to refrain from trading.

Tippers and Tippees

Some courts say that the insider breaches his duty to the corporation if he tips an outsider without legitimate business justification and the tippee trades "on the basis of" the information. But that is not sufficient for liability. The tipper must also receive a benefit for tipping and the tippee must know it. A tippee is liable where (1) she received a tip in breach of an insider-tipper's fiduciary duty, (2) the tipper received a personal benefit for tipping, (3) the tippee knew or should have known that there was a breach of duty (scienter), (4) the tippee knew of the personal benefit, at least before *Salman*, and (5) the tippee uses the tip to trade in securities.

Where Did the "Personal Benefit" Requirement Come From?

In a private exchange of correspondence with Justice Sandra Day O'Connor, Justice Lewis Powell urged a specific intent requirement for insider trading

---

[10] *See* Donna Nagy, "Insider Trading and the Gradual Demise of Fiduciary Principles," 94 *Iowa L. Rev.* 1315, 1357-64 (questioning validity of Rule 10b5-2(b) and noting that it uses the phrase "trust or confidence.").

[11] "*Chevron* deference" is a principle of administrative law pursuant to which a court should defer to an administrative agency's interpretation of a contested statute, so long as the agency's interpretation is not unreasonable. The name comes from *Chevron U.S.A. v. Natural Resources Defense Council*, 468 U.S. 837 (1984). In that case, Justice John Paul Stevens writing for the majority, held that when a legislative delegation to an administrative agency on particular issue is not explicit, a court may not substitute its own interpretation of the statute for a reasonable interpretation made by the agency. There are many exceptions to this rule, which has been narrowed in subsequent cases.

by tipping because he was concerned about the chilling effect that any other, lesser requirement might have on market analysts. Justice O'Connor, recalling her days as a trial court judge in Arizona, and her experience with juries that had difficulty dealing with cases in which intent was an element, urged a more objective standard. "I am not sure about what will be gained by an inquiry into intent, but from my past experience on the bench, I know that a great deal will be lost," she wrote. She added, "If, as a factual matter, the insider did not benefit from his disclosure, then I am not inclined to be concerned with a further inquiry into his motivation."[12]

Justice Powell agreed to amend his draft opinion to include Justice O'Connor's suggestion, the requirement of an actual benefit, but he did not reconcile it with the rest of his draft.

Powell's draft, with Justice O'Connor's addition, was not only confusing, but according to Professor Langevoort, it was a "semantic mess." The difficulty was that Justice Powell was unable to reconcile the notion of a purpose for proving disloyalty with the notion of an actual personal benefit that the insider received. This led to the so-called "mighty comma" issue that split the Second Circuit.[13]

Was proof of a purpose sufficient for showing disloyalty, or was a personal benefit for the insider also required? Unclear. In addition, Justice Powell's illustration of a tip being the same as the tipper's selling the stock and giving the proceeds to a friend or a family member was not helpful. Are tips given outside the circle of friends and family members breaches of the duty of loyalty? Even knowledgeable academics such as Professors Adam Pritchard and Donna Nagy disagree on the answer.

SEC v. Obus[14]

This a somewhat troublesome case. The SEC charged Thomas Strickland, an assistant vice president at General Electric Capital Corp., with insider trading in violation of Section 10(b). In the course of his work, he learned that SunSource, Inc., a publicly traded company, was about to be acquired by Allied Capital Corp. Allied had apparently approached GE Capital to seek financing.

---

[12] Letter from Justice Sandra Day O'Connor to Justice Lewis F. Powell Jr., June 7, 1983, quoted in A.C. Pritchard, "Dirks and the Genesis of Personal Benefit," 68 *S. Methodist L. Rev.* 857 (2015).

[13] *See* Donald Langevoort, "Watching Insider Trading Law Wobble: *Obus*, *Newman*, *Salman*, Two *Martomas* and a *Blaszczak*," Georgetown University Law Center Scholarship, January 8, 2019, Draft, https://scholarship.law.georgetown.edu/facpub/2209.

[14] 693 F.3d 276 (2d Cir. 2013).

The deal book that Strickland saw was marked "Extremely Confidential." A friend of Strikland's, Peter Black, worked at Wynnefield Partners Small Cap. Value L.P.I., which was a large holder of SunSource's stock. The SEC claimed that at some point, Strickland disclosed to Black that SunSource was about to be acquired, although the circumstances were disputed. Nelson Obus was Black's superior and the principal of Wynnefield Partners. Black promptly told Obus what he had learned from Strickland. Obus then called the CEO of SunSource, Maurice Andrien, and told him about the imminent acquisition, although accounts of the call differed. When Black learned of the call, he said to Obus, "What are you doing? You realize, you know, my friend is going to be fired." That same day, Andrien took a call from Alan Weber, a large investor in SunSource. As a result, Andrien was "fairly certain" that the planned acquisition had been leaked.

Two weeks later, a trader at Cantor Fitzgerald called Wynnefield and offered 50,000 shares of SunSource at $5.00 per share. Wynnefield later purchased 287,200 shares of SunSource for $4.75. Eleven days later, Allied announced that it was acquiring SunSource for $10.38 per share. Wynnefield's paper profit was $1.3 million.

Strickland, Black, and Obus were all charged with insider trading, under both the classical and misappropriation theories. Under the misappropriation theory, the SEC argued that Strickland had a duty to GE Capital, his employer, and he breached that duty by tipping Black. The district court granted the defendants' motions for summary judgment under both theories. The SEC appealed only the finding with respect to the misappropriation theory. The Second Circuit vacated the summary judgment ruling and remanded the case for further proceedings.

This was a classic tipping case that raised the issue of scienter. Under Section 10(b) proof of scienter is required for a violation. Under the tipping theory articulated by the Supreme Court in *Dirks*, the tipper must tip material non-public information, in breach of a fiduciary duty of confidentiality owed to shareholders (classic theory) or the source of the information (misappropriation theory), for the personal benefit of the tippee. The tip must be deliberate or reckless, not just negligent. The key issue on the appeal was tippee scienter.

The Second Circuit held that a liable tippee must "know that the tipped information is material and non-public and must have some level of knowledge that by trading on the information, the tippee is a participant in the tipper's breach of fiduciary duty."

With respect to a "tipping chain," as occurred in this case, "a tipper will be liable if he tips material non-public information, in breach of a fiduciary duty, to someone he knows will likely (1) trade on the information, or (2) disseminate the information further for the first tippee's own benefit. The first tippee must both know or have reason to know that the information was obtained and transmitted through a breach and intentionally or recklessly tip the information further for her own benefit. The final tippee must both know or have reason to know that the information was obtained through a breach and trade while in knowing possession of the information. Chain tippee liability may also result from conscious avoidance (e.g., "did not ask [about the source of information] because they did not want to know") *SEC. v. Musella*, 678 F. Supp. 1060 (S.D.N.Y. 1988).

With respect to the individuals, the Second Circuit held that Strickland presented a genuine issue of material fact as to whether he knowingly or recklessly breached a duty to his employer, whether he knew there was a high likelihood that the tip would result in the trading of securities, and whether Strickland tipped for his own personal benefit. With respect to Black, although he did not trade, a jury could find that he knew or had reason to know a tip from Strickland would breach his fiduciary duty to GE Capital, that he tipped Obus in order to improve his standing with Obus, and that he had a reasonable expectation that Obus would trade in SunSource. With respect to Obus, as the result of his call to Andrien and his conversation with Black, a jury could find that Obus believed Black's information was credible and thus knew that it originated from someone entrusted with confidential information and that he knew that Strickland might lose his job as a result of the information he conveyed to Black. Finally, Obus was in possession of material non-public information when he purchased the SunSource stock for Wynnefield.

It was also clear that GE Capital had a policy against sharing client confidential information. As noted, the SEC has tried to codify this obligation in Rule 10b-5(2), which creates an expectation of abstention if there is a promise to respect confidentiality. But as Georgetown Law Professor Donald Langevoort points out, there is a problem because an insider can trade on an anonymous basis without breaching the obligation of confidentiality. The rule seems to create a fiduciary duty once there is a promise of confidentiality, or of what is called "feigned loyalty," so that the breach of the promise becomes intrinsically fraudulent. But does one who promises confidentiality really "feign fidelity"? Is this just a word game?

Professor Langevoort says that *Dirks* describes the essence of a tip as a communication *deliberately intended* to benefit both the tipper and tippee by enabling the latter's trading. This is a form of "conscious fiduciary disloyalty." It prevents insiders from doing indirectly what they cannot do directly. So, if that is correct, there cannot be an innocent or negligent tip. But can there be a "reckless" tip? *Obus* seems to say yes. The Court seemed to say that even if the tipper was not deliberately tipping his friend for personal benefit, he or she could still be liable if he or she acted recklessly in violation of the employer's expectations. Where is the personal benefit that *Dirks* requires? *Obus* seems to say or at least suggest that the personal benefit test does not apply in misappropriation cases. *But see United States v. Conradt*, 2015 WL 480419 (S.D.N.Y. Jan. 22, 2015).

Langevoort has written, "The question remains one of the insider's motivation.... In that sense, I find *Obus*'s styling of the law of reckless tipping at least potentially unsettling." He uses the following example: An associate at a law firm goes home for Thanksgiving and tells her father that she is working on an unannounced merger. He buys the stock. Is the associate a tipper? He says the answer is no, if she did not mean to enrich her father. But was she reckless?

What about tippee scienter? It is required but *Obus* says that it exists if the tippee knew or should have known that the information was acquired through an impropriety of the tipper. The only scienter requirement seems to be an awareness that the information is material and non-public. That does not seem to be sufficient because it ignores the personal benefit requirement. And don't forget that the tippee cannot be liable unless the tipper is also liable. That liability requires a breach and a personal benefit on the tipper's part. Must the tippee know about the breach and personal benefit? *Obus* held that tipper scienter exists where tipper acted deliberately or recklessly (not negligently), knew that the information was non-public and material (or acted with reckless disregard of those facts), and knew (or was reckless in not knowing) that to disseminate the information would violate a fiduciary duty. Is this a different test for scienter from the one we have for misrepresentation under Section 10(b)?

Tippee scienter exists, the court held in *Obus*, when tippee knows that information is material and non-public and "has some level of knowledge that by trading on the information the tippee is a participant in the tipper's breach of fiduciary duty." This test is not consistent with *Dirks*, which requires that the tippee also knows that the disclosure was made for the purpose of receiving a personal benefit.

That part of *Obus* is probably no longer good law in the Second Circuit after *Newman*, which is discussed next.

United States v. Newman[15]

Todd Newman and Anthony Chiasson were portfolio managers at two hedge funds. The government alleged that they received inside information about the upcoming earnings of two corporations from investment analysts at their hedge funds. The inside information was obtained from employees at those two corporations and was being shared among a "cohort of analysts at various hedge funds and investment firms." According to the court, "Newman and Chiasson were several steps removed from the corporate insiders and there was no evidence that either was aware of the source of the inside information."

---

[15] 773 F.3d 438 (2d Cir. 2014).

The court held that to sustain a conviction for insider trading, the government must prove beyond a reasonable doubt that the tippee knew that an insider disclosed confidential information in breach of a fiduciary duty *and* that he did so in exchange for a personal benefit. Here, there was insufficient evidence of a personal benefit received by the insiders, and there was no evidence that Newman and Chiasson knew that they were trading on information obtained from the insiders in violation of their fiduciary duties and in return for a personal benefit. The convictions were reversed and the Supreme Court declined to grant a petition for a writ of certiorari.

The Second Circuit relied heavily on *Dirks*. "The Supreme Court was quite clear in *Dirks*. First, the tippee's liability derives *only* from the tipper's breach of a fiduciary duty, *not* from trading on material, non-public information.... Second, the corporate insider has committed no breach of fiduciary duty unless he [or she] receives a personal benefit in exchange for the disclosure. Third, even in the presence of a tipper's breach, a tippee is liable only if he knows or should have known of the breach" (emphasis in original). *Query*: Is "should have known" the correct standard for scienter? *Obus* used a slightly different formulation: "was reckless in not knowing."

Further, the court held explicitly that "without establishing that the tippee knows of the personal benefit received by the insider in exchange for the disclosure, the Government cannot meet its burden of showing that the tippee knew of a breach." With respect to what constitutes a "personal benefit," the court acknowledged that earlier cases broadly defined the term, and included such things as a "reputational benefit" and the "benefit that one would obtain from simply making a gift of confidential information to a trading relative or friend." But the court held that the benefit must be "of some consequence" and "an exchange that is objective, consequential and represents at least a potential gain of a pecuniary or similarly valuable nature." Quoting another judge, the court held that the "relationship between the insider and the recipient ... [must] suggest a *quid pro quo* from the latter or an intention to benefit the [latter]." The court noted in a footnote that the "tippee did not have to know for certain how information was disclosed ... [but] this is not inconsistent with a requirement that a defendant tippee understands that some benefit is being provided in return for the information." But what about knowledge of the breach of duty? Is that just assumed? The court concluded that the district court erred by not instructing the jury that "the Government had to prove beyond a reasonable doubt that [the defendants] knew that the tippers received a personal benefit for their disclosure." Instead of remanding the case for a new trial, the court vacated the convictions, holding that no reasonable jury could have inferred that the defendants knew or should have known that the information originated with a corporate insider and that the facts in support of the government's theory of liability "are as consistent with an inference of innocence as one of guilt."

In January 2015, the government petitioned for rehearing *en banc*, and the SEC filed an amicus brief in support of the government. Specifically, the SEC took issue with the court's holding that evidence of friendship between an insider who tips and his tippee is insufficient to support an inference that the insider derived a personal benefit from the tipping. The SEC argued that the Supreme Court and prior Second Circuit decisions had held that "disclosing information to a friend . . . is equivalent to the insider himself profitably trading on the information and then giving the trading profits to the friend, which is obviously illegal." The SEC did not take issue with the court's holding that the government had to prove that the tippee knew that the tipper had received a personal benefit, it only took issue with the definition of the personal benefit that was required. However, on April 3, 2015, the Second Circuit denied the petition for rehearing *en banc* and the Supreme Court later refused to issue a writ of certiorari.

The fallout from *Newman* was substantial. Between 2009 and 2014, the U.S. Attorney for the Southern District of New York charged ninety-three people with insider trading. Eighty-eight of those pleaded guilty or were convicted. Since *Newman*, at least twelve other defendants in New York cited *Newman* in asking that their convictions be reversed, their guilty pleas be vacated, or that they be resentenced. As of early February 2014, at least four of those convictions were reversed by the district court. Shortly after *Newman* was decided, a New York district court held that the rule announced by the Second Circuit in *Newman* applied both in "classic" insider cases and "misappropriation" cases. "The elements of tipping liability are the same, regardless of whether the tipper's duty arises under the classical or the misappropriation theory." *United States v. Conradt*, 2015 WL 480419 (S.D.N.Y. Jan. 22, 2015). There is an open question whether the holding in *Newman*, which was a criminal case, applies equally in civil cases brought by the SEC. In those cases, proof of *mens rea* is not required but proof of scienter is.

After *Newman*, there was arguably a higher bar. In *SEC v. Payton & Durant*, 97 F. Supp. 3d 558 (S.D.N.Y. 2015), Judge Jed Rakoff held that an SEC civil action for insider trading must meet the *Newman* personal benefit test, but because the action was a civil action brought under Section 10(b), the SEC only had to meet the "knowing or reckless" test for a tippee's knowledge of a benefit obtained by the tipper. In *SEC v. Bolan & Ruggieri*, File No. 3-16178 (2015), an SEC administrative law judge, Jason Patil, held that the "personal benefit" requirement also applied to SEC administrative proceedings. In an interesting irony, on July 6, 2015, the Ninth Circuit, in *United States v. Salman*, 792 F.3d 1087 (9th Cir. 2015), arguably refused to follow *Newman* and held that the personal benefit test is met when an insider "makes a gift of confidential information to a trading relative or friend." The quotation came from *Dirks*. The Ninth Circuit noted that in *Newman*, the Second Circuit quoted that same language but nevertheless required proof of a personal benefit of "at least a potential gain of a pecuniary or similarly valuable nature." The Ninth Circuit refused to require such a benefit when the inside information comes in the form of a gift to a trading relative or friend. But Salman was a subsequent tippee of the trading relative (who did not receive any benefit). He was convicted, and his conviction was affirmed. What is ironic about the Ninth Circuit's opinion is that it was written by New York Senior District Court Judge Rakoff, sitting by designation in the Ninth Circuit.

Salman v. United States[16]

In the Supreme Court, the circuit split was finally resolved in this important and perhaps somewhat unsatisfactory case. The facts are a bit unusual. Maher Kara, an investment banker, shared confidential information with his older brother Michael, who traded on it. Maher did not know he was trading, but suspected it. Michael also gave the information to his friend and brother-in-law Bassam Yacoub Salman, who traded on it and made a large profit. Maher knew nothing about Salman's trades. The Supreme Court upheld Salman's conviction and put an end to the *Newman* line of cases. The issue was whether proof of a personal benefit was required when Maher disclosed confidential information to Michael. Concluding that Maher would have breached his duty had he himself traded on the information and then made a gift of the proceeds to Michael, the Court held, "To the extent the Second Circuit held that the tipper must also receive something of a 'pecuniary or similarly valuable nature' in exchange for a gift to family or friends, *Newman*, 773 F.3d at 452, we agree with the Ninth Circuit that their requirement is inconsistent with *Dirks*." This appears to be the end of the "something of value" personal benefit test.

Chiarella and *Dirks* concluded that the core of insider trading was a breach of fiduciary duty by an insider. As Professor Langevoort puts it, "it was naturally wrong for fiduciaries (or their confederates) to secretly enrich themselves."[17]

Is the trader motivated to trade by the secret information that he or she acquires? Rule 10b-5(2) seems to define insider trading as a simple awareness that the information in the insider's possession is confidential. Is this the same as motivation? What about "use" of the inside information versus merely

---

[16] 137 S. Ct. 420 (2016).

[17] Donald Langevoort, "'Fine Distinctions' in the Contemporary Law of Insider Trading," 2013 *Colum. Bus. L. Rev.* 429.

possession of it? Could traders break the causal link? ("I would have bought even if I didn't have the inside information.")

As noted, some courts have ignored Rule 10b-5(2) and have continued to require causation. *See, e.g.*, *United States v. Nacchio*, 519 F.3d 1140 (10th Cir. 2008) ("some commentators maintain that the Rule (the authority for which has not been resolved by any circuit) is unlawful because it effectively eliminates fraud from the liability standard") (*dictum*).

Is insider trading really fraud or is it sui generis? The misappropriation theory first described in *O'Hagan* seems to be based on what Langevoort calls "secretive fiduciary disloyalty" to someone who entrusts information to another, expecting fidelity. But is this really a property rights issue, as such a concept would suggest? What if the source's expectation of confidentiality is not explicit but is based on an unwritten norm? What room does Langevoort's definition leave for fraud and scienter, which Rule 10b-5 seems to require?

United States v. Martoma[18]

Matthew Martoma worked with S.A.C. Capital Advisors, a Connecticut hedge fund run by Steve Cohen. He also had some private clients. He primarily invested in pharmaceutical stocks, especially Wyeth, LLC and Elan Corporation plc. He engaged a consultant, Dr. Sidney Gilman, who was part of a "network of experts" who advised pharmaceutical companies in their drug testing. Martoma paid him to "consult" by letting him know what was happening with drug testing. On one occasion, Dr. Gilman told Martoma that Wyeth had experienced problems with one of its drug tests. The information was confidential. Martoma called Cohen and informed him of the test results. Cohen and Martoma reduced their positions in the stocks and sold short, making $80 million in profits and avoiding $194 million in losses.

Martoma was convicted of conspiracy to commit fraud in violation of 18 U.S.C. § 317 and securities fraud under Section 10(b) of the 1934 Act.

The jury was instructed that Dr. Gilman had to have received a personal benefit, but the benefit need not be financial or tangible; it could include some future advantage, such as developing a contact or a friendship or enhancing the tipper's reputation. However, *Newman* had held that "a gift of confidential information to a trading relative or friend was insufficient unless the tipper's goal was to obtain money, property or something of tangible value."

On Martoma's appeal to the Second Circuit, the issue was whether *Salman* had abrogated the *Newman* test for a personal benefit. The Second Circuit affirmed Martoma's conviction, in an opinion written by then Chief Judge Robert Katzmann, over a strong dissent by Judge Rosemary Pooler.

---

[18] 869 F.3d 58 (2d Cir. 2017).

In the majority opinion, the court wrote, "[T]he straightforward logic of the gift-giving analysis in *Dirks*, strongly reasserted in *Salman*, is that a corporate insider personally benefits whenever he 'disclos[es] inside information as a gift ... with the expectation that [the recipient] would trade' on the basis of such information or otherwise exploit it for his pecuniary gain.... That is because such a disclosure is the functional equivalent of trading on the information himself and giving a cash gift to the recipient. Nothing in *Salman*'s reaffirmation of this logic supports a distinction between gifts to people with whom a tipper shares a 'meaningfully close personal relationship'—a term left undefined in *Newman*, but which apparently did not reach two people who 'had known each other for years, having both attended business school and worked ... together,' [citation omitted] and gifts to those with whom a tipper does not share such a relationship."

However, the majority opinion concluded that:

> because there are many ways to establish a personal benefit, we conclude that we need not decide whether *Newman*'s gloss on the gift theory is inconsistent with *Salman*. At trial, the government presented compelling evidence that Dr. Gilman (the tipper) received a different type of personal benefit: $70,000 in consulting fees, which can be seen either as evidence of a *quid pro quo*-like relationship, or simply advance payments for the tips of inside information that Dr. Gilman went on to supply. The government also introduced evidence sufficient to prove Dr. Gilman received a personal benefit by disclosing inside information with the intention to benefit Martoma.

In response to the dissent's argument that someone who gives a gift does not always receive a personal benefit, Chief Judge Katzmann wrote, "[O]ur holding reaches only the insider who discloses inside information to someone *he expects will trade on the information*" (emphasis in original).

In her robust and comprehensive dissent, Judge Pooler criticized the majority for going too far and because, in her view, the jury instructions were plainly erroneous. She wrote:

> I note, in closing, that securities law is a field in which legal and ethical obligations are not coterminous.... This is not surprising, as the Supreme Court has noted, given that securities regulation is built on statutes and that its principles apply broadly to many transactions in the marketplace.... Adhering to the Supreme Court's precedent may challenge us when it leaves unethical conduct unpunished. But there is great wisdom in the Supreme Court's limitations on broad rules, particularly when those rules might otherwise allow

> punishment of the absentminded in addition to persons with corrupt intent. Today, however, the majority severely damages the limitation provided by the personal benefit rule, and casts aside Circuit precedent and Supreme Court rulings to do so.

Judge Pooler's point was that in *Salman*, the Supreme Court did not decide whether the relationship with a friend had to be a "close personal relationship" as *Newman* required. Nevertheless, the majority found that a rejection of the *Newman* test was implicit in the Supreme Court's opinion. Martoma was sentenced to nine years in federal prison.

After the Second Circuit affirmed Martoma's conviction, he asked the Second Circuit to reconsider its decision and it agreed to do so. On June 25, 2018, the Second Circuit "withdrew and amended" its decision. The result was the same: no new trial for Martoma. But the reasoning was more nuanced. In fact, its new understanding of the *Dirks* personal benefit test that started this whole discussion turned on a comma.

In its amended opinion, the Second Circuit reminded us that whether the disclosure of inside information breaches a duty depends in large part on the purpose of the disclosure. The personal benefit test in *Dirks* was designed to test the propriety of the tipper's purpose. "Identifying personal benefits is not . . . the central focus of insider trading law, but simply how courts and juries analyze breaches of fiduciary duty." We will return to the comma in a minute. But first a question. *Dirks* told us that the personal benefit test was one way to test the propriety of the tipper's disclosure. Probably because the breach of duty was a breach of the duty of loyalty, if the tipper received something that he or she should not have (i.e., a personal benefit) in return for the disclosure of the inside information, the tipper was disloyal and the tipper's disclosure was presumably improper. But that is a benefit that the tippee receives.

But what about the tippee? Does the tippee also have to receive a personal benefit in addition to the inside information or is the inside information enough? The Second Circuit analogized the situation to one in which the tipper, instead of giving the tippee information, sold the stock himself and gave the proceeds to the tippee. But again, how does that benefit the tipper? Neither the first nor the amended *Martoma* majority opinion satisfactorily explains (at least to me) the shift in the analysis from a benefit received by the tipper to a benefit received by the tippee.

This is where the comma comes in. The *Martoma* dissent and the majority differed over whether "intent to benefit" is a stand-alone requirement under *Dirks*. "The dissent argues that it is not, claiming instead that the correct formulation is 'a relationship that suggests an intention to benefit' the tippee" (ellipses omitted for clarity). The key sentence of *Dirks* is admittedly ambiguous and we acknowledge that the dissent has offered a plausible reading."

However, the majority concluded, "that is not the only reading. The comma separating the words 'intention to benefit' and 'relationship ... suggesting a *quid pro quo*' phrases can be read to sever any connection between them. The sentence, so understood, effectively reads, 'there may be a relationship between the insider and the recipient that suggests a *quid pro quo* from the latter, or there may be an intention to benefit the particular recipient.' And that is the reading this Court adopted in *Warde* [*SEC v. Warde*, 151 F.3d 42,48 (1998)].... We adhere to *Warde*." *United States v. Martoma*, 894 F.2d 64 (2d Cir. 2017).

In other words, either proof of an intent to confer a personal benefit on the tippee or proof of a relationship that suggests a *quid pro quo* from the recipient is sufficient for tipper liability, and the receipt of such a benefit is sufficient for tippee liability. In dissent, Judge Pooler's reading of the sentence was that the Supreme Court was describing "a relationship ... that suggests an intention to benefit the tippee." As noted above, this sentence and the confusion it caused was the result of Justice Powell's failure to reconcile Justice O'Connor's addition with the rest of his majority opinion in *Dirks*.

If you are confused, you are not alone. I submit that *Martoma* (Amended) is still not the last word. My reading is that under *Salman* and *Martoma* (both versions), it is sufficient for liability on the part of a trading tippee if the tipper disclosed inside information as a gift to a tippee who the tipper expects will trade on the information, thus intending to confer a personal benefit on the tippee. At least in the Second Circuit, there is no longer a requirement of a "meaningfully close personal relationship" between the two. It remains unclear why the court spoke of a personal benefit to the tipper as a legitimate measure of a breach of a duty, and then spoke of an intent on the part of the tipper to benefit the tippee, which seems to have little or nothing to do with the breach of duty. Recall that Justice O'Connor's proposal to Justice Powell was that if the insider received a personal benefit for tipping, that would be objective proof of a breach of duty. This has now morphed into conveying a benefit (i.e., inside information) to a trading relative or friend, which in itself would also confer a benefit on the tipper. But what that benefit actually is remains unclear.

The *Martoma* court held that a tipper's intent to benefit the tippee would be an appropriate personal benefit. "It can allow for the inference that the tipper has not acted simply out of the goodness of his heart because he expects some future benefit.... *Dirks* recognizes that purposely benefiting the tippee with inside information proves that the tipper has received a personal benefit in breach of a fiduciary duty. The question is whether *Dirks* requires that to be proved with evidence of a relationship or not. We think the clear answer is no."

In her dissent, Judge Pooler was direct: "My colleagues assert that under *Dirks*, an intention can be inferred without any objective evidence about relationships. But *Dirks* does not say that, *Newman* remains good law." Does it?

For deception without a breach of fiduciary duty, see *SEC v. Dorozhko*, 574 F.3d 42 (2d Cir. 2009). Oleksandr Dorozhko hacked into the computer of a financial consulting firm and downloaded an earnings report of one of its clients that was about to be released to the market. He bought put options before the release. The Second Circuit held that there is no liability for hacking into a computer to obtain inside information on which to trade unless the hacking involved trickery or deception (e.g., use of fake name). This result was not surprising in light of *Santa Fe Industries v. Green*, 430 U.S. 462 (1977), which requires deception or misrepresentation for liability under Section 10(b). If Dorozhko used his real name while hacking, there would be no deception; if he used a false name, there would be. Plain theft isn't enough for liability. On remand, the SEC's motion for summary judgment was unopposed. 2010 WL 1213430 (March 29, 2010). This seems to be a very fine line to draw and the decision has been criticized.[19]

"In Possession Of" Versus "On the Basis Of" Versus "Use" Debate

The SEC argued that a purchase by an insider in which the purchaser was "in possession of" the inside information is "good enough" in *United States v. Teicher*, 987 F.2d 112 (2d Cir. 1993). In that case, the Second Circuit held, in *dictum*, that a "knowing possession" satisfied the "in connection with" requirement of Section 10(b) and Rule 10b-5. In *United States v. Royer*, 549 F.3d 886 (2d Cir. 2008), the *dictum* became the law of the circuit. But in 1998, the Ninth Circuit disagreed with the SEC and the Second Circuit and held, in *United States v. Smith*, 155 F.3d 1051 (9th Cir. 1998), that in a criminal case, even a defendant who is a traditional insider must "actually use" the material non-public information in making a decision to trade. In civil cases brought by the SEC, however, the Eleventh Circuit held, in *Securities and Exchange Comm'n v. Adler*, 137 F.2d 1325 (1998), that "actual use" was required but that there is a "strong inference" of use if there is possession. In *United States v. Rajaratnam*, 719 F.3d 139 (2d Cir. 2013), the Second Circuit seemed to retreat a bit, and it affirmed the district court's jury instruction that the inside information had to be "a factor, however small, in the defendant's decision to purchase or sell stock." In his petition for a writ of certiorari, Raj Rajaratnam argued that the Second Circuit has erroneously criminalized "trading in possession" without requiring fraudulent interest or actual use. The Supreme Court denied his petition for a writ of certiorari.

---

[19] *See* Elizabeth Odian, "*SEC v. Dorozhko*'s Affirmative Misrepresentation Theory of Insider Trading: An Improper Means to a Proper End," 94 *Marquette L. Rev.* 1313 (2011) (court created a new "affirmation misrepresentation" theory).

What is the issue? Rule 10b5-1, enacted in 2000, defines "on the basis of" as the person making the purchase or sale was "aware" of the material non-public information when purchase or sale was made. Is this satisfactory? What about causation? What if the purchase or sale was made for reasons wholly unrelated to the inside information? What if the seller needed to sell stock to pay her daughter's upcoming tuition bill? Being "aware of" inside information doesn't necessarily mean that is the reason you bought or sold the security. Do courts follow this distinction? Is that rule still the law? The Eighth, Ninth, and Eleventh Circuits have rejected a "possession" standard.[20]

Note that Rule 10b5-1 also creates an affirmative defense to insider trading charges, if the purchaser or seller can demonstrate that before becoming aware of the information, she had either (1) entered into a binding contract to purchase or sell the security, (2) instructed another person to purchase or sell the security for her account, or (3) adopted a written plan for trading securities. In addition, there is a requirement that the contract, instruction, or plan must specify the amount of securities to be bought or sold and the price at which and the date on which the securities were to be bought or sold, including a written formula or algorithm, or computer program for determining the amount of securities to be purchased or sold and the price at which and the date on which the securities were to be purchased or sold, or did not permit the person to exercise any subsequent influence over how, when, or whether to effect purchases or sales; provided, in addition, that any other person who, pursuant to the contract, instruction, or plan, did exercise such influence must not have been aware of the material non-public information while doing so; and the purchase or sale that occurred was pursuant to the contract, instruction, or plan. Some have argued that Rule 10b5-1 actually increases opportunities for insider trading, or what they call "hiding in plain sight" by permitting insiders to use disclosure as a mechanism for reducing the legal risk of actions that might otherwise attract legal scrutiny.[21]

By letter dated February 10, 2021, three U.S. Senators (Elizabeth Warren, Chris Van Hollen, and Sherrod Brown) wrote to the SEC's acting chair to complain that Rule 10b5-1 was being misused and that plans were being modified days or even hours before a major public announcement. Apparently on the day Pfizer announced that its COVID-19 vaccine was found to be 90 percent effective, Pfizer's CEO sold more than 60 percent of his company shares pursuant to his Rule 10b5-1 plan, which was modified the day before Pfizer announced the results of its phase one trial results. The senators said

---

[20] *See* Donald Langevoort, "Rereading Cady, Roberts: The Ideology and Practice of Insider Trading," 99 *Colum. L. Rev.* 1319 (1999).

[21] *See* M. Todd Henderson et al., "Offensive Disclosure: How Voluntary Disclosure Can Increase Returns From Insider Trading," 103 *Geo. L. J.* 1275 (2015).

that this misuse created disadvantages for other investors because the "trigger" price was one of the primary mechanisms leading to large stock sales on the days of "good news" announcements. They recommended that the SEC adopt a four- to six-month cooling-off period between the adoption of a plan and the time when trading may begin, the disclosure to the SEC of the contents of the plans, the enforcement of existing filing deadlines, and the exploration of options to "better align executives' incentives with those of shareholders and the public."

In a speech on June 7, 2021, new SEC Chair Gary Gensler agreed to ask his staff for recommendations to "freshen up" Rule 10b5-1 because corporate stock plans have "real cracks in our insider trading regime" that could be filled if a cooling-off period of four to six months between the adoption of a plan and the execution of its first trade, as some corporations already require, were made mandatory. He also pointed out that there currently are no limitations on when a 10b5-1 plan can be canceled, "meaning that insiders can choose to cancel them whenever they're in possession of material nonpublic information.... In my view, cancelling a plan may be as economically significant as carrying out an actual transaction, because material nonpublic information might influence an insider's decision to cancel an order to sell."[22] "Freshening up" Rule 10b5-1 is now part of Gensler's 2021 agenda.

Private Right of Action

In 1988, Congress created a private right of action in favor of "contemporaneous traders." See Section 20(A) of the 1934 Exchange Act ("contemporaneous traders" can sue violators; damages are limited to illegal profits or losses avoided, less any disgorgement obtained by the SEC; there is joint and several liability for the tipper and the tippee). There are actually very few of these cases because it would be nearly impossible to create a class of contemporaneous traders and individual actions would be too expensive, given the small recovery potential.

Is there any other basis for a private action? The statute says that it does not limit "the right of any person to bring an action to enforce a requirement of this title or the availability of any cause of action implied from a provision of this title."

In 2002, Congress enacted 18 U.S.C. § 1348 (Section 807(a) of the Sarbanes-Oxley Act), which broadly prohibits executing or attempting to execute "a scheme or artifice to defraud any person in connection with ... any security of an issuer of a class of securities registered under Section 12 of the Exchange

[22] J. Dean Seal, "SEC Chair Aims to Seal 'Cracks' in Exec Insider Trading Rules," *Law360*, June 7, 2021.

Act of 1934." The language mirrors the relevant sections of the mail, wire, and bank fraud statutes in Title 18. It has been interpreted as a new criminal insider trading statute. The Justice Department has argued and courts have held that the meaning of the word "defraud" as used in that statute includes the "embezzlement" theory, the fraudulent appropriation of someone else's property to one's own use. The words "insider trading" are not mentioned in the statute but in *United States v. Blaszczak*, 947 F.3d 19 (2d Cir. 2019), remanded, 2021 WL 78043 (Jan. 11, 2021), the DOJ successfully argued that the statute covered insider trading. What is more, the DOJ successfully argued in the Second Circuit that because the complaint alleged a violation of Title 18 and not Title 15 (i.e., Section 10b), there was no requirement to plead the existence of a personal benefit since the crime of embezzlement does not require proof of a personal benefit.

David Blaszczak worked for the Medicare and Medicaid Services Division of Department of Health and Human Services before leaving to become a consultant, and he tipped a friend who worked in a hedge fund about coming changes in Medicare reimbursement rates. Blaszczak was acquitted of a Section 10b charge but convicted of a charge under Title 18. A dissenting opinion from Judge Amalya Kearse in the Second Circuit argued that a change in a Centers for Medicare and Medicare Services regulation was not "a thing of value."

In January 2021, the Supreme Court vacated the Second Circuit ruling upholding the Blaszczak conviction, under the authority of the "New Jersey Bridgegate" case, *Kelly v. United States*, 140 S. Ct. 1565 (2020), and ordered the Second Circuit to rethink its finding in *Blaszczak* in light of *Kelly*'s definition of "property" under the wire fraud statute. The Supreme Court held in *Kelly* that a "scheme to reallocate the George Washington Bridge's access lanes" did not constitute property fraud under 18 U.S.C. §§ 1343 and 666(a)(1)(A) and that the scheme was an exercise "in regulatory power" rather than a "taking of property." The U.S. Solicitor General's Office has taken the position that in a case such as *Blaszczak*, the confidential government information must have economic value in the hands of the relevant government entity to constitute "property" for purposes of 18 U.S.C. §§ 1343 and 1348. The final chapter of this case has yet to be written.

The current law of insider trading is "uncertain." As Harry Sandick and Jeff Kinkle of the Patterson Belknap law firm have recently written, "No one—prosecutors, defense counsel, securities market participants or the public at large—benefits from the current regime of legal uncertainty. In the meantime, courts—like the Second Circuit in *Blaszczak*—continue to render decisions that leave uncertainty about the state of the law."[23]

[23] Harry Sandick & Jeff Kinkle, "Securities Market Urgently Needs Federal Insider Trading Law," *Law 360*, February 12, 2021.

Insider Trading by Congress

The Stop Trading on Congressional Knowledge (STOCK) Act, signed into law on April 4, 2012, prohibits congressional members, staffers, and other federal employees from using nonpublic information gained from their positions for personal benefit. They have a "duty arising from a relationship of trust and confidence" to Congress, the federal government, and U.S. citizens. As a result, tippees can also be held liable if they trade on information learned from government employees.

Attempted Congressional and Other Prohibitions of Insider Trading

In December 2019, the House of Representatives passed the Insider Trading Prohibition Act, one original purpose of which was eliminate the personal benefit requirement. However, when the bill reached the floor for a final vote, the personal benefit requirement was reinstated; tippees had to know that the information was obtained through a breach of duty in exchange for a "direct or indirect" personal benefit, including a "reputational benefit." Unfortunately, another part of the bill eliminated the requirement for proof of a personal benefit: so long as the tippee knew that the inside information had been "wrongfully obtained," the tippee need not know "whether any personal benefit was paid or promised ... to any person in the chain of communication." The bill thus both eliminated and required a personal benefit, and it died in the Senate.

There have been many other attempts to reform the law on insider trading. One of the most recent was the report of "The Bharara Task Force on Insider Trading" in January 2020.[24] Among other things, the report recommended that the requirement for deception or fraud should be eliminated because a requirement that the nonpublic information be "wrongfully obtained" should be sufficient for criminal liability. The report also recommended that the requirement for a "personal benefit" for tippee liability should be eliminated.

---

[24] Preet Bharara is a former U.S. Attorney for the Southern District of New York. The Report of the Task Force does not make clear under whose initiation the task force was created or to whom, if anybody other than the public, the Report was rendered.

Chapter 16

Market Manipulation

What Is Market Manipulation?

Section 9 of the 1934 Act prohibits the manipulation of security prices, and Section 10(b) of the 1934 Act prohibits "any manipulative or deceptive device or contrivance in contravention of such rules and regulations as the Commission may prescribe." In fact, the word "manipulate" appears throughout the securities laws. See, e.g., Section 9: "Manipulation of Security Prices"; Section 10: "Manipulative and Deceptive Devices." Manipulation is "virtually a term of art when used in connection with securities markets." *Ernst & Ernst v. Hochfelder*, 425 U.S. 185 (1976). But what exactly is it?

Common wisdom is that market manipulation led to the enactment of the Securities Exchange Act of 1934 and, as noted above, the word "manipulation" shows up in many sections. For example, Section 2 of the Securities Exchange Act provides: "National emergencies, which produce widespread unemployment and the dislocation of trade, transportation, and industry, and which burden interstate commerce and adversely affect the general welfare, are precipitated, intensified and prolonged by manipulation and sudden and unreasonable fluctuations of security prices and by excessive speculation on such exchanges and markets."

The purpose seems to be to make sure that securities markets be free of conduct that "interferes with the 'natural' forces of supply and demand."[1] But what, exactly, is manipulation and what distinguishes it from ordinary trading?

Those questions have plagued courts, prosecutors, and scholars for decades and have still not been satisfactorily resolved.[2] Most examples of market manipulation that are prosecuted today—and there are relatively few—are accompanied either by clearly unlawful activity or false statements. In "pump and dump" schemes, for example, stock purchases are accompanied

---

[1] *See* Donna M. Nagy et al., *Securities Litigation and Enforcement* (3d ed.) (West Academic Publishing) (2017), 615.

[2] *See, e.g.*, Gina-Gail Fletcher, "Legitimate Yet Manipulative: The Conundrum of Open-Market Manipulation," 69 *Duke L. J.* 479 (2018).

by optimistic but false statements about a stock made by the pumper that are designed to inflate the price of the stock just before the pumper becomes a dumper. But does lawfully purchasing a stock on an open market and without any accompanying false statement solely for the purpose of causing the market price to rise constitute unlawful market manipulation? What if the purchaser wanted the price to increase for the purpose of squeezing the short sellers? Is that an improper purpose? And if it is, can it render an otherwise perfectly lawful purchase of stock unlawful market manipulation? To put that question in a historical context, it is worth recalling that noted Yale law professor J. William Moore wrote in 1934—the year the Securities Exchange Act was enacted—"The term 'manipulation' may, in short, be applied to any practice which has as its purpose the deliberate raising, lowering, or pegging of security prices. *Buying and selling in themselves do, of course, affect price, but in a free and open market this is a natural consequence and not their preconceived purpose. Manipulation leads to an artificial and controlled price*" (emphasis added).[3]

Even though the words "manipulative" and "manipulate" occur throughout the federal securities and other laws, relatively few cases have been brought under Section 9 of the 1934 Act, in large part because until the Dodd-Frank Act, Section 9 was limited to securities traded on national exchanges. Instead, prosecutors seemed to favor Section 10(b) of the 1934 Act, which prohibits "any manipulative or deceptive device or contrivance in contravention of such rules and regulations as the Commission may prescribe," and Rule 10b-5, which prohibits the use of "any device, scheme or artifice to defraud" or engaging "in any act, practice, or course of business which operates or would operate as a fraud or deceit upon any purpose."

The SEC is not the only federal agency that investigates and charges market manipulation, however. The Commodity Futures Trading Commission, for example, enforces its rule, Prohibition on the Employment, or Attempted Employment, of Manipulative and Deceptive Devices—Prohibition on Price Manipulation.[4] Dodd-Frank added additional provisions to the proof of intent component to the market manipulation language that was already contained in the Commodity Exchange Act, including a fraud provision.[5] The Federal Trade Commission and the Federal Energy Regulatory Commission enforce rules against market manipulation that are similar to the 1934 Act's Rule 10b-5.[6]

---

[3] James William Moore & Frank Wiseman, "Market Manipulation and the Exchange Act," *U. Chicago L. Rev.* (1934).

[4] 17 C.F.R. Part 180.

[5] Dodd-Frank Wall Street Reform and Consumer Protection Act, 111-203 (July 21, 2010).

[6] 17 C.F.R. § 240, Rule 10b-5.

Why do we even care about market manipulation, especially if it takes place through open market purchases? Conventional wisdom holds that market manipulation interferes with pricing consistent with the normal supply and demand forces in the market. In theory, efficient markets "impound" all publicly available information about a stock in the stock price. In a "perfectly efficient" market (the "strong-form efficiency," which doesn't actually exist in reality), the market price closely resembles the true value of the stock. In a manipulated market, by contrast, the market price has been "artificially" moved in one direction or the other and is unrelated to the true value of the stock. Sanjay Wadhwa, at the time an Associate Director of the SEC's Enforcement Division in the New York Regional Office and currently SEC Deputy Director of Enforcement, said that "the fair and efficient functioning of the markets requires that prices of securities reflect genuine supply and demand. Traders who pervert these natural forces by engaging in layering or some other form of manipulation invite close scrutiny from the SEC." That may be so, but "close scrutiny" rarely results in prosecutions—much less successful ones.

Part of the reason may be that there is no satisfactory definition of market manipulation. The statute does not define it. The SEC's attempt at rulemaking simply refers back to Section 9. In the *Hochfelder* case, 425 U.S. 185 (1976), the Supreme Court made it clear that although the 1934 Securities Exchange Act was intended "principally to protect investors against manipulation of stock prices," manipulation cases (there an attempt to defraud investors into investing in non-existent "escrow" accounts) nevertheless required proof of intent. "There is no indication that Congress intended anyone to be made liable for such practices unless he acted other than in good faith." But what if the improper intent is accompanied by conduct that is otherwise lawful? Keep this question in mind. We will return to it below. It is very important.

The word "manipulative" as used in Sections 10(b) and 15(c)(1) has never had any precise meaning. Although there is a short definition in the SEC's Investor.Gov website ("Market manipulation is when someone artificially affects the supply or demand for a security (for example, causing stock prices to rise or fall dramatically)"), the question still remains what constitutes "artificially" affecting supply and demand? Timothy Snider called it a "murky miasma of questionable analysis and unclear effects."[7]

Open questions abound: What is "interference" with supply and demand? Is purchasing or selling a stock on an open market "interference"? What if a broker releases a positive report on a company, the clients buy, and the price goes up? Is that an interference with supply and demand or is that just the normal operation of the market? What about "day traders" who trade for the purpose

---

[7] Timothy Snider & Thomas Russo, *Regulation of Commodities Futures and Options Market* (2d ed.) (Shepard's/McGraw-Hill) (1995) 12.01.

of driving the price up and then sell at the end of the day? What is "forcing a security's price to trade at an artificial level"? Is there a difference between an artificial and non-artificial price? What if the purpose of the manipulation is to "restore the stock to its true value"? If you are finding it difficult to answer those questions, you are not alone. The most common response is the equivalent of Justice John Paul Stevens's definition of pornography in *Jacobellis v. Ohio* (378 U.S. 184 (1964)): "I know [manipulation] when I see it."[8]

According to Professor Louis Loss, there is no satisfactory definition. Although there is a definition in the SEC's "fast answer" website, it is neither a legal definition nor a statement of SEC policy. Neither the Securities Exchange Act nor the Commodity Exchange Act attempts to define the term. "The law governing manipulations has become an embarrassment—confusing, contradictory, complex, and unsophisticated."[9]

Is manipulation "interference with supply and demand" as Professor Nagy suggests? What does "interference" mean? What about "inducing people to trade"? What if a broker releases a positive report on a company and the clients buy the stock and the price goes up? Can intent alone make an otherwise lawful practice unlawful? What about forcing a security's price to trade at an artificial level? Is there a difference between an artificial and a non-artificial price? What if the purpose of the manipulation is to "restore the stock to its true value"?[10] There are no good answers to most of these questions.

Elements of Manipulation

The traditional elements of a manipulation prosecution are thought to be the following:

- a manipulative act,
- damage,
- reliance on an efficient market free of manipulation,
- scienter,
- "in connection with" purchase or sale of a security, and
- the use of mail or national exchange.

---

[8] Definitions include intentional interference with supply and demand, exercising unsupported price pressure, and reducing price accuracy and liquidity. *See generally* Albert Kyle & S. Viswanathan, "How to Define Illegal Price Manipulation," 98 *Am. Econ. Rev.* 274 (2008).

[9] Edward McDermott, "Defining Manipulation in Commodity Futures Trading," 74 *Nw. U. L. Rev.* 202 (1979).

[10] *See United States v. Hall*, 48 F. Supp. 2d 387 (S.D.N.Y. 1999) ("A defendant may be guilty of manipulation even if in fact a stock is trading below its actual value.").

Even though these elements have been recently reiterated by the Second Circuit Court of Appeals, the theoretical basis for them remains elusive. In particular, can a "manipulative act" be based on intent alone if the underlying act is lawful? We examine that question below.

The Theoretical Basis for Prohibiting Manipulation

In 1991 in the *Harvard Law Review*, Professor Daniel Fischel (later Dean of the Chicago Law School) and David Ross, a Ph.D. candidate, tried to define manipulation as trades made with "bad intent."[11] They concluded that trades that meet the following criteria are manipulative:

- the trading is intended to move prices in a certain direction,
- the trader has no belief that the prices would move in this direction but for the trade, and
- the resulting profit comes solely from the trader's ability to move prices, not from his or her possession of valuable information.

This generated some academic debate. For example, Professor Steve Thel said that manipulation was the buying of a security for the purpose of increasing the price or selling a security for the purpose of decreasing the price.[12] Perhaps, but isn't that the purpose of many corporate stock buybacks?

Are there any problems with this definition? Could a trade made with bad intentions nevertheless actually be beneficial to the market? Could a trader with the best of intentions nevertheless execute a detrimental trade? Yet both definitions are based almost entirely on intent, without clearly observable harm.

Is there a relationship between manipulation and fraud? Is manipulation just a species of fraud? For certain types of conduct, it is. For example, fictitious transactions like wash sales. But for other types of transactions, those involving real trades, the comparison does not work. Take Fischel's example: a trader who trades with bad intent attempts to move the price with no belief that but for the trade, the price would move in that direction. Has the trader engaged in any objectively bad conduct? The trader's conduct is the same as that of other traders; the only difference is intent. But fraud requires underlying bad conduct such as false statements. Bad intent alone cannot create fraud, but it can create manipulation, at least under Fischel's definition. Should the law prohibit such trades? Are they likely to occur without some prohibition? Does

---

[11] Daniel Fischel & David Ross, "Should the Law Prohibit Manipulation in Financial Markets?" 105 *Harv. L. Rev.* 503 (1991).

[12] *See* Steve Thel, "$850,000 in Six Minutes—The Mechanics of Securities Manipulation," 79 *Cornell L. Rev.* 219 (1994).

trading actually affect market price? If so, why are there millions of trades each day that do not change the price?

Some trades can affect price by supplying information to the market (this is the so-called information hypothesis) or if supply and demand are not perfectly elastic because perfect substitutes do not actually exist (the "price pressure hypothesis").[13] Fischel and Ross also say that it is difficult to identify manipulative trades. There are some characteristics that might help, like trading at the end of the day, short sales, or making bids at successively higher prices. But those practices in and of themselves say nothing about intent. They also argue that there is an unacceptable social cost to prohibiting manipulation, because we might prohibit certain beneficial trades, such as short selling.

Allen and Gale

In 1992, University of Pennsylvania's Wharton School Professor Franklin Allen, an economist, and then Boston University Professor Douglas Gale, an economist who is now teaching at New York University, wrote about trade-based manipulation (a trader attempting to manipulate a stock simply by buying and then selling, without taking any publicly observable actions to alter the value of the firm or releasing false information to change the price) and concluded that it was possible when it is unclear whether the purchaser of a large block of shares has good information about the firm's prospects or is simply trying to manipulate the stock price for profit.[14]

Aggarwal and Wu

In 2003, Professor Rajesh Aggarwal, of Northeastern University, and University of Houston's Professor Guojun Wu, considered what happens when a manipulator can trade in the presence of other traders who seek out information about the stock's true value. They concluded that in a market without manipulators, the information seekers improve market efficiency by pushing prices up to the level indicated by the informed party's information. In a market with manipulators, the information seekers play a more ambiguous role. More information seekers imply greater competition for shares, making it easier for a manipulator to enter the market and potentially worsening market efficiency. Using evidence from SEC cases, they conclude that potentially

---

13 *See* Matthijs Nelemans, "Redefining Trade-Based Market Manipulations," 42 *Val. U. L. Rev.* 1169 (2008).

14 *See* Franklin Allen & Douglas Gale, "Stock-Price Manipulation," 5 *Rev. of Fin. Studies* 503 (1992).

informed parties such as corporate insiders, brokers, underwriters, large shareholders, and market makers are likely to be manipulators.[15]

They also conclude that illiquid stocks are more likely to be manipulated and that manipulation increases stock volatility. Prices and liquidity are higher when the manipulator sells than when the manipulator buys. Their overall conclusion is that, not surprisingly, market manipulation may have important impacts on market efficiency.

Ledgerwood and Carpenter

Shaun Ledgerwood and Paul Carpenter are economists at the Brattle Group who have confronted the dearth of successful market manipulation cases and have proposed a different way of looking at market manipulation. In addition to the traditional academic thesis that market manipulation required either market power—the ability to unilaterally move prices by "flexing economic muscles"—or fraud or deceit—the introduction of false or misleading information into the market—they posit a third way of manipulating a market—uneconomic trades. In their hypothesis, there is a "framework" for this third way that includes a "trigger" that uses price-making trades to inject false information into the market about the value of the assets traded and thus causes a directional price movement, a "target" that is the position held by the trader that will benefit from the directional price movement, and a "nexus" that links the "trigger" and the "target." This hypothesis is based on the theory of "uneconomic trading" by a trader that is intentionally designed lose money at the beginning of the manipulation.

They argue that "the historical precedent of manipulation cases tried before the CFTC, FERC (Federal Energy Regulatory Commission), and SEC provide a patchwork of specific types of behaviors determined to be illegal, with no functional linkage to a common economic logic across the cases tried by each agency, much less across agencies." They criticize this "I know it when I see it" approach and contend that "the framework that we propose could clarify what does and does not constitute manipulation for both market participants and enforcement agencies. Such certainty would ultimately improve market efficiency through improving market liquidity and reducing bid-asked spreads."[16]

It is certainly true that there have been instances in which traders would deliberately pay less than or more than a market price in order to take advantage

[15] Rajesh Aggarwal & Guojun Wu, "Stock Market Manipulation: Theory and Evidence," 79 *J. of Bus.* 1915 (2006) (based on a paper prepared in 2003).

[16] Shaun Ledgerwood & Paul Carpenter, "A Framework for Analysis of Market Manipulation," Review of Law and Economics, Vol. 8, No. 1 (2012).

of a subsequent change in the price that would benefit other securities that they held. The case brought against Amaranth Advisors L.L.C. by the FERC in 2007 in which Amaranth bought natural gas futures contracts at a high price and then liquidated the position at a lower price during a settlement window is one example. Although that conduct generated a loss, it turned out that Amaranth had acquired short positions in swap and options positions that benefited from the losses in the price-making trades.[17] But how widespread such conduct is or will become and whether or not this new theory of market manipulation will gain traction remains to be seen. Stay tuned!

Is Intent Alone Enough?

This is the question that I asked you earlier to keep in mind. There has been a sharp split among the federal circuits with respect to the key question in market manipulation law: can trading activity alone ever be considered illegal manipulation under federal law? Under what circumstances can the purchase of a stock on the open market in and of itself become prohibited market manipulation?

Fischel and Ross have concluded that there is no objective definition of manipulation and that "the only definition that makes any sense is subjective—it focuses entirely on the intent of the trader.... Manipulative trades could be defined as profitable trades made with 'bad intent.'" In other words, they were trades intended to move prices in a direction different from the direction in which they would have gone but for the trade. This is what the academics call "open market manipulation." Fischel and Ross's conclusion was that because such trading is likely to be self-deterring and because the enforcement of a prohibition is likely to be costly, "actual trades should not be prohibited as manipulative regardless of the trader's intent." Their definition of manipulation as being subjective generated considerable academic debate. Could a trade made with bad intentions nevertheless actually be beneficial to the market? After all, rising prices could be said to "lift all boats" except possibly those owned by the short sellers. Could a trader with the best of intentions nevertheless execute a detrimental trade? Short sellers borrow stock and immediately sell it in the expectation that the price will decline so that they can repurchase it at a lower price. Does that meet the Fischel definition of manipulation?

Section 9(a)(2) of the 1934 Securities Exchange Act prohibits the use of the mails, interstate commerce, or any facility of a national exchange to effect transactions in a security creating actual or apparent active trading in the security or raising or depressing the price "for the purpose of inducing the

[17] *CFTC v. Amaranth Advisors, L.L.C., Amaranth Advisors (Calgary) ULC, and Brian Hunter*, 07 Civ. 6682 (S.D.N.Y. May 21, 2007).

purchase or sale of such security by others." But must the purchaser actually be able to influence the market price of the security or is a naked intent enough for criminality? Fischel believes that at a minimum, the purchaser must be able to affect the stock price. "If trading has no effect on price because of the substitution effect (i.e., the buying and selling of securities signals to others that the securities at issue are under- or over-priced and they will revise their own expectations about value accordingly), a successful manipulation is impossible." And even if there is a relationship between trading and price movements, "a successful manipulation is still unlikely to occur."

Fischel's definition focused entirely on the intent of the trader. Since manipulation in his view had to be subjective, a trader who buys or sells for the purpose of moving the stock price in one direction or the other is by definition a manipulator. That definition was unsatisfactory to him because all purchases tend to move the stock price upward. Why should the intent of the purchaser make a difference, especially when one is talking about a criminal statute? Does the manipulator commit fraud? We know that for certain types of conduct, manipulation is just a species of fraud. For example, fictitious transactions like wash sales and matched orders are clearly manipulative and fraudulent and perhaps for that reason, they are explicitly prohibited by Section 9(a)(1). But for other types of transactions, those involving real trades, the comparison does not work. Take Fischel's example: a trader who trades with bad intent attempts to move the stock price with no belief that but for the trade, the price would still move in that direction. Has the trader engaged in any objectively bad conduct? The trader's conduct is the same as that of other traders; the only difference is intent. Bad intent alone cannot create fraud but it can create manipulation under Fischel's definition. Should the law prohibit such trades without knowing the intent of all the traders? Because trades are based on expectation of future prices and because the future cannot be known, buyers and sellers can act on different expectations of future prices and, obviously, with different intents.

As noted, some trades can affect price by supplying information to the market. The manipulator must appear to be informed, otherwise the trades cannot cause prices to rise. But if the trader appears to have too much information, prices will rise simultaneously with the trade, in which case the trader cannot profit from later price increases. All of this led Fischel to conclude that in reality, successful manipulation is very difficult to pull off.

Fischel argued that it was also difficult to identify manipulative trades. There are some characteristics that might help, like trading at the end of the day (i.e., "marking the close"), short sales, or making bids at successively higher prices. But even those practices say nothing about intent, at least not directly, and those trading with manipulative intent rarely reveal it.

In 2018, an economist and two law professors attempted to answer that question by asking who is being harmed and who is helped if the practice of market manipulation is left unregulated and how this would change if the practice were instead legally prohibited.[18] They identified three types of market manipulation that should be prohibited:

1. *Naked Open-Market Manipulation*, where the trader purchases a number of shares with an upward push on prices and then sells the shares under circumstances where the downward push on prices is less severe, resulting in the average sale price exceeding the average purchase price, where the trader had a good reason to believe that the likelihood of this price reaction was sufficiently great that it will yield net gains from trading.
2. *Open Market Manipulation With an External Interest*, where a trader has an economic interest in the price of a security independent of the price at which it can be bought or sold in the open market, such as a corporate executive whose compensation is based on the price of the company's stock at a particular moment in time.
3. *Misstatement Manipulation*, where a trader makes a materially false statement concerning an issuer that pushes down its price, then purchases shares in the market, then waits until the truth comes out, and then resells the shares.

In each of these cases, the investor's purpose was to profit from the expected price movement alone, similar to a wash sale where the resulting price change is socially undesirable, and the trade otherwise has no socially redeeming features.

Judge Frank Easterbrook of the Seventh Circuit came up with his own definition of market manipulation: "manipulation should be defined as conduct in which profit flows solely from the trader's ability to conceal his position from other traders and the trades do not move prices more quickly in the direction that reflects long-run conditions of supply and demand." In other words, if the trader does not disclose a position in the stock being traded, purchases or sales could be manipulative. Unfortunately, that definition was no more helpful than Professor Fischel's "subjective" definition. What exactly are "long-run conditions of supply and demand"?

What if the trader thinks the price will move in one direction and the prices move in the opposite direction? Has the trader still engaged in market manipulation? And what about the fact that traders do not need to disclose the

---

[18] Merrit Fox et al., "Stock Market Manipulation and Its Regulation," 35 *Yale J. Reg.* 67 (2018).

information they possess that motivates their trades? In fact, they rarely do. In April 2014, the SEC charged five New Jersey traders and two brokerage firms with engaging in illegal high-speed trading known as "layering" or "spoofing." The complaint, which was immediately settled, alleged that the defendants would trick investors into buying and selling specific stocks at prices that were manipulated by orders that were placed and then immediately canceled. *In the Matter of Visionary Trading LLC*, SEC Rel. 71817 (April 2014). Sanjay Wadhwa, at the time the SEC Associate Director of Enforcement in New York, said that "the fair and efficient functioning of the markets requires that prices of securities reflect genuine supply and demand. Traders who pervert these natural forces by engaging in layering or some other form of manipulation invite close scrutiny from the SEC." Spoofing occurs when a broker places an order that he or she intends to cancel before execution. Layering is a more sophisticated form of spoofing in which multiple orders are made and then canceled before execution. Both create a false appearance of market activity that can induce investors to buy.

Some say Congress was concerned about "bear raids" when it adopted the 1938 "uptick rule" adopted by the SEC. Bear raids were attempts by a trader or traders to force down the price of a stock in order to cover a "short" position. A "short sale" is any sale of a security the seller does not own or any sale that is consummated by the delivery of a security borrowed by the seller. A "naked short sale" occurs when the seller does not actually borrow the stock prior to the trade but promises to deliver it to the buyer at some later date. If the seller does not do so, that is referred to as a failure to deliver. The SEC now prohibits naked short sales. The uptick rule, Rule 10a-1(a)(1), provided that a short sale must either be above the last traded price or at the last traded price when the most recent movement between traded prices was upward. The uptick rule was replaced with Regulation SHO in 2005. A modified uptick rule in Regulation SHO was adopted in 2010. See Section 201 (Circuit Breaker).

The drafters of the 1933 and 1934 Acts were most concerned about "pools" in which perceived combinations of issuers, underwriters, and speculators allegedly caused wild fluctuations in security prices by their trading activities. "Pools" are agreements among issuers, underwriters, and others to raise the price of a security after a public offering by active trading or other means, followed by then selling the stock at the inflated price before the inevitable collapse. Do pools still exist? Yes they do.[19]

We have seen that Section 9(a)(2) of the 1934 Act makes it unlawful for any person, alone or with others, to effect a series of transactions creating actual or apparent active trading or raising or depressing the price, for the purpose

[19] *See United States v. Goodman* (D. Mass. Sept. 12, 2005) (guilty plea) (fraudulent IPO pool alleged).

of inducing the purchase or sale of the security by others. Would this apply to a publicly announced corporate stock buyback program for the purpose of raising the stock's price? Perhaps, but recall that Rule 10b-18 provides a safe harbor for corporate buybacks of stock that meet all four conditions relating to manner of purchase, the time of the repurchase, the price paid, and the volume of the shares repurchased. It is worth repeating that all four conditions must be met to qualify for the safe harbor.

Note also that the Dodd-Frank Act removed the words "registered on a national securities exchange" from Section 9(a)(2) and as a result, Section 9 now covers manipulative conduct in the trading of most securities, whether or not registered. This solved the IPO problem of IPOs not traded on national exchange.

What about day traders? SEC's Regulation T is one of many attempts to curb market manipulation by limiting the use of margin accounts. The SEC defines "pattern day traders" as day traders who execute four or more trades within five business days, provided that the number of day trades represents more than 6 percent of the customer's total trades in the margin account for that same five-business day period. A "day trade" is defined as the purchasing and selling or the selling and purchasing of the same security on the same day in a margin account.[20] In order to prevent market manipulation, the SEC's Regulation T requires pattern day traders to have minimum equity into the customer's account of $25,000 prior to any day trading activities, and this minimum must be maintained at all times. Each day trading account is required to meet the $25,000 requirement independently, using only the financial resources available in that account. If the account falls below that amount, the customer will not be permitted to day trade until the customer deposits cash or securities into the account to restore the account to the $25,000 minimum equity level. The customer will be allowed to trade up to four times the customer's maintenance margin excess in the account. If the customer exceeds this day trading buying power limitation, there will be a margin call.

Types of Manipulation

There are three main types: (1) "fictitious" securities transactions, (2) actual trading motivated by a manipulation purpose, and (3) misleading recommendations regarding real securities, such as "touting." Certain specific manipulations include wash sales, matched orders, marking the close (attempt to influence closing price), "painting the tape," "chumming" (as in throwing bait to shareholders), circular transactions, "pump and dump," "distort and

---

[20] https://www.sec.gov/files/daytrading.pdf.

short," and many others. Most of these create the appearance of real trading activity in order to raise the price of a stock.

Touting

Congress was concerned about statements by paid shills, "tipster sheets," and articles in newspapers and periodicals that appeared to be unbiased opinions endorsing certain securities but that were in fact bought and paid for. This was called "touting." As a result, the 1934 Act contains Section 17(b), which mandates that if a person is paid to promote a security, then the person must disclose the nature, source, and amount of compensation. Touting came back to life in the internet era when touting appeared in online message boards, discussion forums, and social media. The SEC created the Office of Internet Enforcement to deal with such activity, and the SEC conducted a series of "internet sweeps" that resulted in more than twenty-five enforcement actions, including actions against such well-known people as Steven Seagal and Floyd Mayweather for touting cryptocurrencies. Section 17(b) is a strict liability statute that is violated when the action is committed regardless of the actor's intent or whether the actor was even aware of Section 17(b).

Pegging

This is an attempt to maintain a security at a specific price. It is usually done in connection with a public offering and is an attempt to stabilize the price at the offering price. It is prohibited by Section 9(a)(6), which prohibits "any series of transactions for the purchase or sale of any security ... for the purpose of pegging, fixing or stabilizing the price of the security in contravention of rules that may be prescribed by the SEC."

In 1955, the SEC adopted Rule 10b-6, prohibiting any underwriter, issuer, broker, or other participant in the distribution process from bidding for, purchasing, or advising others to purchase any security being distributed until he has completed his part in the distribution. This rule in effect replaces Section 9(a)(2) with a blanket prohibition on all trading by certain individuals during distributions. However, Rule 10b-6 has many exceptions and is a nightmare.[21] Perhaps as a result, the SEC essentially replaced Rule 10b-6 with Regulation M (for Anti-Manipulation) that prohibits underwriters and other "distribution participants" from trading securities with an average daily trading volume of $100,000 or more during a "restricted period," or a period

---

21 *See generally* Lewis Lowenfels, "Rule 10b-13, Rule 10b-6 and Purchase of Target Company Securities During an Exchange Offer," 69 *Colum. L. Rev.* 1392 (1969).

beginning the day prior to the fixing of an offering price and ending when the trader has completed its participation in the distribution. In other words, underwriters may no longer purchase stock after an offer but before the distribution has been completed for the purpose of pegging or supporting the price to the stock in the offering. Pegging, at least in theory, no longer exists.

Other Prohibitions

As noted, prohibitions against market manipulation are found in Section 9 (wash sales, etc.), Section 10(b), and Rule 10b-5. Most of the few manipulation cases that have been brought are brought under Rule 10b-5. NYSE and FINRA also have rules prohibiting manipulation, as do other exchanges. Many other countries have similar prohibitions. For example, European Union member states have adopted Section 1(2)(a) MAD 2003/6/EC: "market participants shall refrain from trading when their transactions would secure the price at an abnormal level."

Recall that Section 10(b) provides that it is "unlawful to use or employ, in connection with the purchase or sale of any security, any manipulative or deceptive device or contrivance." But what is a "contrivance"? According to various dictionaries, it is a "device or gadget," something that is used to "bring something about," an "artificial arrangement or development," or a "clever plan." The Rule 10b-5 prohibitions do not precisely delineate manipulation but courts have interpreted and qualified the type of activity that constitutes manipulation; nevertheless, there is still some ambiguity.

Private Rights of Action

There is an implied private right of action for manipulation under Section 10(b). *ATSI Communications v. Shaar Fund*, 493 F.3d 87 (2d Cir. 2007). The Private Securities Litigation Reform Act (PSLRA) applies. Therefore, heightened standards for pleading scienter apply. In *Fezzani v. Bear Stearns*, 716 F.3d 18 (2d Cir. 2013) (rehearing denied, Jan. 30, 2015), a private right of action, the Second Circuit held that a market manipulation claim under Section 10(b) could not be maintained against an individual who parked penny stocks in his account to facilitate a scheme by a broker to make it appear that there was trading volume. The broker falsely represented that the stock was trading in an active bona fide market. But the individual could only be primarily liable (no aiding and abetting liability is available) if he made a false statement, under *Janus* (and *Stoneridge*). He did not make any false statement and the federal claims were dismissed. The strong and arguably correct dissent argued that the individual was a primary violator because he engaged directly in market manipulation, and that does not necessarily require a misrepresentation (*But see Wilson v. Merrill Lynch*, 671 F.3d 120 (2d Cir. 2011).) Who is right? In denying the petition for rehearing, which the SEC had urged, the Second Circuit panel clarified that it has never required that reliance by a victim be based on an oral or written communication to the victim by the defendant, and that reliance may be based on a showing of "market activity" upon which the victim relied. But it found that in this case, there was no claim that there existed a market in any sense of the word for the shares that the broker sold to the victim.

Other Types of Manipulations

Contract-Based Manipulations (called market manipulations with "external interests"), in which the trader can trigger a contract right or benefit by trading. *Example*: Purchases by a corporate officer that raise the price of her company's shares enough to trigger a bonus in her compensation package.

Trading Combined With Disclosure. Example: An analyst makes a purchase and then makes a favorable recommendation to her clients, even though she privately believes there is no basis for such a recommendation. Is this manipulation or outright fraud? *Zweig v. Hearst Corp.*, 521 F.2d 1129 (9th Cir. 1975) (could be evidence of securities fraud). In another example, Foster Winans, a *Wall Street Journal* columnist who wrote a column called "Heard on the Street," was accused of leaking information about upcoming articles to a friend who then traded on that information. In *Carpenter v. United States*, 484 U.S. 19 (1987), Winans's conviction for violating the federal securities laws and mail and wire fraud statutes was affirmed by an equally divided Supreme Court; the court could not agree on a misappropriation theory for insider trading. Who did he defraud? *The Wall Street Journal*? How?

What about an internet blogger who buys stock and then touts it on her blog? Who is she defrauding? What if she said, "I just bought this stock and you should too"?

Short Squeeze. This an attempt to artificially increase the price of a stock in order to force short sellers to purchase stocks to cover their losses. In the case of GameStop, a seller of internet games and equipment, its stock rose from $3 per share in April 2020 to $483 per share on January 12, 2021. Its short interest ratio was 84 percent in April 2020, leading some to argue that its price increase was the result of a short squeeze. The SEC investigated and concluded that although there were periods of price increases and covering of positions by short sellers, the real reason for the price increase was the positive sentiment of the purchasers, who were purchasing the stock through online brokers such as Wallstreetbets.[22]

Famous Cases of Manipulation

In *United States v. GAF Corp.*, 928 F.2d 1253 (2d Cir. 1991), GAF wanted to sell a large block of Union Carbide's outstanding stock and solicited bids from investment banking firms. James Sherwin, GAF's vice chairman, asked employees of Jeffries & Co. to arrange for the price of Union Carbide to close at or above $22 per share on two specified days and indemnified Jeffries against any loss (this request was disputed at trial). The stock was trading slightly below $22. The alleged purpose was to attract buyers and thereby maximize the profits to be earned from the sale. On the first of the days in question, Jeffries bought 60,000 shares near the close of trading day and on the second day, bought 40,000 shares, also near the close of trading. The price closed at $22 on both days. Three days later, Jeffries sold its shares at a loss. GAF sold 5 million shares of Union Carbide in a negotiated transaction a week later.

Both the company and Sherwin were indicted. The government alleged that the "end of the day" trades were evidence of manipulation, even though such trades are not uncommon. Was there manipulative intent? Price increases that accompany trades do not establish manipulative intent. What about the guarantee against loss? It could have been a means to induce Jeffries to trade as GAF's agent. What about the purpose to increase GAF's profits? Unlikely, since the difference was so small and since the negotiated price would have taken into account all prior trading information.

There were three trials: a mistrial because of prosecutorial error, a hung jury, and a conviction on all counts. The Second Circuit reversed and remanded for a new trial. The government then dropped all charges.

In *United States v. Milken*, 759 F. Supp. 109 (S.D.N.Y. 1990), Wickes Corp. had 8 million shares of a $2.50 convertible exchangeable preferred outstanding, issued in April 1985. The indenture contained a redemption feature that gave Wickes an option to redeem the stock prior to May 1988 if the closing price of Wickes common stock equaled or exceeded $6-1/8 for at least twenty of the thirty consecutive trading days prior to the call for redemption. About a week before the last redemption date, the stock price had closed at or above the threshold price on nineteen of twenty-eight days. Michael Milken, who worked for Drexel Burnham Lambert, Wickes investment adviser, asked a

[22] *See* SEC "Staff Report on Equity and Options Market Structure Conditions in Early 2021" October 14, 2021, at 43; Joshua Bautz, "What Is the SEC Going to Do About GameStop?" NYSBA Latest News, February 4, 2021, https://nysba.org/what-is-the-sec-going-to-do-about-gamestop/.

third party, Ivan Boesky, to purchase enough Wickes stock to cause it to close at or above $6-1/8, and he guaranteed Boesky against loss.

On the appointed day (April 23, 1986), Boesky, through his chief trader, bought 1.9 million shares, and the stock closed at the threshold price. Wickes then called the preferred, and Drexel received a fee of $2.3 million. The stock price then declined, and Boesky had a loss. This would be called alleged "contract-based manipulation." The United States was unable to link Milken directly to the Wickes purchase, although several witnesses believed he "was behind the manipulation."

Is there an alternative benign explanation? What if Boesky thought the stock was a good investment and sufficiently close to the threshold price that it would be met in the ordinary course and would then rise?

Milken was indicted but the charges were dropped in a plea bargain agreement. When Milken was sentenced on other violations, the judge said that the Wickes evidence against Milken was "fairly ambiguous."

In *United States v. Mulheren*, 938 F.2d 364 (2d Cir. 1991), John Mulheren was chief trader and general partner of Jamie Securities Co. In 1985, Ivan Boesky purchased 3.4 million shares of Gulf & Western Industries Inc., or 4.9 percent of the outstanding stock. Carl Ichan, his friend, also owned a "position of magnitude." Boesky had discussions with Marvin Davis, G&W's chairman, about taking control of the company, increasing his position in the company, or selling his shares back to the company at $45 per share. The press speculated about the possibility of a takeover, but Mulheren denied reading the articles. After the close of trading on October 16, 1985, Boesky again offered to sell his stock at $45. Davis said the company would buy his stock back "but only at the price at which the stock last traded on the NYSE at the time of the transaction." Davis told Boesky to have his investment banker contact G&W's banker to arrange the deal. Boesky then called Mulheren and said that he "liked" G&W stock but would not pay more than $45 for it and "it would be great if it traded at 45." Mulheren: "I understand." (*Query*: Why would Boesky limit the price to $45 if a higher price would help him even more?)

Shortly thereafter, Jamie Securities, Mulheren's broker, placed an order to buy 50,000 shares at the market price and the order was filled at prices of $44-3/4 and $44-7/8. A few minutes later, Jamie placed another order for 25,000 shares at $45 or less. All shares were purchased at $45. Boesky then sold his stock back to G&W at $45, and thereafter, the stock closed at $43-5/8. Jamie sold its position at the end of the day at a loss.

Mulheren was indicted and convicted at trial on charges that he conspired to manipulate and did manipulate the price of the stock, in violation of Section 10(b) (he was not charged under Section 9(a)(2) because there was no evidence that he intended to induce the purchase or sale of a security by others). But the Second Circuit reversed, finding that there was a lack of evidence of

Mulheren's intent and that Boesky's conversation with Mulheren was at best ambiguous. The observable characteristics of the transaction were "at least as consistent with innocence as they were with guilt." The court declined to accept the government's invitation to infer intent from Mulheren's conduct.

The Second Circuit wrote, "Unlawful manipulation occurs, the argument goes, even though the investor has not acted for the 'purpose of inducing the purchase or sale of such security by others,' an element the government would have had to prove had it chosen to proceed under the manipulation statute, § 9(a)(2) [of the 1934 Securities Exchange Act]. Mulheren was not charged with violating § 9(a)(2). When the transaction is effected for an investment purpose, the theory continues, there is no manipulation, even if an increase or diminution in price was a foreseeable consequence of the investment. . . . None of the traditional badges of manipulation are present in this case. Mulheren conspicuously purchased the shares for Jamie's account in the open market. . . . Jamie was conspicuously identified as the ultimate buyer of the G&W securities. . . . We acknowledge that this case treads dangerously close to the line between legitimate inference and impermissible speculation. We are persuaded, however, that to come to the conclusion it did, the jury must have engaged in false surmise and rank speculation."

What if there was proof that Mulheren's "sole purpose" was to help Boesky? Would that have made Mulheren's open market purchase unlawful? Can a bad intent make an otherwise lawful act unlawful? The court had "misgivings" about the government's view of the law that Rule 10b-5 is violated when one trades in the open market for the sole purpose of affecting the price of the stock

In *Markowski v. SEC*, 274 F.3d 525 (D.C. Cir. 2001), Michael Markowski was the CEO of Global America, Inc. Global had underwritten an IPO for Mountaintop Corp., an Alaska vodka producer. In after-market trading, Global dominated the market for Mountaintop securities and absorbed all unwanted securities, thereby accounting for a majority of all purchases and sales. This had the effect of supporting the price of Mountaintop securities, similar to "pegging." The ostensible reason for Global's purchases was not to profit from later sales of the stock but to "maintain customer interest in Global generally and to sustain confidence in its other securities." Global's chief trader Joseph Riccio explained that "if we do that on one stock, they [presumably holders of Global's stocks] will hit us on all the stocks." Unfortunately for Markowski, the effort failed; Global went out of business and the Mountaintop stock dropped 75 percent in one day.

The National Association of Securities Dealers (NASD) found that Markowski had violated Rule 10b-5 by manipulating the stock market and NASD's rules prohibiting "non–bona fide" bid quotations. It imposed a fine and a censure. The SEC affirmed the NASD's finding of violations and the imposition of disciplinary action and also found that Markowski had violated a restriction agreement governing his firm's inventory and failed to cooperate with the NASD investigation. An appeal to the District of Columbia Circuit Court of Appeals followed.

In a unanimous opinion, the D.C. Circuit affirmed the SEC's order. Citing and quoting from the Fischel and Ross article,[23] the court acknowledged that there was a debate among academics as to whether intent alone could result in actionable manipulation. "Liability for manipulation wholly independent of fictitious transactions in fact raises interesting questions. Without such transactions, the core of the offense can be obscure. It may be hard to separate the 'manipulative' investor from one who is simply over-enthusiastic, a true believer in the object of the investment.... Legality would thus depend entirely on whether the investor's intent was 'an investment purpose' or 'solely to affect the price of the security (quoting from the Second Circuit's opinion in the *Mulheren* case).'"

The court concluded, however, that those arguments were of "little use" to Markowski because Congress had already determined that manipulation can be illegal solely because of the actor's purpose, citing Section 9(a)(2) of the Securities Exchange Act, which made it unlawful "to effect ... [the] raising or depressing the price of ... a security, for the purpose of inducing the purchase or sale of such security by others." Of course, that is not what Markowski was charged with doing. The court also cited the prohibition on certain issuer repurchases even though they are "perfectly real transactions." In other words, intent alone can, in fact, make an otherwise lawful transaction unlawful.

Professor Gina-Gail Fletcher, a scholar of open-market manipulation at Duke Law School, has written that the decision was "disconcerting" because the sole basis for liability was the defendant's manipulative intent. "[I]ntent is inadequate as an explanation of why otherwise legitimate transactions are manipulative.... Under the current approach to open-market manipulation, intent plays an outsized role in determining liability."[24]

Manipulation in Futures Markets

A commodity futures contract is a standardized agreement to buy or sell a fixed quantity and grade of a commodity to be delivered at a specified time in the future. Prior to the expiration of the futures contract, there is little cause for concern because they are easily traded and there are good substitutes available. However, near the time of expiration, demands of "short traders" are

---

[23] Daniel Fischel & David Ross, "Should the Law Prohibit Manipulation in Financial Markets?" 105 *Harv. L. Rev.* 503 (1991).

[24] Gina-Gail Fletcher, "Legitimate Yet Manipulative: The Conundrum of Open-Market Manipulation," 69 *Duke L. J.* 479 (2018).

inelastic, and the owner of the contract has market power, leading to noncompetitive pricing. The owner can extract a high price from the shorts. Manipulation occurs when there is ability and intent to create artificially high or low prices, through the use of market power.

Concealment of true positions might give rise to manipulation under Judge Easterbrook's definition, but is it natural to conceal? Concealment might be necessary in order to profit from the ability to predict correctly future conditions.

Secret purchases would allow a manipulator to obtain market power and permit the manipulator to buy at a price that did not reflect the coming squeeze caused by the exercise of his market power at expiration.

Manipulation in the futures market is risky. In 1979 and 1980, the Hunt family secretly took substantial long positions in silver. Prices rose and then fell as silver stocks increased. The price declines resulted in margin calls that the Hunts were unable to meet, and they lost over $1 billion.[25]

In *Cargill Inc. v. Hardin*, 452 F. 2d 1154 (8th Cir. 1971), Cargill hedged its inventory of soft red winter wheat by selling May 1963 wheat futures. Contracts traded until May 21 and could be satisfied at par by the delivery of soft winter wheat. Cargill learned that the Spanish government was interested in buying soft red winter wheat and concluded that the market would be tight. Cargill liquidated its short position and began acquiring long positions. There followed a series of purchases and sales of wheat and contracts, the result of which was that Cargill obtained market power and was able to sell its wheat at just below the maximum price.

The Eighth Circuit concluded that Cargill had manipulated the market price by acquiring and holding long positions in the May 1963 futures, that the shorts had insufficient supply of wheat available for delivery, that Cargill received an artificially high price in the liquidation of its futures contracts, and that the squeeze was intentional. But what really happened is that Cargill was able to sell its position at the highest price because it had market power.

Other Examples of Manipulation

Among the many different types of market manipulation--some of which do not even have a name--are the following:

- Pump and Dump (boosting the price through false statements).
- Trash and Cash or Distort and Short (the opposite).

[25] *See* Jeffrey Williams, *Manipulation on Trial: Economic Analysis and the Hunt Silver Case*, Cambridge University Press 1995.

- Market Timing (making buy or sell decision based on prediction of future movement; it may not be unlawful but it is certainly frowned upon. There is debate about whether it works.).
- Altering the end-of-day price. "Marking the close" occurs when a trader makes the last trade of the day at a price significantly different from the current price and allows market-on-close orders to be executed at a price that is advantageous to the manipulator. This is sometimes called "price positioning." *See SEC v. Masri*, 523 F. Supp. 2d 361 (S.D.N.Y. Nov. 21, 2007) (SEC claim dismissed for insufficient proof of intent).
- Layering (making orders with no intent to have them executed to trick others to buy or sell at an artificial price).
- The Bear Raid (short sellers conspire to dump huge quantities of borrowed shares into the market, driving the price down).
- In November 2007, a bear raid allegedly took place against Citigroup. In that case, short interests jumped to almost four times the average and trading volume increased nearly four times the average. On November 1, 2007, the stock dropped 6.9 percent, and the short positions closed on November 7 were 53 percent higher than the positions opened on November 1. The short sellers gained $640 million.

Recent Cases

Wilson v. Merrill Lynch, 671 F.3d 120 (2d Cir. 2011). This was an auction-rate securities case in which the complaint was dismissed because disclosure that the broker might step in to buy securities in the auction in order to prevent the auction from failing was adequate. Judge Robert Katzmann held that the complaint was not a "well-pleaded complaint." The Second Circuit declined to accept the SEC's evaluation of the disclosure at issue. What is a "well-pleaded complaint"? (*Hint*: The basis for federal jurisdiction must appear in the complaint; one cannot rely on "anticipated defenses" to establish federal jurisdiction.)

Anschutz v. Merrill Lynch, 690 F.3d 98 (2d Cir. 2012). High-volume, high-frequency trading as market manipulation.

City of Providence v. BATS Global Markets Inc., 878 F.3d 36 (2d Cir. 2016). Several market participants, including the City of Providence, Rhode Island, sued seven national securities exchanges, alleging that they engaged in market manipulation in violation of Rule 10b-5 by giving certain high-frequency traders (HFT) three trading advantages: proprietary data feeds, co-location services, and complex order types, that were not made available to other market participants. These three benefits, it was alleged, gave the HFTs access to and the ability to trade on market information before it became publicly available. The plaintiffs alleged that by making these services to the HFTs, the exchanges were engaging in fraudulent, manipulative conduct. The district court dismissed the complaint. Of relevance to this discussion, the district court found that the defendants did not themselves manipulate the market, the HFTs did, and that aiding and abetting is not an available allegation after *Central Bank*. On December 19, 2017, the Second Circuit reversed, finding that the plaintiffs properly alleged that the exchanges were "co-participants with the HFT firms in the manipulative scheme and profited by that scheme." The Supreme Court denied the petition for certiorari, and the case continues.

High-Volume, High-Frequency Trading as Market Manipulation

HFT is the new "market manipulation" but in itself, it may not be unlawful. Today, three-fourths of all equity trading volume is due to HFTs using sophisticated, computer-generated algorithms to move in and out of stock positions in fractions of seconds. As the result of high-frequency trading abuses, the SEC has adopted two new regulations, Regulation NMS (National Market Systems) to "modernize and strengthen the national market system ... for equity securities" and Regulation SCI that is designed to reduce the occurrence of system problems and to improve the resilience and communication when systems problems do recur.[26]

The SEC also requires exchanges and brokers to accept the most competitive bid or offer price posted at any trading venue and to inform the investing public of the best national bid and offer prices by displaying them on national data feeds.

The SEC's first high-frequency market manipulation case was brought against Athena Capital Research in October 2014. Athena was a high-frequency trading firm that placed a large number of aggressive, rapid-fire trades in the final two seconds of almost every trading day during a six-month period to manipulate the closing process of thousands of NASDAQ-listed stocks. Athena used an algorithm code named "Gravy" in order to engage in "marking the close." Because of volume, the price was artificially pushed in Athena's favor. Athena was charged with violating Section 10(b) of the 1934 Act.[27]

---

[26] Mary Jo White, "Equity Market Structure in 2016 and for the Future," Address, Securities Traders Ass'n, Sept. 14, 2016.

[27] https://www.sec.gov/files/Market%20Manipulations%20and%20Case%20Studies.pdf.

Athena agreed to a cease-and-desist order and a censure and agreed to pay a fine of $1 million.[28]

A good article to begin with is Professor Thomas Lin's article "The New Market Manipulation,"[29] which picks up on Michael Lewis's *The Flash Boys: A Wall Street Revolt*,[30] and adds legal analysis to Lewis's factual narrative.

Much of the concern about high-frequency trading is about whether it increases market volatility and diminishes liquidity. In response, the Commodity Futures Trading Commission has implemented rules on manipulative and deceptive devices and rules that require registration of proprietary traders who engage in algorithmic trading or who use direct electronic access. The relevant regulation is called Regulation Automated Trading (or Reg AT).

It is believed that high-frequency trading was responsible for the "flash crash" of May 6, 2010, and for the crashes of August 2 and October 15, 2014.

---

[28] https://www.sec.gov/litigation/admin/2014/34-73369.pdf.

[29] Thomas Lin, "The New Market Manipulation," 66 *Emory L. J.* 1253 (2017).

[30] Michael Lewis, *The Flash Boys: A Wall Street Revolt* (W.W. Norton 2014).

Chapter 17

The SEC

When the 1933 Securities Act was passed, the Federal Trade Commission had authority to enforce it and to regulate issuers. When the 1934 Securities Exchange Act was passed, a question arose whether the FTC should continue its regulatory and enforcement functions or whether a new agency should be created. President Franklin Roosevelt was indifferent but was persuaded to create a new agency, the Securities Exchange Commission, to replace the FTC in those roles. The first chair was Joseph P. Kennedy, formerly Ambassador to the United Kingdom and father of President John Kennedy.

The SEC's Division of Enforcement was created in 1972; before that, the functions were handled by various operating divisions. The SEC's authority to investigate is found in Section 21 of the 1934 Securities Exchange Act.

The SEC's Organization Today

The SEC is composed of five commissioners, appointed by the president and confirmed by the Senate. The president may appoint one of the commissioners to serve as the chair; no more than three commissioners may belong to the same political party. The commissioners serve for five-year staggered terms.

There are six divisions of the SEC:

1. *The Division of Corporation Finance.* This division has the most contact with issuers and, among other things, reviews filings. The division also provides administrative interpretations of the federal securities statutes, provides "no-action" letters with interpretive guidance, and offers guidance on financial reporting issues.
2. *The Division of Economic and Risk Analysis.* This division, created in 2009, conducts internal analyses, but has little interaction with investors, registrants, or market participants.
3. *The Division of Enforcement.* This division pursues the commission's civil complaints and suits against violators of the securities laws and performs investigations. It has subpoena power and,

with the approval of the commission, can bring civil and administrative actions against violators.

4. *The Division of Examinations.* This division conducts the SEC's National Exam Program through which the SEC inspects registered entities like broker-dealers and investment advisers, to ensure their compliance with the federal securities laws.
5. *The Division of Investment Management.* This division oversees the mutual fund, investment company, and investment adviser regulation.
6. *The Division of Trading and Markets.* This division oversees the broker-dealer industry and the capital markets generally, including the self-regulatory organizations, such as the stock exchanges and FINRA.

In addition to the divisions, the SEC has various offices, including the Office of Chief Accountant, the Office of International Affairs, the Office of Compliance, Inspections and Examinations, the Office of the General Counsel, and the Officer of Investor Education and Advocacy.

The SEC has only civil jurisdiction; it can sue in a federal court to seek injunctions, impose penalties, and seek disgorgement. Only the Department of Justice, through the U.S. Attorneys, can bring criminal cases, however.

The SEC can also bring administrative proceedings presided over by an SEC administrative law judge. In those cases, the SEC can seek a cease and desist order, can seek to preclude violators from serving as officers or directors of a public company, and can also seek disgorgement. Under Section 929P(a) of Dodd-Frank, the SEC can also seek penalties in administrative cases. Specifically, it can now obtain the same remedy in an administrative proceeding that it could in a federal court. It can also bring proceedings against regulated persons (*e.g.*, accountants) to revoke or suspend registration or to impose bars or suspensions from employment. Some have argued that SEC administrative proceedings violate due process by limiting the respondent's rights (*see, e.g.*, *Stilwell v. SEC*, 14 Civ. 7931 (S.D.N.Y. October 1, 2014) (subsequently settled)), but others argue that the availability of review by a federal court of appeals is sufficient to protect those rights. Administrative proceedings are posted on an SEC website,[1] and the SEC's Rules of Practice and Enforcement Manual are publicly available.

The full commission hears appeals from decisions by administrative law judges. Decisions by the full commission are then appealable to a federal court of appeals. The SEC can also hear appeals from enforcement actions

---

[1] https://www.sec.gov/litigation/admin.htm.

and disciplinary proceedings by self-regulatory organizations such as FINRA, NASD, or NYSE.

How Investigations Work

An SEC investigation is begun as a Matter Under Inquiry (MUI). An MUI can last sixty days. The SEC staff begins investigations privately. The staff develops facts through informal inquiry, interviewing witnesses, examining brokerage records and trading data, and other methods. In a preliminary investigation, no process is issued or testimony compelled. Then, the staff may seek a Formal Order of Investigation if it appears that the law has been or is about to be violated. Until 2009, only the SEC commissioners could issue a Formal Order of Investigation, but in that year, first as an experiment, the SEC delegated the authority to issue such orders to the head of the Enforcement Division. The delegation was made permanent the following year, after which the director began to "sub-delegate" the authority to senior officers in the division. After Donald Trump became president, the acting SEC Chair Michael Piwowar rescinded the delegation and returned the authority to the director of the Enforcement Division. On February 9, 2021, the Acting SEC Chair Allison Herren Lee restored the authority to issue Formal Orders of Investigation to the senior officers of the Division, about thirty in total, such as regional directors and associate directors. The restoration of delegation is expected to enable the investigative staff to act more swiftly in launching investigations.

Once a Formal Order is issued, the SEC staff can compel witnesses by subpoena and can compel the production of books, records, and other documents. The subpoena is not self-enforcing but can be enforced in federal district court. Witnesses can assert constitutional and attorney-client privileges.

If the SEC issues a subpoena to a third party, there is no obligation to notify the target (although it *may* do so). *SEC v. Jerry T. O'Brien Inc.*, 467 U.S. 735 (1984).

The defendant has the right to make a Wells Submission.

The Wells Notice and the Wells Submission

Why is it called a Wells Notice? In 1972, SEC Chairman William Casey appointed a committee to review and evaluate the commission's enforcement policies and practices. John Wells, a partner at the New York law firm then called Royall, Koegel & Wells, was the chair. The committee made forty-three recommendations. One was that a prospective defendant should be notified of the substance of the staff's charges and probable recommendation in advance of the submission of the staff memorandum to the commission and be afforded an opportunity to submit a written statement to the staff, which would be forwarded to the commission together with the staff memorandum.

But the SEC did not adopt the Wells Committee recommendation and did not adopt a formal rule. Instead, the notice, called a Wells Notice, is given on a "strictly informal basis." Whether or not it is formal, do not take it lightly. It means that the SEC staff has carefully considered the facts and the law and is considering bringing an action. The SEC Enforcement Manual specifies what should be in a Wells Notice, including stating the specific charges being considered, affording the prospective defendant an opportunity to provide a voluntary statement (in writing or on videotape) to argue why the commission should not bring charges or to bring any other facts to the commission's attention. The notice must advise that the submission may be used by the commission in any subsequent action and that it may be discoverable by third parties. The manual also speaks to setting reasonable limitations on length (typically not to exceed forty pages).

The Wells Submission is the formal opportunity for respondents to persuade the SEC staff and the commission in writing that an enforcement recommendation is not warranted. See SEC Securities Act Release 5310 (1972). The Wells process is better suited for legal rather than factual arguments. Shorter is better. One benefit is that the commission will hear a rebuttal to the staff's recommendation. One danger is that the submission can be used in later proceedings.

Wells submissions may be admissible under Rule 801(d)(2) of the Federal Rules of Evidence. At least the SEC has taken that position. But there is an argument that Wells submissions are actually "offers of compromise" under Rule 408 of the Federal Rules of Evidence and are therefore neither discoverable nor admissible.[2]

Warning: Be careful; your legal theories might change and the submission might be factually or legally mistaken. Once the investigation is closed, the Freedom of Information Act may require the production of a Wells submissions, but there are exceptions and typically the respondent is provided an opportunity to object to the production of a Wells submission under FOIA.

There is no general duty for a company that has received a Wells Notice to disclose the existence of the SEC Investigation or the Wells Notice, nor is there an obligation to do so under Regulation S-K. "The securities laws do not impose an obligation on a company to predict the outcome of investigations." *In re Lions Gate Entertainment Corp. Securities Litigation*, 2016 WL 297722 (S.D.N.Y. Jan. 22, 2016). Once the Wells submission is received,

---

[2] *See* Joshua Naftalis, "Wells Submissions to the SEC as Offers of Settlement Under Federal Rule of Evidence 408 and Their Protection from Third Party Discovery," 102 *Colum. L. Rev.* 1912 (2002).

the commission considers the staff's recommendation and can then authorize bringing of a case in federal court or an administrative action.

If it is an administrative action commenced by an Order Instituting Proceedings, the administrative law judge, who is independent from the commission, presides over a public hearing and makes an initial decision (findings and conclusions) and recommends a sanction if warranted. Preponderance of evidence is the burden of proof standard. Both the division and the defendant may appeal to the full commission and the parties may then appeal further to a federal court of appeals. Cease and desist orders are handled administratively. Is there a right to a jury trial in an administrative proceeding where penalties are sought? In 1977, in *Atlas Roofing Co. v. Occupational Safety and Health Review Commission*, 430 U.S. 442 (1977), the Supreme Court held that Congress could create statutory "public rights" and assign them to administrative agencies for adjudication without violating the Seventh Amendment's injunction that the jury trial right is to be "preserved," and held that the Seventh Amendment was never intended to establish the jury as the exclusive mechanism for fact finding in civil cases. What is a "public right"? (*Hint*: Those that "arise between the government and persons subject to its authority in connection with the performance of the constitutional functions of the executive or legislative departments." (*See Crowell v. Benson*, 285 U.S. 22 (1932).)

If the case is brought in federal court, all the normal rules of civil procedure and evidence apply but there is no right to a jury trial in profit disgorgement cases. *SEC v. Rind*, 991 F. 2d 1486 (9th Cir. 1993). Is there such a right in cases involving penalties? Probably yes.[3]

Up to 90 percent of all investigations are settled. Settlement with the SEC requires court approval. Often cases are filed and settled on the same day. Be aware of the SEC's "Policy Statement Concerning Cooperation." It requires a case-by-case analysis but can be helpful. 17 C.F.R. § 202. (Exchange Act Release 61340 (2010).

Administrative Sanctions

When the SEC determines administrative sanctions, it considers "the egregiousness of the defendant's actions, the isolated or recurrent nature of the infraction, the degree of scienter involved, the sincerity of the defendants' assurances against future violations," the defendants' recognition of the

---

[3] *See Tull v. United States*, 481 U.S. 412 (1987) (petitioner had a right to a jury trial in a claim filed in a federal court where the bulk of the government's case was for a civil penalty for violations of the Clean Water Act. The Supreme Court held that this was similar to an action in debt and the case was brought in a tribunal that offered a jury trial).

wrongful nature of his conduct, and the likelihood that the defendant's occupation will present opportunities for future violations. *See Steadman v. SEC*, 603 F.2d 1126 (5th Cir. 1979). The SEC determines sanctions using a "public interest" standard. *See* Section 15(b)(6) and 21B(c) of the 1934 Act. It also "weighs the effect of [its] action or inaction on the welfare of investors as a class and on standards of conduct in the securities business generally." *Arthur Lipper Corp.*, 46 S.E.C. 78, 100 (1975).

Settlements With the SEC

In *SEC v. Citigroup*, 752 F.3d 285 (2d Cir. 2014) (rehearing *en banc* denied, Apr. 3, 2015), the Second Circuit considered the refusal of Judge Jed Rakoff, a district court judge in the Southern District of New York, to accept a settlement between Citigroup and the SEC in a case arising out of Citigroup's alleged negligent misrepresentation of its role in structuring a fund whose assets were collateralized by subprime securities tied to the U.S. housing market. The proposed consent decree permanently enjoined Citigroup from violating Section 17(a) of the 1933 Act, required disgorgement of $160 million, and imposed prejudgment interest of $30 million and civil penalty of $95 million. The proposed decree made various other internal changes in Citigroup's procedures and provided that the judgment could not be used to offset any damages awarded in any related private action (a common feature of SEC consent decrees). There was no admission of guilt or liability. [A parallel action against an individual resulted in a defense verdict.]

A hearing was held in which Judge Rakoff asked numerous questions (*e.g.*, Why did the defendant neither admit nor deny liability? How could a fraud of this magnitude result only in a charge of simple negligence? How was the amount of the judgment determined?) After the questions were answered in written submissions, Judge Rakoff refused to approve the consent judgment. He found the proposed judgment was "neither fair, nor reasonable, nor adequate, nor in the public interest ... because it does not provide the court with a sufficient evidentiary basis to know whether the requested relief is justified under any of these standards." He ordered the case to proceed to trial. The Second Circuit reversed and remanded, holding that Judge Rakoff abused his discretion in refusing to accept the settlement.

First, the Second Circuit dismissed the popular but erroneous perception that Judge Rakoff conditioned his approval on an admission of liability; he did not, and the court added that if he had, there would have been no basis in the law for doing so.

Second, the court held that the proper standard for reviewing a proposed consent decree is for the district court to "determine whether the proposed consent decree is fair and reasonable. With the additional requirement that the public interest would not be disserved ... in the event the consent decree included injunctive relief. Absent a substantial basis in the record for concluding that the proposed decree does not meet those requirements, the district court is required to enter the order."

Third, the court noted that the "adequacy" requirement mentioned by Judge Rakoff is one that applies only in class action settlement; it does *not* apply to SEC settlements. The Second Circuit set forth four findings that a lower court must make when considering whether to approve an SEC settlement: (1) basic legality of the decree, (2) whether the terms are clear, (3) whether the decree reflects an actual resolution of the actual claim, and (4) whether the decree is "tainted by improper collusion." According to the court, it was an "abuse of discretion" for the district court to require that the SEC establish the "truth" of the allegations. "Trials are primarily about the truth. Consent decrees are primarily about pragmatism."

The Second Circuit then reversed and remanded for further proceedings, although a concurring opinion by Judge Raymond Lohier would have reversed and ordered Judge Rakoff to enter the consent decree. He later did so, somewhat reluctantly. He called the Second Circuit's standard "very modest" and one that provided "no meaningful oversight whatsoever" over SEC settlements.

The Second Circuit opinion has been criticized for lowering the bar for court approval of consent decrees almost to the point of non-existence. For example, Professor Eric Gerding of Colorado Law School wrote that "[The] court's message to trial judges seems to be 'unless the SEC hands you facts that this consent decree is illegal, unrelated to the complaint, or collusive/corrupt, you must approve."[4]

Some have also argued that the Second Circuit's standard will be difficult to apply. "It is not clear how a district court could consider substantive factors—such as deterrent—if adequacy is beyond its purview.... The court had earlier determined [that the test was] whether the 'proposed decree ha[d] an *adequate* deterrent effect for it to be in the public interest ... An ideal standard of review would achieve a middle ground between the Circuit and [lower] court decisions."[5] Who is right?

In June 2013, then SEC Chair Mary Jo White announced that, "in certain cases" involving "particularly egregious conduct, a large number of harmed investors, significant risk to investors or the markets, obstruction of our investigation or where the defendant presents a particular future threat to

---

[4] Eric Gerding, "The Second Circuit's Mistakes in Reversing Rakoff," The Conglomerate, June 5, 2014.

[5] "*SEC v. Citigroup Global Markets, Inc.*," 128 *Harv. L. Rev.* 1288 Feb. 10, 2015.

investors or the market," the SEC will insist on an admission of wrongdoing as a condition of settlement.[6] Would such an admission be admissible in a private civil case? Is it an "offer of compromise" under Rule 408 of the Federal Rules of Evidence? These remain open questions.

In *Parklane Hosiery Co. v. Shore*, 439 U.S. 322 (1979), the Supreme Court held that a finding against a defendant following a four-day trial in a case brought by the SEC could be used as offensive collateral estoppel in a private civil action because the defendant had a "full and fair" opportunity to litigate. What about settlements? They usually do not result in collateral estoppel.

"Obey the Law" Injunctions

Where there is no ill-gotten gain to be disgorged, the SEC often resorts to injunctive relief in the form of an "obey the law" order. However, in *SEC v. Goble*, 682 F.3d 934 (11th Cir. 2012), the Eleventh Circuit vacated a broad injunction requiring North American Clearing Inc. to comply with specified provisions of the securities laws. The company and three executives booked a sham transaction to free up operating funds. FINRA found out about it, the transaction was reversed and the company went out of business. Richard Goble, a director, went to trial and was found to have aided and abetted the violation of Section 10(b) and certain books and records requirements of Section 17(a) of the Exchange Act. The court entered an injunction permanently restraining Goble from violating the securities laws and from obtaining a securities license or participating in the securities business. On appeal, the Section 10(b) charges were dismissed but the books and records charge was upheld. The "obey the law" injunction was stricken as being inconsistent with Rule 65 of the Federal Rules, which requires that an injunction specify why it was issued and in reasonable detail the act or act being restrained. The court held that the defendant would need to review hundreds of pages of the Federal Reporters, law reviews, and similar material before he could "grasp the conduct proscribed by § 10(b)." The case was remanded with instructions to craft an injunction that addresses compliance with the books and records requirement in language "that allows Goble to understand his obligations under the injunction."

In *SEC v. Goldman Sachs & Co.*, 40 F. Supp. 2d 579 (S.D.N.Y 2014), Judge Katherine Forrest was "skeptical of the utility" of an "obey the law" injunction, and she rejected the SEC's request for such an injunction. ("After all, everybody is required to obey the law.") In that case, the SEC conceded that such injunctions are rarely if ever enforced through contempt proceedings.

---

[6] *See* James Stewart, "S.E.C. Has a Message for Firms Not Used to Admitting Guilt," *New York Times*, June 21, 2013.

Civil Penalties

In 1990, Congress passed the Securities Enforcement Remedies and Penny Stock Reform Act, giving the SEC authority to seek civil money penalties in enforcement cases in federal court against both individuals and corporations. As noted, Dodd-Frank now gives the SEC the authority to seek penalties in administrative cases as well. Prior to the enactment of the Reform Act, the SEC's penalty authority was limited to the ability of the SEC to seek penalties in federal district court for insider trading violations.

In 2006, in its "Statement Concerning Financial Penalties," the SEC said that two factors will be considered in whether to seek a financial penalty against a corporation: the presence or absence of a direct benefit to the corporation as a result of the violation, and the degree to which a penalty will recompense or further harm the injured shareholders. The statement also listed seven additional factors that will be considered, such as the level of intent on the part of the perpetrators.

What is the point of a civil penalty against a corporation? Who actually pays? (*Hint*: The current shareholders.)

Section 21(B) of the 1934 Act authorizes the SEC to seek civil penalties if it finds that the penalty is "in the public interest." Section 21(d)(3)(B) establishes three tiers of wrongdoing with different maximum penalties for each tier and violation. The highest (third tier) is $100,000 for an individual and $500,000 for an entity, for each "act or omission." Section 21(B) has six factors for the SEC to consider in determining whether a penalty is "in the public interest." Is the district court bound by these factors in considering the public interest? *See SEC v. Citigroup*, 752 F.3d 285 (2d Cir. 2014). Some have argued that the SEC has too much discretion in deciding who to target and how much to seek. "There are multiple reasons to be concerned. Particularly for the public corporations, the source of the largest sums garnered and circulating and temporal problems may prevent optimal deterrence.... [T]he SEC's approach is suboptimal."[7]

Fair Fund Distributions

Section 308 of Sarbanes-Oxley created the Fair Fund. Amounts obtained by SEC as civil penalty or in settlement may be put into a fund for the benefit of the "victims." Note that these funds cannot be used as an offset against civil damages in private actions. But, why not, if the fund is for the benefit of the "victims"? Is there a possibility of double recovery? Almost certainly yes. Note

[7] Sonia Steinway, SEC "Monetary Penalties Speak Very Loudly" But What Do They Say? A Critical Analysis of the SEC's New Enforcement Approach," 124 *Yale L.J.* 209 (2014).

that by contrast, in antitrust cases brought by the Federal Trade Commission, the amount paid to the FTC as a penalty *can* be used as an offset in a private case.

The Fair Fund is distributed in the same way a civil settlement fund is distributed. The defendant has nothing to do with the administration of the fund. The SEC recently gave the Enforcement Division greater authority over Fair Fund distributions in administrative matters. SEC Rel. No. 34-70049 (2013). The Director of the Enforcement Division can now select the Fair Fund Administrators.

SEC's "Temporary Freeze" Authority

Section 1103 of Sarbanes-Oxley gives the SEC the authority to seek a temporary restraining order from a federal district court if, during a lawful investigation, it shall appear to the commission that it is likely that the issuer will make extraordinary payments to a director, officer, partner, controlling person, agents, or employees. The court may require an escrow of the payment for forty-five days. Notice and a hearing is required unless they are impracticable or contrary to the public interest. Only one additional forty-five-day extension is allowed. See Section 21C(e)(3) of the 1934 Act. If an SEC action is commenced during the period of the injunction, the escrow continues.

This authority was used to prevent Vivendi, a French corporation, from paying an approximately $20 million severance payment that had been awarded by an arbitral tribunal to its former CEO Jean-Marie Messier, who was simultaneously being investigated for fraud by the SEC.[8] Messier later settled with the SEC and gave up his right to the severance payment. He was later found not liable in a private civil class action.

Cooperation With the SEC

The SEC has a formal and published "Cooperation Policy" that encourages defendants and their counsel to cooperate.[9] In 2015, the Filip Memorandum was replaced by the Yates Memorandum, written by Sally Yates, then-Deputy Attorney General, the key provision of which was an "all or

---

[8] Linda Thomsen & Donna Norman, "Sarbanes-Oxley Turns Six: An Enforcement Perspective," 3 J. Bus. & Tech. L. 393 (2008).

[9] *See also* "Memorandum From Mark Filip, Deputy Attorney General, Department of Justice, to Heads of Department Components Regarding Principles of Federal Prosecution of Business Organizations" (Aug. 28, 2008) (the "Filip Memorandum," which replaced the "Thompson" and "McNulty" memoranda).

nothing" requirement of cooperation for a corporation or an individual that wanted to negotiate a settlement.

Some Statistics

In fiscal year 2020, the SEC brought 715 enforcement actions, including 405 standalone actions. These actions addressed issuer disclosure and accounting violations, foreign bribery (FCPA violations), investment advisory issues, securities offerings, market manipulation, insider trading, and broker misconduct. The SEC obtained judgments and orders totaling approximately $4.68 billion in disgorgement and penalties, and returned more than $600 million to harmed investors. The SEC also awarded $175 million to thirty-nine whistleblowers.[10]

Special Problems Relating to "Parallel Proceedings" and Other Matters

There is generally no prohibition against the SEC sharing information with the Department of Justice (except in special circumstances). *See SEC v. Dresser Industries, Inc.*, 628 F.2d 1368 (D.C. Cir. 1980). But is that true after there is an indictment? May the DOJ use the SEC as its investigating agency at that point?[11]

Key criminal offenses: violations of the securities laws (up to $5 million and twenty years in prison), mail and wire fraud, obstruction of justice and making false statements, retaliation against whistleblowers, attempt and conspiracy, aiding and abetting.

What is "willful" violation of the securities laws? There is a split among courts—some require specific intent to violate the law; others require intent to perform an act that violated the law. The most common interpretation is that the defendant must have known that his or her conduct was wrongful, although not necessarily unlawful.

Filing of false certifications under Section 906 of the Sarbanes–Oxley Act can be punished by up to $1 million and ten years.

Sarbanes–Oxley created a new criminal offense: "knowingly executing or attempting to execute a fraudulent scheme in connection with the securities of a public company or fraudulently obtaining money or property in

---

[10] *SEC Division of Enforcement Annual Report for Fiscal Year 2020*, https://sec.gov/files/enforcement-annual-report-2020.pdf.

[11] *See* Marc Steinberg, "Parallel Proceedings," 8 *Corp. L. Rev.* 335 (1985).

connection with the purchase or sale of such securities." 18 U.S.C. § 1348 (up to twenty-five years).

Sarbanes–Oxley also created a new offense: destruction of documents. It prohibits knowingly altering, destroying, concealing, covering up, falsifying, or making a false entry in any record, document, *or tangible object* with intent to impede, obstruct, or influence the investigation or proper administration of any matter within the jurisdiction of any U.S. department or agency or in relation to or contemplation of any such matter or case (up to twenty years in prison). 18 U.S.C. § 1519 (emphasis added). This is in addition to the general witness and document tampering statute that makes it a crime "corruptly" to alter, destroy, or conceal a document or record or to attempt to do so with the intent to impair the document's or object's integrity or availability for use in an official proceeding or to corruptly persuade another person to do so. Arthur Andersen's conviction in the Enron affair for destroying documents was later reversed by the Supreme Court but Arthur Andersen had ceased to exist in the meantime.[12]

What is a "tangible object"? We know at least that it is not a red grouper. In *Yates v. United States*, 574 U.S. 528 (2015), a fisherman was convicted under 18 U.S.C. § 1519 for throwing undersized groupers overboard to avoid prosecution. (The groupers in question were no more than one-and-one-quarter inches shorter than the required length.) He was sentenced to thirty days in jail. The Supreme Court, employing the well-known Latin canon *noscitur a sociis* ("A word is known by the company it keeps."), reversed the conviction and held that the phrase "tangible object" meant "tangible objects used to preserve and record information." It emphatically did not mean fish.

Whistleblowers

The bounty provision of ITSFEA (permissive bounty) has been replaced by Section 21(F) of the 1934 Act (by Dodd-Frank), which *requires* the SEC to pay a whistleblower 10 to 30 percent of the sanctions collected in a successful enforcement action where $1 million or more is recovered. What is the corporation's legal duty in the face of a whistleblower complaint? How do you determine significance of the complaint *ab initio*?

On April 2, 2015, the *New York Times* reported a new SEC crackdown on the use of employment agreements to restrict the ability of whistleblowers to report to the SEC. Note that the rules enacted after Section 21(F) became law do *not* require the whistleblower first to report to the company's

---

12 *See Arthur Andersen LLP v. United States*, 544 U.S. 696 (2005). *See also* James Kelly, "The Power of an Indictment and the Demise of Arthur Andersen," 48 *Texas L. Rev.* 509 (2006).

internal channels. Dodd-Frank also extended the statute of limitations, prohibits the enforcement of pre-dispute arbitration clauses and waivers, and creates new private rights of action. As noted above, it also allows penalties against non-regulated persons or entities in administrative proceedings.

The Foreign Corrupt Practices Act

Remember that in addition to its criminal provisions, the FCPA has a "books and records" provision in the Securities Act. As a result, the FCPA is enforced both by the SEC and by the Department of Justice. This is covered further in Chapter 20.

The SEC as a Plaintiff; the SEC's Civil Authority

Section 21(a)(1) of the 1934 Securities Exchange Act gives the SEC authority to make such investigations as it deems necessary to determine whether any person has violated, is violating, or is about to violate any of the securities laws or rules and regulations of the SEC. Section 21(b) gives the SEC authority to require the attendance of witnesses and the production of documents. Section 21(c) authorizes judicial enforcement of the investigative power of the SEC, including the refusal to obey a subpoena.

Section 21(d)(1) authorizes the SEC to seek injunctions against Exchange Act violations and a similar provision in the 1933 Act, Section 20(b), authorizes the SEC to seek injunctions against violations of that Act as well. Those provisions also give the SEC authority to "transmit such evidence as may be available concerning such acts or practices as may constitute a violation [of the 1933 or 1934 Act] to the Attorney General, who may, in his discretion, institute the necessary criminal proceedings."

Section 21(d)(3) of the 1934 Act authorizes the SEC to seek monetary penalties whenever a violation of the Act has been found to have been committed. The penalties are authorized in three tiers, from $5,000 for a natural person and $50,000 for any other person, to $100,000 for a natural person and $500,000 for any other person.

Section 21A of the Exchange Act specifically authorizes civil actions by the SEC (and civil penalties) for insider trading.

Section 21C of the Exchange Act authorizes the SEC to bring cease and desist proceedings and administrative actions and Section 21B authorizes the SEC to impose civil penalties in administrative proceedings.

There are similar provisions in the Securities Act. For example, Section 8A allows the SEC to issue cease and desist orders and bar orders against officers and directors who have violated the antifraud provisions of the 1933 Act and

Section 20(d) authorizes the SEC to seek civil penalties for violations of the Securities Act.

Where Can the SEC Litigate?

When the SEC is a plaintiff, it can appear in two fora and can refer cases for criminal prosecution in a third forum.

First, the SEC can bring administrative charges. Such charges are governed by the SEC's Rules of Practice and if an evidentiary hearing is required, the proceeding will take place before an administrative law judge. Neither the Federal Rules of Civil Procedure nor the Federal Rules of Evidence applies to such a hearing. Rather, the SEC's own Rules of Practice apply. In such proceedings there is typically a charge by the SEC (an "Order Initializing Proceedings") followed by an answer by the respondent. At the public hearing there can be examination and cross-examination of witnesses and the administrative law judge (ALJ) is required to make findings of fact and conclusions of law. Upon a petition for review by the commission filed by either party, the SEC, whose review is de novo, may affirm, reverse, or modify the ALJ's decision.

An issue recently arose as to whether the SEC's ALJs were constitutionally appointed. Although the Commission has the constitutional authority to appoint ALJs, it delegated that authority to the staff. Thus, SEC ALJs were selected by the staff and appointed by the SEC's Office of Administrative Law Judges with input from other parts of the SEC and/or the Office of Personnel Management. The selection of the ALJs was subject to approval by the SEC's Office of Human Resources. In *Lucia v. SEC*, 138 S. Ct. 2044 (2018), the Supreme Court decided that the ALJs were "officers of the United States" under Article II, Section 2, Cl. 2 of the U.S. Constitution and must be appointed by the president, the courts, or the head of a department. The Supreme Court declined to decide whether the ALJs may be removed only for cause or directly by the president for no reason. The SEC, to nobody's surprise, changed its selection procedures.

Can there be an appeal taken from an administrative decision of the SEC? Yes, if the charges are brought under the Securities Act or the Securities Exchange Act. Both statutes provide for an appeal to the federal appeals court in which the respondent resides or works or to the District of Columbia Circuit. In such an appeal, the SEC findings are conclusive, provided they are supported by "substantial evidence." But no such appeal can be taken if the respondent did not first appeal the ALJ's decision to the full SEC. In other words, the respondent is required to "exhaust all administrative remedies" first.

In *Bebo v. SEC*, 2015 WL 4006165 (E.D. Wis. March 3, 2015), *aff'd*, 799 F.3d 765 (2015), the court heard plaintiff's claim that Dodd-Frank was unconstitutional on its face because it gave the SEC "unfettered discretion" whether to bring administrative penalty proceedings or to bring such claims in federal court and that the choice could affect the defendant's Seventh Amendment right to a jury trial. The court found that the plaintiff's claims were "compelling and meritorious," but that it lacked jurisdiction because the plaintiff had to litigate her claims first to the SEC and then to the Seventh Circuit. The Seventh Circuit affirmed. The Supreme Court then denied Ms. Bebo's petition for a writ of certiorari.

Second, the SEC can bring civil charges in a federal district court. In such cases, the proceedings are governed by the Federal Rules of Civil Procedure and the Federal Rules of Evidence apply. Typically, in such cases the SEC will be seeking injunctive relief and, as we will see, sometimes different rules will apply depending on whether the SEC is seeking a penalty or merely disgorgement.

Is there a right to a jury trial in federal court when the SEC is the plaintiff? That depends on the type of relief that the SEC is seeking. The Seventh Amendment guarantees the right to a jury trial in suits at common law where the value in controversy exceeds $20. If the SEC seeks to impose a penalty, there is a Seventh Amendment right to a jury trial on the issue of liability (the court decides the quantum of the penalty); if the SEC is seeking only injunctive relief or disgorgement (both of which are equitable remedies), there is no right to a jury trial.

Third, the SEC can refer the case to the Justice Department for criminal proceedings, in which the SEC does not participate as a party, but in which it is not uncommon for an SEC lawyer from the Division of Enforcement to be assigned temporarily to the Department of Justice as a "Special Assistant United States Attorney." In some cases, those lawyers will actively participate in the trial. In those cases, all of the normal criminal rights and procedures apply.

The SEC's Burden of Proof

The burden of proof in SEC civil cases is clearly "preponderance of the evidence," although in the past there was some doubt about that question because the relevant statutes are silent. Some respondents argued that a higher burden ("clear and convincing evidence") should apply to SEC cases because of the severity of penalties that could be imposed. But in *Steadman v. SEC*, 450 U.S. 91 (1981), the Supreme Court, by reference to the Administrative Procedure Act (which refers to findings based on "substantial evidence"), held that "preponderance of the evidence" was the appropriate test for the SEC's burden. *Query*: Is that the correct test if the SEC is seeking only injunctive relief? Probably yes, in light of *Herman & MacLean v. Huddleston*, 103 S. Ct. 683 (1983).

There have been cases in which the defendants have argued that the more rigorous "clear and convincing" standard should apply to SEC cases in which the relief could be, in the words of Professors Donna Nagy, Richard Painter, and Margaret Sachs, "loss of livelihood."[13] But in *SEC v. Moran*, 922 F. Supp. 867 (S.D.N.Y. 1996), the court refused to apply that higher standard to an insider trading case in which money damages and injunctive relief were sought. Nagy, Painter, and Sachs raise the question whether the "clear and convincing" standard of *Collins Sec. Corp. v. SEC*, 562 F.2d 820 (D.C. Cir. 1977), survives the Supreme Court's decision in *Steadman v. SEC*, 450 U.S. 91 (1981), which endorses the "preponderance of the evidence" test without any obvious exceptions. It probably does not.

Statute of Limitations

There are no statutes of limitations that explicitly apply to actions brought by the SEC with the single exception of actions for monetary civil penalties in insider trading cases under Section 21A(d)(5) of the 1934 Act. That being the case, are there any periods of limitations for the bringing of SEC cases? Yes. The general federal five-year statute of limitations applies.

For many years, the SEC took the position that since its actions were vindicating the public interest, there should be no statutes of limitations applied at all in actions under Section 10(b). However, in 1996, the U.S. Court of Appeals for the District of Columbia Circuit held, in *Johnson v. SEC*, 87 F.3d 484 (D.C. Cir. 1996), that where the SEC was seeking a penalty as opposed to relief that merely remedied the damages done to third parties by the violation, the general federal five-year statute of limitations found in 28 U.S.C. § 2462 should apply. At issue in that case was a six-month suspension of a broker's supervisor. The D.C. Circuit held that because of the "collateral consequences" of censure and suspension, the SEC's sanction had "punishment-like qualities." "Unlike restitution or disgorgement, the sanctions here do not attempt to restore the stolen funds to their rightful owner. To the contrary, the sanctions in this case impose a punishment for Johnson's violation of a standard laid down in the Exchange Act, and qualify therefore as a 'penalty' within the meaning of § 2462."[14]

---

[13] Donna M. Nagy et al., *Securities Litigation and Enforcement* (3d ed.) (West Academic Publishing) at 769.

[14] *See also SEC v. Bartek*, 484 F.3d 949 (5th Cir. 2012) (court engaged in a fact-specific inquiry, focusing on the intent, nature, and long-term consequences of the sanction.) *See generally* Mauro Wolf & Melissa Geller, "The New Statute of Limitations

Fortunately, both the Supreme Court and Congress have resolved the issue. In *Kokesh v. SEC*, 137 S. Ct. 1635 (2017), the Supreme Court held that claims for disgorgement were punitive and thus subject to the general federal five-year statute of limitations. And then in *Liu v. SEC*, 140 S. Ct. 1936 (2020), the Court held that because disgorgement was an equitable remedy, recovery had to be limited to the net income or net profit generated from the unlawful conduct, allowing the defendant to offset expenses. However, Congress quickly came to the rescue of the SEC and on January 1, 2021, Congress passed a statute that gave the SEC a ten-year statute of limitations for claims of disgorgement in cases where there were allegations of intentional misconduct (e.g., Rule 10b-5 and Section 17(a)(1)).

What is the takeaway from these cases? Stale claims should be analyzed carefully. The SEC may not be able to get around the statute of limitations. The Sarbanes–Oxley Act's two-year/five-year statute of limitations does not apply to the SEC. If any statute of limitations explicitly applies to the SEC, and there is an issue with respect to whether one does at all, it is only the general federal five-year statute of limitations, except with respect to disgorgements, as to which the statute of limitations is ten years if the claim includes intentional misconduct.

When Does the Statute of Limitations Begin to Run?

In private securities litigation, the statute of limitations begins to run when the plaintiff discovers the fraud or when a "reasonably diligent plaintiff" would discover the "facts constituting the violation." However, as we will see, the rules are different for the SEC as a plaintiff.

In *Gabelli v. SEC*, 133 S. Ct. 1216 (2013), the SEC charged Marc Gabelli and a colleague with allowing one investor in a Gabelli Fund to engage in "market timing" in exchange for the investor's agreement to invest in a different fund managed by Gabelli. The *quid pro quo* was not disclosed. The SEC's complaint was not brought within five years from the date of the violation, but the SEC argued that because the allegation "sounded in fraud" the general

---

Battle Post-*Gabelli*," ABA Journal, January 3, 2014. *But see SEC v. Rind*, 991 F.2d 1486 (9th Cir. 1993) (permanent injunction and disgorgement ordered; statute of limitations defense stricken because "of the important public function served by Commission enforcement activity"). *See SEC v. Graham*, 2014 WL 1891418 at *8-10 (S.D. Fla. May 12, 2104) (SEC claims for disgorgement, injunctive relief, and declaratory relief are subject to the five-year statute of limitations in 28 U.S.C. § 2462); *but see SEC v. Amerindo Inv. Advisors, Inc.*, 2014 WL 405339 at *9 (S.D.N.Y. Feb. 3, 2014) (holding that *Gabelli v. SEC*, 568 U.S. 442 (2013), "applies only to civil penalties and does not prevent a finding of liability or an awarding of other kinds of remedies"). Can these cases be reconciled?

federal five-year statute of limitations did not apply. The Supreme Court held that "if" the general federal five-year statute of limitations (28 U.S.C. § 2462) applies (and that is a big "if"), then the statute begins to run from the date of the fraud and not from the date on which the fraud was discovered. Of course, that case concerned only when the statute of limitations began to run and not whether the statute was implicated at all.

However, in *Merck & Co. v. Reynolds*, 559 U.S. 633 (2010), the Supreme Court held that the two-year statute of limitations for a securities fraud claim (under the preexisting statute) did not begin to run in that case until the plaintiff in fact discovered the fraud or a reasonably diligent plaintiff would have discovered the "facts constituting the violation," whichever comes first. In that case, there was evidence that some of the facts relating to the fraud were revealed in the publication of a medical journal article, so the Supreme Court explained that "discovery of facts constituting the violation" was defined to include discovering evidence of scienter. The statute did not begin to run until the plaintiff "discover[ed] the fraud."[15]

How to distinguish the two cases? If you thought that one way to distinguish *Gabelli* might be the difference between the plaintiffs, you would be correct. *Gabelli* suggested that *Merck* was different because the government (i.e., the SEC) had more tools to root out and discover fraud than an individual plaintiff and that such a difference justified a different commencement date for the statute of limitations.

The Supreme Court pointed out that the SEC was in the business of discovering fraud, whereas private plaintiffs are not. "The SEC, for example, is not like an individual victim who relies on apparent injury to learn of a wrong. Rather, a 'central mission' of the Commission is to 'investigate potential violations of the federal securities laws.'... Unlike the private party who has no reason to suspect fraud, the SEC's very purpose is to root it out, and it has many legal tools at hand to aid in that pursuit." For that reason, the Supreme Court created and applied a different statute of limitations rule for the SEC. The statute begins to run when the fraud is committed, regardless of when it is discovered.

Scienter and Section 17

Scienter is a required element of proof for the SEC in actions under Section 17(a)(1) of the Securities Act but not under Section 17(a)(2) or (3). *See*

---

[15] *See City of Pontiac Gen. Employees' Ret. Sys. v. MBIA, Inc.*, 637 F.3d 169 (2d Cir. 2011) (limitations period does not begin to run until a reasonably diligent plaintiff would be able to plead facts constitute a securities law violation with sufficient detail and particularity to survive a motion to dismiss).

Aaron v. SEC, 446 U.S. 680 (1980). The language of Section 17(a)(1) plainly evinces an intent on the part of Congress to proscribe only knowing or intentional misconduct, whereas the language of Section 17(a)(2) is devoid of any suggestion of a scienter requirement and the language of Section 17(a)(3) focuses on the effect of a particular conduct on members of the investing public rather than the culpability of the person responsible. As a result, Sections 17(a)(2) and (3) are referred to as "non-scienter" fraud sections and there is an incentive for the SEC to bring cases under those two sections rather than under Section 17(a)(1). Even though the SEC need not prove scienter in such cases, it must still prove violation of the applicable standard of care. *SEC v. Ginder*, 752 F.3d 569 (2d Cir. 2014).

Is it necessary for the defendant in a Section 17(a) case brought by the SEC to be the speaker or maker of an untrue statement in order to be liable? No. It is sufficient for liability that the defendant had "knowledge of the fraud and assisted in its perpetration." *SEC v. First Jersey Sec. Inc.*, 101 F.3d 1450 (2d Cir. 1966).

Proving Scienter in Section 10(b) Cases

We know that in order to prove a violation of Section 10(b), the SEC must prove that the defendant acted with scienter. *Aaron v. SEC*, 446 U.S. 680 (1980). We also know that the pleading rules for scienter set forth in the Private Securities Litigation Reform Act (PSLRA) (that the complaint must "state with particularity facts giving rise to a strong inference that the defendant acted with the required state of mind") do not apply, at least explicitly, to the SEC as a plaintiff.

But during the legislative history of the PSLRA, there was some comment to the effect that the PSLRA was intended to copy the existing Second Circuit rule for the pleading of scienter. *See, e.g.*, *Lentell*, 396 F.3d at 168. In the Second Circuit, prior to the PSLRA, the plaintiffs were required to allege "those [facts] which they assert give rise to a strong inference that the defendants had 'the requisite state of mind.'" *See Tellabs, Inc. v. Makor Issues & Rights, Ltd.*, 551 U.S. 308 (2007), quoting and adding emphasis to *Ross v. A.H. Robins Co.*, 607 F.2d 545, 558 (2d Cir. 1979). Thus, even prior to the PSLRA, it seems to have been the case that, at least in the Second Circuit, the SEC as a plaintiff would have been required to plead scienter under a heightened pleading standard. Indeed, after the PSLRA, the Second Circuit held that the PSLRA "raised the nationwide pleading standard to that previously existing [in the Second Circuit] and no higher."

The Supreme Court's decision in *Tellabs* holds that in deciding whether a complaint meets a heightened pleading standard for scienter (there the PSLRA), the court must consider the complaint in its entirety, including plausible opposing inferences to the inferences of scienter, and that the "strong" inferences of scienter that must be pleaded must be "powerful or cogent" and "compelling" and such that a reasonable person "would deem the inference of scienter ... at least as compelling as any opposing inference one could draw from the facts alleged." Given the fact that the PSLRA pleading standard is similar if not identical to the Second Circuit's pre-PSLRA standard, there is some reason to believe that that heightened pleading standard applies equally to the SEC, at least in the Second Circuit.[16]

Is proof of "motive and opportunity" sufficient to prove scienter? Yes, in the Second Circuit. *See Novak v. Kasaks*, 216 F.3d 300 (2d Cir. 2000). No, in the First, Fifth, Sixth, Seventh, Eighth, and Eleventh Circuits (although proof of "motive and opportunity" may be relevant to a "totality of the circumstances" inquiry). *See Aldridge v. A.T. Cross Corp.*, 284 F.3d 72 (1st Cir. 2002). It should be noted that in those circuits where "motive and opportunity" is not sufficient to allege and prove scienter, most if not all of the cases are interpreting the pleading requirement of the PSLRA. *Query*: What would be the result in those circuits if the SEC were the plaintiff?

Is proof of recklessness sufficient to prove scienter? The Supreme Court has never decided this question and as recently as *Tellabs* has noted that it has previously reserved the question. But in doing so, the court noted that "every Court of Appeals that has considered the issue has held that a plaintiff may meet the scienter requirement by showing that the defendant acted intentionally or recklessly, though the Circuits differ on the degree of recklessness required." Some circuits require that the recklessness pleaded must be "severe" (e.g., the Fourth, Fifth, Eighth, and Eleventh), or "extremely reckless" (the D.C. Circuit), or "reflecting some degree of intentional or conscious misconduct" (the Ninth), or "bordering on an intent to deceive" (the Third), or "the functional equivalent of intent" (the Seventh).

It seems clear that the SEC, as plaintiff, will be bound by the pleading standards for scienter in the circuit in which it chooses to file suit.[17]

In *SEC v. Payton & Durant*, 14 Civ. 4644 (S.D.N.Y. Apr. 6, 2015), Judge Rakoff held that in a civil insider trading case brought by the SEC, the complaint is generally subject to the heightened pleading standards of Federal Rule 9(b) but where "matters are 'peculiarly within the [defendant's] knowledge,' 'slightly relaxed' pleading standards are appropriate."

---

[16] *But see SEC v. Lucent Techs. Inc.*, 363 F. Supp. 2d 708, 717 (D.N.J. 2005) (holding and collecting cases supporting the proposition that the SEC need not satisfy the PSLRA's heightened pleading requirement for scienter) (Third Circuit).

[17] *See, e.g.*, *SEC v. Shanahan*, 6476 F.3d 536 (8th Cir. 2011) (holding the SEC to a "severe recklessness" standard); *Dolphin & Bradbury, Inc. v. SEC*, 512 F.3d 634, 639 (D.C. Cir. 2008) (holding the SEC to an "extreme recklessness" standard).

May the SEC use the doctrine of "collective scienter" to prove scienter for a corporate defendant? The doctrine of collective scienter attaches corporate liability on the basis of the collective knowledge of the corporation's employees, regardless of whether those employees had any role in making the false statements. Most courts have rejected the notion of collective scienter; all of those decisions have been in the context of private securities litigation. It remains an open question whether the SEC may use that doctrine to plead and prove scienter and some have argued that even though the SEC may use that doctrine, it should not do so.[18]

Reliance

Reliance, sometimes referred to as "transaction causation," is one of the elements of proof for a civil plaintiff alleging a violation of Section 10(b). But there is no requirement that reliance be shown in SEC injunctive relief or penalty cases or in criminal cases brought by the Department of Justice under Section 10(b). *See United States v. Haddy*, 134 F.3d 542 (3d Cir. 1998); *SEC v. Rana Research, Inc.*, 8 F.3d 1358 (9th Cir. 1993). The same is true for proof of reliance by individual investors in SEC actions under Section 17. *See SEC v. Manus*, 1981 U.S. Dist. LEXIS 15317 at *20 (S.D.N.Y. Oct. 7, 1981).

Loss Causation

Under the PSLRA and consistent judicial opinions, a private plaintiff must plead and prove loss causation in order to prove and recover for a violation of Section 10(b). Under the PSLRA (Section 21D(b)(4) of the Exchange Act), the plaintiff has the burden of proving that the act or omission of the defendant alleged to violate [the Exchange Act] caused the loss for which "the plaintiff seeks to recover damages." *See also Dura Pharmaceuticals v. Broudo*, 544 U.S. 336 (2005); *In re Omnicom Grp. Inc. Sec. Litig.*, 597 F.3d 501 (2d Cir. 2010).

It seems clear that in civil cases, the requirement to plead and prove loss causation does not apply to the SEC. But does it apply in criminal cases where the prosecutor is trying to enhance a sentence? The Second and Fifth Circuits

---

[18] *See, e.g.*, Bradley Bondi, "Dangerous Liaisons: Collective Scienter in SEC Enforcement Actions," 6 *NYU Journal of Law & Business* 1 (Fall 2009) (Professor Bondi was, at the time of that writing, counsel to a commissioner at the SEC) ("The theory of collective scienter is a radical departure from the principles of corporate liability and runs contrary to the objectives of the federal securities laws.... If the SEC seeks to utilize collective scienter, the Commission should issue guidance on the circumstances in which the theory would be pursued.... A wholesale resort to collective scienter would harm the SEC's overall goals and should be avoided.").

have applied the *Dura* holding in such cases. *United States v. Rutkoske*, 506 F.3d 170 (2d Cir. 2007); *United States v. Olis*, 429 F.3d 540 (5th Cir. 2005). However, the Ninth Circuit has adopted a more general principle, looking not at the precise loss caused by the fraud in the *Dura* sense but to the total losses "resulting from the fraud." *United States v. Berger*, 587 F.3d 1038 (9th Cir. 2009).

Aiding and Abetting Liability

Following the Supreme Court decision in *Central Bank v. First Interstate Bank*, 511 U.S. 164 (1994), there was some question in the lower courts whether the Court's decision to eliminate aiding and abetting liability under Section 10(b) applied to cases brought by the SEC. As a result, Congress passed Section 20(e) of the 1934 Act that made it clear that the SEC may bring actions for injunctive relief and/or penalties against those persons who "knowingly aid or abet" primary violations. In such cases, the SEC must prove (1) the existence of a primary violation, (2) knowledge of the violation by the aider or abettor, and (3) "substantial assistance" in the achievement of the primary violation. *See SEC v. DiBella*, 587 F.3d 553 (2d Cir. 2009). As noted in Chapter 11, "substantial assistance" has been defined as proof that the defendant "in some sort associated himself [or herself] with the venture, that [he or she] participated in it as something that he [or she] wished to bring about and that he [or she] sought by his [or her]action to make it succeed." *SEC v. Apuzzo*, 689 F.3d 204 (2d Cir. 2012). Also as noted above, a provision of Dodd-Frank later added that aiding and abetting liability applied to reckless behavior as well as to knowing behavior.

Chapter 18

Arbitration of Securities Disputes

Arbitration of securities disputes in the United States can be traced back to the birth of the country. The first bonds were issued by the federal government in 1789 to finance the government's decision to assume the debts of the colonies and the debts the Continental Congress incurred during the Revolutionary War. In 1792, a group of brokers agreed to trade only among themselves on behalf of their customers and this agreement was memorialized in what became known as the "Buttonwood Agreement."[1] In 1817, another group of brokers, including four signers of the Buttonwood Agreement, created the New York Stock and Exchange Board, known then as the "Board of Brokers." The board's rules forbade such things as fictitious trades, called "wash sales," and imposed penalties for the violation of the rules. Also among the rules in the board's constitution was a requirement that the board members arbitrate disputes before the full board and that "all questions of dispute in the purchase or sale of Stocks shall be decided by a majority of the Board."[2]

In time, the requirement that disputes be decided by the full board was replaced by the creation of an Arbitration Committee composed of five members and that committee began the practice of hearing disputes not only among board members but also between members and their customers.[3] Some, including Professor Jill Gross, have traced the use of arbitration to resolve such

[1] According to the SEC Historical Society, in the wake of the market crash of 1792, twenty-four brokers met under a buttonwood tree at 68 Wall Street and pledged to deal only with each other and to charge only minimum commission rates. The commodity that they were trading—first in the Tontine Coffee House in lower Manhattan—was government bonds, then called "stocks." SEC Historical Society, "The Institution of Experience: Self-Regulatory Organizations in the Securities Industry, 1792-2010."

[2] Rule 17, "Transcript of Constitution of the New York Stock & Exchange Board," Feb. 25, 1817. *See generally* Stuart Banner, "The Origin of the New York Stock Exchange, 1791-1860," 27 *J. Legal Studies* 113 (1998).

[3] *See generally* Jill Gross, "The Historical Basis of Securities Arbitration as an Investor Protection Mechanism," 2016 *J. Disp. Resol.* 171 (2016).

disputes to the use of such a mechanism in England, where disputes among members of trade groups were resolved by arbitration as early as the fourteenth century.[4]

One of the reasons for the arbitration of securities disputes in the nineteenth century was to ensure that industry norms would be enforced, even if they were otherwise unlawful and not enforceable in court. This allowed the NYSE to protect its good name and reputation, thus perpetuating the near monopoly that the exchange enjoyed.[5] This was important for at least two reasons. First, many of the practices of the NYSE could not be enforced in a court of law, and second, arbitration was seen as a necessary mechanism for ensuring investor protection, especially because there were no federal securities laws at the time.

Nevertheless, perhaps aided by the U.S. Supreme Court, there was a strong perception that the arbitration of securities disputes was a relatively new phenomenon. It was not. Below, we will discuss the modern history of the arbitration of securities disputes but first, we will briefly review arbitration generally.

Arbitration Generally: A Review

Arbitration is "a process by which parties consensually submit a dispute to a non-governmental decision-maker, selected by or for the parties, to render a binding decision resolving a dispute in accordance with neutral, adjudicatory procedures affording each party an opportunity to present its case."[6] Some arbitrations are governed by institutional rules (e.g., ICC, AAA) and others are "ad hoc" in which the parties agree on the rules that should apply. There are many advantages in arbitrating disputes rather than litigating them. Often—but not always—arbitration is faster and less expensive than litigation while still providing a forum for a full and fair hearing on the merits. One other benefit is that, generally, the parties can choose their own arbitrators. Still another benefit is that the decision of the arbitrator or arbitrators is typically final and not appealable.

Arbitration is a contract-based dispute resolution mechanism. The parties to the arbitration must have contracted to adopt arbitration as their dispute resolution mechanism. The arbitration clause in a typical contract includes agreement with respect to the type of arbitration (institutional or ad hoc), the

---

[4] Katherine Stone, "Rustic Justice: Community and Coercion Under the Federal Arbitration Act," 77 *N. C. L. Rev.* 931 (1999).

[5] Jill Gross, *supra*, at 176-177.

[6] Gary Born, *International Arbitration: Law and Practice* (Wolters Kluwer) (2012), p. 4.

seat or situs of the arbitration (the state or country whose arbitration laws will prevail if the rules of the arbitration are insufficient; this is not necessarily the place where the arbitration will be held), and the language and the scope of the arbitration. Generally speaking, the award of the arbitrator or arbitrators is final and unappealable. A court order is necessary to enforce the award.

The Federal Arbitration Act (FAA) was passed in 1925. The FAA expresses and represents an explicit recognition of the importance, irrevocability, and enforcement of arbitral awards and lists the very few grounds on which they can be set aside. An amendment also incorporates the so-called New York Convention, a multinational treaty for the recognition and enforcement of international arbitration awards.

The key provision of the FAA was that arbitration agreements in any "maritime transaction or contract evidencing a transaction involving commerce shall be valid, irrevocable and enforceable save on such grounds as exist at law or in equity for the revocation of any contract." The Supreme Court later ruled that the FAA created "an emphatic federal policy in favor of arbitral dispute resolution."[7] Even though it preceded the enactment of the federal securities laws and for a very long time was not used as a vehicle for resolving disputes under those securities laws, it could have been so used, since securities transactions were "transaction[s] involving commerce." If there is a valid arbitration agreement, a U.S. court has the power to stay court proceedings and compel arbitration.

For example, *Moses H. Cone Memorial Hospital v. Mercury Constr.*, 460 U.S. 1 (1983), held, "The FAA creates a body of federal substantive law establishing and regulating the duty to arbitrate." But what about *Erie Railroad Co. v. Tompkins*, 304 U.S. 62 (1938) (no federal common law)? Is arbitration procedural or substantive?[8]

Does the FAA preempt state laws governing the enforceability of arbitration agreements? Section 2 of the FAA establishes a rule of federal substantive law regarding enforceability. *See Robert Lawrence Co. v. Devonshire Fabrics Inc.*, 271 F.2d 402 (2d Cir. 1959). *See also Prima Paint Corp. v. Flood & Conklin Mfg. Co.*, 388 U.S. 395 (1967) (creates the "separability" doctrine). What about the application of state procedural rules on an arbitration held under the FAA? The law is unsettled. *See Volt Information Sciences v. Board of Trustees of Leland Stanford Junior University*, 489 U.S. 468 (1989). The Court approved a choice of law provision that incorporated a state law that provided for a stay of arbitration if there is litigation involving a party that is not a party to the arbitration, even though the FAA did not permit such a stay.

---

[7] *Marmet Health Care Ctr. v. Brown*, 132 S. Ct. 1201 (2012).

[8] *See* David Kochery, "The Enforcement of Arbitration Awards in the Federal courts: *Erie v. Tompkins*," 39 *Cornell L. Rev.* 74 (1953).

But see Mastrobouono v. Shearson Lehman Hutton, 514 U.S. 52 (1995). In that case, the contract apparently permitted punitive damages (by referring to rules that permit punitive damages) but selected New York as governing law. New York law does not permit arbitrators to award punitive damages. The Supreme Court said that the choice of law provision would not be interpreted to require the application of state law "limiting the authority of arbitrators" and that the arbitration clause covers the arbitration. So the parties' choice of New York law did not incorporate the procedural limitations in New York law on the power of arbitrators to award punitive damages. *Lesson*: It is better to be as specific as possible in drafting an arbitration clause.

It is widely held that the enforceability of the arbitration clause itself is separate from the enforceability of the rest of the contract (the so-called "separability doctrine"). In other words, even if the rest of the contract is invalid, the arbitration clause will be separately enforceable and the question of validity will be decided by an arbitral tribunal.

First Options v. Kaplan[9]

This is a very important case. The arbitral award was rendered against both an investment company and its owners with respect to debts owed to a securities clearing house. The owners, Mr. and Mrs. Kaplan, argued that they had never signed the arbitration agreement from which the tribunal drew its power and that they were not bound by its award. The Supreme Court held that unless the arbitration agreement explicitly provided otherwise, the scope of the arbitration agreement was a matter for the courts to decide independently (i.e., without regard to the arbitral finding on the matter). In dicta, the Court suggested that in some situations, the "arbitrability question itself" may be submitted to arbitration and that the courts must defer to arbitrators decisions on the limits of their own jurisdiction. The Supreme Court said there must be "clear unmistakable evidence" that the parties intended the arbitrators to decide the question of arbitrability. What does this mean, especially where there are standard form contracts such as those in the securities industry? Here is the troublesome language from the opinion: "If the parties agreed to submit arbitrability to arbitration, then the court's standard for reviewing the arbitrator's decision about the matter should not differ from the standard courts apply when they review any other matter that the parties have agreed to arbitrate. That is to say, the court should give considerable leeway to the arbitrator, setting aside his or her decision only in certain narrow circumstances."

Professor William "Rusty" Park from Boston University, a leading expert on international arbitration, notes that the term "arbitrability" in the dictum

[9] *First Options of Chicago, Inc. v. Kaplan*, 514 U.S. 938 (1995).

can cover many different matters. He thinks that the Court meant only that the scope of the arbitration clause should properly be delegated to the arbitrators in a separate agreement that is chronologically subsequent to the principal agreement. He adds that if there was a separate agreement in which the parties agreed that the arbitrators had sole competence to decide on their jurisdiction to hear the first agreement, then they could do so. But the suggestion that the arbitrators can determine their own jurisdiction with respect to the identity of the parties, some of which may be non-signatories, on the basis of a single agreement containing both an arbitration clause and a submission of arbitrability to the arbitrators is like "Baron Münchhausen pulling himself up by his own pigtail."[10] What if the arbitration agreement in *First Options* provided that "the arbitrability question itself is subject to arbitration"? Would those eight words change the fact that in the *First Options* case, Carol and Manuel Kaplan had not agreed to arbitration?

The doctrine of Kompetenz-Kompetenz (or in French, Compétence-Compétence) means that the arbitrators could look into their own jurisdiction without waiting for a court to do so. They would not be required to stop the proceedings to refer a jurisdictional issue to a judge. But their decision as to jurisdiction could still be reviewed by a court at any time. In the French model, by contrast, the courts must wait until after there is an award to review an arbitrator's decision as to jurisdiction.

Class Action Arbitration

The FAA does not mention class arbitration. In *Stolt-Nielsen S.A. v. AnimalFeeds Int'l Corp.*, 130 S. Ct. 1758 (2010), the Supreme Court said there can be no class action arbitrations unless the parties agree. But what kind of agreement is required? Ambiguity and silence are not good enough. Class procedures may not be inferred "solely from the parties' agreement to arbitrate." The following year, in *AT&T Mobility LLC v. Conception*, 131 S. Ct. 1740 (2011), the Supreme Court ruled that the FAA preempted a California case that held that class action waivers contained in consumer agreements were unconscionable. The Court held that the California rule was preempted by the FAA. While the Court did not hold that the parties could not agree to a class action arbitration, it suggested that class action arbitrations threatened the foundations of the FAA, informality and finality, in response to the dissent's concern that unless class action arbitrations were permitted, it would be difficult if not impossible for small claimants to afford the expense of litigation.

---

[10] *See* William Park, "Arbitral Jurisdiction in the United States: Who Decides What?," *Int. A.L.R.* Issue 1 33 (2008).

In 2013, the Supreme Court decided *American Express Co. v. Italian Colors Restaurant*, 133 S. Ct. 2304 (2013), holding that a class action waiver clause in a contract was enforceable unless it deprived the claimant of the right to litigate the claim, as opposed to the ability to bring the claim. Since the claimant still had the ability to pursue the claim in a court, the claimant was not being deprived of any rights.

In a five-to-four decision in 2019, the Supreme Court held that to be enforceable, class action requirements had to be explicit, because unlike the individualized arbitration envisioned by the FAA, class action arbitration "sacrifices the principal advantage of arbitration—its informality—and makes the process slower, more costly, and more likely to generate procedural morass than final judgment." Ambiguity, like silence, is not sufficient and anything short of a clear and express consent to class action arbitrations will not suffice. *Lamps Plus, Inc. v. Varela*, 137 S. Ct. 1407 (2019). In other words, there is a presumption against class action arbitrations unless there is an explicit consent in the agreement.

Who decides? *Green Tree Financial Corp. v. Bazzle*, 539 U.S. 444 (2003), says that the arbitrators decide. That was a plurality decision. Is class arbitration a question of arbitrability (typically decided by a court) or contract construction (typically decided by an arbitrator)? The Supreme Court has now decided that the question is one of contract construction rather than arbitrability. However, in *Lamps Plus*, the Court held that a state rule of contract construction, *contra proferentum* (ambiguity in a contract is construed against the drafter) did not apply to the FAA, which required the clear agreement of the parties before there can be a class action arbitration. There must be the requisite "affirmative contractual basis for concluding that the parties agreed to class action arbitration."

Some courts have said that a reference to American Arbitration Association rules (permitting class arbitration) in the agreement is good enough, but the *Lamps Plus* case seems to have put that argument to rest.

Does it matter who decides? Yes, because the scope of judicial review of an arbitral decision is very narrow. For example, in *Oxford Health Plan v. Sutter*, 133 S. Ct. 2064 (2013), the parties agreed that the arbitrator could decide whether the agreement authorized class arbitration. He held that it did. The Supreme Court upheld his decision as within his powers (even if he was wrong on the merits). The clause in question did not mention class actions: "No civil action concerning any dispute arising under this Agreement shall be instituted before any Court, and all such disputes shall be submitted to final and binding arbitration." But unless the contract "unmistakably provides otherwise," the question whether class-wide arbitration is available is to be determined by a court and not by the arbitrators. *Opalinski v. Robert Half International Inc.*, 761 F.3d 326 (3d Cir. 2014) (the availability of class-wide arbitration is a substantive "question of arbitrability" to be decided by a court absent clear agreement otherwise). *See also Reed Elsevier, Inc. v. Crockett*, 734 F.3d 594 (6th Cir. 2013). Does *Lamps Plus* affect those cases?

Class Action Waivers in Arbitration Agreements

What about class action waivers? Some federal courts have stricken class action waivers under the "vindicating statutory rights" doctrine. So long as the prospective litigant effectively may vindicate its statutory cause of action in the arbitral forum only in a class action, the federal statute that provides the cause of action will continue to serve its remedial and deterrent function, and the disputant can argue that the arbitration agreement containing a class action waiver is unenforceable because it would preclude that party from vindicating its federal statutory rights.

For example, the Second Circuit, in *In re American Express Merchants Litigation*, 634 F.3d 187 (2d Cir. 2011) (*Amex II*), an antitrust class action, the court reconsidered its earlier decision that class action waivers in credit card agreements were unenforceable under the FAA in light of *AT&T Mobility LLC v. Conception*, 131 S. Ct. 1740 (2011), and concluded that that decision did not change its earlier analysis, which was a "vindication of a statutory right" analysis, and that was part of the substantive law of arbitrability. The motion to compel arbitration (as opposed to proceeding with the class action) was denied, after a showing that individual lawsuits were uneconomic. The Second Circuit distinguished between preemption of state action (*AT&T*) and conflict between two federal laws (not decided).

However, as noted above, in *American Express Co. v. Italian Colors Restaurant*, 133 S. Ct. 2304 (2013), the Supreme Court reversed the Second Circuit again. It held that the "no class arbitration" clause was enforceable. The "effective vindication" theory did not apply because the contract did not eliminate the right to sue. The statutory remedy under the antitrust laws in fact existed before the class action rules were even adopted. Justice Scalia, for the Court, did not hold that there was or was not such an exception, but rather, the Court declined to apply it if indeed it did exist.

In 2012, in a per curiam opinion, the court ruled that the FAA preempted a West Virginia Supreme Court rule that held void as against public policy predispute arbitration clauses in nursing home contracts with respect to negligence claims. *Marmet Health Care Center v. Brown*, 565 U.S. 530 (2012) (U.S. Supreme Court) (per curiam) (states cannot prohibit a particular type of arbitration). But the court said that states could consider "whether arbitration clauses are unenforceable under common law principles that are not specific to arbitration and preempted by the FAA."

In *DIRECTV, Inc. v. Imburgia*, 136 S. Ct. 463 (2015), the Court dealt with a consumer arbitration agreement that contained a class action waiver clause and a provision that "if the law of your state" made such waivers unenforceable, the entire arbitration agreement was void. The California Court of Appeals had held that California law made class action waivers unenforceable, even though the Supreme Court had subsequently held that the California rule was preempted by the FAA. The Supreme Court held the waiver clause enforceable and required the arbitration to go forward because the reference to "law of your state" obviously meant the "valid" law of your state. Because there is a federal policy favoring arbitration, California's interpretation did not give due regard for that policy. Interestingly, the majority opinion was written by Justice Breyer and Justices Thomas, Sotomayor, and Ginsberg dissented.

Refusal to Recognize and Enforce an Arbitral Award

When can a court refuse to recognize and enforce an arbitral award? The FAA has four narrow grounds:

1. award was procured by fraud, corruption or undue means;
2. evident partiality or corruption among arbitrators;
3. arbitrators were guilty of misconduct or where rights of any party have been prejudiced; and
4. when arbitrators have exceeded their power.

What about "manifest disregard of the law" as a reason for setting aside an arbitration award? *Hall Street Associates v. Mattel Inc.*, 552 U.S. 576 (2008), rejected that as a ground for vacating an award. Or did it? *Stolt-Nielsen S.A. v. AnimalFeeds Int'l Corp.*, 130 S. Ct. 1758 (2010): "*Hall Street*, did not, we think, abrogate the manifest disregard doctrine altogether." As a result, there is now a split in the circuits. The Second Circuit says "manifest disregard" can be used to set award aside. *See, e.g.*, *Stolt-Nielsen* (decided after *Hall Street*); *see also Coffee Beanery Ltd. v. W.W. LLC*, 2008 U.S. App. LEXIS 23645 (6th Cir. 2008). The Fifth Circuit says it cannot. *See Citigroup Global Markets v. Bacon*, 562 F.3d 349 (5th Cir. 2009); *see also McKool Smith, P.C. v. Curtis International Ltd.*, No. 15-11140 (5th Cir. May 23, 2016). In *Walia v. Dewan*, No. 13-722, 2014 WL 1343626 (US Apr. 7, 2014), the Supreme Court passed on the opportunity to resolve the circuit split. At the moment, the Fifth, Seventh, Eighth, and Eleventh Circuits reject manifest disregard of the law as a ground for setting aside an international arbitral award, while the Second, Fourth, Sixth, and Ninth Circuits recognize it. One of the questions these cases raise is whether a "manifest disregard of the law" is an act beyond the arbitrator's powers under the FAA, 9 U.S.C. § 10(a)(4), thus permitting a court to set the award aside.

One of the most recent cases dealing with the issue was *Daesang Corp. v. NutraSweet Co.*, 167 A.D. 3d 1 (N.Y. App. Div. 1st Dept. 2018), reversing a lower court's decision setting aside an arbitral award on the ground that the arbitrators "manifestly disregarded" the law. Quoting from the arbitral award that explicitly discussed the legal claim being made and the controlling law, the court said "the foregoing suffices to show that the resolution in the partial award of the (relevant) issue—whether or not that resolution was correct, a question on which we express no opinion—does not meet the high standard required to establish manifest disregard of the law, namely a showing that 'the arbitrators knew of the relevant principle, appreciated that this principle controlled the outcome of the disputed issue, and nonetheless willfully flouted the governing law by refusing to apply it.'"

Federal Court Jurisdiction

The Supreme Court is currently considering whether federal courts have subject matter jurisdiction to confirm or vacate an arbitration award. Section 4 of the FAA provides explicitly that a petition to compel arbitration may be filed in "any United States District Court which, save for [the arbitration] agreement, would have jurisdiction without it." However, there is no similar language in Sections 9 and 10. In *Vaden v. Discover Bank*, 566 U.S. 49 (2009), the Court (Justice Ginsberg) interpreted the language of Section 4 and held that "the court should assume the absence of an arbitration agreement and determine whether the court would have jurisdiction without it." This is sometimes called the "look-through" approach.

But can the "look-through" approach also be used to infer federal jurisdiction under Sections 9 and 10? In *Badgerow v. Walters*, 975 F.3d 469 (5th Cir. 2020), cert. granted, 2021), the Supreme Court took up that question. Specifically, that case presents the question whether federal courts have subject matter jurisdiction to confirm or vacate an arbitration award under Sections 9 and 10 when the only basis for jurisdiction is that the underlying dispute involved a federal question. The Fifth Circuit held, contrary to the positions taken by the Third and Seventh Circuits, that the "look-through" approach could be used under Sections 9 and 10 to determine whether a federal court has jurisdiction to determine whether it could vacate a FINRA award dismissing the petitioner's claim so long as the underlying dispute involved a federal question, notwithstanding that there is no explicit grant of federal jurisdiction for review or enforcement of an arbitral award. In other words, could the Court's decision in *Vaden* to "look through" the arbitral proceedings for federal jurisdiction arising out of the underlying dispute under Section 4 be applied to the entire FAA as a whole?

Curiously, as the Supreme Court noted in the *Hall Street* case, the FAA is "something of an anomaly" because it "bestows no federal jurisdiction but rather requires for access to a federal court an independent jurisdictional basis over the parties' dispute." (quoting *Moses H. Cove Memorial Hospital v. Mercury Const. Corp.*, 460 U.S. 1, 25 n.32 (1983)). If the look-through approach is sufficient for federal jurisdiction at the end of an arbitration, is it similarly sufficient at the beginning? Should the FAA be read as a whole, or is it correct to imply federal jurisdiction only for Section 4? Chief Justice Roberts may have tipped his position when he remarked that the FAA was an "odd creature in that ... it doesn't by itself give rise to jurisdiction ... because [litigants] recognize that people arbitrate all sorts of disputes, and they don't want all the 380,000 cases brought in federal court, just like you don't want [the enforcement of settlement agreements] being brought in federal court just because it arose out of a federal case." (Transcript of oral argument, p. 46). Stay tuned!

History of Securities Arbitration

As noted above, in 1817, the constitution of the predecessor of the NYSE provided for internal resolution of disputes among members. In 1872, that constitution was expanded to provide for the arbitration of claims by customers against members.

In 1934, after the Securities Exchange Act was passed, the SEC recommended to Congress that the NYSE, which was then a "self-regulatory organization" (SRO), be encouraged to offer customers a standard arbitration contract and to create an independent arbitral tribunal for the claims of customers that could be chosen as an alternative to the long-standing arbitration committee. The NYSE did not adopt the recommendation and arbitrations continued under the auspices of the NYSE's arbitration committee.

In 1975, President Ford's regulatory reform program contained, as one of its four principal points, concerns for responsiveness to consumers, including the handling of investor complaints. As a result, the arbitration facilities of the SROs, which were not entirely independent, were transformed into modern forums. An industry task force became the Securities Industry Conference on Arbitration (SICA). Uniform arbitration rules (the Uniform Code) were adopted by SICA in 1979 and revised again in 1989. The SEC reviewed SRO arbitrations in 1986 and 1987 and requested changes to the Uniform Code. In 1994, the NASD appointed an Arbitration Policy Task Force, known as the Ruder Commission, which reported in 1996 that securities arbitration is a "relatively efficient, fair, and less costly forum for resolution of disputes involving public investors, member firms and firm employees."[11] Today, SICA is composed of representatives of the SROs, the Securities Industry and Financial Markets Association, and three public members.

In 1987, the AAA adopted Securities Arbitration Rules for securities arbitrations. However, the program was not successful, and the rules were abolished in 1999. Instead, securities arbitrations are heard by the AAA under its generic rules. AAA securities filings dropped from a high of 635 in 1993 to only thirty-three in 2006.

Notwithstanding the long history of securities arbitrations in this country, for years the Supreme Court refused to recognize the arbitration of securities disputes as legitimate and in fact refused to enforce pre-dispute arbitration agreements in contracts for the purchase or sale of securities. The leading case was *Wilko v. Swan*, which originally applied only to the Securities Act and was later extended to the Securities Exchange Act.

Wilko v. Swan[12]

This case illustrated a judicial hostility to securities arbitrations. The Supreme Court declined to enforce an arbitration agreement relating to a dispute claiming a violation of a Section 12(2) of the 1933 Securities Act. The Supreme Court refused to stay a court action pending arbitration, as the FAA would require. The Court noted that the Securities Act provided a "special right to recover for any misrepresentation" and that "any condition, stipulation or provision binding any person acquiring any security to waive compliance with any proviso of the 1933 Act or the rules and regulations of the Commission shall be void." The Supreme Court said that an agreement to arbitrate was such a provision that cannot waive any provision of the 1933 Act. It held that arbitrations lacked the judicial system's ability to provide investors with the level of protection necessitated by the Securities Act.

However, the Court's attitude seemed to soften in *Scherk v. Alberto Culver*, 417 U.S. 506 (1974), in which it relied on the international aspects of a complex pre-dispute agreement to differentiate *Wilko*, noting that "uncertainty will almost inevitably exist with respect to any contract touching two or more countries, each with its own substantive and choice of law rules." The Supreme Court held that enforcing such contractual provisions is an "indispensable

---

[11] David Ruder, "Securities Arbitration Reform: Report of the Arbitration Policy Task Force to the Board of Governors of the National Association of Securities Dealers, Inc." (1996).

[12] 346 U.S. 427 (1953).

precondition" to achieving orderliness and predictability in international business transactions.[13]

Wilko was nearly put to rest in *Shearson/American Express, Inc. v. McMahon*, 482 U.S. 220 (1987); the Court enforced a pre-dispute arbitration agreement, finding that arbitration did not deprive investors of an adequate means of enforcing the Securities Exchange Act.

Wilko was completely overturned in *Rodriquez de Cuijas v. Shearson/ American Express, Inc.*, 490 U.S. 477 (1989), in which the Court noted the SEC's oversight of the SRO arbitration procedures and firmly established that securities laws disputes can be arbitrated.[14]

FINRA

The Financial Industry Regulatory Authority (FINRA) was created in 2007 as the result of the consolidation of the NASD, which created its own arbitration rules in 1968, and the member, regulatory, enforcement, and arbitration divisions of the NYSE. FINRA is a self-regulated organization but it is also regulated by the SEC. Its dispute resolution program is administered out of four regional offices: New York, Boca Raton, Chicago, and Los Angeles. Its headquarters are in Washington, D.C., and New York.

Virtually all securities arbitrations today are under the auspices of FINRA through its FINRA Dispute Resolution, a division of FINRA. In 2011, it had a pool of 2,854 industry arbitrators and 3,557 non-industry arbitrators. Each year FINRA administers between 4,000 and 8,000 arbitrations and mediations. In 2011, 4,729 cases were filed.

FINRA arbitrations are required if a broker-dealer firm includes a pre-dispute arbitration agreement (PDAA) in its customer contracts or if a customer without a PDAA demands an arbitration pursuant to FINRA's Rule 12200.[15]

If the amount in dispute is less than $50,000, there is one arbitrator and the dispute is decided on the papers. If it is between $50,000 and $100,000, one or three arbitrators will be appointed. If it is more than $100,000, three arbitrators are required. FINRA arbitral awards may be appealed to the FINRA National Adjudicating Council and in rare cases, to the FINRA Board of Governors.

---

[13] *See* Francis Giberson, "Arbitration of International Securities Transactions—*Scherk v. Albert-Culver Co.*," 16 *B. C. L. Rev.* 491 (1975).

[14] *See* William Hermann, "Arbitration of Securities Disputes: Rodriguez and New Arbitration Rules Leave Investors Holding a Mixed Bag," 65 *Indiana L. Rev.* 697 (1990).

[15] *See* Jill Gross, "The Customer's Non-Waivable Right to Choose Arbitration in the Securities Industry," 10 *Brook. J. Corp. Fin. & Com. L.* (2016).

FINRA Procedures

When member firms decide to use mandatory arbitration clauses in their customer agreements, they must follow certain FINRA rules. For example, the rules establish minimum disclosure requirements regarding the use of arbitration clauses; prohibit pre-dispute arbitration agreements from including conditions that, among other things, limit or contradict FINRA rules; and prohibit class actions claims in FINRA arbitration. Accordingly, FINRA rules prohibit member firms from incorporating provisions that would prevent customers from bringing or participating in judicial class actions by adding waiver language into customer agreements (class action waivers) and prohibit member firms from enforcing arbitration agreements against members of a certified or putative class action. If member agreements fail to comply with FINRA rules, the members may face disciplinary action.[16]

An issue has recently arisen as to whether FINRA's jurisdiction applies to cases brought under the 1933 Securities Act as well as the 1934 Securities Exchange Act. The argument against jurisdiction is based on FINRA's statutory authority as a sanctioning body, which comes from Sections 15A and 19 of the 1934 Act. Those sections give FINRA authority to discipline members for violations of "this chapter" and "rules and regulations thereunder." The issue was raised in an action brought in a Maryland federal court against FINRA by Scottsdale Capital Advisors Corp. in March 2016. In that case, the plaintiff sought an injunction prohibiting FINRA from enforcing the 1933 Securities Act. FINRA relied on its Rule 2010, a catchall rule, for its jurisdiction. The federal district court upheld FINRA's jurisdiction and the Fourth Circuit affirmed. "Congress, through the Exchange Act, intended to channel objections to FINRA's authority through the agency and the courts of Appeals. In so doing, it is clear Congress sought to preclude federal district court jurisdiction.... We hold [Scottsdale's] challenge to FINRA's authority is the type of claim Congress intended to be reviewed within the statutory scheme." *Scottsdale Capital Advisors Corp. v. FINRA*, 844 F.3d 414, 422-24 (4th Cir. 2016).

Some FINRA Statistics. Damages are awarded in about 50 percent of the cases. In 2011, 74 percent of customer claimant cases resulted in monetary recovery for the investor. Average processing time from service of the claim to close of the case is about fourteen months.

Types of causes of action handled by FINRA include margin calls, churning, unauthorized trading, failure to supervise, negligence, omission of facts, breach of contract, breach of fiduciary duty, unsuitability, misrepresentation, and online trading. Many cases concern manipulation.

---

[16] *See* FINRA Regulatory Notice 21-16, April 2021.

In January 2011, the rules were changed to give the investor the option of having an all-public (i.e., non-industry) panel as opposed to the typical panel that consisted of two public and one non-public arbitrators. Only customers can choose the selection method.

Can collective actions be arbitrated in FINRA? The staff consistently interpreted the rules to say "no" but in 2010, a federal court in New York said that the staff's interpretation of the rules was incorrect. As a result, the rules were changed in April 2012 to expressly preclude certain collective actions. FINRA Rule 13204. That rule was approved by the SEC in June 2012. But is that rule still valid?[17]

FINRA recently charged Charles Schwab with violating FINRA rules by including provisions in a PDAA that required customers to waive their right to bring class actions against the firm. FINRA regulates what language can be contained in PDAAs. In February 2013, a FINRA panel, citing *AT&T Mobility LLC v. Conception*, 131 S. Ct. 1740 (2011), held that the FINRA rule prohibiting class action waivers was unenforceable and preempted by the FAA.

Schwab sued FINRA in federal court in California, but in May 2012 the court dismissed the complaint, holding that it lacked jurisdiction because Schwab had not exhausted its administration remedies, *Charles Schwab & Co. v. FINRA* (N.D. Cal. May 11, 2012). In 2014, the FINRA Board of Governors affirmed the panel decision that Schwab violated FINRA rules. You may well ask how that could be so since the FINRA rules preclude class action arbitration. It is true, however, because FINRA arbitrators *may* consolidate more than one party's claims into a single arbitration. That would be a "class action" in sheep's clothing. There have been few if any such cases, however.

Discovery can be ordered by the arbitrators who have great flexibility. Non-party discovery is permitted pursuant to subpoena. General rules of discovery apply, such as privilege protection. FINRA publishes detailed discovery guides specifying what documents must be produced by the customer or the institution. Simplified arbitration rules apply to claims under $50,000.

Suitability. Nearly one-third of FINRA cases involve "unsuitability." New rules went into effect in July 2012. For example, FINRA Rule 2090: "Know your customer"; Rule 2111 provides that a broker must have a reasonable basis to believe that the recommended transaction or strategy is suitable for the customer. Note that these rules do not impose a fiduciary duty on the broker, but they come close.

---

[17] *See Cohen v. UBS Financial, Inc.*, 799 F.3d 174 (2d Cir. July 2015); *Lloyd v. J.P. Morgan Chase & Co.*, 791 F.3d 265 (2d Cir. 2015). ("Rule 13204 says nothing about class action and collective action waivers, and cannot be read to bar enforcement of them." It merely says that "class action claims may not be arbitrated under the Code.")

Appeal. As noted, the grounds for challenging an arbitrator's decision are very limited. *See* Section 10, Federal Arbitration Act.

Notwithstanding the popularity of securities arbitration in FINRA, in 2010, Dodd-Frank provided that the SEC should decide whether the public interest and the protection of investors required the SEC to ban arbitration clauses in customer agreements and expressly authorized the SEC to adopt such a rule. Investor advocates who wanted the ability to choose their own forum urged the SEC to do so, but the securities industry pushed back, arguing that the right to mandate the arbitration of securities disputes was a "vital component of this system because such agreements help shape the public policy in favor of arbitration that has been recognized by both Congress and the U.S. Supreme Court."[18] Lost in the debate was the fact that securities arbitration was originally viewed as an investor protection mechanism.

At the "SEC Speaks" Forum on February 24, 2018, Rick Fleming, Director of the SEC's Office of Investor Advocate, argued that mandatory arbitration of securities disputes was "draconian" and "stripped away the right of shareholders to bring a class action." He argued that the SEC should refuse to accelerate the effective date of an issuer's registration statement if the statement contained a forced arbitration provision, citing Section 8(a) of the Securities Act. "Consider," he argued, "how different the federal securities laws would be in the absence of civil litigation.... Would investors even be able to pursue claims under Rule 10b-5?"

Arbitration of Shareholder Disputes Based on an Arbitration Clause in the Company's Constituent Documents

In two Delaware cases, one by the Delaware Chancery Court and the other by the Delaware Supreme Court, the courts upheld a forum selection clause in a corporate bylaw for intra-company lawsuits and a fee-shifting bylaw for unsuccessful litigants against the company. *Boilermakers Local 154 Retirement Fund, et al. v. Chevron Corp.*, 73 A.3d 934 (Chancery Ct. Del. 2013); *ATP Tour, Inc. v. Deutscher Tennis Bund*, 91 A.3d 554 (Supreme Ct. Del. 2014) (*en banc*). After *ATP*, the Delaware Corporate Law Council, a committee of the Delaware State Bar Association, proposed an amendment to the Delaware Corporation Law that would prohibit fee-shifting bylaws. In 2015, the legislature adopted an amendment that authorized forum selection clauses in corporate governing documents (although prohibiting clauses that designate only courts outside Delaware unless contained in a written shareholder

---

[18] Pre-Dispute Arbitration Resource Center, Securities Industry & Financial Markets Association.

agreement) and invalidating fee-shifting provisions in charters and bylaws. On June 24, 2015, the Delaware governor signed the law.

In two cases in Maryland, the courts upheld the enforceability of a bylaw that required shareholder claims to be resolved by binding arbitration. *Corvex Mgt. L.P. v. CommonWealth REIT* (Baltimore City Court May 8, 2013); *Katz v. CommonWealth REIT* (Maryland Cir. Ct. Feb. 19, 2014). What is the theory of those cases? (*Hint*: That bylaws are like a contract between the corporation and its shareholders. But are they really?) Would such a requirement be a way to forestall derivative actions or shareholder class actions? Are there any public policy issues? Some other countries, such as Finland and Austria, expressly recognize that an arbitration clause in a company's constituent documents could bind certain stakeholders. How would the company disclose the consequences?

What if a given shareholder voted against the provision? Senior Counsel Perry Herzfeld, an Australian lawyer with the law firm Eleven Wentworth, says he is not bound.[19] Is he right? How would that be enforced? Professor Ann Lipton of Tulane Law School has argued that corporate charters and bylaws are not the same as contracts because corporate law is premised on fiduciary obligations and is, for FAA purposes, noncontractual. She argues, therefore, that corporations cannot (or should not be permitted to) require shareholders to arbitrate disputes rather than to litigate them.[20]

In its IPO filing, the Carlyle Group included a clause that would prohibit shareholders from filing class actions, requiring them to arbitrate instead. After considerable pressure, including from the SEC, it withdrew the provision.[21]

Could you actually arbitrate a securities class action? Yes, at least in theory. *See Green Tree Financial Corp. v. Bazzle*, 539 U.S. 444 (2003). In that case, the contract was silent as to whether it permitted class arbitration. South Carolina law said that in that case, class arbitration was permitted. The Supreme Court remanded so that the arbitrator could interpret the meaning of the arbitration clause, which the majority thought was ambiguous. AAA now has rules for arbitrating class actions, including class certification and notice. Could the contract require or prohibit the application of the Private Securities Litigation Reform Act (PSLRA)? Is any of this realistic or likely?[22] Recall that recent

---

[19] *See* Perry Herzfeld, "Prudent Anticipation: The Arbitration of Public Company Shareholder Disputes," 24 *Arbitration International* No. 2 (2008).

[20] Ann Lipton, "Manufactured Consent: The Problems of Arbitration Clauses in Corporate Charters," 104 *Geo. L. J.* 583 (2016).

[21] *See* Kevin Roose, "Carlyle Drops Arbitration Clause From I.P.O. Plans," *New York Times DealBook*, Feb. 3, 2012.

[22] *See* Farah Usmani, "Inequities in the Resolution of Securities Disputes: Individual or Class Action; Arbitration or Litigation," 7 *Fordham J. Corp. & Fin. L.* 193 (2001).

Supreme Court cases, including *Lamps Plus*, require that a class action clause in an arbitration agreement must be explicit before it can be enforced.

Should Arbitration of Securities Disputes Be Mandated? Fasten Your Seat Belts

In a 2017 report titled "A Financial System That Creates Economic Opportunities [for] Capital Markets," the U.S. Department of the Treasury recommended that "the states and the SEC continue to investigate the various means to reduce costs of securities litigation for issuers in a way that protects investors rights and interests, including allowing companies and shareholders to settle disputes through arbitration." In support of that recommendation, the Treasury Department cited the increase in securities class actions and concluded that "securities class actions can significantly benefit attorneys at the expense of shareholders." No factual support was cited for that conclusion.[23]

Similarly, in July 2017, SEC Commissioner Michael Piwowar said, in a speech to the Heritage Foundation, that the SEC was open to the idea of allowing companies to include mandatory arbitration provisions in their corporate charters. "Come to us and ask for relief to put in mandatory arbitration into [your] charters." Jay Clayton, the SEC chair at the time, said that the SEC would not prejudge the issue.

However, on February 11, 2019, Clayton announced that the SEC's Division of Corporate Finance had decided not to enforce Rule 14a-8(i)(2) against a corporation that had chosen *not* to include a shareholder proposal in its proxy statement that would include mandatory arbitration in its governing documents. The company did not want to include such a provision in its documents on the ground that it would violate New Jersey law (the company was incorporated in New Jersey) even though there was no binding New Jersey precedent. The New Jersey Attorney General had opined that implementation of the proposal would nevertheless violate New Jersey law. Clayton endorsed the position of the Division of Corporate Finance not to recommend enforcement. "A court is a more appropriate venue to seek a binding determination of whether a shareholder proposal can be excluded."

That may not be the end of the matter, however. In *Salzberg v. Sciabacucchi*, No. 346, 2020 WL 1280785 (Del. Mar. 18, 2020), three corporations in Delaware each adopted a provision in its certificate of incorporation providing that federal district courts were the exclusive forum for the resolution of any complaint asserting a class action arising under the 1933 Act against the corporation. The Delaware Supreme Court unanimously decided that federal

[23] *See* Mark Kantor, "Treasury Suggests Arbitration of Securities Actions," Amer. Bar Ass'n, Alternate Dispute Resolution, Section of Litigation, October 9, 2017.

forum-selection provisions were consistent with Section 115 of the Delaware General Corporate Law, especially when the claims were brought under the 1933 Securities Act (recall *Cyan v. Beaver County Employees Retirement Fund*, 138 S. Ct. 1061 (2018)). What is significant here is that, in a footnote, the Delaware Court dismissed concerns that "the next move" might be a provision that required arbitration of internal corporate claims, because, "at least from our state law perspective," such provisions would violate Section 115's ban on charter or bylaw language that "prohibit[s] bringing [internal corporate claims] in the courts of this state." (n. 169).

But does that end the debate? Probably not. The U.S. Supreme Court has held that the Federal Arbitration Act establishes an "equal treatment principle" that forbids states from discriminating against arbitration agreements. Would a state statute that forbade language in corporate documents that mandated an arbitral forum for certain disputes violate that principle? Although the SEC has yet to approve such a requirement in corporate documents, at least one commissioner, Hester M. Pierce, has left the door open to the idea.[24]

Recent Supreme Court Cases Relating to Arbitrations

In *Henry Schein Inc. v. Archer and White Sales Inc.*, 139 S. Ct. 524 (2019), the Supreme Court flatly rejected an argument that even though an arbitration clause clearly required the arbitrators, not a court, to determine their own jurisdiction, a court could determine that on the merits, the arbitration would be a waste of time since the claim was "wholly groundless." The FAA contains no such exception and the Supreme Court is "not at liberty to rewrite the statute passed by Congress and signed by the President."

As noted above, in *Lamps Plus Inc. v. Varela*, 139 S. Ct. 1407 (2019), the Supreme Court rejected a claim that an ambiguous arbitration clause permitted a class action arbitration. The plaintiff was an employee of Lamps Plus whose employee information had been hacked, causing a fraudulent income tax return to be filed in his name. The plaintiff persuaded the district court to compel a class action arbitration against the employer even though the arbitration agreement was ambiguous. The Supreme Court held that, consistent with *Stolt-Nielsen* and other precedents, more than an ambiguous agreement is required to ensure that the parties did in fact agree to a class action arbitration, especially since an individual arbitration is "the traditional individualized arbitration" contemplated by the FAA.

---

[24] *See* https://www.sec.gov/news/speech/speech-pierce-092418.

FINRA Rule 12200 Versus "Forum Selection" Clauses

As noted above, FINRA is a self-regulatory organization established under Section 15A of the Securities Exchange Act. It is authorized to exercise "comprehensive oversight over all securities firms that do business with the public." Pursuant to FINRA Rule 12200, all FINRA members are required to submit customer disputes to FINRA arbitration whenever a customer demands arbitration.

Recently, however, FINRA members have been including forum-selection clauses in their broker-dealer agreements with customers pursuant to which the parties agree that all actions and proceedings "arising out of" the agreement would be brought in a designated federal district court.

There is a split in the circuits with respect to the question whether FINRA Rule 12200, which requires arbitration if demanded by the customer, trumps a forum selection that designates a federal district court as the venue for all proceedings "arising out of" the broker-dealer contract. The Second and Ninth Circuits have held that such clauses require litigation in federal court, whereas the Third and Fourth Circuits have held that they do not. The Second and Ninth Circuits regard Rule 12200 as merely a "default obligation" that can be waived by the parties. The Third and Fourth Circuits disagree because the clauses were not "sufficiently specific to impute to the contracting parties the reasonable expectation that they are superseding, displacing or waiving the arbitration obligation created by FINRA Rule 12200." The Third Circuit went even further, holding that an action to compel arbitration under that rule does not "arise out of" the forum-selection clause but rather "arises out of" the FINRA rule.[25] The circuit split has not yet been resolved.

In *UBS Financial Services, Inc. v. West Virginia University Hospitals, Inc.*, 660 F.3d 643 (2d Cir. 2011), the Second Circuit held that the decision whether a forum-selection clause that prohibited the defendants from proceeding with an arbitration outside of New York County even though FINRA Rule 12213(a)(1) provides that the FINRA director of dispute resolution will decide "the hearing location for the arbitration," had to be taken in the first instance by the FINRA arbitrators. "[V]enue is a procedural issue that FINRA's arbitrators should address in the first instance." Whether this rule could be applied to the circuit split described above remains to be seen.

---

[25] *See Reading Health System v. Bear Stearns & Co.*, 900 F.3d 87 (3d Cir. 2018); *but see Goldman, Sachs & Co. v. Golden Empire Schools Fin. Auth.*, 764 F.3d 210 (2d Cir. 2014).

More FINRA Statistics

In 2019, there were 3,753 new arbitration cases filed at FINRA, of which 2,363 were customer cases and 1,394 were intra-industry. There were 4,011 cases closed and 4,808 cases were pending. The average overall turnaround time in months was 14.2; for regular hearings, it was 16.9; for special proceeding decisions, it was 7.0; and for paper decisions, it was 5.8.

Chapter 19

International Securities Fraud

In this chapter, we discuss primarily securities actions in the United States against foreign companies with foreign shareholders and whose stock is traded on foreign exchanges (the so-called F-cubed companies).

Extraterritoriality Background

For many years, federal courts never addressed the issue of the extraterritorial application of the U.S. laws. Although there was a generally understood presumption that unless Congress explicitly specified otherwise, the laws of the United States did not apply extraterritorially, it was not until *Kook v. Crang*, 182 F. Supp. 388 (S.D.N.Y. 1960), that a federal court explicitly applied that presumption to a case under the 1934 Act. However, by 1968, the federal courts had carved out an exception to that presumption because they concluded that extraterritorial application of the securities laws was necessary "to protect American investors." *Schoenbaum v. Firstbrook*, 405 F.2d 200 (2d Cir.), *modified en banc* 405 F.2d 215 (2d Cir. 1968). By 1975, that carve-out was made even more explicit in *Bersch v. Drexel Firestone Inc.*, 519 F.2d 974 (2d Cir. 1975). Foreign transactions would be covered by the U.S. securities laws if the foreign transactions were "directly caused" by "acts (or culpable failures to act) within the United States." *Bersch* at 993. The notion was that until Congress decided to act, federal courts could fill in the gap in the hope that "by finding jurisdiction" for frauds occurring abroad, "we may encourage other nations to take ... reciprocal action against fraudulent schemes aimed at the United States from foreign sources." *SEC v. Kasser*, 548 F.2d 109 (3d Cir. 1977).

The "conduct" test seemed fairly clear. It required that "only domestic conduct constituting the relied-upon misrepresentations sufficed." *See Morrison*, 561 U.S. 247 (2010), *Brief for Respondents*, p. 5. In *Bersch*, the lower court found that domestic conduct constituted an "essential link" in the fraud that had taken place in the United States. The Second Circuit reversed because the statements at issue were made abroad and reached their victims abroad. Thus, Section 10(b) would apply only when "all the elements of a defendant's conduct necessary to establish a violation" occurred in the United States, that is, when the misrepresentations were made in the United States.

This was a bright-line test (the so-called "location of the lies" test) but it did not last long. Soon, other courts focused on the materiality of the domestic acts and conflated the "conduct" test with a separately articulated "effects" test. As a result, the law became, as the National Australian Bank's counsel, George Conway, argued in *Morrison*, "a collection of conclusions" and a set of "potentially incompatible statements of applicable rules" that were essentially impossible to apply in a consistent and predictable fashion. As a result, the filing of the so-called "F-cubed" cases expanded greatly, "generating excessive levels of conflict with other countries."[1]

Against this background, the Supreme Court rejected the "conduct and effects" test in the *Morrison* case and concluded that the issue was not one of jurisdiction but one of extraterritorial application of the U.S. laws. In other words, a return to the pre-1968 law. Whether the "new" test turned out to be a bright-line test or easy application remains to be seen. This issue is apparently still alive and well, at least insofar as it applies to private cases.

Class Certification Issues

Rule 23 and Supreme Court decisions provide that absent class members are bound by the result and are precluded from suing again. That is one reason why they must receive notice that complies with the requirements for due process. But what if some of the class members are foreigners? Will a judgment (in favor of the defendant) be given preclusive effect in other countries? Why does this matter? What is the correct test? Is it "near certainty" or "more likely than not"? In *In re Vivendi Universal S.A. Securities Litigation*, 2007 WL 861147 (S.D.N.Y. Mar. 22, 2007), the district court held that class certification is permissible so long as the "plaintiffs are able to establish a probability that a foreign court will recognize the res judicata effect of a U.S. class action judgment." However, *Bersch v. Drexel Firestone, Inc.*, 519 F.2d 974 (2d Cir. 1975), held that an American court should abstain from entering a judgment against a foreign company when it is a "near certainty" that a foreign court might not recognize or enforce it. Recall that Rule 23 requires that a class notice must advise putative class members about "the binding effect of a class judgment on members." How could that be done if it is even a "possibility" that the judgment might not be held by a foreign court to be "binding" on class members?

---

[1] Hannah Buxbaum, "Multinational Class Actions Under Federal Securities Law: Managing Jurisdictional Conflict," 46 *Colum. J. Transnat'l L.* 14 (2007).

It should be understood that the "binding" that we are talking about here is the "binding" effect of a judgment in favor of the defendant foreign corporation in its home country. There is no question that a foreign member of a class that lost its case could not sue again in an American court; the question of interest, however, is whether that class member could sue again in a foreign court that does not recognize the binding *res judicata* effect of the U.S. judgment. Because there are very few bilateral treaties mandating such recognition, there is no satisfactory answer to that question.

The other question of interest is whether the American courts could or more properly should exercise jurisdiction over foreign companies in the first place. We know that for decades they have been doing so, but did they have the right to do so? We turn to that question next.

Jurisdiction or Extraterritoriality?

Does a U.S. court have "jurisdiction" over F-cubed companies? Is this a subject matter jurisdiction issue, as the courts have assumed for decades, or do the U.S. securities laws simply not apply abroad?

Bersch v. Drexel Firestone, Inc., 519 F.2d 974 (2d Cir. 1975), established the "conduct and effects" test and held that whether a foreign corporation could be sued in a U.S. court for violating the U.S. securities laws was a questions of "subject matter jurisdiction." The court had jurisdiction if the alleged unlawful conduct took place in the United States (at least beyond merely preparatory activities) or if the conduct occurring overseas has a substantial "effect" inside the United States. That test lasted forty years but the cases were not uniform. Most circuits had weighed in. They all thought that the issue was one of subject matter jurisdiction. The problem with the test was simply that it was very hard to apply. Along came the *Morrison* case.

Morrison v. National Australia Bank Ltd.[2]

National Australia Bank was an Australian company whose shares were traded on the Australian Stock Exchange Limited. Only its America Depository Receipts (ADRs) were traded on an American stock exchange. The plaintiffs claimed that a subsidiary, HomeSide Lending, Inc., a Florida company, misstated certain risks to its business model and as a result, National Australian Bank had to write down its investment. The two lower courts dismissed the complaint and affirmed the dismissal because there was no "subject matter jurisdiction." The acts that took place in the United States were "at most, a link in the chain of an alleged overall securities fraud scheme that culminated

[2] 561 U.S. 247 (2010).

abroad" that did not meet the conduct test. *In re National Australia Bank Securities Litigation*, 2006 WL 3844465 (S.D.N.Y. Oct. 25, 2006). The Second Circuit affirmed that judgment. 547 F.3 167 (2008).

The Supreme Court affirmed, but not for the same reasons as the lower courts. Rather, it held that the issue was not one of subject matter jurisdiction at all but was rather a "merits" question, to wit, the extraterritorial reach of Section 10(b). "It is a 'longstanding principle of American law' that legislation of Congress, unless a contrary intent appears, is meant to apply only within the territorial jurisdiction of the United States." *Morrison*, 561 U.S. 247 (2010), citing *EEOC v. Arabian Americas Oil Co.*, 499 U.S. 244, 248 (1991).

Thus, the Supreme Court held that the "conduct and effect" test that had been used for decades was fatally flawed. The Court looked at the statutory text and found no evidence of an intent to extend the securities laws extraterritorially. The Court applied the "presumption against extraterritoriality" and held that Section 10(b) applies "only in connection with the purchase or sale of a security listed on an American stock exchange and the purchase and sale of any other security in the United States." (*Query*: What does the latter part mean? Why did the Court not say simply "the sale of a security in the United States"?)

The Supreme Court intended to create a bright-line test, but did it? Did the court misspeak? Does the statute apply to transactions outside the United States even if the securities are cross-listed on a U.S. exchange? No, it doesn't, but for a while it looked as if it might. Post-*Morrison* cases have now clearly rejected that so-called "listing" theory.

In order to see why that is so, it is necessary to read the opinion as a whole. The Court clearly wanted to limit the extraterritorial reach of Section 10(b), and it did so notwithstanding the fact that National Australian Bank had ADRs listed in the United States backed by common shares. Those common shares were "listed" on an American exchange, but they were not tradable on that exchange. Clearly, the Court meant to exclude from the reach of Section 10(b) shares that were listed *and tradable* on an American exchange.[3] But the Court did not say so explicitly.

Much of the post-*Morrison* litigation concerns the second prong of the test. The "domestic transaction" test is difficult to apply in today's modern, electronic, cross-border world where different components of a transaction

[3] Why would that be the case? When an ADR is listed on a U.S. national exchange, common shares are also listed to back up the ADR. But those common shares are not tradable. In the *Morrison* case, copies of the ADRs with common shares were made part of the record before the Court, so the Court was certainly aware of the existence of the common shares.

occur in different physical locations or in cyberspace.[4] Lower courts have struggled with that part of the *Morrison* test.

Some Illustrative Post-*Morrison* Cases

When is a "purchase" made? In *Plumbers Union Local #12 Pension Fund v. Swiss Re*, 753 F. Supp. 2d 166 (S.D.N.Y. 2010), Judge John Koeltl held that the term "purchase" includes "contract to purchase." An individual is a purchaser when he or she incurred "irrevocable liability to take and pay for the stock." The plaintiffs had argued that the purchase occurs when the investor places a buy order. The court rejected the argument.

In *Quail Cruises Ship Management Ltd. v. Agenciade Viageus*, 645 F.3d 1307 (11th Cir. 2011), the focus was on where the transaction closed and where title to the securities was transferred. The court held that it was sufficient at the pleadings stage to allege that the transfer of title took place in the United States.

In *SEC v. Goldman Sachs*, 790 F. Supp. 2d 147 (S.D.N.Y. 2011), Judge Barbara Jones held that a transaction is deemed to occur in the United States where a party incurs "irrevocable liability" in the United States to complete the transaction. The court cited *Plumbers*, but that case only concerned *when* not *where* a purchase took place. The court held that merely placing an order from the United States that is executed on a foreign exchange is not sufficient for the purchase to be deemed to have been made in the United States.

In *Basis Yield Alpha Fund v. Goldman Sachs Group*, 798 F. Supp. 2d 533 (S.D.N.Y. 2011), Judge Barbara Jones held that it was sufficient to allege that the parties incurred "irrevocable liability" to purchase or sell in the United States. A Cayman Island fund purchased securities issued by two structured finance vehicles marketed by Goldman Sachs. The plaintiffs alleged that the defendants, one of whom operated out of New York, made fraudulent statements. They did not allege that any purchase or sale occurred in the United States. In the case of securities not traded on an exchange, the court must first determine when a purchase or sale occurs before it can determine where it occurs. The court held that under the Exchange Act, a purchase occurs when the parties incur "irrevocable liability" to complete the transaction. The court then extended the concept of *when* a sale took place to *where* it took place. This is key. The court extended a temporal concept to a geographical concept. The court then said, without citing authority, that to state a claim under Section 10(b), the plaintiff must allege that the parties incurred "irrevocable liability" to purchase or sell in the United States.

---

[4] *See* John Roesser & Louis Russo, "How Morrison Inadvertently Broadens Extraterritorial Actions," *N.Y. L.J.*, Aug. 17, 2012.

Where did the concept of "irrevocable liability" come from? Perhaps it came from *Riseman v. Orion Research, Inc.*, 749 F.2d 915 (1st Cir. 1984), which held that a sale takes place when the investor has incurred an "irrevocable liability" to take and pay for the stock and then the seller is "irrevocably bound" to sell his shares.

In *In re Optimal U.S. Litigation*, 813 F. Supp. 2d 351 (S.D.N.Y. 2011), a U.S. issuer was a sub-fund of a foreign fund. Shares in the U.S. fund were sold to foreign investors. Investors were directed to mail their subscription materials to a manager outside the United States. The plaintiffs argued that the shares were issued in New York and therefore "purchased" in New York. The court (Judge Scheindlin) said the pleading was adequate under *Morrison* and that defendant's argument was better made at the summary judgment stage. But after *Absolute Activist*, which we will discuss in a moment, was decided, the district court issued a show cause order, and the plaintiffs withdrew their allegation that the purchase took place in New York. They argued only that the purchases were "in connection with" the purchase of shares on the NYSE.

Absolute Activist Value Master Fund v. Ficeto, 677 F.3d 60 (2d Cir. 2012), is one of the two most important post-*Morrison* cases. This case holds that a transaction is domestic when the title to the shares is transferred within the United States or if the purchaser incurs "irrevocable liability" within the United States to take and pay for a security or to deliver a security even if title is actually transferred outside the United States. The district court's dismissal of the complaint was affirmed by the Second Circuit with leave to replead.

In that case, an offshore hedge fund purchased stock in U.S. companies that was traded on over-the-counter bulletin boards or pink sheets. The issuers were registered with the SEC. Offshore funds purchased the shares directly from the issuer in a PIPE (Private Investment in Public Equity) transaction, not on the secondary market.[5] The complaint alleged that the defendants, a broker-dealer and two individuals, engaged in a "pump and dump" scheme. The defendants would acquire the securities for their own account, and the plaintiffs, which were offshore funds, acquired securities in the same companies. The complaint alleged that the defendants pumped up the prices of the securities and also took sizable commissions based on the transactions by the offshore funds. One of the principals of the broker-dealer had power of attorney from the funds. The district court dismissed the case.

The district court said that there was no sale of the security listed on an American exchange because the PIPE transaction involved shares purchased directly from the company. Even if the shares had been listed on a U.S.

---

[5] Investors commit to purchase a number of restricted shares, and the company agrees to file a registration statement so shares can be sold to the public. Such a transaction dilutes existing shares.

exchange, there would be no cause of action because the transaction was not consummated on the exchange. The district court also said there had been no transaction in the United States, although the opinion is unclear as to why not. Apparently the location of the funds offshore was enough.

The Second Circuit (with Chief Judge Robert Katzmann writing the majority opinion) reversed. It adopted the "title passing" or "irrevocable liability" test. The issue was to determine the locus of the purchase or sale. At the pleading stage, it is sufficient to allege facts leading to a plausible inference that the parties incurred "irrevocable liability" within the United States, that is, "that the purchaser incurred 'irrevocable liability' within the United States to take and pay for a security or that the seller incurred 'irrevocable liability' within the United States to deliver a security." Is the court confusing *when* liability is incurred with *where* it is incurred? As noted, "irrevocable liability" is the traditional test for determining when a purchase or sale takes place. Does it work as well for establishing the locus of the transaction? What if the purchase takes place electronically? Is the court begging the question? Perhaps.

What are some of the factors that courts might look at? (*Hint*: Formation of the contract, placement of purchase orders, passing of title, exchange of money.) Residence or citizenship is irrelevant. The focus is not on the place where the deception originated but on the locus of purchases and sales. The court found that there were insufficient allegations to the effect that purchases or sales took place within the United States. Only a few allegations actually mentioned the location of the transactions. The complaint did not unequivocally allege the existence of domestic securities transactions. But the plaintiff was given leave to replead.

There was a related SEC case, *SEC v. Ficeto*, 839 F. Supp. 2d 1101 (C.D. Cal. 2011), alleging manipulation of stocks on the Over-the-Counter Market Bulletin Board and Pink Sheets. The SEC alleged that defendants engaged in matched orders, "marking the close" transactions, and wash sales. The California district court held that the trades on the over-the-counter market were subject to U.S. antifraud provisions notwithstanding that some of the foreign parties were outside the United States. The defendants argued that since the shares were not listed in the United States, the court had to apply the "domestic transaction" test. The court disagreed, stating that Section 10(b) applied to frauds committed in the U.S. over-the-counter markets. "We do not agree that *Morrison* held that fraud on the domestic over-the-counter market does not fall within the prohibitions of Section 10(b) except where the trades qualify independently as 'domestic transactions.'" The court read *Morrison* as dealing with the dichotomy between foreign and domestic exchanges and not between exchanges and the over-the-counter market. Therefore, the court did not engage in the "irrevocable liability" analysis. Is this decision consistent with *Morrison*? It does not appear to be.

On August 15, 2014, the Second Circuit decided the other most important post-*Morrison* case, *Parkcentral Global Hub Ltd. v. Porsche Automobile Holding SE*, 763 F.3d 198 (2d Cir. 2014), and completed the *Morrison*, *Absolute Activist*, and *Porsche* trilogy. The case concerned statements made by *Porsche* concerning its purchases of VW stock primarily in Germany with respect to stock traded only on exchanges in Europe. The plaintiffs, hedge funds, argued that there was a violation in the United States because the securities-based swap agreements that they entered into were concluded in the United States. Note that the plaintiffs did not buy Porsche stock, just swap agreements that were based on the price of Porsche stock. The court held that while a domestic transaction or listing is necessary to state a claim under Section 10(b), it is not sufficient to make a particular invocation of Section 10(b) appropriately domestic. "A rule making the statute applicable whenever the plaintiffs' suit is predicated on a domestic transaction, regardless of the foreignness of the facts constituting the defendant's alleged violation, would seriously undermine *Morrison*'s insistence that Section 10(b) has no extraterritorial application."

The court continued:

> If the domestic execution of the plaintiffs' agreements could alone suffice to invoke Section 10(b) liability with respect to the defendant's alleged conduct in this case, then it would subject to U.S. securities laws conduct that occurred in a foreign country, concerning securities in a foreign company, traded entirely on foreign exchanges, in the absence of any congressional provision addressing the incompatibility of U.S. and foreign law nearly certain to arise. This is a result *Morrison* plainly did not contemplate and that the Court's reasoning does not, we think, permit.

This means that the "bright-line" test articulated in *Morrison* and repeated in *Absolute Activist* is not so bright after all. The *Porsche* case makes it clear that a domestic transaction is not alone sufficient for a domestic claim, but that all of the relevant facts need to be analyzed.[6]

The *Porsche* decision was not well received. In *Stoyas v. Toshiba Corp.*, 896 F.3d 933 (9th Cir. 2018), *cert. denied*, 139 S. Ct. 2766 (2019), the Ninth Circuit held that *Porsche* ignored the broad language of Rule 10b-5; speculated about congressional intent, which *Morrison* "rebuked"; and "relied heavily on the foreign location of the alleged deceptive conduct, which *Morrison* held to be irrelevant." We do not know whether the Second Circuit or the Ninth

---

[6] *See* Jonathan Richman, "So Much for Bright-Line Tests on Extraterritorial Reach of U.S. Securities Laws?" Harvard Law School Forum on Corporate Governance and Financial Regulation, Sept. 2, 2014.

Circuit test will prevail, as the Supreme Court has so far declined to take up the issue.

A Few Questions and Some Answers

What if the transfer of shares occurs only by book entry in the United States and the share accounts are actually held in France? The U.S. securities laws do not apply.

What if the payment for the securities is done in part by transfer of funds from one U.S. bank to another? The U.S. laws do not apply. *MVP Asset Management v. Vestbirk*, No. 10 CV 02483 (E.D. Cal. 2012).

What about a purchase outside the United States of shares in an offshore feeder fund that in turn made corresponding investments in a domestic fund? The U.S. laws do not apply. Foreign investors do not get the benefit of a "pass-through" effect. *In re Banco Santander Optimal Securities Litigation*, 732 F. Supp. 2d 1305 (S.D. Fla. July 30, 2010).

Manipulative activity in the over-the-counter market is subject to Section 10(b). *See SEC v. Ficeto*, 839 F. Supp. 2d 1101 (C.D. Cal. 2011). But the test seems to be different. Apparently over-the-counter markets are the equivalent of American stock exchanges.

In general, the *Morrison* tests also apply to the 1933 Act.

With respect to Section 17(a), a federal court in New York has held that an offer is domestic if the offeror attempts to dispose of the securities or solicits an offer to buy the securities in the United States. *SEC v. Goldman Sachs*, 40 F. Supp. 2d 579 (S.D.N.Y 2014). This is true even if the offeree is outside the United States.

What if a foreign investor buys derivative instruments outside the United States referring to securities traded on the NYSE? The statute does apply because the purchase was "in connection with" a security listed on the NYSE. *SEC v. Compania Internacional Financiera*, 2011 WL 3251813 (S.D.N.Y. July 29, 2011). Is this right? What does the "in connection with" test have to do with extraterritorial jurisdiction? If the underlying shares themselves were purchased abroad, would there be jurisdiction just because the derivative instrument was listed? In this case, foreign investors purchased "contracts for difference" (CFDs), which were securities that allowed the purchaser to have a position in future price movements of the underlying security without actually owning it. The CFD prices were the same as the prices of the underlying securities, and the broker purchased the actual underlying security on the NYSE. The district court held that the Exchange Act applied because the purchase was "in connection with" a security listed on the NYSE. But this doesn't seem right and is probably based on the mistake in *Morrison*. It should not be enough that the underlying shares were listed in the United States because they were not purchased by the plaintiff. The plaintiff purchased CFDs. The SEC later dropped the case.

What principles emerge from these cases? There are several:

- Section 10(b) does not apply to purchases on foreign exchanges even if the investors are in the United States at the time.
- The existence of securities, including ADRs, listed on a U.S. exchange, is irrelevant if the transaction giving rise to the claims of violations is in fact executed on a foreign exchange.
- Section 10(b) does apply to purchase of a security that is executed on a U.S. exchange, no matter where the purchaser is.
- One court has held that purchases of ADRs in the over-the-counter market are not subject to Section 10(b). Is it correct? Off-exchange transactions effected outside the United States are not covered by Section 10(b).
- What if there is an off-exchange transaction between a U.S. party and a foreign party? Courts look to where the "irrevocable liability" is incurred or where title passes.
- Determining where "irrevocable liability" is incurred is often a factual inquiry. And it can be very difficult to do.
- Section 10(b) applies to U.S. transaction between a U.S. buyer and a U.S. seller.
- Section 10(b) does not apply to a foreign defendant that makes misrepresentations that affect the value of a reference security for a swap transaction between domestic market participants.
- Section 12(a)(2) is subject to *Morrison,* but Section 17 is subject to a different *Morrison* analysis.
- What about Section 5 of the 1933 Act (use of mail or interstate commerce to sell security without a registration statement)?
- The Investment Advisers Act does apply to advisers in the United States with respect to conduct outside the United States.
- Section 10(b) may be applicable to purchases outside the United States of derivative instruments that refer to U.S.-listed securities depending on the "economic reality." *See Elliott Ass'n. v. Porsche Automobile*, 759 F. Supp. 2d 469 (S.D.N.Y. 2010).
- Purchasers of ADRs (or American Depositary Shares, ADSs) on a domestic exchange can have claims under Section 10(b). *In re Vivendi*, 765 F. Supp. 2d 512 (S.D.N.Y. 2011).

Professor Roberta Karmel (a former SEC commissioner) has written that the Supreme Court's new test is producing a raft of litigation, and it is unlikely that consistency in the application of the *Morrison* standard will occur.[7] She points out that *Morrison* wrongly assumed that title to securities purchases and sales passes in a discrete geographical location, ignoring the reality of modern banking and securities transactions.

What about cases brought by the SEC? What about criminal cases brought by the United States? *United States v. Vilar*, 729 F.3d 62 (2d Cir. 2013), held that *Morrison* applies to a Section 10(b) criminal case and reaffirmed the "irrevocable liability within the United States" test in *Absolute Activist*. Even though reliance, economic loss, and loss causation need not be proved in criminal cases, that difference does not justify an extraterritorial application of the Exchange Act in a Section 10(b) criminal case.

In *United States v. Georgiou*, 777 F.3d 125 (3d Cir. 2015), the Third Circuit also held that the "irrevocable liability" test applied to criminal securities fraud cases. *But see United States v. Bowman*, 260 U.S. 94 (1922) (Crimes against government caused by fraud can be prosecuted no matter where committed.). Some have argued, citing *Bowman*, that *Vilar* extended *Morrison* further than it should go.[8]

The Various *Vivendi* Cases

In *In re Vivendi Securities Litigation*, 765 F. Supp. 2d 512 (S.D.N.Y. 2011), a class action presided over by Judge Richard Holwell, the plaintiffs' argument after *Morrison* was that ordinary shares were listed in the United States in connection with the ADR program. They were, but not for trading purposes. The court held that cross-listing was irrelevant and said that the Supreme Court must have meant "listed and traded" not just "listed." As we have already seen, Judge Holwell was correct.

In *Liberty Media Corp. v. Vivendi Universal, S.A.*, 874 F. Supp. 2d 169 (S.D.N.Y. 2012), before Judge Scheindlin, shares of Multithematiques, a Vivendi subsidiary, were transferred in France from a French subsidiary of Vivendi to a French subsidiary of Liberty Media. The agreement to do so was signed in Colorado and the signature page was then faxed to and countersigned in New York. The actual exchange of stock took place in France. The court held that "irrevocable liability" was incurred in the United States (because the contract to make the exchange was signed in the United States) and that it did not have to reach the issue of where title was transferred. The agreement was "irrevocable" because it was binding (even though it was later

---

[7] Roberta Karmel, "The Application of Morrison to SEC and Criminal Cases," *N.Y. L. J.*, Oct. 17, 2013.

[8] D. Herz-Roiphe, "Innocent Abroad? *Morrison*, *Vilar* and the Extraterritorial Application of the Exchange Act," 123 *Yale L. J.* 1875 (2014).

changed). The court said that incurring "irrevocable liability" was the same as "entering" into a binding contract and that it did not matter if the contract was later amended. Note that this case was decided before *Porsche*. Would the outcome have been different after *Porsche*?

Current *Morrison* Issues

In *In re Vivendi Securities Litigation*, 838 F.3d 223 (2d Cir. 2016), the Second Circuit affirmed the district court's holding that U.S. shareholders who acquired stock in a three-way merger among three foreign companies did not incur "irrevocable liability" in the United States even though they were present in the United States when they purchased their shares. The court wrote:

> In *Absolute Activist*, we used the concept of irrevocable liability to determine what constitutes a domestic purchase or sale under *Morrison*. We reasoned that when parties to a transaction incur irrevocable liability in the United States, defined as becom[ing] bound to effectuate the transaction or entering into a binding contract to purchase or sell securities, the transaction is domestic and § 10(b) applies.... To the extent that plaintiffs rely on the merger [between Vivendi, Canal Plus and Seagram] as the transaction at issue, the location of the Americans who acquired ordinary shares as a result of the merger, who plaintiffs admit were not parties to it, is not relevant to the question of whether the merger qualifies as a domestic purchase or sale.

The transaction at issue was a complicated one, however, and this passage from the Second Circuit's opinion is not entirely clear. The merger was completed in Europe; shareholders in the United States who had owned Seagram shares before the merger received Vivendi ordinary shares after the merger. That fact alone did not make the transaction domestic, and it did not matter where the receiving shareholders were physically located.

In *In re Petrobras Securities Litigation*, 862 F.3d 250 (2d Cir. 2017), the Second Circuit examined a class action by holders of Petrobras securities and conducted a holistic analysis of the transaction's domestic connections in order to decide whether there were individual issues of fact with respect to who bought or sold stock and how the transactions came about that might predominate over class-wide issues. The court reversed the lower court's decision that there were class-wide issues of domesticity and held instead that "on the available record, the investigation of domesticity appears to be an 'individual question' requiring putative class members to 'present evidence that varies from member to member.'" In making that ruling, the Second Circuit clarified the *Morrison* test, citing as support its own opinion in *City of Pontiac Policemen's & Firemen's Retirement System v. UBS AG*, 752 F.3d: "The mere *listing* on a domestic exchange is not sufficient to establish domesticity if the relevant securities transaction did not *occur* on a domestic exchange" (emphasis in original). The court went further: "The location or residence of the buyer, seller or broker will not necessarily establish the situs of the transaction. Rather, plaintiffs demonstrate the location where irrevocable liability was incurred or legal title transferred by producing evidence 'including, but not limited to, facts concerning the formation of the contracts, the placement of purchase orders, ... or the exchange of money.'"

There have been several recent cases discussing the application of *Morrison* to the trading of ADRs. First, in *Stoyas v. Toshiba Corp.*, 191 F. Supp. 3d 1080 (2016), the district court for the Central District of California held that ADRs traded over the counter did not satisfy *Morrison*'s requirement of trading on a national exchange. The district court also held that "unsponsored" ADRs (i.e., ADRs sold by a depositary bank without any involvement of Toshiba) did not meet the second prong of the *Morrison* test. However, on July 17, 2018, the Ninth Circuit reversed the district court and held that because purchases of ADRs were (or could be) "domestic transactions in other securities," the plaintiffs should be given an opportunity to amend their complaint in order to attempt to allege a domestic violation of the Exchange Act. *Automotive Industries Pension Trust Fund v. Toshiba Corp.*, No. 16-56058.

In *In re Volkswagen "Clean Diesel" Mktg. Sales Practices & Product Liab. Litig.*, 2017 WL 66281 (N.D. Cal. Jan. 4, 2017), *reversed in part after an amended complaint had been filed*, 2017 WL 2798525 (N.D. Cal. June 28, 2017), the court held that the ADRs in that case were not independent from Volkswagen, which had taken steps to make them available to investors in the United States. The depositary agreements were signed in New York and governed by New York law. *Morrison* was therefore satisfied.

One of the consequences of *Morrison* has been the increase in collective (i.e., versions of class) actions outside the United States, especially in EU countries. The Netherlands permits such actions, but only for injunctive or declaratory relief. France allows associations representing consumers or investors to bring an opt-in class action for monetary compensation. The United Kingdom permits some collective actions, but its "loser pays" system makes them generally unsatisfactory. As a result, they are rare.

The End of *Morrison* in SEC Cases?

In Title IX of Dodd-Frank, Congress enacted the Investor Protection Act, which amended Section 27(b) of the 1934 Act. Dodd-Frank Section 929P(b) provides that the district courts shall have jurisdiction of an action brought by the SEC or the United States alleging violations of Section 17(a) of the Securities Act or a violation of any antifraud provision of the 1934 Act involving (1) conduct within the United States that constitutes significant steps in furtherance of the violation, even if the securities transaction occurs outside the United States and involves only foreign investors; or (2) conduct occurring outside the United States that has a foreseeable substantial effect within the United States.

There are corresponding sections for corresponding provisions of the Exchange Act and the Investment Advisers Act. Does this test sound familiar? It is taken from *Bersch v. Drexel Firestone Inc.*, 519 F.2d 974 (2d Cir. 1975). It is the old "conduct and effects" test. This statute applies only to SEC actions, not to private civil actions. This is important.

Is this statute effective in light of *Morrison*? Probably yes, at least for cases brought by the SEC or the Department of Justice. How did that happen?

Congress jumped the gun and wrote that statute while *Morrison* was pending in the Supreme Court but before it was decided. Congress assumed, as did most observers, that the *Morrison* case would either affirm or reject the "conduct or effect" test or at least draw a bright line for lower courts to apply. Few observers expected the court to reject the test entirely.

Morrison was decided on the last day on which the House and Senate conferees considered the two bills. The statute was then passed, without any changes, about a week after the *Morrison* decision came down. In *Morrison*, the Supreme Court held that the issue was not one of jurisdiction, which both *Bersch* and the statute assumed, but one of extraterritorial application of a statute, which is a merits issue. Interestingly, the title of the relevant statutory section is "Extraterritorial Jurisdiction" even though the text of the statute does not explicitly refer to extraterritoriality but instead refers to the "conduct or effect" test for subject matter jurisdiction, which Justice Scalia and the Supreme Court said was not the correct test. There was a plausible argument, therefore, that the statute is not effective because it dealt with subject matter jurisdiction, not extraterritoriality. The language of Dodd-Frank is certainly unclear.[9] In Dodd-Frank, Congress also asked the SEC to make recommendations about changing the law for private civil cases and after eighteen months of study, the SEC passed the ball back to Congress with no recommendation for future legislation.[10]

---

[9] *See* Chaim Levin, "Dodd-Frank, Morrison and Global Securities Transactions," *N.Y. L. J.*, Aug. 19, 2014, p. 4; *see also* Richard Painter, "The Dodd-Frank Extraterritorial Provision: Was it Effective, Needed or Sufficient?" 1 *Harv. Bus. L. Rev.* 196 (2011).

[10] "SEC Study on the Cross-Border Scope of the Private Right of Action Under 10(b) of the Securities Exchange Act of 1934" (April 2012).

Was the Dodd-Frank Act effective in overturning *Morrison* for cases brought by the SEC? In *SEC v. Traffic Monsoon, LLC*, 245 F. Supp. 3d. 1275 (D. Utah Mar. 28, 2017), a district court in Utah held that Dodd-Frank Section 929P(b) gave federal courts jurisdiction under the "conduct and effect" test, even though the "plain language" of the statute did not overturn *Morrison*. On appeal, the Tenth Circuit affirmed the district court, holding that "it is clear to us that Congress undoubtedly intended that the substantive antifraud provisions should apply extraterritorially when the statutory conduct-and-effects test is satisfied." *Scoville v. SEC*, 913 F.3d 1204 (10th Cir. 2019) (This is the appeal of the *Traffic Monsoon* case; the name was changed). In other words, if the "conduct or effect" test could be met, there was extraterritoriality in cases under the 1934 Act brought be the SEC or the Department of Justice.

Traffic Monsoon petitioned for a writ of certiorari in the Supreme Court, in a case styled *Scoville v. SEC*, Docket No. 18-1566, June 20, 2019. (Scoville was the owner of Traffic Monsoon, a Ponzi scheme that sold advertising services to persons outside the United States.) An *amicus* brief was filed in support of the petition by five prominent securities law professors who argued that because the words of the amendment were clear, there was no need to look behind the words to determine whether Congress intended to extend the scope of Section 10(b) extraterritorially even though the words of the amendment did not do so and despite the presumption against territoriality. Nevertheless, the Supreme Court denied the petition for certiorari on November 3, 2019.

The takeaway is simple: The "conduct or effect" test may be alive and well for the SEC and the Department of Justice, but it is probably at the end for private cases. It is highly unlikely—especially given the SEC's failure to take a position on private cases—that the *Morrison* test will ever be reconsidered for private cases.

Post-*Morrison* Filings

What has the effect of *Morrison* been on filings? Not as much as you might think. There has been a fairly large increase in filings against non-U.S. companies, despite *Morrison*. Many of the cases recently filed have been the so-called Chinese Reverse Merger (CRM) cases. In a reverse merger, a private company is merged with a listed and publicly traded "shell" company with little or no operations. In that way, the private firm (here, a Chinese company) can get a U.S. listing without having to go through the expensive disclosures required by an IPO.

This trend is not likely to continue because the rules against reverse mergers have been made stricter. Also, the threat of litigation has deterred many potential reverse mergers.

From 2008 to mid-2012, 85 percent of the filings against Chinese issuers included accounting-related allegations. In 2011, the U.S. Public Company Accounting Oversight Board expressed concern about the quality of the auditing process for Chinese companies that gained U.S. listings through reverse mergers.[11]

Even without taking the CRMs into consideration, the number of filings post-*Morrison* has remained flat. That may be because many of the non-U.S. companies that are being sued may have ADRs in the United States. However, the effect of *Morrison* would be to reduce the scope of the claims and as a result to reduce the settlement amounts.

In cases against non-U.S. companies, there are far fewer allegations of breach of fiduciary duty (15 percent) than there are in cases against U.S. companies (31 percent). These cases typically involve mergers, where the claim is that the directors of the target company breached their fiduciary duty to shareholders by accepting a price that was too low.

Also, cases against non-U.S. companies that allege insider trading are half as likely as are such cases against U.S. companies. Why? Perhaps there are less stringent insider trading laws in other countries.

Settlements in cases against non-U.S. companies are smaller. In 2011, for example, the median settlement against a non-U.S. company was $5 million as compared to $10 million in cases against U.S. companies.

Discovery Under the Hague Convention

The *Hague Convention on the Taking of Evidence in Civil or Commercial Matters* (1970) governs foreign discovery in domestic cases. It allows foreign litigants to take a deposition of an involuntary or voluntary witness before a local judicial authority by means of letters rogatory (Article 1), to take a deposition of a voluntary witness before a diplomatic or consular officer (Article 16), to take a deposition of a voluntary witness before a "person commissioned by the court" (Article 17), or use national internal procedures for litigants in the national courts (Article 27). Letters rogatory pursuant to Federal Rules of Civil Procedure 28(b) may be used but they are subject to the Hague Convention. Parties and their representatives may be present; a judge of the requesting court may also be present (but almost never is). (Article 8.) The "national court" has the discretion under Article 9 to refuse implementation of any procedures that may violate or strongly implicate its sovereign interest.

Some countries, such as France, will not permit the obtaining of pretrial discovery documents. They have blocking statutes that preclude such discovery

[11] "Activity Summary and Audit Implications for Reverse Mergers Involving Companies from the China Region," March 14, 2011.

unless the relevant ministry agrees. But the Supreme Court, in *Societe Nationale Industrielle Aerospatiale v. U.S. District Court for the Southern District of Iowa*, 482 U.S. 522 (U.S. 1987), relegated the French blocking statute to secondary status. The French courts have only once (as far as we know) enforced their own blocking statute. *In re Avocat Christopher X*, Cour de Cassation, Paris, crim. Dec. 12, 2007, Bull.crim. No. 2007-83228. The next year, the French Supreme Court refused to uphold a lower court's refusal to prosecute a violation of the French blocking statute but it reaffirmed that the statute applied to documents located in the United States, so long as there is a French victim who files a complaint. French Supreme Court, Criminal Chamber, Pourvoi no. 06-84.098. The French statute is a criminal statute that criminalizes all evidence gathering that does not strictly follow the Hague Convention procedures. But in *In re Activision Blizzard, Inc. Stockholder Litigation*, 86 A.3d 531 (Del. Ch. 2014), Vice Chancellor J. Travis Laster decided that Delaware's "powerful interest in the efficient and effective handling of disputes involving the internal affairs of a Delaware corporation" outweighs France's "preference for its own method of litigation." He gave defendant Vivendi, Activision Blizzard's parent, an opportunity to use the Hague Convention but only if it did not lead to any delay in Delaware. There may be a distinction between taking a deposition and obtaining documents. Some writers think the Supreme Court needs to give more guidance.[12]

Discovery in Aid of Foreign Arbitrations

In 28 U.S.C. § 1782, a U.S. district court is permitted to order a person residing in the district to give testimony or to produce documents for use in a proceeding in a foreign or international tribunal, including criminal investigations. There is a circuit split on the question whether such an order may be made with respect to a private commercial arbitration abroad. The Fourth and Sixth Circuits hold that it may be, and the Second, Fifth, and Seventh Circuits hold that it may not be. One question is whether a private commercial arbitration is a "foreign tribunal." On March 22, 2021, the Supreme Court granted certiorari to decide the issue in a UK arbitration between Servotronics and Rolls-Royce, arising out of a fire in a Boeing facility during a ground test of a Rolls-Royce engine in Charleston, South Carolina. Boeing sought compensation from Rolls-Royce, and they settled. Thereafter, Rolls-Royce demanded that the manufacturer of a faulty engine valve that caused the fire, Servotronics, pay for the damage. The dispute was sent to arbitration in London. During

---

[12] *See, e.g.*, Pierre Grosdidier, "The Fraud Blocking Statute," website of the Association of Corporate Counsel, August 31, 2014, https://www.acc.com/resources-library/french-blocking-statute-hague-evidence-convention-and-case-law-lessons-french.

the arbitration, Servotronics sued Boeing in Illinois, seeking documents to be used in the arbitration. The Seventh Circuit rejected Servotronics' claim. The Supreme Court will most likely resolve the circuit split.

Chapter 20

The Foreign Corrupt Practices Act

First, an explanation. The Foreign Corrupt Practices Act (FCPA) is not technically speaking a part of the federal scheme of securities regulation or enforcement. However, for reasons that are explained below, the FCPA is enforced against issuers by the SEC and the Department of Justice and against non-issuers only by the DOJ. For that reason, it is necessary to understand the basic framework of the FCPA when studying securities regulation and enforcement.

Background

After more than two years of study and debate, the U.S. Congress, in 1977, passed this country's and the world's first attempt to regulate business conduct with foreign governments in foreign markets, the Foreign Corrupt Practices Act.

The passage of the FCPA was brought about by the revelations of corporate bribery that surfaced during the Watergate scandal and the publicity accompanying some high-profile bribery cases, including the Lockheed scandal in which Lockheed made payments to the Prime Minister of Japan, the husband of the Queen of the Netherlands, and various Italian political parties. The perception in Congress was that such payments were an embarrassment to the United States and, to quote Senator Frank Church, "[W]e cannot close our eyes to this problem. It is no longer sufficient to simply sigh and say that is the way business is done. It is time to treat the issue for what it is: a serious foreign policy problem."[1]

The FCPA had its genesis in the work of the Watergate Special Prosecutor, followed up by the SEC and the Church Committee, a Senate subcommittee on multinational corporations headed by Senator Church. The SEC said in its "Report of the SEC on Questionable and Illegal Corporate Payments and

---

[1] *See generally* Mike Koehler, "The Story of the Foreign Corrupt Practices Act," 73 *Ohio St. L. J.* 929 (2012).

Practices" that it found that "falsification of corporate financial records [was] designed to disguise or conceal the source and application of corporate funds misused for illegal purposes as well as the existence of secret 'slush funds' disbursed outside the normal financial accountability system."[2] The Church subcommittee found that Gulf Oil, Northrop, Mobil Oil, and Lockheed, among others, had made "questionable payments to foreign government officials in connection with a business purpose." Senator William Proxmire said that "I fear that ... many companies will continue paying bribes if they can get away with it because the potential rewards are so great and the risks are minimal.... And so we come to the need for a remedy."

Finding the remedy, however, did not prove easy. Somewhat surprisingly, "the SEC wanted no part in policing the morality of American business or in determining what is an improper foreign corporate payment. Rather the SEC, true to its mission, was focused on ensuring disclosure of material foreign corporate payments to investors by companies subject to its jurisdiction."[3] SEC Chairman Roderick Hills testified before the Senate that "[The SEC] would prefer not to be involved in civil enforcement of such prohibitions ... [T]he enforcement of such provisions does not easily fit within the Commission's mandate."[4] The State Department was similarly reluctant: "We need to move carefully.... [W]e believe it would not be advisable for the United States to try to legislate the limits of permissible conduct by our firms abroad ... It would be not only presumptuous but counterproductive to seek to impose our specific standards in countries with different histories and cultures. The Deputy Legal Advisor of the State Department, Mark Feldman, told a House committee, "[W]e would be opposed to any legislation that would be directed to conduct of U.S. citizens abroad in their relations with foreign officials which is based on a general proposition that U.S. citizens should behave well abroad."[5] The Defense Department was concerned about America's competitive position. General Howard Fish, director of the Defense Security Assistance Agency, testified, "I think it is important that any legislation protect the rights of all concerned. You have to make sure that you protect the competitive

---

[2] U.S. Sec. & Exch. Comm'n, "Report of the Securities and Exchange Commission on Questionable and Illegal Corporate Payments and Practices "(1976), reprinted in *Special Supplement*, Sec. Reg. & L. Rep. (BNA) No. 353 (May 19, 1976).

[3] Koehler, *supra*.

[4] Statement of Roderick Hills, *Foreign Corrupt Practices and Domestic and Foreign Investment Disclosure Hearing Before the S. Comm. On Banking, Hous., and Urban Affairs, 95th Cong.* (1977) 124-125.

[5] *The Activities of American Multinational Corporations Abroad*, Hearings before the Subcomm. on Int'l Econ. Policy of the H. Comm. on Int'l Relations, 94th Cong. (1975), statement of Mark B. Feldman, Deputy Legal Advisor, U.S. Dep't of State.

position of the U.S. firms and the workingman, who is working in these industries."[6] The chair of the Association of the Bar of the City of New York, Robert Von Mehren, testified, "We oppose criminalization." A 1976 report by a Ford administration task force opposed criminalization and favored "systematic and informative reporting" instead. Senator Church summarized the problem as follows: "Our Government has initiated no real concern with this problem.... It prefers to stick its head in the sand and hear no evil, see no evil, and pretend there is no problem."[7]

However, the various U.S. government agencies with relevant responsibility took very different positions on the desirability of such a statute. Secretary of Commerce Elliot L. Richardson testified that "in the bribery area we are moving into uncharted national and international waters in which legislative remedies may be capable of achieving only part of the objectives we seek."[8]

As a result, passage of the FCPA, including both the prohibition of bribery provision and the books and records provision, did not come about until after President Gerald Ford established a "Task Force on Questionable Corporate Payments Abroad" in 1976 (which ultimately rejected the proposal that in addition to full disclosure there should be criminal sanctions) and until after Jimmy Carter, who campaigned against the recommendations of the Ford Task Force, was elected president.

The long legislative history of the FCPA makes it hard to ascertain the precise motivation for the law. Clearly, it was seen as a foreign policy initiative that would in part rectify the damage done by scandals such as the Lockheed scandal. But it was also seen in purely moral terms. This is how Representative Steven Solarz put it: "What is at stake here is really, in a number of significant respects, the reputation of our own country, and I think that we have an obligation to set a standard of honesty and integrity in our business dealings not only at home but also abroad which will be a beacon for the light of integrity for the rest of the world."[9]

Others believed that a strong statute would make it easier for U.S. companies to resist pressures to pay bribes. According to James Weldon, Acting Director, Bureau of Enforcement, the Civil Aeronautics Board, "U.S. corporations may have more success in resisting requests for such payments if such

---

[6] Colloquy between Rep. Edward Biester and General Howard Fish, Director, Defense Security Assistance Agency, H. Subcomm. on Int'l Econ. Policy, H. Comm. on Int'l Relations, 94th Cong. (1975).

[7] Koehler, *supra* at 971.

[8] Koehler, *supra* at 972.

[9] Koehler, *supra* at 944.

payments are unlawful under U.S. law and if there exists some reasonable likelihood of detention and prosecution in the United States."[10]

There is also a strain in the legislative history, especially in the comments made by Senator William Proxmire, that such a law would create an example that other countries "would perforce be constrained to follow" although there does not appear to be a powerful argument that the true motivation of the law was to eliminate bribery entirely in the foreign countries.

The U.S. business community was decidedly mixed. As noted above, some companies thought that such a law would make it easier for them to resist bribery requests, while others thought that the law would put them at a competitive disadvantage.[11]

In any event, the law was passed shortly after Jimmy Carter became president. It criminalized bribery of foreign officials and required full disclosure of the bribe under a "books and records" amendment to the federal securities laws. Although prosecution under the law had a slow beginning, lately it has picked up steam. From 1977 to 1998, there were only twenty-five corporate foreign bribery cases brought. However, from 2000 to 2011 there were 324 violations prosecuted, the vast bulk of which were in 2010.

In May 2010, U.S. Attorney General Eric Holder said that "[s]ince 2004, we have prosecuted 37 different corporations for foreign bribery–related offenses, levying criminal penalties in excess of $1.5 billion.... Also in this time period, we have criminally charged nearly 80 individuals. And the pace is accelerating. Let me be clear, prosecuting individuals is a cornerstone of our enforcement strategy.... The risk of heading to prison is real, from the boardroom to the warehouse."[12]

Why the Joint SEC-DOJ Jurisdiction?

The Ford Task Force opined that "the criminalization approach" to foreign bribes would represent "little more than a policy assertion, for the enforcement of such a law would be very difficult if not impossible. Successful prosecution of offenses would typically depend upon witnesses and information beyond the reach of U.S. judicial process. Other nations, rather than assisting in such prosecutions, might resist cooperation because of considerations of national preference or sovereignty." Its solution was to require disclosure to

---

[10] Statement of James Weldon, Subcomm. on Int'l Econ., Policy, H. Comm. on Int'l Relations, 94th Cong. (1975).

[11] Koehler, *supra* at 975.

[12] Statement of U.S. Attorney General Eric Holder, Organisation for Economic Co-Operation and Development, Paris, France, May 31, 2010.

"supplement current SEC disclosure that would avoid the difficult problems of defining and proving 'bribery.'"[13]

This position gave birth to the "books and records" provisions of the FCPA. The general counsel of the Commerce Department put it like this: "If I give you money, I am going to have to report the payment to the Department of Commerce, perhaps to the SEC, and it will therefore be in the public record ... [and] it is our guess that the extorter will be substantially deterred. We believe that a combination of sunlight and encouragement of other nations to enforce their own laws represents a much more effective way to end the corrupt payments than does direct, unilateral criminalization by this country of actions taking place in foreign jurisdictions." There is also some legislative history to the effect that there was concern that the FCPA, if enforced only by the DOJ, might not survive a constitutional challenge. At the congressional hearings in 1976, for example, Richard Darman, Assistant Secretary for Policy, U.S. Department of Commerce, asked, "What reason is there to enact a provision of law which an overwhelming majority of responsible legal scholars, law enforcement officials, and serious analysts of this issue, view to be essentially unenforceable."[14] In his testimony, Robert Von Mehren, Chair of the Committee on Foreign Payments of the New York City Bar, said that "the writs of our grand juries and courts do not run as to non-United States citizens outside out boundaries."[15]

Yogi Berra once said that "when you come to a fork in the road, take it."[16] In typical Washington fashion, the Congress and President Carter followed Yogi's advice. As a result, the FCPA appears in two places in the U.S. Code, in Title 15, § 78dd-1 (Article 30 of the 1934 Act) (for issuers) and in Title 15 § 78dd-2 (for non-issuer "domestic concerns"). The SEC and the DOJ have joint civil jurisdiction to enforce the FCPA, and only the DOJ has criminal jurisdiction.

The Impact of Global Corruption

There is no question that global corruption exists. The question is what can be done about it. It seems clear that despite good intentions, neither the FCPA nor even more aggressive laws such as the UK's 2010 Bribery Act has

---

13 Koehler, *supra* at 986.

14 Koehler, *supra* at 1000.

15 Koehler, *supra* at 1001.

16 Yogi Berra & Dave Kaplan, *When You Come to a Fork in the Road, TAKE IT!*, Hyperion, 2002.

significantly reduced it.[17] A joint report of the SEC and the DOJ concluded that bribery is bad for business, anti-competitive, leads to distorted prices, and disadvantages honest businesses. Bribery has destructive effects within businesses by undermining employee confidence and raising the cost of doing business. It also has the potential to impact the health, safety, and welfare of humanity if public service and infrastructure projects are being awarded based on self-interest rather than objective analysis of the most qualified provider. And even where awarded to the most qualified in the first instance, corruption may allow the provider to cut corners or perform to lower health and safety standards than are required by contract.[18] The report concluded that "companies that pay bribes to win business ultimately undermine their own long-term interests and the interests of their investors."

About 90 percent of all FCPA enforcement actions against companies involve a third party providing some service to the company, such as a distributor, consultant, customs broker, freight forwarder, tax consultant, political lobbyist, or sales agent. Companies are liable if they were aware that the unlawful actions were "substantially certain" to occur, aware of a "high probability" that they would occur, or where the company consciously avoided knowing or was "willfully blind" to the third party's corrupt conduct.

What the FCPA Prohibits

There are two principal provisions in the FCPA: the anti-bribery provision and the accounting provision.

Anti-Bribery Provision. The FCPA prohibits making any payments, offers, promises to pay or authorize the payment of any money, or offer, gift, promise to give, or authorization of the giving of anything of value made for the purpose of (1) influencing any act or decision of a foreign official in his or

---

[17] A 2019 Report of the United Kingdom's House of Lords Select Committee on the Bribery Act 2010 concluded the Bribery Act "is an excellent piece of legislation which creates offences which are clear and all-embracing" but the actual statistics were disappointing. In 2017, for example, only seven defendants were "proceeded against" in magistrates' courts for violation of Section 1 of the act, of whom only three were found guilty and sentenced. Only nine defendants were "proceeded against" for violations of Section 2 of the act, of whom only six were found guilty, and four of whom received suspended sentences.

[18] A good example of this is the 2019 collapse of the Brumadinho Dam in Brazil in which 259 people died. Twelve million cubic meters of toxic tailings were released. An investigation found that the dam's owner, Vale SA, failed to inspect the dam as required, as did its auditor, TÜV Süd, a German company contracted to inspect the dam. Both companies were charged with crimes, and Vale was required to pay $7 billion to the families of the people killed.

her official capacity, (2) inducing a foreign official to do or omit to do any act in violation of the lawful duty of such official, (3) securing any improper advantage, or (4) inducing a foreign official to use his or her influence with a foreign government or instrumentality thereof to affect or influence an act or decision of such government or instrumentality. The payment, offer, or promise must be made in order to assist in obtaining or retaining business for or with, or directing business to, any person. This last provision is known as the "business purpose" test and is broadly interpreted. In one of the few litigated cases, *United States v. Kay*, 359 F.3d 738 (5th Cir. 2004), the court held that bribes paid to obtain favorable tax treatment that reduced a company's customs duties and sales taxes on imports could constitute payments made to "obtain or retain" business. In addition, to violate the FCPA, the offer, promise, or payment must be made "corruptly." This means that the offer, promise, or payment must be intended to induce the recipient to misuse his or her official position. However, a violation does not require that the intended corrupt act be successful. An attempt is sufficient for a violation.

Criminal liability under the anti-bribery provision requires that the act be "willful." This is a more stringent requirement than the "corrupt intent" requirement for civil liability. Willfulness is not defined by the FCPA but in criminal law generally willfulness means "voluntary and with a bad purpose." *Bryan v. United States*, 524 U.S. 184 (1998). Courts have also held that the violator need not even be aware of the existence of the FCPA to violate it.

"Anything of value" is broadly interpreted and might include giving gifts such as fur coats, travel to sporting events, expensive rounds of golf, and trips to Disney World. Payments and gifts to third parties may also violate the FCPA.

A "foreign official" includes any officer or employee of a foreign government, or any department, agency, or instrumentality thereof, or of a public international organization, or any person acting in an official capacity for or on behalf of such government or department, agency, instrumentality, or organization. This includes low-ranking employees. Examples include officials of government-owned banks, physicians in government-owned hospitals, and customs officials.

An "instrumentality" of a foreign government is broadly defined to include state-owned and state-controlled entities that are not part of the government entity itself but that are entities that the government "treats as its own." *See United States v. Esquenazi*, 752 U.S. 912 (11th Cir. 2014), *cert. denied*, 83 U.S.L.W. 3189 (U.S. Oct. 6, 2014).

The act prohibits payments to foreign officials, not to foreign governments.

This provision includes both criminal and civil liability and is enforced against both issuers and non-issuers. The criminal aiding and abetting statute applies. Individuals and companies may be liable. For criminal cases, the general federal five-year statute of limitations applies.

"Facilitating payments" are excluded from the reach of the FCPA anti-bribery prohibition. What is a "facilitating payment"? In general, it is a payment to expedite or secure the performance of a routine governmental action. These payments are sometimes called "grease payments." The distinction between facilitating payments and prohibited bribes is not always easy to determine. For that reason, most companies prohibit the making of "facilitating payments."

The FCPA anti-bribery prohibition does not apply in cases of extortion or duress because true extortionate demands under imminent threat of physical harm cannot be said to have been made with corrupt intent or for the purpose of obtaining or retaining business.[19]

The Accounting Provisions. These include the "books and records" provision and the "internal controls" provision.

- *Books and Records.* Issuers are required to keep books, records, and accounts that, in reasonable detail, accurately and fairly reflect the transactions and dispositions of the assets of the issuer. "In reasonable detail" means that the issuer's records should reflect transactions in accordance with accepted methods of recording economic events and effectively prevent off-the-books slush funds and payment of bribes. (There is no generally accepted accounting category for the payment of bribes.) There is no materiality threshold. Reasonable detail also means sufficient to satisfy prudent officials in the conduct of their own affairs.
- *Internal Controls.* Under this provision, issuers are required to devise and maintain a system of internal accounting controls sufficient to provide reasonable assurances that:
  - transactions are executed in accordance with management's general or specific authorizations;
  - transactions are recorded as necessary to permit preparation of financial statements in conformity with generally accepted accounting principles or any other criteria applied to such statements and to maintain accountability for assets;
  - access to assets is permitted only in accordance with management's general or specific authorizations; and
  - the recorded accountability for assets is compared with the existing assets at reasonable intervals and appropriate action is taken with respect to any differences.

---

[19] SEC & DOJ, "A Resource Guide to the U.S. Foreign Corrupt Practices Act," Second Edition, 2020.

- This requirement gives companies flexibility to develop an appropriate system of controls that is appropriate to their needs and circumstances.
- Section 13(a) of the 1934 Act, which requires the filing of periodic reports, requires the disclosure of payments associated with the bribery of foreign officials and the failure to do so may result in a violation of Section 10(b).
- There are several requirements of the Sarbanes-Oxley Act of 2002 that may have FCPA implications, including its requirements that principal officers certify the integrity of company financial reports; that issuers report on the management's conclusion with respect to the effectiveness of the company's internal controls; and that prohibit the altering or destroying of records, documents, and tangible objects with the intent to obstruct or impede an actual or potential federal investigation.

There is potential criminal liability in addition to civil liability for violating the accounting provisions of the FCPA, but criminal cases are brought only by the DOJ. Both individuals and corporations may be liable. Under the federal civil and criminal laws, aiding and abetting liability is also possible

Section 10A of the 1934 Act requires that independent auditors who discover illegal acts, such as the payment of bribes to domestic or foreign officials, are required to report such acts to appropriate levels within the company and if the company fails to take the appropriate action, to notify the SEC.

Affirmative Defenses

There are two affirmative defenses to FCPA violations: First, that the money was spent as a part of demonstrating a product or service or performing a contractual obligation. Second, that the payment was lawful under written laws of the foreign country. However, this second defense is essentially dead. It is highly unlikely that the written laws of any foreign country affirmatively permit the payment of bribes. *See United States v. Kozeny*, 582 F. Supp. 2d 667 (S.D.N.Y. 2008); *aff'd*, 667 F.3d 122 (2d Cir. 2011).

Discovery of FCPA Violations and Dealing With the SEC and the DOJ

The majority of (in fact nearly all) FCPA cases are settled and do not result either in a trial, a civil verdict, or a criminal conviction. Most violations are discovered by the companies themselves, often during due diligence performed in connection with a proposed merger or acquisition or when investigating whistleblower complaints. These issues must be considered:

- Does the merger agreement deal with FCPA violations?
- Are red flags discovered during due diligence, such as:
  - cash payments to third parties,
  - unusually large commissions to agents or large discounts to distributors,
  - undocumented payments or payments made for work that cannot be substantiated,
  - the agent or consultant has no relevant experience,
  - the third party is closely associated with a foreign official,
  - the third party is recommended or requested by a foreign official,
  - the third party is a shell company incorporated in an offshore jurisdiction, and
  - the third-party requests payment to an offshore bank account.[20]
- Will the deal be terminated if a violation is discovered?
- Is there a post-termination remediation process?
- What if post-closing violations are discovered?

If there are any such issues, the participants may take advantage of the DOJ Opinion Process, pursuant to which the DOJ will entertain requests for opinions in anticipation of a potential acquisition. *See, e.g.*, DOJ Opinion Release 08-02.

The DOJ publishes a *Resource Guide to the U.S. Foreign Corrupt Practices Act* that provides that, where a company voluntarily self-discloses misconduct, fully cooperates, and timely and appropriately remediates, there will be a presumption that the DOJ will decline prosecution absent aggravating circumstances. A public website reports DOJ declinations. In cases where the company does not voluntarily self-disclose but later fully cooperates, the department will recommend a 25 percent reduction from the low end of the sentencing guidelines. Full cooperation could include production of documents and voluntary waiver of the attorney-client privilege.[21]

---

[20] With thanks to Miller Canfield, "Record Level of FCPA Enforcement in 2020 Highlights Key Risk Areas," February 22, 2021, https://www.millercanfield.com/resources-FCPA-Key-Risk-Areas.html.

[21] https://www.justice.gov/criminal-fraud/fcpa-resource-guide.

The SEC in 2001 published a similar framework for evaluating cooperation.[22] In 2010, the SEC announced a new cooperation program for individuals in which the SEC considers four factors:

1. the assistance provided by the cooperating individual in the SEC's investigation,
2. the importance of the matter,
3. the societal interest in ensuring that the cooperating individual is held accountable for misconduct, and
4. the appropriateness of a cooperation credit in light of the profile of the cooperating individual.

Both the SEC and the DOJ have corporate compliance programs in which they evaluate whether a company's compliance program is well designed, applied in good faith, and works in practice.

Consequences of Violations of the FCPA

There are several possible consequences of a violation:

- *Criminal penalties.* Corporations are subject to a fine of up to $2 million and individuals are subject to a fine of up to $5 million and up to twenty years imprisonment. Under the Alternative Fines Act, the fines may be significantly higher. The Sentencing Guidelines apply.
- *Civil penalties.* For anti-bribery violations, civil penalties can be up to $21,400 per violation and may include forfeiture and disgorgement. Violations of the accounting provisions may result in fines up to $192,768 for individuals and up to $963,837 for corporations. It should be noted that these statutory penalties are almost meaningless when the Sentencing Guidelines are applied and the SEC obtains disgorgement. Penalties may also include suspension and debarment. In 2020, corporate fines and penalties levied by the Justice Department and the SEC totaled $2.78 billion, a record.
- *Settlement.* The most common form of resolution, by far, is an agreed-upon settlement. Some of these can be substantial. For example, the Siemens settlement was $1.6 billion, not counting the $50 million that Siemens spent for lawyers who conducted the

[22] "Report of Investigation Pursuant to Section 21(a) of the Securities Exchange Act of 1934 and Commission Statement on the Relationship of Cooperation to Agency Enforcement Decisions" (often referred to as the Seaboard Report).

investigation. BAE paid a settlement of $400 million, and Halliburton paid $579 million, in addition to remedial undertakings such as future reporting to the SEC/DOJ and/or compliance monitors.

Recent Examples

In January 2021, the DOJ announced a settlement with Deutsche Bank AG of a years-long investigation into bribery.[23] In a criminal case brought by the U.S. Attorney for the Eastern District of New York, the prosecutors alleged that Deutsche Bank had covered up bribes paid to third-party intermediaries called "business development consultants" (BDCs) who had access to foreign officials who were decision makers for potential business ventures in Saudi Arabia, Abu Dhabi, and Italy. Deutsche Bank profited by about $35 million from the BDCs' efforts. The BDCs managed hundreds of millions of dollars for the Saudi royal family. Deutsche Bank recorded the payments to the BDCs as "referral fees" that were paid to a shell company in the British Virgin Islands. The bank also paid millions to a BCD in Abu Dhabi that was a proxy for a sovereign-wealth fund official, including the financing of a mega-yacht. In the settlement, Deutsche Bank paid $79 million in criminal penalties. In a related matter with the SEC, Deutsche Bank paid $43 million in disgorgement and pre-judgment interest.

In December 2020, Halliburton agreed to pay a settlement of $29 million to the SEC in a case alleging payments to a former employee in Angola who was a friend of a government official who controlled the local-contracting requirement.[24] Angola required the use of local suppliers for a minimum percentage of contract value in contracts with the government. Because of evidentiary difficulties, the SEC charged a books and records violation, not a violation of the anti-bribery section of the FCPA. Halliburton had allegedly ignored its internal requirements for competitive bidding and entered into a temporary consulting services agreement with the former employee in violation of company procedures. Of interest is that the SEC settlement order went far beyond accounting controls and included other business controls such as procurement policies.

In 2020, Airbus entered into a deferred prosecution agreement with the Department of Justice and agreed to pay combined penalties of nearly $4 billion, although the DOJ agreed to credit a portion of the amount the company

---

[23] https://www.justice.gov/opa/pr/deutsche-bank-agrees-pay-over-130-million-resolve-foreign-corrupt-practices-act-and-fraud.

[24] https://www.sec.gov/news/press-release/2017-133.

paid to a French investigative agency, the Parquet National Financier.[25] Airbus had been charged with conspiracy to violate the FCPA, the Arms Export Control Act, and the International Traffic in Arms Regulations. Airbus had used third-party business partners to bribe government officials in multiple countries around the world, in order to win business from both private companies and entities that were state-owned or state-controlled. When the settlement was announced, the DOJ stated that the resolution with Airbus was reached "based on the voluntary and timely nature of its disclosure to the department as well as the Company's cooperation and remediation."

---

[25] https://www.justice.gov/opa/pr/airbus-agrees-pay-over-39-billion-global-penalties-resolve-foreign-bribery-and-itar-case.

Chapter 21

Regulating Fintech: Cryptocurrencies and Digital Assets[1]

The modern world of cryptocurrencies and digital assets had its beginning with the fall of Lehman Brothers during the 2008 financial crisis. One enterprising person (the word "person" is used advisedly because we don't really know whether it was one or more than one person or even an entity, not a person) who called "himself" Satoshi Nakamoto, invented something called "Bitcoin."[2] The ostensible concern was that the existing global financial system was failing and that something was needed to replace it. Whether Lehman was failing in fact, the events of 2008 were sufficient to prompt a serious look at the errors of the system and to propose an alternative. So-called fiat currency was in jeopardy.

Nakamoto's idea was to create an alternate financial system that did not rely on governments. One component of his idea was to create a network of computers that would remember financial transactions and to create a new currency called "Bitcoin." In preexisting financial systems, currencies either had intrinsic value, such as those built on gold and silver, or government backing, such as the American dollar. Nakamoto's Bitcoin would be neither of those.

However, pre-existing systems also enabled the growth of capital and technological innovation. The practice of buying stocks on margin was at first an engine of growth in the securities market and then fuel for the Crash of 1929

[1] Much of the material in this chapter is inspired by *Fintech Law in a Nutshell*, (West Academic Publishing) (2020), written by my Georgetown Law colleague and former Cravath lawyer Professor Chris Brummer.

[2] In January 2021, the London Court of Appeal reinstated a libel case brought by Craig Wright against Magnus Granath who challenged Wright's claim that he was in fact Satoshi Nakamoto. A similar case in the United States over who owns Bitcoin is headed for trial in federal district court in Florida.

and the resulting Depression. The ensuing Securities Act of 1933 required comprehensive disclosures by companies wishing to sell their securities to investors and to update the disclosures periodically. As we saw in Chapter 2, the definition of "securities" the sale of which would require that disclosure has been somewhat difficult to apply and, as we will see, is now at the heart of the dispute over whether cryptocurrencies and digital assets are "securities" the sale of which would be governed by the federal securities laws.

Fintech is as much a creature of the explosion of the world of personal computers beginning in the late 1980s as it is a creature of the 2008 financial collapse. Computers became inexpensive, ubiquitous, and, most important, easy to use. Electronic exchanges replaced traditional stock markets and information was exchanged at lightening speeds. Michael Lewis's *Flash Boys*[3] is but one of many chronicles of the change. Another consequence of the computer revolution was the rise of securitization, in which assets were pooled and prospective cash flows could be estimated by computers, and lenders could buy interests in the pools at whatever level of risk they deemed appropriate for their needs, thereby displacing investment advisers. Similarly, credit default swaps—basically insurance offered to creditors based on the perceived risk of default by borrowers—used computers to determine the risk, and electronic trading systems were developed to facilitate trading of over-the-counter derivatives based on the swaps. The oversight of the Commodities Futures Trading Commission (CFTC) had been significantly reduced, but the 2008 financial crisis led to a renewed effort toward more robust government intervention.[4] Swaps, in particular, were subjected to more oversight.

Fintech thus came at a most auspicious time. The overseers were busy regulating swaps and securitizations, and they missed the birth and significance of fintech. The emergence of the internet allowed the creation of far more data and the creation of networked communities. New sources of data were available; automation and machine learning enabled much faster transactions; artificial intelligence more and more mimicked human features of logic and deduction. This led to the use of artificial intelligence in creating blockchain operating systems, and cryptocurrencies can be preprogrammed to specify the conditions under which payments should take place.

Fintech is based largely on small start-ups that have more expertise in technology than they do in finance. Using cryptocurrencies and blockchains, incumbent financial institutions can settle payments for customer accounts faster and less expensively. But, because fintech firms are young and untested, they present unique challenges for agencies such as the SEC, which regulates

---

[3] Michael Lewis, *The Flash Boys: A Wall Street Revolt* (W.W. Norton) (2014).

[4] The CFTC does not in fact regulate currency, only the derivatives based on currencies.

the registration of securities and the CFTC, which regulates currency derivatives. The SEC, for example—at least prior to the new *Ripple* litigation—has been unable to decide whether cryptocurrencies and digital assets were securities that it could regulate. We will discuss this further below.

What Types of Regulation Are Available to Federal Regulators?

Before that question is answered, it is worth considering the types of regulation that might fulfill the regulators' charge of protecting investors. That is not an easy question to answer; in fact, it is not even clear that persons who buy cryptocurrencies and digital assets are even "investors" in the traditional sense. In the typical "investment contract" the "investor" contributes money to a common enterprise in the expectation of profit derived from the entrepreneurial or managerial efforts of others. Why should they need the protection of the federal government, and if they do, what type of protection would that be?

One way regulators can decide what types of regulation are appropriate is the creation of pilot programs and regulatory "sandboxes" in which regulations can be tested. But such pilot programs are difficult to create and assess. Georgetown University Law Professor Chris Brummer uses the SEC's 2016 pilot program on "tick sizes" (the price increments at which stocks are bought and sold) as an example of the difficulty of creating and evaluating pilot programs.

What, Exactly, Is Fintech?

Brummer has concluded that fintech is a term of art that describes "a confluence of technologies applied in financial markets to facilitate lending, payment, investments and capital markets operations." That may appear to be a disappointing definition—perhaps of necessity—because it does not really define those technologies and without such a definition, it is nearly impossible to ascertain whether and, if so, what type of regulation is called for. But it is the best definition that we have at the moment. Some technological innovations, such as "crowdfunding," are relatively easy to identify and to regulate for the protection of users and investors. But others, such as decentralized autonomous organizations, are more difficult to regulate.

What, Exactly, Are "Cryptocurrencies and Blockchains"?

Similarly, some innovations, such as "digital assets," are nearly impossible to define, much less regulate. Brummer's definition of "cryptography," for example, "refers to algorithmic techniques used to protect information by encrypting it in formats accessible to individuals only if they possess a special key." A simpler way to describe that may be "you cannot see what is in my wallet unless you say the secret word." I would define a cryptocurrency as an intangible digital "something" that is encrypted and that can be used a medium of exchange that is separate from any other typical financial institution or entity. One of the claimed advantages of cryptocurrencies and other digital assets is that they claim independence from banks and regulatory agencies. Cryptocurrencies are traded over a network that uses peer-to-peer technology in order to eliminate any outside interference or regulation.

One way to understand these innovations is to understand how networks work. In general, networks share information between and among parties that have no relationship with each other. A principal problem with networks is the issue of "trust." How do parties with no relationship establish trust? Normally, a third-party intermediary who acts as a trusted recordkeeper establishes that trust. For example, if I need to know who you are, I can "trust" the government to tell me. If I need to know whether you have enough money, I can "trust" your bank or credit card company to tell me. This is called a "centralized" approach in which the centralized intermediary acts as the "single source of truth." There are obvious downsides to such a system, not the least of which is the opportunity for hackers to obtain access to the central repository of all information. But how could one maintain a "single source of truth" without a "single point of failure or control"? The answer? "Distribute." In a distributed network, there is no single point of failure.

A "distributed ledger" is a database in which every participant in the system owns his or her own copy of the data, and the system is managed by "consensus." These are sometimes called "peer-to-peer" networks because participants can communicate with each other without the verification of an outside entity. Instead, transactions are verified by a "consensus" in which participants will independently verify the output. Each participant updates its own copy of the data according to a globally agreed-upon set of rules, and the "true" version is the one that most participants have "agreed" to. Once agreed to, the output becomes a "block." Changes are recorded as new entries and old entries are never deleted or changed. Once an entry is made to the database, it is practically impossible to remove or change. It is "immutable." The network stores records that are confirmed through a peer-to-peer network of computers. A "blockchain" is a special kind of distributed ledger in which transactions are linked together and in which transactions are initiated directly by an owner via a private key. They are described further below.

"Digital assets" are intangible assets with respect to which the definitive record of ownership is maintained on a blockchain. They are not necessarily currencies. But they are sometimes used as a medium of exchange or keys for unlocking online services or—and here is a major problem—consideration given to investors who invest their capital in certain digital ventures. "Smart contracts" are sometimes stored on blockchains. They are immutable and are automatically executed in a decentralized way by each participant in the network independently. This results in a level of confidence and certainty not possible by existing traditional automation techniques.

Blockchains are not necessarily a silver bullet. They are inefficient due to required redundancy, and they are vulnerable to hacking and unintentional coding errors.

Initial Coin Offerings (ICOs) (sometimes called "token sales") are the sale of a newly created cryptoasset directly to investors as a means of raising capital for new or existing businesses or projects. Tokens offered in such offerings can be assigned any combination of rights or entitlements. They are sometimes traded via secondary markets.

Digital assets and cryptocurrencies can be used as currencies but unlike traditional currencies, they have no physical form. Use of digital assets and other cryptocurrencies as currencies is entirely voluntary. It should be noted that some countries restrict the transacting in cryptocurrencies and some impose jail sentences for their use. Examples are China, Saudi Arabia, Egypt, Zambia, Mexico, Bangladesh, Vietnam, Morocco, Algeria, Bolivia, Ecuador, and Nepal.[5]

Digital assets may also be used as utility tokens that permit access to certain encrypted services or systems or as digital tokens that serve as consideration for investments the same way that people receive stocks and bonds for their investments. That definition, of course, suggests the need for SEC regulation of digital assets as securities. The SEC's 2017 report on the results of its investigation of "The DAO" is a through illustrative guide to the thicket of digital assets and the regulatory issues that they pose.

Our discussion of cryptocurrencies and digital assets requires some definitions:

- Some digital currencies such as blockchain and Ethereum's Ether are used as currencies. Historically, currencies have either been things of value, such as gold and silver or proxies, such as paper bills, for things of value held by government entities, called "fiat currencies." Currencies traditionally fulfill three objectives: a unit of account, a medium of exchange, and a store of value. Currencies, especially fiat currencies, tend to retain their value. Digital currencies such as blockchain can be used to buy goods and

[5] BDO, Cryptocurrency: The Top Things You Need to Know, https://www.bdo.com/insights/assurance/financial-reporting/cryptocurrency-the-top-things-you-need-to-know.

services such as coffee at the local Starbucks. When used in that fashion digital currencies generally present no securities law issues.

- Digital "coins" or "tokens" have no intrinsic value and are not backed by any governmental entity. Their values come from those who use them. But they have uses beyond that of a currency; they can be used to unlock and gain access to digital systems such as a video game. Used in that sense, they are called "utility tokens." But they can also be used as markers in return for an investment, very much like a stock certificate is a "marker" for an investment in a corporation.
- Transactions in digital assets and cryptocurrencies are recorded in digital ledgers that consist of databases that store the records of those who transact in the cryptocurrencies or digital assets. The digital ledgers are themselves stored in peer-to-peer networks that can be accessed by the network users. A well-known type of such a digital ledger is a blockchain. A blockchain tracks information and transactions engaged in by pseudonymous participants in "blocks" of information instead of recording them one at a time. There are rules that determine when and how new "blocks" can be added to preexisting ones to form a "chain" of blocks. One of those rules is called a "hash," which enables participants in the network to verify that their encrypted information has not been—and cannot be—manipulated. In the Bitcoin blockchain, new blocks of information can be created every ten minutes; in the Ethereum blockchain, a block is created every ten seconds. The rules as to when information can be added to a blockchain are called a "consensus mechanism." The person who wishes to use the blockchain must provide a valid cryptographic "hash" or solve a series of cryptographic problems. When that is performed correctly, the user receives a reward in the form of a digital asset "coin" for "mining" the system. This operation is called "proof of work." In other systems, the user is empowered to form new "blocks" by ownership of a certain number of digital asset tokens. This is called a "proof of stake" system, and such systems are called "forged" or "minted" when new blocks are added, not "mined."
- A "fork" occurs when the rules used to verify transactions are changed. A "soft fork" occurs when the rules are tightened; a "hard fork" occurs when the rules are loosened. If the fork occurs with respect to a coin, the coin using the old rule set is called the "original coin" and the coin using the new ruleset is called the "forked coin."

- A "chainsplit" occurs where two blockchains, one using the old set of rules and one using a new set of rules with re-written software, exist simultaneously. All "forks" result in "chainsplits." If the fork is a "hard fork," then the split will be permanent and previous blocks or transactions will be considered valid or invalid, depending on the software.
- In August 2017, Bitcoin hard forked into Bitcoin (BTC) and Bitcoin Cash (BCH).
- Ethereum hard forked after a hack, and the forked Ethereum became the standard and the original Ethereum became known as Ethereum Classic.
- Do forks result in taxable realizations? Probably not, if they merely result in a persistent chainsplit, since the fork merely changes one piece of paper for another. But this is a difficult concept to apply. The IRS has stated that cryptocurrencies should be treated and subject to tax treatment as if they were property, rather than currencies.
- "Smart contracts" are agreements expressed as computer code so that the agreement executes itself. It can be defined as an "agreement between two or more parties for an automated, independent commercial result from the satisfaction or non-satisfaction determined objectively through code, or a specific factual condition." Smart contracts can result in lower transaction costs and improved trust. There are challenges for mainstream adoption, including negotiating contracts written in computer codes, parole evidence issues, risk allocation for cyber security, and user interfaces.

Three Current Cryptocurrency-Digital Asset Systems

Bitcoin. As noted above, this was the first and largest digital asset provider. It uses a distributed ledger technology called Bitcoin blockchain. Assets are transferred using public and private keys, which are algorithms. Bitcoins can be used as payment but because the system is slower than a credit card payment, it is generally not satisfactory. But when they are used, the transactions become final in minutes. The value of Bitcoins has fluctuated a great deal. There is a cap of 21 million Bitcoins.

Ethereum. This was created in 2014 by a Russian-born Canadian and was supported by a not-for-profit foundation that he formed. It also uses blocks to store information. Its coins are called "Ether" (or in fractions of Ether called "gas"). Its users can create "smart contracts" by programming the system to transfer digital assets when certain conditions, such as dates or the rendering of a service, are satisfied. Users can create applications on top of the Ethereum blockchain, just like the App Store. There is no cap on the number of Ethers that are possible.

XRP. This is a network that is similar in many respects to Bitcoin and Ethereum, but it permits its users to choose a set of "validators" who make proposals for projects that are voted on until a consensus is achieved. There are 150 validators. XRP is a creation of Ripple Labs Inc., which controls seven validators and holds 6.5 billion XRPs plus an escrow account of additional XRPs. Each month, 1 billion XRPs are released and made available to market makers for sale to institutional investors. XRPs can be used as a bridge between fiat currencies, and the owners of Ripple hope to make a profit from their enterprise.

The Regulatory Question: Are These Cryptocurrencies and Digital Assets "Securities" That Must Be Regulated?

As we have seen in Chapter 2, the Supreme Court's *Howey* test for what constitutes a security has, with some slight interpretations and modifications, been the guiding test for more than seventy years. Basically, it requires the investment of money in a common enterprise with the expectation of profit due to the efforts of others. In an address during the SEC's Securities Enforcement Forum 2021 webcast on November 4, 2021, SEC Chair Gary Gensler recalled the *Howey* test and called on lawyers to advise their crypto clients to register. "Think about that Supreme Court test, the *Howey* test, then get them to come in, get them to register."[6] But the question is not as simple as Gensler made it seem. In the typical digital asset scheme such as those described above, there is the investment of money. But the "common enterprise" test may or may not be met, depending on the structure of the digital system. And the "from the efforts of others" test is, most of the time, not met because there is no common entity that generates digital assets and there is no central issuer because the assets are created by "miners." Bitcoin is a good example of such a system.

In the Ethereum system, by contrast, there was an investment of money, and the Ethereum Foundation, the creator of Ethereum, promised to create a network that would reward its users with digital asset tokens. However, as the system evolved, the Ether's use eventually depended on the ingenuity of independent software developers that made it more like a commodity. In

---

[6] Al Barbarino, "Gensler to Attys: Don't Help Crypto Cos. Hide From the SEC," Law360, November 4, 2021, https://www.law360.com/articles/1437927.

a well-known 2018 address titled "When Howey Met Gary (Plastic[7])," SEC Commissioner William Hinman said that although Ether may have been a security when created, it no longer was: "Current offers and sales of Ether are not securities transactions."

Professor Brummer pointed out that Ripple's XRP was closer to a true security. He might have been prescient. Ripple's XRP is in fact currently the target of a lawsuit brought by the SEC in 2020 in the U.S. District Court for the Southern District of New York alleging that it was a security and that its issue should have been the subject of a registration statement under Section 5 of the 1933 Securities Act.[8] This case is described further below.

The Decentralized Autonomous Organization

The DAO is the best current example of a digital asset that has been found to be a security under the federal securities laws. Although the SEC, after investigation, decided not to pursue an enforcement action against The DAO, it issued a report in July 2017 that described in some detail—some of it hard to understand—why the SEC had nevertheless concluded that DAO Tokens were securities that should have been registered with the SEC pursuant to Section 5 of the 1933 Securities Act.

The DAO was an unincorporated organization created by a German corporation, Slock.it UG, as a "virtual" organization. It had no physical presence. It offered units called "DAO Tokens" in exchange for Ether (from Ethereum) through a DAO block on the Ethereum blockchain. Tokens with a value of about $150 million in U.S. dollars were ultimately distributed.

The purpose of The DAO was to use technology to supplant traditional mechanisms of corporate governance and management by formulating digital "rules" based on a corporation's bylaws or imposed by applicable corporate law. The rules, in the form of "smart contracts," would solve governance issues.

The DAO was created through a "crowdfunding contract" pursuant to which users would exchange Ethers for DAO Tokens, described by the founders as similar to "buying shares in a company and getting ... dividends." All "investors" would be able to vote on proposals that should be undertaken by The DAO and placed on a "whitelist" of such proposals that had been

[7] This is a reference to *Gary Plastic Packaging Corp. v. Merrill Lynch, Pierce, Fenner & Smith*, 756 F.2d 230 (2d Cir. 1985) (if otherwise exempt CD is sold in a way that caused expectation of profit from broker, it can become a security).

[8] On November 16, 2021, Ripple's CEO Brad Garlinghouse argued that digital assets should fall under the regulatory purview of the Commodity Futures Trading Commission, not the SEC. Elise Hansen, "Ripple Labs Wants Smaller Role for SEC in Crypto Oversight," Law360, November 16, 2021, https://www.law360.com/articles/1441008.

submitted by "Contractors" that could provide the Token-holders a return on their investments and that were approved by the Token-holders.[9] A board of "Curators" appointed by Slock.it would then review the proposals, and its approval was required before the proposals were submitted for a vote.

There was a secondary market for DAO Tokens but it was threatened by an attack on the DAO system by hackers who exploited a flaw in its software and that resulted in a "hard fork" imposed by the Ethereum blockchain in order to protect those DAO Token-holders who had already invested. Platforms could receive orders for DAO Tokens from non-Platform customers and execute buy and sell transactions.

The SEC concluded that the DAO Tokens were securities that should have been registered before they were sold. The SEC applied the traditional *Howey* test, finding that the investors invested money, with a reasonable expectation of profits, derived from the managerial efforts of others, in a common enterprise. The SEC reminded readers that the definition of a security was "a flexible rather than a static principle" and that "form should be disregarded for substance."

> The emphasis should be on economic realities underlying a transaction, and not on the name appended thereto. Those who offer and sell securities in the United States must comply with the federal securities laws, including the requirement to register with the Commission or to qualify for an exemption from the registration requirements of the federal securities laws. The registration requirements are designed to provide investors with procedural protections and material information necessary to make informed investment decisions. These requirements apply to those who offer and sell securities in the United States, regardless whether the issuing entity is a traditional company or a decentralized autonomous organization, regardless whether those securities are purchased using U.S. dollars or virtual currencies, and regardless whether they are distributed in certificated form or through distributed ledger technology.

The clear warning set forth in the SEC's DAO Report has laid down a clear marker and it will be interesting to see whether it can be enforced, as the SEC has chosen to attempt to do in the pending *Ripple* litigation in New York.

Two years after the SEC's DAO Report, its staff issued a "Framework for 'Investment Contract' Analysis of Digital Assets." That report urged those who were considering an Initial Coin Offering or otherwise engaging in the offer, sale, or distribution of a digital asset to consider whether the federal securities laws apply. The report then reviewed the Supreme Court's *Howey*

[9] Because of a flaw in the structure, the voting was tilted in favor of "yes" votes.

case that set forth four tests for whether an investment contract is a security, but it reminded readers that "these factors are not intended to be exhaustive in evaluating whether a digital asset is an investment contract or any other type of security, and no single factor is determinative." In other words, be forewarned and be careful.

SEC v. Ripple Labs

On December 22, 2020, nearly two years after the SEC's "Investment Contract Analysis" was issued, the SEC sued Ripple Labs and two of its senior executives for selling 14.6 billion XRP tokens without filing a registration statement. The complaint, filed in the U.S. Court for the Southern District of New York, alleged that the defendants were told by their law firm in 2012 that the XRP tokens might be considered "investment contracts" and thus securities, and the defendants were advised to consult with the SEC. Nevertheless, the defendants did not heed the legal advice, did not consult with the SEC, and continued to market the tokens. The complaint, which is long and detailed (seventy-one pages) follows the *Howey* path in alleging that the tokens met the four elements of the *Howey* test and were investment contracts, not currencies. At issue is something called an "XRP," units (of something) that were marketed to purchasers who wished "to engage in speculative investment trading." They were related in some fashion to something called the "XRP Ledger," which "operates as a peer-to-peer database, spread across a network of computers that records data respecting transactions." Each server on the network evaluates the proposed transactions from a subset of servers it trusts, known as the server's "unique node list." The company that sold the XRPs was a subsidiary of Ripple Labs, and it owned 80 percent of the outstanding XRPs. The founders owned the remaining 20 percent. Lacking financing, the owners of Ripple decided to sell XRPs to finance its operations. Purchasers were told that the XRPs were a "speculative investment." The Ripple owners acknowledged that the XRPs had some "securities-type characteristics." If you are confused by this, you are not alone. One of Ripple's lawyers, Andrew Ceresney, formerly the SEC's Director of Enforcement, said that the SEC's complaint "stretches *Howey* beyond recognition."

The complaint alleged, *inter alia*, that Ripple's founders control the enterprise, and its users expect to receive a profit from their work and managerial expertise. The case is in its early stages; Ripple's lawyers have succeeded in getting discovery from the SEC about its internal debates with respect to whether digital assets were "securities." In a virtually unheard of turn of events, in April 2021, the U.S. Magistrate Judge who was handling discovery issues, Judge Sarah Netburn, granted the defendants' motion for leave to require the SEC to produce documents "expressing the agency's interpretation or views" on cryptocurrencies. Obviously, the purpose was to determine whether the SEC ever considered cryptocurrencies such as XRP as a currency rather than a security. Nearly simultaneously, Judge Netburn denied an SEC request for eight years of personal financial information from the top two executives of Ripple Labs. Stay tuned.

The Delaware Blockchain Initiative

Delaware became the first state to recognize blockchain for corporate finance. In May 2016, Delaware's governor announced the launch of a Delaware Blockchain Initiative. In September 2016, Vice Chancellor Laster encouraged corporate shareholders to "take back the voting and stockholding infrastructure of the U.S. securities market" by using a "plunger" to clean up the plumbing. "That plunger is distributed ledger technologies, the technology that drives bitcoin."

After several costly failures to record shareholder certificates properly (for example, Dell Inc. recorded paper certificates in the wrong name and as a result, Dole Food Co. Inc. recorded 133 percent of the total number of shares outstanding in a vote approving a going-private transaction[10]), the Delaware General Corporate Law was amended to permit Delaware corporations to use blockchain to record ownership of their shares. This became known as the Delaware Blockchain Initiative. But in 2018, political pressures from incumbent intermediaries caused the Delaware Head of the Blockchain Initiative to resign and Delaware hit the pause button.

Should the Regulation of Cryptoassets Be Strengthened?

In March 2019, Timothy Massad, former Chair of the Commodity Futures Trading Commission, wrote a powerful monograph on behalf of the Brookings Economic Studies program arguing that the time had come to strengthen the federal government's regulation of cryptoassets.[11] Massad argued that Congress should pass legislation providing the SEC (or the CFTC)

---

[10] In 2013, the CEO and largest shareholder of Dole Food Co. took it private, in a deal that had to be approved by the shareholders. When the vote was taken, 49 million shares were voted, which exceeded the number of shareholders by about 13 million. https://www.bloomberg.com/opinion/articles/2017-02-17/dole-food-had-too-many-shares.

[11] Timothy G. Massad, "It's Time to Strengthen the Regulation of Crypto-Assets," Report of the Economic Studies Program of the Brookings Institute, March 2019, https://www.brookings.edu. Full disclosure: Mr. Massad was a partner of mine at the Cravath firm before he joined the Treasury Department.

with authority to regulate the offering, distribution, and trading of cryptoassets, increasing the resources of both the SEC and the CFTC to implement new and existing authorities pertaining to cryptocurrencies. He also said that "the Financial Stability Oversight Council or the Treasury Department should issue a report recommending congressional action to strengthen and clarify regulation of the sector."

Massad's recommendations appear to have gained some traction. On August 3, 2021, the new SEC Chair Gary Gensler told an Aspen Security Forum that the cryptocurrency market, valued at more than $1.5 trillion, "lacked the typical investor protection guardrails that the SEC is commissioned with providing and has become rife with fraud scams and abuse in certain applications." He repeated the SEC's current position that many of the cryptotokens are offered and sold as securities and said that "we have taken and will continue to take our authorities as far as they go."[12]

Recent Statistics

A study completed by Professors Douglas Eakeley and Yulia Guseva of Rutgers Law School at the end of 2020, *Crypto-Enforcement Around the World*, published in the Columbia Law School Blog on Corporations and the Capital Markets (The CLS Blue Sky Blog) concluded that out of twenty-three financial market jurisdictions around the world, only fourteen had either commenced enforcement actions or issued official warnings concerning cryptocurrencies or cryptoassets.[13] By far the leading jurisdiction was the United States, which brought more enforcement actions against digital-asset issuers, broker-dealers, and other crypto market participants than most other major jurisdictions combined. Actions brought by the SEC also resulted in more serious penalties.

Of interest, global enforcement appears to have peaked in 2018 and has declined dramatically since then. Enforcement in the United States appears to have peaked in 2019 and to have fallen since then. Actions brought by the SEC were nearly four times greater than actions brought by the CFTC. Nearly half of the cases brought by the SEC resulted in suspension of trading. Slightly more than half of the cases (twenty-nine) were brought by the SEC in federal courts rather than in administrative courts (twenty-two). Most of the cases alleged violations of the 1934 Exchange Act.

---

[12] Dean Seal, "Gensler Calls for Amped-Up Regulation of Crypto 'Wild West,'" Law 360, Aug. 3, 2021, https://www.law360.com/articles/1409345/print.

[13] https://clsbluesky.law.columbia.edu/2020/11/24/crypto-enforcement-around-the-world/.

Chapter 22

Regulation of Attorneys

The Role of Counsel

Lawyers play an essential role in delivering the rule of law to their clients.[1] Not only do they counsel and advise their clients but they are often the most important, sometimes the only, way many clients learn what their obligations under the law actually are. Counsel help to ensure that their clients comply with the law, and they are also advocates for their clients. Sometimes those two roles conflict. The lawyer must resolve the conflicts "through the exercise of sensitive professional and moral judgment, guided by the basic principles underlying the Rules [of Professional Conduct]."[2]

Lawyers who "appear and practice before the SEC" have a special responsibility. As former SEC Chairman Manual F. Cohen put it, "I believe that the privilege of appearing and practicing before the Commission imposes on [lawyers] a corresponding obligation to assist in achieving the protection of investors and the public interest that the securities laws are designed to bring about."[3]

What does it mean "to appear and practice before the commission"? Actually, the definition, found in SEC Rule 205.2, is quite broad. It includes:

- transacting any business with the commission, including communications in any form;
- representing an issuer in a commission administrative proceeding or in connection with any commission investigation, inquiry, information request, or subpoena;

[1] Louis Craco, "Carpe Diem: An Opportunity to Reclaim Lawyers' Independence," 27 *Pace L. Rev.* 1 (2006).

[2] *See* New York State Rules of Professional Conduct, Preamble, Para. 3.

[3] Address by Hon. Manuel F. Cohen, "The Lawyer's Role in Securities Regulation," before the ALI-ABA Conference on Current Problems of Broker-Dealer Regulation, June 7, 1968.

- providing advice in respect of the U.S. securities laws or the commission's rules or regulations thereunder regarding any document that the attorney has notice will be filed with or submitted to, or incorporated into any document that will be filed with or submitted to, the commission, including the provision of such advice in the context of preparing, or participating in the preparation of, any such document;
- advising an issuer as to whether information or a statement, opinion, or other writing is required under the U.S. securities laws or the commission's rules or regulations thereunder to be filed with or submitted to, or incorporated into any document that will be filed with or submitted to, the commission; and
- somewhat surprisingly, investigating evidence of a material violation reported under the up-the-ladder reporting requirements.

In recent years, there has been an increasing interest on the part of the SEC in regulating lawyers who "appear and practice" before it. In the well-known decision by the full SEC in *In the Matter of Carter and Johnson*, 475 SEC 471 (Feb. 28, 1981), the commission reversed a decision of an administrative law judge holding that two prominent Wall Street lawyers had violated the antifraud provisions of the securities laws as well as the standards of professional responsibility by assisting their client's management in concealing the company's true financial condition and in not informing the board of directors concerning the management's refusal to make adequate disclosures. The administrative law judge's decision was reversed because, according to the commission, "certain concepts of proper ethical and professional conduct were not sufficiently developed, at the time of the conduct here at issue, to permit a finding that either respondent breached applicable ethical or professional standards." But in a stern warning, the commission then stated that "we are today giving notice of an interpretation by the Commission of the term 'unethical or improper professional conduct' [as follows]: When a lawyer with significant responsibilities in the effectuation of a company's compliance with the disclosure requirements of the federal securities laws becomes aware that his client is engaged in a substantial and continuing failure to satisfy those disclosure requirements, his continued participation violates professional standards unless he takes prompt steps to end the client's non-compliance."

When a lawyer becomes aware of such activities, what steps should the lawyer take? For a thorough discussion of the obligations of a lawyer who is asked to render a formal legal opinion in connection with a securities transaction, see Darrell Rice and Marc Steinberg, "Legal Opinions in Securities Transactions," 16 *J. Corp. L.* 375 (1991). Consider also the following:

- Professor Mark Sargent, "Lawyers in the Perfect Storm," 43 Washburn L. J. (2003):

  > Lawyers' role as gatekeepers is complex and ambiguous, unlike the role of auditors who are required by law to be independent. Auditors are required to play a quasi-adversarial role vis-à-vis their auditing clients. Their job is to protect the investing public by casting a dispassionate disinterested eye on management's financial and accounting disclosures and placing their own reputation on the line by certifying the corporate financial statement. They function in essence as reputational intermediaries, drawing on their professional reputations to vouch for their auditing clients' financial disclosures. [But] lawyers *are* advocates. They have obligations to act on behalf of the corporate client that makes their role quite different from the quasi-adversarial role of an auditor.... (emphasis in original).

- Professors Deborah Rhode, of Stanford Law School, and Professor Paul Paton of the University of Alberta: "For lawyers, a place to start is with conditions that compromise independent professional judgment." Deborah Rhode & Paul Paton, "Lawyers, Ethics and Enron," 8 *Stan. J.L. Bus & Fin.* 9 (2002). Remember that under most states' professional responsibility codes, lawyers are ethically obligated to give "independent" and "candid" legal advice. *See, e.g.*, New York State Code of Professional Conduct Rule 2.1 ("In representing a client, a lawyer shall exercise independent professional judgment and render candid advice.")

Lawyers are also advocates who are obligated to act on behalf of their corporate clients. Did the Enron lawyers betray the public interest by acting as advocates? Rhode & Paton: "Allegiance to management's short-term financial interests may compromise their obligation to the broader public as well as to the entity itself, which is, at least in theory, the lawyer's client." What is the lawyer's obligation to the "broader public"?

Lawyers are not only advocates; they are also gatekeepers. They can refuse to do the necessary legal work on a questionable transaction. Remember that NYS Rules of Professional Conduct 2.1 requires the lawyer to use "independent professional judgment and provide candid" legal advice.

Are lawyers (or should they be) the social conscience of the client? Robert Weber, the former general counsel of IBM, has said that he is not a Jiminey

Cricket for IBM.[4] "I have never been, am not now, nor will I ever be IBM's Jiminey Cricket.... When we take on the role of conscience to the Company, we abandon the disciplined confines of legal reasoning." Others disagree. For example, Michael Cardozo, a partner at the Proskauer Rose law firm in New York and former corporation counsel of the City of New York, has written, "I cannot emphasize strongly enough that the government lawyer must not only give legal advice, but must forcefully express views on the desirability and morality of the particular policy question at issue," and he points out that Rule 2.1 of the Model Rules of Professional Conduct authorizes lawyers not only to give legal advice but to refer to "other considerations" such as "moral, economic, social and political factors relevant to the client's situation."[5]

What was the regulatory response to the Enron scandal? More regulations of lawyers. Congress passed Section 307 of Sarbanes-Oxley ("Forcing lawyers to see"). It required that the SEC adopt rules requiring "up the ladder" reporting of a "material violation" determined according to an objective standard, but not outside the corporation. Lawyers who do not receive an adequate response must continue to report "up the ladder," even to the board.

The Origin of SEC Rule 205: Standards of Professional Conduct for Lawyers

After the Enron scandal, the ABA created a task force charged with examining the "systematic issues relating to corporate responsibility arising out of the unexpected and traumatic bankruptcy of Enron and other Enron-like situations."[6] As noted, Sarbanes-Oxley Section 307 required the SEC to prescribe minimum standards of professional conduct for attorneys appearing and practicing before the commission in the representation of issuers. This was the first time that Congress entered the area of attorney regulation, typically the realm of state regulators.

The SEC promulgated Rule 205 in response to Section 307. At the heart of Rule 205 (17 C.F.R. § 203) is Rule 205.3(a), which provides that a lawyer "appearing and practicing before the Commission in the representation of an issuer owes his or her professional and ethical duties to the issuer *as an organization*" (emphasis added). Thus, even though the lawyer may work with the

---

[4] *See* New York State Judicial Institute on Professionalism in the Law, "A Convocation on Lawyer Independence and In-House Corporate Counsel," Nov. 9, 2012, ww2.nycourts.gov.ip/jipl/index.shtml. Full disclosure: I chair the Judicial Institute.

[5] Michael Cardozo, "The Conflicting Ethical, Legal, and Public Policy Obligations of the Government's Chief Legal Officer," Vol. 22, *The Professional Lawyer* No. 3 (2014).

[6] *Report of the ABA Task Force on Corporate Responsibility*, March 32, 2003.

issuer's officers, directors, and employees, they are not the lawyer's clients; the organization is.

Rule 205 required lawyers to report "up the ladder" if he or she has "credible evidence" that it is "reasonably likely" that a "material violation" of federal or state securities law, including a breach of fiduciary duty, or a "similar violation of federal or state law," is occurring or is likely to occur. The lawyer must continue reporting up until he or she has received an "appropriate response."

Prior to the enactment of Rule 205, the lawyer's responsibility to report wrongdoing by a corporate client was unclear. The tension was between the lawyer's duty to maintain the client's confidences and the lawyer's duty not to assist a client in a crime or fraud. The SEC's solution was to require lawyers who appeared and practiced before it to report evidence of material violations of the securities laws within the issuer itself, "up the ladder."

The lawyer's duty to maintain the client's confidences—different from the attorney-client privilege—is at the core of the lawyer's professional responsibility. For example, the early version of ABA Model Code Rule 1.6 permitted but did not require a lawyer to reveal a client's confidential information to the extent that the lawyer believed it to be reasonably necessary to (1) prevent reasonably certain death or substantial bodily harm, or (2) establish a claim or defense on behalf of the lawyer. State regulations varied.

In 2003, the ABA House of Delegates amended Model Code Rule 1.6 to permit—but not require—a lawyer to reveal a client's confidences "to prevent the client from committing a crime or fraud that is reasonably certain to result in substantial injury to the financial interests or property of another and in furtherance of which the client has used or is using the lawyer's services." The rule also permits disclosure to "prevent, mitigate or rectify substantial injury to the financial interests or property of another that is reasonably certain to result or has result from the client's commission of a crime or fraud in furtherance of which the client has used the lawyer's services."

These changes were not universally popular. Some claimed that they "eroded the core value of client confidentiality." To that end, the Comments to the Rule made it clear that the rule was a "limited exception to the rule of confidentiality" and permitted only limited disclosure "to prevent the client from committing a crime or fraud." Again, state rules varied, although the majority of state rules were similar to the ABA's Model Code.

The ethical rules of at least forty-two states permit lawyers to reveal a client's crime or fraud under certain circumstances. In New York, that permission is limited to preventing "reasonably certain death or substantial bodily harm" or to prevent the client from committing a crime (not a civil fraud). *See, e.g.*, New York Rules of Professional Conduct, Rule 1.6. The ABA Model Rules are broader (to prevent conduct that is "reasonably certain to result in substantive injury to financial interests or property of another").

New York Rules of Professional Conduct Rule 3.3 (Conduct Before a Tribunal) requires a lawyer who represents a client before a tribunal to take "reasonable remedial action" if he or she "knows" that a person is engaging, or has engaged, in criminal or fraudulent conduct "relating to a proceeding," including, if necessary, disclosure to the tribunal. This includes depositions.

Also, the same rule provides that if a lawyer, the lawyer's client, or a witness called by the lawyer has offered "material" evidence that the lawyer "has come to know of its falsity," the lawyer shall take "reasonable remedial measures including, if necessary, disclosure to the tribunal."

The SEC's original proposal, in response to Sarbanes-Oxley, was to require lawyers representing issuers and appearing before the commission to bring evidence that a material violation of the securities laws has occurred, is occurring, or is about to occur to the issuer's "chief legal officer" or to both its CEO and CLO. The CLO was required to conduct an inquiry and if there was evidence that the reporting lawyer was correct, to take "all reasonable steps to cause the company to adopt an appropriate response and to advise the reporting attorney of such." The issuer also had the option to create a Qualified Legal Compliance Committee to handle the report of the lawyer concerning the material violation.

Evidence of a material violation means credible "evidence, based upon which it would be unreasonable, under the circumstances, for a prudent and competent attorney not to conclude that it is reasonably likely that a material violation had occurred, is ongoing, or is about to occur." Note the double negative. Why? In a letter to the SEC, dated April 7, 2003, a number of law professors criticized the use of a double negative: "The very phrasing of the Commission's rule with its double negative will be read by many lawyers as encouraging them to hide in the folds that the double negative creates.... The Commission's standard is an invitation to inaction."

Professor George Cohen of the University of Virginia Law School said, in testimony before the House Committee on Financial Services, that "this definition, which triggers the 'up the ladder' reporting duty, is troublesome because its use of a double negative makes the standard difficult to understand, interpret or apply.... It is barely possible to read the SEC's definition out loud without tripping ... over the words."

Under the SEC proposal, if the reporting lawyer did not receive an "appropriate response," the lawyer was required to report the evidence to the issuer's audit committee, another committee of independent directors, or the full board of directors. What is an "appropriate response"? Probably a finding of no violation or the undertaking of remedial actions.

Must (or May) the Reporting Lawyer Tell the SEC if No "Appropriate Response" Is Received?

A proposed rule prepared by the SEC and released for comment would have required an outside lawyer to withdraw from the representation of the issuer if an appropriate response was not received from the client and to notify the SEC in writing of the withdrawal and that it was based on "professional considerations." The proposal would also have required the lawyer to "disaffirm any false or materially misleading submission to the SEC in which he or she has participated in preparing." An in-house lawyer in that situation would not be required to resign but must similarly disaffirm any "tainted" documents filed with the SEC and must inform the SEC.

This proposal became known "noisy withdrawal" and was roundly criticized by the bar. One of the concerns was that the rule would require the disclosure of confidential client information. The ABA supported the "up the ladder" reporting requirement but opposed the "noisy withdrawal" requirement, believing that the SEC was trying to mandate through regulation what was not in the statute.[7] A replacement proposal by the SEC—known as "noisy withdrawal lite—would have required the issuer, not the lawyer, to make the disclosure to the SEC.

There was a vigorous debate about whether the SEC rules preempted inconsistent state rules. Proposed SEC Rule 205.6(c) said that an attorney who complies in good faith with the SEC rules shall not be subject to discipline or otherwise liable under inconsistent standards imposed by any state or other United States jurisdiction where the attorney is admitted or practices.[8] California has advised lawyers admitted in that state that "given the apparent conflict between the provision of the Part 205 Rules permitting disclosure of client confidences to the SEC and the fiduciary duty of California attorneys to maintain client secrets and confidences, it may be safer for California attorneys not to accept the SEC's invitation to disclose client confidences to the SEC, at least until such time as the preemption and good faith issues have been decided by a Court of competent jurisdiction." *See State Bar of California Ethics Hotline* Spring 2014.

In order to address the criticism relating to the waiver of the attorney-client privilege, the SEC also proposed an amendment that would have provided that when information related to a material violation was shared with the SEC

---

[7] Clifton Barnes, "ABA, States and SEC Hash Out Lawyers' Responsibility in Corporate Setting," *Bar Leader*, November/December 2003, https://www.americanbar.org/publications/bar_leader/2003_04/2802/corporate.html.

[8] *See, e.g.*, John Villa, "Hidden Storms for Those in Safe Harbors: The SEC's Professional Conduct Rules and the Federal Preemption Doctrine," *ACC Docket* 22 (February 2004).

pursuant to a confidentiality agreement, the sharing "shall not constitute a waiver of any otherwise appliable privilege or protection to such persons." This proposal did not satisfy the critics, however. A principal argument of the critics was that it was up to the states or courts to decide when there has been a waiver of the attorney-client privilege and that there was a real possibility that a lawyer might disclose client-confidential information in reliance on the rule only to find after-the-fact that the privilege had been waived.

In the end, the SEC withdrew—or at least never again mentioned—the "noisy withdrawal" proposal and replaced the proposed rule stating that the disclosure of client-confidential information did not constitute a waiver of the privilege with a rule—still in existence—that "where the standards of a state or other United States jurisdiction where an attorney is admitted or practices conflict with this part, this part shall govern."[9]

Under Rule 205.3(d), "an attorney appearing and practicing before the Commission in the representation of an issuer may reveal to the Commission, without the issuer's consent, confidential information relating to the representation to the SEC without the issuer's (i.e., client's) consent to the extent the attorney reasonably believes necessary:

- to prevent the issuer from committing a material violation that is likely to cause substantial injury to the financial interest or property of the issuer or investors; or
- to prevent the issuer from committing perjury or an act in violation of 18 U.S.C. § 1001 that may perpetrate a fraud on the SEC in an SEC investigation or administrative proceeding, or to rectify the consequences of a material violation by the issuer that caused or may cause substantial injury to the financial interest or property of the issuer or investors in furtherance of which the attorney's services were used."

It remains to be seen whether the SEC's rule that "where the standards of a state or other United States jurisdiction ... conflict with this part, this part shall govern" can or will be enforced. I am aware of no case in which a lawyer who voluntarily disclosed client confidential information to the SEC without the client's consent has been disciplined by a state disciplinary committee, or sued by the client, or even accused of violating state rules of professional responsibility. In fact, I am not aware of any case in which a lawyer has even made such a disclosure.

---

[9] *See generally* Susan Koniak, George Cohen & Roger Cramton, "Legal and Ethical Duties of Lawyers After Sarbanes-Oxley," 49 *Villanova L. Rev.* 725 (2004).

The Lawyer as Whistleblower

The SEC's whistleblower award rules were adopted in 2011 to implement the whistleblower provisions of the Dodd-Frank Act. The rules generally exclude lawyers from eligibility for whistleblower awards if they try to use information obtained while performing their professional duties to blow the whistle on a client or an employer. In particular, the lawyer may not use information obtained through a privileged communication or in connection with the legal representation of a client.

But there are three exceptions to the general lawyer whistleblower exclusions: the confidential client information may be disclosed to the SEC without the client's consent if such disclosure is otherwise permitted by the SEC's attorney conduct rules, the applicable state attorney conduct rules, or "otherwise."

Is there a conflict between a lawyer's ability to maintain the duty of confidentiality and the lawyer's ability to claim a whistleblower's "bounty" under Dodd-Frank? Some have argued that there is.[10] When the SEC's three exceptions were published, the SEC said that they were similar to the rules "as adopted by the vast majority of states" but that was an exaggeration. The "vast majority" of states had not adopted such rules.[11] Of course, the statute does require that the information transmitted by the lawyer to the SEC be "original," and the SEC has taken the position that information obtained through a privileged communication is not derived from the lawyer's "independent knowledge or analysis" unless it would be permitted to be disclosed under Rule 205.

In October 2013, the New York County Lawyers Association's Committee on Professional Ethics fired the first shot, opining that New York lawyers "presumptively may not ethically serve as whistleblowers for a bounty against their clients under [the Dodd-Frank Act] because doing so generally gives rise to a conflict between the lawyers' interests and those of their clients."[12] The opinion continued that "even when disclosure is permitted under the New York Rules ... preventing wrongdoing is not the same as collecting a bounty." This issue remains open and there have been no satisfactory resolutions. Lawyers have been warned to "decide whether the misconduct he or she perceives

---

[10] *See* Jennifer Pacella, "Advocate or Adversary: When Attorneys Act as Whistleblowers," 28 *Geo. J. Legal Ethics* 1027 (Fall 2015).

[11] *See* Latham & Watkins Client Alert White Paper, "Will Award-Seeking Whistleblower Lawyers Be Caught Between Conflicting SEC and State Ethics Rules?" No. 1596, October 21, 2013, https://www.lw.com/thoughtLeadership/SEC-whistleblower-ethics-conflict.

[12] NYCLA Opinion at 15.

is so brazen and he or she is so otherwise blameless that the risks of a state disciplinary investigation are worth taking."[13]

Will the SEC rules result in marginalizing the role of lawyers and excluding them from sensitive discussions? Will clients have a greater incentive to hide things from the lawyers? Will clients circumscribe assignments given to outside law firms? Some have made those arguments but it remains to be seen whether they will gain any traction.[14]

Other Sarbanes-Oxley Provisions of Interest

Audit committees can hire independent counsel and advisers. (Section 301) (Is there a difference between "separate" and "independent"?) Can (should) other parts of the corporation also be authorized to hire separate counsel?

Section 806 of Sarbanes-Oxley provides that "no [public] company or any officer, employee, contractor, subcontractor or agent of such company may discharge, demote, suspend, threaten, harass or in any other manner discriminate against an employee in terms and conditions of employment because of [whistleblowing or other protected activity]." *See* 18 U.S.C. § 1514A. In *Lawson v. FMR LLC*, 134 S. Ct. 1158 (2014), the Supreme Court held that the protected class of employees included "employees of privately held contractors and subcontractors, for example, investment advisers, law firms, accounting enterprises, who perform work for the public company."

Discipline of Lawyers by the SEC

Rule 102(e) of the SEC Rules of Practice permits the SEC to initiate disciplinary proceedings against a lawyer who lacks integrity or competence, engages in unprofessional conduct, or has been determined to have violated the federal securities law. Sanctions include censure, suspension, or bar. A violation of Rule 205 constitutes a violation of Rule 102(e). Rule 102(e) does not establish rules of conduct; rather it permits the SEC to discipline layers who have engaged in unprofessional conduct by violating other rules or regulations.

---

[13] Latham & Watkins Client Alert, *supra* 8.

[14] *See* Ernest Badway, "'The Empire Strikes Back': The SEC's New Assault on Lawyers," *N.J. Law Journal*, February 2, 2009 ("Government regulation of attorney conduct, especially during an SEC investigation . . . may create potential client conflicts and chill zealous defense.")